Inaugural Meeting of the Society for Computation in Linguistics (SCiL 2018)

Salt Lake City, Utah, USA
4 – 7 January 2018

Editors:

Gaja Jarosz
Brendan O'Connor
Joe Pater

ISBN: 978-1-5108-5551-9

TABLE OF CONTENTS

Preface: SCiL 2018 Editors' Note

Gaja Jarosz, Brendan O'Connor and Joe Pater
University of Massachusetts Amherst

This volume contains research presented at the inaugural meeting of the Society for Computation in Linguistics (SCiL), held in Salt Lake City, January 4-7 2018, in conjunction with the annual meeting of the Linguistic Society of America.

These proceedings include the full length paper submissions that were peer-reviewed as papers and accepted for either oral or poster presentation at SCiL 2018. The first 5 papers in the proceedings are those that were accepted as oral presentations, while the remaining 12 papers were presented as posters. Submissions to SCiL also included abstracts, which were presented as talks or posters at the conference. Further information, including the schedule and abstracts, can be found at our website: https://blogs.umass.edu/scil/scil-2018/.

In total, we received 55 submissions to the conference, 34 abstracts and 21 papers. 18 of the submissions (44%) included a female author. We accepted 13 submissions as talks, and 27 as posters. Six of the talks (46%) included a female author, and 12 of the posters (44%) included a female author. We thank our reviewers for their indispensible help in selecting the research for presentation at the conference:

Adam Albright, Jacob Andreas, Michael Becker, Emily Bender, Leon Bergen, Su-Lin Blodgett, Sam Bowman, Miriam Butt, Alexander Clark, Jennifer Culbertson, Robert Daland, Brian Dillon, Ewan Dunbar, Jason Eisner, Josh Falk, Robert Frank, Richard Futrell, Adamantios Gafos, Matt Goldrick, Sharon Goldwater, Thomas Graf, John Hale, Bruce Hayes, Jeff Heinz, Kasia Hitczenko, Tim Hunter, Gerhard Jaeger, Dan Jurafsky, Roni Katzir, Tracy Holloway King, Greg Kobele, Sandra Kuebler, Andrew Lamont, Tal Linzen, Giorgio Magri, Rob Malouf, Andrea E. Martin, Nazarré Merchant, Elliott Moreton, Emily Morgan, Becca Morley, Tim O'Donnell, Alexis Palmer, Lisa Pearl, Heather Pon-Barry, Christopher Potts, Ezer Rasin, Philip Resnik, James Rogers, Nathan Schneider, Stephanie Shih, Andrea Sims, Noah Smith, Paul Smolensky, Morgan Sonderegger, Ed Stabler, Mark Steedman, Tom Wasow.

We also thank Coral Hughto, Su-Lin Blodgett and Andrew Lamont for their help in recruiting and assigning reviewers to papers, and everyone who indicated a willingness to review whose services we couldn't use. Andrew Lamont also helped enormously with the production of this volume.

The conference also included invited talks by Jacob Andreas, Emily M. Bender, Sam Bowman, Chris Dyer, Jason Eisner, Robert Frank, Matt Goldrick, Sharon Goldwater, Paul Smolensky, which formed a special session on "Perceptrons and Syntactic Structures at Sixty", funded by NSF conference grant BCS-1651142 to the University of Massachusetts Amherst. Thanks to Tom Maxfield for logistical help.

Statistical learning theory and linguistic typology: a learnability perspective on OT's strict domination

Émile Enguehard
ENS
emile.enguehard@ens.fr

Edward Flemming
MIT
flemming@mit.edu

Giorgio Magri
CNRS
magrigrg@gmail.com

Abstract

This paper develops a learnability argument for strict domination by looking at the generalization error of learners trained on OT and HG target grammars. The argument is based on both a review of error bounds in the recent statistical learning literature and simulation results on realistic phonological test cases.

1 Introduction

According to **Optimality Theory** (OT; Prince and Smolensky 2004), constraint interaction in natural language phonology is severely constrained by the hypothesis of **strict domination**. According to this hypothesis, "the constraints [are] arranged in a hierarchy" and "each constraint is strictly more important than — takes absolute priority over — all the constraints lower-ranked in the hierarchy. [...] Strict domination thus limits drastically the range of possible strength-interactions between constraints to those representable with the algebra of total order" (Prince and Smolensky, 1997). This hypothesis of strict domination has been challenged in the recent phonological literature (Pater, 2009; Potts et al., 2010; Pater, 2016), which has therefore started to explore an implementation of constraint-based phonology which does away with strict domination, known as **Harmonic Grammar** (HG; Legendre et al., 1990a,b; Smolensky and Legendre, 2006). Section 2 re-assesses the OT versus HG debate, concluding that HG over-generates for many natural constraint sets and that natural language phonology thus supports OT's hypothesis of strict domination.

Why should constraint interaction in natural language phonology display strict domination? Legendre et al. (2006) conjecture that "demands of learnability [might] provide a pressure for strict domination among constraints" although they admit that "it remains an open problem to formally characterize exactly what is essential about strict domination to guarantee efficient learning." Riggle et al. (2009; 2010) take a closer look at this alleged connection between strict domination and learnability. They look at **error bounds** in terms of a classical measure of the learning complexity of a hypothesis class, namely its **Vapnik-Chervonenkis** (VC) dimension (Vapnik and Chervonenkis, 1971). But they find that the VC dimension is the same for OT and HG, despite OT typologies being smaller than HG typologies because of strict domination. They conclude that, "though there may be factors that favor one model [OT or HG] over the other, the complexity of learning [...] is not one of them."

Yet, VC dimension is an old measure of learning complexity (it dates back to the seventies) which is inevitably coarse as it applies to completely arbitrary classifiers. Since Schapire et al. (1998), statistical learning theory has instead focused on a special class of classifiers, namely **voting classifiers** which aggregate the "votes" of more basic classifiers scaled through corresponding weights. For this special class of classifiers, better error bounds have been developed, which take into account the **margin** of "confidence" with which a classifier succeeds on the data. More recently, Koltchinskii and Panchenko (Koltchinskii and Panchenko, 2002; Koltchinskii et al., 2003b; Koltchinskii et al., 2003a; Koltchinskii

Proceedings of the Society for Computation in Linguistics (SCiL) 2018, pages 1-11.
Salt Lake City, Utah, January 4-7, 2018

and Panchenko, 2005) have further refined margin theory through error bounds which depend not only on the margin but also on the rate of decay of the weights of the basic classifiers: the bounds get better (that is provide guarantees for a smaller generalization error) as the rate of decay increases.

Crucially, HG and OT grammars can be construed as voting classifiers with the phonological constraints playing the role of the basic classifiers. Section 3 thus brings Koltchinskii and Panchenko's result to bear on the debate between HG and OT, through the well known characterization of OT as a special case of HG with weights decreasing fast, specifically exponentially.

Section 4 complements these theoretical results with simulation-based estimates of the generalization error (codes and data are provided as online supplements). We look at two test cases related to vowel harmony and syllable types. We compute the corresponding typologies of OT grammars and HG-non-OT grammars (namely HG grammars with no OT correspondent). For both types of target grammars, we compute the generalization error of the hypothesis that performs better (that is, has the largest margin) on a training set of cardinality n. We show that on average the generalization error decreases faster as a function of n for the OT targets than for the HG-non-OT ones. Section 5 concludes the paper and discusses various issues to explore in future research.

2 The OT versus HG debate

As reviewed above, HG fundamentally differs from OT because it does away with strict domination and therefore allows for **gang effects** in which multiple violations of lower-weighted constraints outweigh a violation of a higher-weighted constraint (see section 3 for details). Bane and Riggle (2009) show that sets of constraints drawn from the phonological literature yield much richer typologies in HG than in OT as a result of gang effects, and that many of the additional patterns derived under HG are unattested. The same point is made by the investigation of Kaun's (2004) analysis of the typology of rounding harmony discussed in section 4. However these constraint sets were developed in the context of OT, so these results leave open the possibility that a revised HG constraint set could provide a closer match

to natural language typology. In this section we see that there is reason to doubt that the problem of typological over-generation faced by HG phonology can be solved in this way. The evidence comes from classes of problematic gang effects that arise from basic and uncontroversial constraints.

For example AGREE(place) penalizes heterorganic clusters, and *g penalizes voiced velar stops. The weighting of these constraints in figure 1a derives a pattern in which only [g] undergoes place assimilation because IDENT(place) outweighs each markedness constraint individually, but heterorganic [g] violates both constraints, which together outweigh IDENT(place). This pattern cannot be derived by any ranking of these constraints in OT: to block general place assimilation, IDENT(place) must outrank AGREE(place), but that ranking prevents assimilation of [g] as well.

Place assimilation targeting only [g] is unattested (velars resist place assimilation more than coronals and labials and voicing does not affect place assimilation (Jun, 2004)), but once HG is adopted, it is hard to avoid predicting the existence of this process because its derivation does not depend on the specific formulations of AGREE(place) and *g. The prediction follows as long as there is some constraint that penalizes heterorganic consonant clusters over homorganic clusters, which is necessary to account for place assimilation, and some constraint that penalizes [g] more than [b, d] and voiceless stops, which is necessary to account for a variety of phenomena, including languages such as Thai that allow voiced stops but not [g] (Ohala, 1983).

Variants of this configuration are easy to generate, e.g. *p (Hayes, 1999) can replace *g to derive place assimilation that only targets [p], or AGREE(place) can be replaced by AGREE(voice) to derive a pattern in which mixed-voicing clusters are tolerated unless they contain [g], in which case devoicing applies. Neither pattern has been reported in spite of thorough investigations of the typologies of place and voicing assimilation. More generally, HG predicts that any markedness constraints that mention the same feature specification in compatible contexts should be able to gang up on faithfulness constraints regulating that feature.

Furthermore, in HG any set of markedness constraints that can penalize a single segment should be

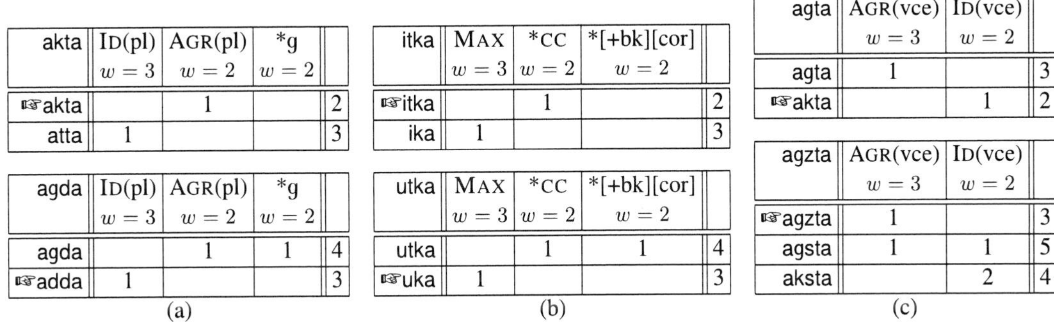

(a)

akta	ID(pl) $w=3$	AGR(pl) $w=2$	*g $w=2$	
☞akta		1		2
atta	1			3

agda	ID(pl) $w=3$	AGR(pl) $w=2$	*g $w=2$	
agda		1	1	4
☞adda	1			3

(b)

itka	MAX $w=3$	*CC $w=2$	*[+bk][cor] $w=2$	
☞itka		1		2
ika	1			3

utka	MAX $w=3$	*CC $w=2$	*[+bk][cor] $w=2$	
utka		1	1	4
☞uka	1			3

(c)

agta	AGR(vce) $w=3$	ID(vce) $w=2$	
agta	1		3
☞akta		1	2

agzta	AGR(vce) $w=3$	ID(vce) $w=2$	
☞agzta	1		3
agsta	1	1	5
aksta		2	4

Figure 1: Examples of unattested phonological patterns predicted by HG gang effects

able to gang up on a MAX constraint because deletion of a segment eliminates all of its constraint violations. For example, a constraint against consonant clusters, *CC, and a markedness constraint that penalizes particular VC sequences, e.g. *[+back][cor] (cf. Flemming 2003), can together derive the unattested pattern in figure 1b: pre-consonantal coronals are deleted only if the preceding vowel is back.

Many potential gang effects involving deletion are likely to be ruled out by independent principles. E.g. an alternative repair may be universally preferred due to a fixed ranking among faithfulness constraints (Steriade, 2008). This cannot be the case in the current example because it is a variant of a well-attested process of cluster simplification. On this basis, we can make the generalization that HG predicts the existence of variants of attested deletion processes in which deletion applies only in the presence of additional constraint violations. This set includes many unattested processes.

Another general class of problematic predictions of HG concerns iterative processes in which a markedness constraint can motivate multiple violations of faithfulness. For example, if voicing assimilation is motivated by a constraint like AGREE(voice), then mappings like /agta/→[akta] and /agzta/→[aksta] eliminate just one violation of AGREE(voice) at the cost of $n-1$ violations of IDENT(voice) with a cluster of n obstruents. In HG, the relative weighting of these two constraints establishes a maximum number of consonants that will undergo assimilation (a maximum of 1 in figure 1c) — an unattested phenomenon. In OT, the equivalent ranking derives unbounded assimilation because one violation of AGREE(voice) is worse than any number of violations of IDENT(voice).

Examples of gang effects have been posited by analysts (see Pater 2016 for a review), but alternative OT analyses have been proposed in a number of cases, as in the much discussed case of Japanese loanword devoicing (Pater, 2009; Kawahara, 2006). On balance, the evidence for HG gang effects is weak compared to the evidence that they result in substantial typological over-generation, supporting OT's hypothesis of strict constraint domination.

3 The perspective of statistical learning

We turn now to results from statistical learning theory and bring them to bear on OT's hypothesis of strict domination. The presentation is kept informal with technical details relegated to the final appendix.

3.1 Binary classification

The statistical learning framework of binary classification assumes a **set of instances** $\mathcal{X}$ and a **set of labels** $\mathcal{Y} = \{+1, -1\}$. A classifier can then be construed as a function which assigns a label $y = +1$ or $y = -1$ to an instance x in the set $\mathcal{X}$. We are interested in classifiers with a special shape, as follows.

We start with a collection $\mathcal{H}$ of functions $h : \mathcal{X} \to [-1, +1]$ that take an instance and return a number between -1 and $+1$. Using the functions in $\mathcal{H}$, we construct the collection $\mathcal{F}$ of all weighted sums $f = \sum_{k=1}^{K} w_k h_k$ of an arbitrary finite number K of functions h_k in $\mathcal{H}$ through some corresponding weights w_k. We restrict ourself to weights which are non-negative and sum up to 1 (whereby $\mathcal{F}$ is the convex hull of $\mathcal{H}$). A function $h \in \mathcal{H}$ or a function $f \in \mathcal{F}$ maps instances in $\mathcal{X}$ to numbers between -1 and $+1$. The sign of these numbers can in turn be interpreted as a classification label. Thus, $\mathrm{sign}(h)$ with $h \in \mathcal{H}$ is called a **basic classifier** and $\mathrm{sign}(f)$

with $f = \sum_{k=1}^{K} w_k h_k \in \mathcal{F}$ is called a **voting** (or an **ensemble**) **classifier**, because it aggregates and averages the "votes" of the basic classifiers.

We consider a probability distribution $\mathbb{P}$ on $\mathcal{X} \times \mathcal{Y}$ that generates labels from instances according to the conditional probability $\mathbb{P}(y|x)$. The **generalization error** $Err_{\mathbb{P}}(f)$ of a classifier $f \in \mathcal{F}$ relative to $\mathbb{P}$ is the probability of misclassification of f, namely the probability under $\mathbb{P}$ of a labeled instance (x, y) such that f assigns to the instance x a label $\text{sign}(f(x))$ different from the intended label y:

$$Err_{\mathbb{P}}(f) = \mathbb{P}\big[\text{sign}(f(x)) \neq y\big]$$

As the generalization error measures the probability of misclassification, a classifier with a smaller generalization error is better than a classifier with a larger generalization error. The learner's ideal goal would be to find a classifier $f \in \mathcal{F}$ with the smallest possible generalization error, that is a classifier which maps instances to their most probable label. Unfortunately, the generalization error $Err_{\mathbb{P}}(\cdot)$ cannot be minimized directly, because it is defined in terms of the probability $\mathbb{P}$ which is unknown to the learner. Indeed, the learner only has at its disposal a training set $T = ((x_1, y_1), \ldots, (x_n, y_n))$ consisting of n labeled instances $(x_i, y_i) \in \mathcal{X} \times \mathcal{Y}$ sampled independently according to $\mathbb{P}$.

The goal of statistical learning theory is to provide **error bounds**, that is bounds on the generalization error $Err_{\mathbb{P}}(f)$ of an arbitrary classifier $f \in \mathcal{F}$ based on parameters such as the shape of f or its performance on the training set T. Of course, we want our error bounds to be as low as possible, thus providing guarantees for the smallest possible generalization error. In this section, we focus on a state-of-the-art error bound due to Koltchinskii and Panchenko (2005, theorem 2, page 1464; henceforth KP), recalled in appendix A.1. Sections 3.2 and 3.3 discuss the two crucial properties of KP's bound qualitatively. This will suffice to make a connection with OT's strict domination in section 3.4.

3.2 KP's bound depends on the margin

The condition $\text{sign}(f(x_i)) = y_i$ that a voting classifier $sign(f)$ classifies correctly the data pair (x_i, y_i) is equivalent to the inequality $y_i f(x_i) > 0$. Thus, the size of the real number $y_i f(x_i)$ can be intuitively interpreted as the margin of confidence with

which f succeeds at assigning the correct label y_i to the instance x_i: the larger $y_i f(x_i)$ is above zero, the larger the confidence. Given a training set $T = ((x_1, y_1), \ldots, (x_n, y_n))$ that f classifies correctly, we focus on the most dangerous training pair, namely the one that f classifies with the smallest confidence. That smallest margin of confidence is called the **margin** $\delta_T(f)$ of f on the training set T:

$$\delta_T(f) = \min_{i=1,\ldots,n} y_i f(x_i) \tag{1}$$

Since the margin $\delta_T(f)$ represents the worst-case confidence of f on the training set T, it is intuitive that KP's bound (like earlier bounds, since Schapire *et al.* 1998) depends on the margin in such a way that the error bound is large (that is, worse) when the margin $\delta_T(f)$ is small (namely close to 0). See appendix A.2 for details on the dependence of KP's bound on the margin. In conclusion, KP's bound says that, all else being equal, the learner should pick a classifier in $\mathcal{F}$ which correctly classifies the training set T with the largest margin $\delta_T(f)$. We will use this fact extensively in section 4.

3.3 KP's bound depends on the effective dimension

Consider a representation of a voting classifier $f \in \mathcal{F}$ as a sum of basic classifiers in $\mathcal{H}$, namely $f = \sum_{k=1}^{K} w_k h_k$ with non-negative weights w_k which sum up to 1 and are therefore each smaller than 1. We assume without loss of generality that $w_1 \geq w_2 \geq \cdots \geq w_K$. Intuitively, the number K of basic classifiers in the representation of f can be interpreted as the **dimension** of f. Yet, the weights in the tail of the representation of f might be tiny whereby the corresponding basic classifiers contribute only little and should be discounted when determining the dimension of f. KP thus consider the alternative notion (2) of **effective dimension** $d_T(f)$ of the classifier f. Intuitively, we split K as $K = d + (K - d)$ and replace $K - d$ with the sum $\sum_{j=d+1}^{K} w_j$ of the $K - d$ weights in the tail, thus taking into account the smallness of the smallest weights. If the weights decrease fast, the tail weights will be small and the effective dimension $d_T(f)$ will therefore be small.

$$d_T(f) = \min_{0 \leq d \leq K} \left[d + \left(\sum_{j=d+1}^{K} w_j \right)^2 \frac{2 \log n}{\delta_T(f)^2} \right] \tag{2}$$

The novelty of KP's error bound is that it depends not only on the margin $\delta_T(f)$ of the classifier f but also on its effective dimension $d_T(f)$ and thus on the decay of the weights in a representation of f. In the sense that (for a fixed margin) KP's bound is small (that is, better) when the effective dimension is small because of a fast decay of the weights. For instance, the bound is smaller for exponentially decaying weights than for polynomially decaying weights (assuming that the margin is the same in the two cases). See appendix A.3 for details on the dependence of KP's bound on the decay of the weights. In conclusion, KP's error bound says that, all else being equal, the learner should pick a classifier in $\mathcal{F}$ which correctly classifies the training set T and whose weights decay fastest, possibly exponentially. We now make explicit the implications of this conclusion for the OT versus HG debate.

3.4 KP's bound and OT's strict domination

The connection between the classification framework reviewed above and the framework of constraint-based phonology can be drawn as follows. Let the space of instances consist of triplets (u, s, s') where u is an underlying form and s, s' are corresponding candidate surface forms. We interpret s as the intended **winner** and s' as the intended **loser**. The **HG grammar** relative to constraints $C_1, \ldots, C_K$ and weights $w_1, \ldots, w_K \geq 0$ is consistent with the triplet (u, s, s') provided $\sum_{k=1}^{K} w_k h_k(u, s, s') > 0$ where $h_k(u, s, s')$ is the constraint violation difference

$$h_k(u, s, s') = C_k(u, s') - C_k(u, s) \qquad (3)$$

Without loss of generality, we assume the weights w_k sum up to 1. Furthermore, we assume that there are a finite number of underlying forms and a finite number of surface forms (for discussion of this assumption, see Alber *et al.* 2015). Thus, we can assume without loss of generality that

$$-1 \leq h_k(u, s, s') \leq +1 \qquad (4)$$

for every triplet (u, s, s'). In fact, if the inequalities (4) fail for the original constraints, we can divide them by the largest number of constraint violations without affecting the typological predictions. In conclusion, an HG grammar can be construed as a classifier $f \in \mathcal{F} = \mathrm{conv}(\mathcal{H})$ in the convex hull of the collection $\mathcal{H}$ of the constraint violation differences h_k in (3) which take values in $[-1, +1]$ by (4).

The **OT grammar** relative to constraints $C_1, \ldots, C_K$ and a constraint ranking π is consistent with the triplet (u, s, s') provided there exists a constraint C_k such that each of the constraints π-ranked above C_k assigns the same number of violations to the two mappings (u, s) and (u, s') while the constraint C_k assigns less violations to the winner mapping (u, s) than to the loser mapping (u, s'). The following well known result says that the latter condition is equivalent to the HG consistency condition relative to exponentially decaying weights (Prince and Smolensky, 2004; Keller, 2000; Keller, 2005). The constant Z in (5b) is arbitrary and can be used to normalize the weights.

Theorem 1 *Consider an arbitrary ranking π. Without loss of generality, assume that π is (5a), whereby C_1 is ranked at the top, C_2 is ranked below it and so on, until the bottom ranked C_K.*

$$
\begin{array}{lll}
a. \quad C_1 & b. \quad w_1 = \frac{1}{Z}\left(\frac{\Delta+\delta}{\delta}\right)^{-1} & (5) \\
\quad\;\; \downarrow & \\
\quad\;\; C_2 & \quad\;\; w_2 = \frac{1}{Z}\left(\frac{\Delta+\delta}{\delta}\right)^{-2} \\
\quad\;\; \vdots & \quad\;\; \vdots \\
\quad\;\; C_K & \quad\;\; w_K = \frac{1}{Z}\left(\frac{\Delta+\delta}{\delta}\right)^{-K}
\end{array}
$$

The HG grammar corresponding to the weights in (5b) for an arbitrary $Z > 0$ and

$$\Delta = \max\left\{\,|h_k(u, s, s')|\,\big|\, k = 1 \cdots K\right\}$$
$$\delta = \min\left\{\,h_k(u, s, s')\,\big|\, h_k(u, s, s') > 0\right\}$$

is consistent with a triplet (u, s, s') if and only if the OT grammar corresponding to π is.

Theorem 1 says that OT's strict domination corresponds to a restriction to the subset of the HG typology corresponding to weights which decay exponentially, as in (5b). KP's bound provides a learnability rationale for this restriction: fast decaying weights ensure a smaller effective dimension (as long as the margin does not shrink) and thus a smaller (that is, better) error-bound. Thus, a learner of an OT grammar would have a better guarantee of a low generalization error, and we may conjecture that it will actually have a lower generalization error in practice.

4 Empirical simulations

To complement the theoretical perspective of section 3, we now turn to simulations of margin-based learning on two test cases. Our experiments found OT target grammars to be easier, on average, to learn than HG-non-OT ones. Furthermore, we found that this learning procedure yields weights with a lower effective dimension on OT targets than on HG-non-OT ones.

4.1 Test cases

Our first test case is based on the analysis of rounding harmony by Kaun (2004). It models progressive harmony between two vowels of the same backness. As it posits two levels of height and backness, it assumes 8 underlying forms consisting of one of 4 possible triggers (i.e., the four rounded vowels which differ for height and backness) and of one of 2 possible targets (the unrounded vowels of corresponding backness of both possible heights). Each underlying form has 2 candidate surface forms, one with harmony and one without. The constraint set consists of 7 constraints (see the online supplementary materials). The typology (computed with OT-Help2; Staubs *et al.* 2010) consists of 37 OT grammars and 26 HG-non-OT grammars.

Our second test case is based on the analysis of syllable structure by Prince and Smolensky (2004, Part II). This analysis involves 5 constraints in its simpler variant. As in Bane and Riggle (2009), the set of underlying forms consists of all 13 strings of length 1 to 3 of symbols in $\{C, V\}$ (except CV which has only one possible output). Furthermore, we used their procedure to precompute all possibly optimal outputs, yielding a total of 56 surface forms.[1] The typology (computed with OT-Help2) consists of 12 OT and 13 HG-non-OT grammars.

---

[1]Note that what we call underlying and surface forms do not really correspond to actual forms but to patterns of constraint violations. For instance in our second test case, the underlying forms /tat/ and /bat/ are a single "underlying form" /CV/, and the surface forms (say for /tat/) [ta] and [da] are a single "surface form" [CV]. This means that the admittedly low number of data points we have should not be compared to the number of words human learners are exposed to; our data points exemplify all the possible patterns of small length for each phenomenon.

4.2 Procedure

Algorithm 1 features the pseudo-code for our simulation procedure. For each grammar G in the typology, we build the set of instances $\mathcal{X}_G$ in (6). We consider all triplets (u, s, s') where: u is an underlying form; s is the corresponding winner surface form according to the grammar G; and s' is a loser candidate for u different from s. We represent (u, s, s') as the vector $h(u, s, s')$ whose components are the constraint violation differences $h_k(u, s, s')$ in (3).

$$\mathcal{X}_G = \{x = h(u, s, s') \mid G \text{ maps } u \text{ to } s\} \quad (6)$$

We sample a training set T by drawing uniformly with replacement n data points from $\mathcal{X}_G$ (we assume all labels are equal to $y = 1$, because we only generate positive data). Based on the considerations in section 3.2, we compute the weights w^* which maximise the empirical margin on the training set T over all non-negative weight vectors $w \geq 0$. The margin (1) can be made explicit as in (7) in the specific case considered

$$\delta_T(w) = \min\{w^\mathsf{T} x \mid x \in T\} \quad (7)$$

We do this for n ranging from 3 to an arbitrary number N. This procedure is repeated 250 times, so we can compute the average generalization error $Err(n, G)$ that a margin-based learner trying to learn G makes after seeing n data points.

Algorithm 1: Learning simulation procedure.

1 **for** G *in the typology* **do**
2   **for** $n = 3, \ldots, N$ **do**
3   **for** $m = 1, \ldots, 250$ **do**
4   Randomly select $T \in \mathcal{X}_G^n$
5              $w^* \leftarrow \arg\max_{w \geq 0} \delta_T(w)$
6              $Err(m) \leftarrow \mathbb{P}(w^{*\mathsf{T}} x \leq 0 \mid x \in \mathcal{X}_G)$
7          $Err(n, G) \leftarrow \frac{1}{250} \sum_m Err(m)$

4.3 Results

Figure 2 plots the error $Err(n, G)$ averaged over target OT-grammars G (solid red lines) and averaged over target HG-non-OT grammars (dashed blue lines). We observe a learnability advantage for OT grammars in practice, as the generalization error of

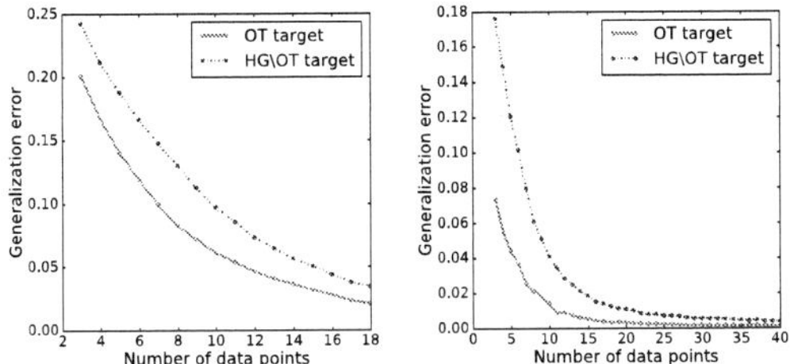

Figure 2: Average of the generalization error $Err(n, G)$ over OT and over HG-non-OT target grammars as a function of n, for rounding harmony (left) and syllable types (right) data.

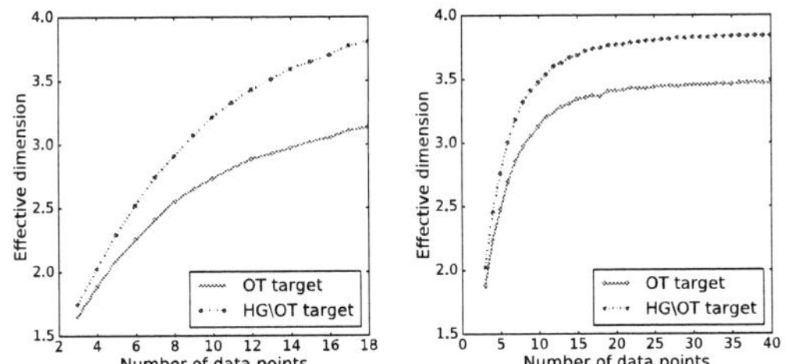

Figure 3: Average effective dimension of the learner's weights over OT and HG-non-OT target grammars as a function of n, for rounding harmony (left) and syllable types (right) data.

a margin-based learner on OT target grammars is lower for any given number n of data points than that of the same learner on HG-non-OT targets.

The error obtained in the simulations cannot be straightforwardly compared to Koltchinskii and Panchenko's error bound (8), as we do not know the value of the constant K which appears in the bound. Yet, figure 3 shows a lower effective dimension — as defined in (2) — of the weights w^* selected by the learner when trained on OT target grammars (red solid line) than on HG-non-OT targets (blue dotted line). Thus, we can speculate that the easier learnability of OT grammars compared to HG-non-OT grammars is related to the lower effective dimension of the HG weights that generate them.

Of course, the advantage of OT that we observe *on average* could be due to just a couple of very "easy" OT grammars that drag the average down. For instance, in the case of harmony, both the grammar with systematic harmony and the one with no harmony at all only depend on only one constraint (respectively ALIGN-L/R([RD]) and DEP(LINK)) and both belong to the OT typology. Figure 4 thus plots the generalization error $Err(n, G)$ for each individual OT (red dashed lines) and each individual HG-non-OT (blue dotted lines) target grammar G. The overall pattern is that most OT grammars are eas-

ier to learn than most HG-non-OT grammars. In the case of syllable structure, there are indeed only a few exceptions to this general pattern. The pattern is admittedly somewhat less clear in the case of vowel harmony, as discussed below in section 5.A.

5 Conclusions and open issues

This paper has argued that OT's strict domination seems to be warranted by phonological typology (section 2) and that strict domination might provide a learnability advantage (*pace* Riggle *et al.* 2009; 2010). This learnability argument is twofold: first, a review of recent results in the statistical learning literature (section 3) lets us conclude that learners of OT grammars will infer them with greater chance of success for the same amount of data. Second, simulation results on realistic test cases (section 4) show that OT target grammars are indeed easier to learn under certain assumptions. We conclude with various open issues that we would like to address in future research.

(A) As remarked above, figure 4 shows that several of the "hardest" grammars are part of the OT typology in the harmony case. As a tentative explanation, we note that in this test case, there are few underlying and surface forms, and many constraints, some of which are closely related. For instance, there are three different variants of ALIGN-L/R([RD]) for different features of the trigger vowel. Thus, in most grammars of the HG typology, not all constraints have to be active (in the sense of having non-zero weights). Certain OT grammars are harder than certain HG-non-OT grammars by virtue of requiring more active constraints. Future work will try to get a cleaner picture by comparing only OT and HG-non-OT grammars that require a comparable number of active constraints.

(B) For consistency with the classification framework of section 3.1, the simulations described in section 4 define the error in terms of the number of triplets (u, s, s') where the loser s' incorrectly beats the winner s (see line 6 in algorithm 1). We might instead want to redefine the error in terms of the number of underlying forms u mapped to a winner different from s. For the results from statistical learning theory in section 3 to still be relevant, we would need to extend them from classifiers of the form $f(x) =$

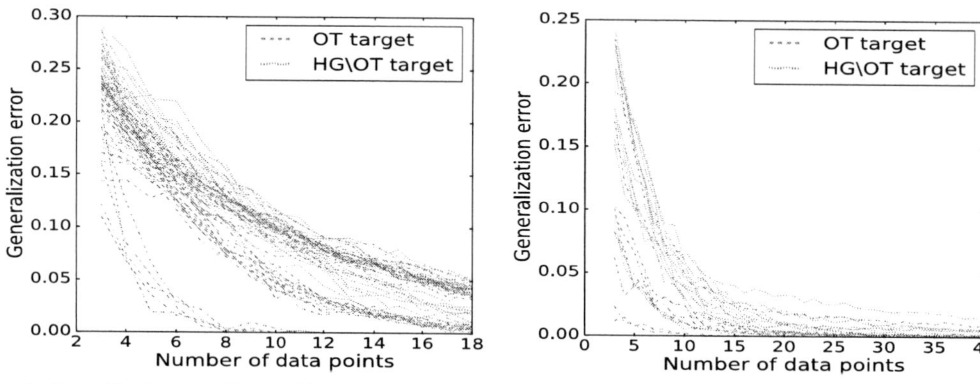

Figure 4: Generalization error $Err(n, G)$ as a function of n, for rounding harmony (left) and syllable types (right) data, for each OT target grammar G (red line) and each HG-non-OT target grammar G (blue line).

$\sum_k w_k h_k(x)$ to $f(x) = \min_{t \in S(x)} \sum_k w_k h_k(x, t)$, where S is a function from x to some finite set.

(C) The simulations reported in section 4 assume a uniform distribution over triplets (u, s, s') all consistent with some target grammar G. Future research will look at different data distributions (e.g., a Zipfian distribution over the underlying forms u) and the addition of some noise in the training data.

(D) The learner tested in section 4 simply looks for weights which maximize the margin but is oblivious to whether the target grammar is an OT or an HG-non-OT grammar. For OT targets, theorem 1 suggests the more specific learning strategy in algorithm 2. We consider each ranking π, construct the corresponding exponentially decaying weights w_π in (5), and determine the ranking $\pi*$ whose weights $w_{\pi*}$ maximize the margin. We denote by $Err_{OT}(n, G)$ the average error of the OT grammar corresponding to π^* on the target grammar G.

$Err_{OT}(n, G)$ is generally quite high when G is a HG-non-OT grammar. This is not surprising, since we're trying to learn a grammar outside the search space. Yet, figure 5 shows that even when the target grammar G is OT, $Err_{OT}(n, G)$ (red solid line) is slightly higher than the error $Err(n, G)$ (dashed blue line) obtained with the general learning procedure in algorithm 1. This is puzzling, as one might have expected that the restriction of the search space in algorithm 2 should have led to a lower error. Towards a possible explanation, we observe that the weights $w_{\pi*}$ obtained by algorithm 2 result in a very low margin, and thus a very high effective dimension compared to the weights w^* obtained through algorithm 1, as shown in figure 6.

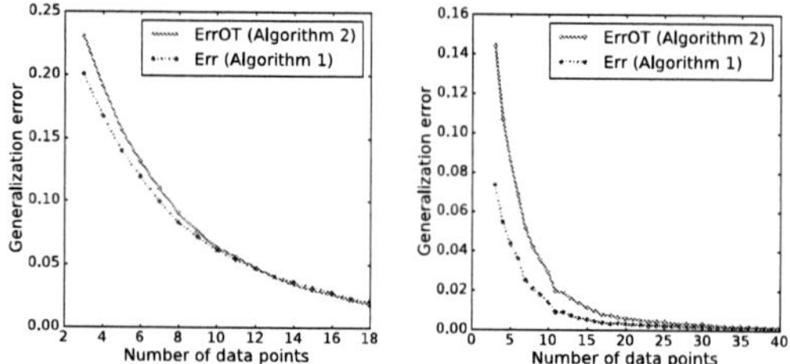

Figure 5: Average over OT target grammars of the generalization errors $Err(n, G)$ in algorithm 1 and $Err_{OT}(n, G)$ in algorithm 2, for harmony (left) and syllable types (right) data.

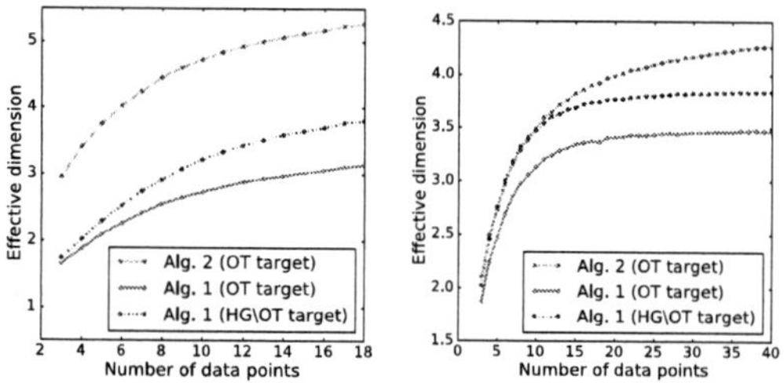

Figure 6: Effective dimension of the weights in algorithm 1 averaged over OT and over HG-non-OT target grammars; effective dimension of the weights in algorithm 2 averaged over OT target grammars.

Evidently, margin-based learning is incompatible with the strategy (5) for computing exponentially-decaying weights corresponding to OT rankings. One possibility for future research is to base weights not on full rankings, but on RCD's (Tesar and Smolensky, 1998) hierarchy $H_1 \gg H_2 \gg \cdots$ (H_1 consists of constraints never loser preferring in T; H_2 consists of constraints which are only loser-preferring on triplets (u, s, s') of T where some constraint in H_1 is winner-preferring; and so on). For instance, one could pick weights w_H so that the constraints in H_1 all have the same weight, the constraints in H_2 all have the same exponentially smaller weight, and so on. A strategy of this kind might reach a compromise between fast decay and large margin.

Algorithm 2: Learning simulation for OT targets.

1 **for** G *in the typology* **do**
2   **for** $n = 3, \ldots, N$ **do**
3   **for** $m = 1, \ldots, 250$ **do**
4   Randomly select $T \in \mathcal{X}_G^n$
5        $\pi^* \leftarrow \arg\max_\pi \delta_T(w_\pi)$
6        $Err_{\mathrm{OT}}(m) \leftarrow \mathbb{P}(w_{\pi^*}^T x \le 0 | x \in \mathcal{X}_G)$
7      $Err_{\mathrm{OT}}(n, G) \leftarrow \frac{1}{250} \sum_m Err_{\mathrm{OT}}(m)$

Acknowledgments

The research reported in this paper was partially supported by the *MIT France Seed Fund* (project title: 'Phonological Typology and Learnability') and by the *Agence National de la Recherche* (project title: 'The mathematics of segmental phonotactics'). We thank an anonymous reviewer for helpful comments.

Appendix: more details on KP's bound

A.1 The exact formulation of Koltchinskii and Panchenko's (2005, theorem 2, p. 1464) error bound discussed in section 3 is as follows:

Theorem 2 *Suppose that $\mathcal{H}$ is a VC-subgraph class with VC-dimension V (see for instance Mohri et al. 2012). Consider a voting classifier $f = \sum_{k=1}^K w_k h_k \in \mathcal{F} = conv(\mathcal{H})$ which classifies correctly a training set $T = ((x_1, y_1), \ldots, (x_n, y_n))$ sampled i.i.d. according to a distribution $\mathbb{P}$. For every $t > 0$, the generalization error $Err_{\mathbb{P}}(f)$ of f is bound as follows with probability at least $1 - e^{-t}$:*

$$Err_{\mathbb{P}}(f) \le K \left(\frac{V d_T(f)}{n} \log \frac{n}{\delta_T(f)} + \frac{t}{n} \right) \quad (8)$$

where K is a universal constant, $\delta_T(f)$ is the margin of the classifier f on the training set T defined in (1) and $d_T(f)$ is its effective dimension defined in (2).

A.2 Since $\sum_{k=1}^K w_k \le 1$, the choice $d = 0$ in the definition (2) of the effective dimension yields $d_T(f) \le \frac{2}{\delta_T(f)^2} \log n$. KP's bound (8) thus becomes

$$Err_{\mathbb{P}}(f) \le K \left(\frac{V \log n}{n \delta^2} \log \frac{n}{\delta} + \frac{t}{n} \right) \quad (9)$$

which decreases as $1/n$ when $n \to \infty$ and increases as $1/\delta^2$ when $\delta \to 0$.

A.3 The effective dimension $d_T(f)$ which appears in KP's bound (8) depends on the decay of the weights in a representation of f. The following corollary (see Koltchinskii and Panchenko 2005, example on p. 1465) details the dependence of the bound on the decay. The proof of the corollary is provided in the online supplement, based on class notes by Panchenko (2004, class 21), as it has not appeared in the literature.

Corollary 1 *Consider a classifier $f = \sum_{i=1}^K w_k h_k$ in $\mathcal{F}$ which classifies correctly a training set $T = ((x_1, y_1), \ldots, (x_n, y_n))$ with margin $\delta = \delta_T(f)$, namely $y_1 f(x_1), \ldots, y_n f(x_n) > \delta$.*

- *If the weights w_k decay polynomially, i.e. $w_k \le k^{-B}$ for some $B > 1$, KP's bound (8) becomes:*

$$Err_{\mathbb{P}}(f) \le K \left(\frac{C_B}{\delta^{2/(2B-1)}} \frac{V}{n} \log^2 \frac{n}{\delta} + \frac{t}{n} \right) \quad (10)$$

where $C_B \to 1$ as $B \to \infty$.

- *If the weights w_k decay exponentially, namely $w_k \le e^{-k}$, KP's bound (8) becomes:*

$$Err_{\mathbb{P}}(f) \le K \left(\frac{V}{n} \log^2 \frac{n}{\delta} + \frac{t}{n} \right) \quad (11)$$

The two bounds (10) and (11) decrease as $1/n$ when $n \to \infty$, just as in the general case (9). The substantial improvement concerns the growth of the bound when $\delta \to 0$. The general bound (9) grows as $1/\delta^2$ when $\delta \to 0$. The bound (10) for the case of polynomial decay instead grows only as $1/\delta^{2/(2B-1)}$, which is slower than $1/\delta^2$ because $2/(2B-1) \le 2$ as $B > 1$. Furthermore, the bound (11) for the case of exponential decay grows only as $\log 1/\delta$ when $\delta \to 0$, which is substantially slower than $1/\delta^2$. When $B \to \infty$, the bound (10) for the case of polynomial decay becomes the bound (11) for the case of exponential decay.

References

Birgit Alber, Natalie DelBusso, and Alan Prince. 2015. From intensional properties to universal support. Università degli Studi di Verona and Rutgers University.

Maximilian Bane and Jason Riggle. 2009. Evaluating Strict Domination: The typological consequences of weighted constraints. In *Proceedings of the 45th annual meeting of the Chicago Linguistics Society*, pages 13–27.

Max Bane, Jason Riggle, and Morgan Sonderegger. 2010. The VC dimension of constraint-based grammars. *Lingua*, 120.5:1194–1208.

Edward Flemming. 2003. The relationship between coronal place and vowel backness. *Phonology*, 20:335–373.

Bruce Hayes. 1999. Phonetically-driven phonology: the role of Optimality Theory and inductive grounding. In Michael Darnell, Edith Moravscik, Michael Noonan, Frederick Newmeyer, and Kathleen Wheatly, editors, *Functionalism and Formalism in Linguistics*, volume 1: General Papers, pages 243–285. John Benjamins, Amsterdam.

Jongho Jun. 2004. Place assimilation. In B. Hayes, R. Kirchner, and D. Steriade, editors, *Phonetically Based Phonology*, pages 58–86. Cambridge University Press.

Abigail Kaun. 2004. The typology of rounding harmony. In Bruce Hayes, Robert Kirchner, and Donca Steriade, editors, *Phonetically based phonology*, pages 87–116. Cambridge University Press.

Shigeto Kawahara. 2006. A faithfulness ranking projected from a perceptibility scale: The case of [+voice] in Japanese. *Language*, 82:536–574.

Frank Keller. 2000. *Gradience in Grammar. Experimental and Computational Aspects of Degrees of Grammaticality*. Ph.D. thesis, University of Edinburgh, England.

Frank Keller. 2005. Linear Optimality Theory as a model of gradience in grammar. In Gisbert Fanselow, Caroline Féry, Ralph Vogel, and Matthias Schlesewsky, editors, *Gradience in Grammar: Generative Perspectives*, pages 270–287. Oxford University Press, Oxford.

Vladimir Koltchinskii and Dmitry Panchenko. 2002. Empirical margin distributions and bounding the generalization error of combined classifiers. *Ann. Statist.*, 30:1–50.

Vladimir Koltchinskii and Dmitry Panchenko. 2005. Complexities of convex combinations and bounding the generalization error in classification. *Ann. Statist.*, 33.4:1455–1496.

Vladimir Koltchinskii, Dmitry Panchenko, and Savina Andonova. 2003a. Generalization bounds for voting classifiers based on sparsity and clustering. In *Lecture Notes in Artificial Intelligence 2777*, pages 492–505.

Vladimir Koltchinskii, Dmitry Panchenko, and Lozano. 2003b. Bounding the generalization error of convex combinations of classifiers: Balancing the dimensionality and the margins. *Ann. Appl. Probab.*, 13:213–252.

Gèraldine Legendre, Yoshiro Miyata, and Paul Smolensky. 1990a. Harmonic Grammar: A formal multi-level connectionist theory of linguistic well-formedness: An application. In Morton Ann Gernsbacher and Sharon J. Derry, editors, *Annual conference of the Cognitive Science Society 12*, pages 884–891, Mahwah, New Jersey. Lawrence Erlbaum Associates.

Gèraldine Legendre, Yoshiro Miyata, and Paul Smolensky. 1990b. Harmonic Grammar: A formal multi-level connectionist theory of linguistic well-formedness: Theoretical foundations. In Morton Ann Gernsbacher and Sharon J. Derry, editors, *Annual conference of the Cognitive Science Society 12*, pages 388–395, Mahwah, NJ. Lawrence Erlbaum.

Gèraldine Legendre, Antonella Sorace, and Paul Smolensky. 2006. The optimality theory/harmonic grammar connection. In Paul Smolensky and Gèraldine Legendre, editors, *The Harmonic Mind*, pages 903–966. MIT Press, Cambridge, MA.

Mehryar Mohri, Afshin Rostamizadeh, and Ameet Talwalkar. 2012. *Foundations of Machine Learning*. MIT Press, Cambridge, MA.

John J. Ohala. 1983. The origin of sound patterns in vocal tract constraints. In Peter F. MacNeilage, editor, *The production of speech*, pages 189–216. Springer-Verlag, New York.

Dmitry Panchenko. 2004. Statistical learning theory. Lecture notes for the class 18.465 (Topics in Statistics), Department of Mathematics, MIT.

Joe Pater. 2009. Weighted constraints in Generative Linguistics. *Cognitive Science*, 33:999–1035.

Joe Pater. 2016. Universal grammar with weighted constraints. In Joe Pater and John J. McCarthy, editors, *Harmonic Grammar and Harmonic Serialism*, pages 1–46. Equinox, London.

Christopher Potts, Joe Pater, Karen Jesney, Rajesh Bhatt, and Michael Becker. 2010. Harmonic Grammar with Linear Programming: From linear systems to linguistic typology. *Phonology*, 27(1):1–41.

Alan Prince and Paul Smolensky. 1997. Optimality: From neural networks to universal grammar. *Science*, 275:1604–1610.

Alan Prince and Paul Smolensky. 2004. *Optimality Theory: Constraint Interaction in generative grammar*. Blackwell, Oxford. As Technical Report CU-CS-696-93, Department of Computer Science, University of Colorado at Boulder, and Technical Report TR-2, Rutgers Center for Cognitive Science, Rutgers University, New Brunswick, NJ, April 1993. Also available as ROA 537 version.

Jason Riggle. 2009. The complexity of ranking hypotheses in Optimality Theory. *Computational Linguistics*, 35(1):47–59.

Robert E. Shapire, Yoav Freund, Peter Bartlett, and Wee Sun Lee. 1998. Boosting the margin: a new explanation for the effectiveness of voting methods. *The Annals of Statistics*, 26.5:1651–1686.

Paul Smolensky and Gèraldine Legendre. 2006. *The Harmonic Mind*. MIT Press, Cambridge, MA.

Robert Staubs, Michael Becker, Christopher Potts, Patrick Pratt, John J. McCarthy, and Joe Pater. 2010. OT-Help 2.0. Software package. Software Package. University of Massachussetts, Amherst.

Donca Steriade. 2008. The phonology of perceptibility effects: the P-map and its consequences for constraint organization. In Kristin Hanson and Sharon Inkelas, editors, *The nature of the word: essays in honor of Paul Kiparsky*, pages 151–179. MIT Press, Cambridge.

Bruce Tesar and Paul Smolensky. 1998. Learnability in Optimality Theory. *Linguistic Inquiry*, 29:229–268.

Vladimir N. Vapnik and Alexey Y. Chervonenkis. 1971. On the uniform convergence of relative frequencies of events to their probabilities. *Theory of Probability and its Applications*, 16(2):264–280.

Detecting language impairments in autism: A computational analysis of semi-structured conversations with vector semantics

Adam Goodkind[1]**, Michelle Lee**[2,3]**, Gary E. Martin**[4]**, Molly Losh**[3]**, and Klinton Bicknell**[1]
[1]Dept. of Linguistics, Northwestern Univ., Evanston, IL 60208
[2]Clinical Psychology, Feinberg School of Medicine, Northwestern Univ., Chicago, IL 60611
[3]Dept. of Communication Sciences and Disorders, Northwestern Univ., Evanston, IL 60208
[4]Dept. of Communication Sciences and Disorders, St. John's Univ., Staten Island, NY 10301
`{a.goodkind, michelleannemarie2017}@u.northwestern.edu,`
`marting@stjohns.edu, {m-losh, kbicknell}@northwestern.edu`

Abstract

Many of the most significant impairments faced by individuals with autism spectrum disorder (ASD) relate to pragmatic (i.e. social) language. There is also evidence that pragmatic language differences may map to ASD-related genes. Therefore, quantifying the social-linguistic features of ASD has the potential to both improve clinical treatment and help identify gene-behavior relationships in ASD. Here, we apply vector semantics to transcripts of semi-structured interactions with children with both idiopathic and syndromic ASD. We find that children with ASD are less semantically similar to a gold standard derived from typically developing participants, and are more semantically variable. We show that this semantic similarity measure is affected by transcript word length, but that these group differences persist after removing length differences via subsampling. These findings suggest that linguistic signatures of ASD pervade child speech broadly, and can be automatically detected even in less structured interactions.

1 Introduction

From its earliest descriptions (Kanner, 1943), autism spectrum disorder (ASD) has been associated with language impairment, and pragmatic language impairment in particular. Problems with pragmatic language are a key component of current diagnostic criteria for ASD, and both atypical and idiosyncratic language are noted as features of ASD un-der current standards used in both the DSM-IV and DSM-5 (American Psychiatric Association, 2000, 2013). However, current methods for assessing pragmatic language impairment are often subjective, can be very time intensive, and distal from underlying mechanisms. Computational models of language production in ASD thus have the potential to improve diagnostic assessments, contribute to research into the basis of language impairment in ASD, and may also show strong utility in clinical treatment as objective and quantitative measures of response to intervention.

Additionally, evidence that more subtle language differences are evident at elevated rates among relatives of individuals with ASD points towards pragmatic language as a genetically meaningful domain in ASD, with potential for informing molecular genetic studies, which examine more specific ties to component phenotypes in ASD that may segregate independently and relate to distinct genetic underpinnings (Losh, Sullivan, Trembath, & Piven, 2008). The development of computational tools for quantifying language impairment in ASD, such as the present study, may therefore contribute to future studies of ASD genetics as well. This can be accomplished by applying the present study's methods to large-scale datasets, which are appropriate for broad genetic studies. In addition, the methods presented below provide a continuous measure of pragmatic impairment, which can be more readily compared against genetic data.

The pragmatic language impairments in ASD are

Proceedings of the Society for Computation in Linguistics (SCiL) 2018, pages 12-22.
Salt Lake City, Utah, January 4-7, 2018

evident in a range of linguistic features. For instance, limited frequency and diversity of complex syntax has been shown to significantly impact narrative and conversational quality in ASD (Losh & Capps, 2003; Prud'hommeaux, Roark, Black, & Van Santen, 2011). Individuals with ASD produce more non-contingent discourse in narrative and conversation (Capps, Kehres, & Sigman, 1998; Losh & Capps, 2003, 2006). In a similar vein, people with ASD tend to fixate on a single topic, even though a conversation may have moved away from that single topic in another direction (Nazeer & Ghaziuddin, 2012). Additionally, both inappropriate semantic and pragmatic language has been demonstrated (Tager-Flusberg & Sullivan, 1995). From a semantic standpoint, one way these differences may manifest is when children with ASD use very uncommon words in a context in which a common word suffices. Children with ASD can also fail to make common pragmatic inferences, such as understanding the semantics of a question like *Can you close the door?* but failing to understand its pragmatics, and so responding by saying *Yes, I can.*

Given this evidence that individuals with ASD exhibit such pragmatic impairments, prior work has used computational models to distinguish individuals with ASD from typically developing individuals, using distributional semantic word models (Rouhizadeh, Prud'hommeaux, Roark, & Van Santen, 2013; Losh & Gordon, 2014). For example, both Losh and Gordon (2014) and Lee et al. (2017) used Latent Semantic Analysis (Deerwester, Dumais, Furnas, Landauer, & Harshman, 1990) with transcripts from picturebook narratives, a narrative recall task, and a less structured narrative elicitation task. Both studies showed that narratives from individuals with ASD diverged significantly in vector semantic space from a gold standard (either the original narrative, or a narrative derived from the TD group of participants) compared to (non-gold standard) typically developing controls.

Narrative recall and picturebook description tasks afforded clear gold standards for comparisons, with a very clear objective semantics to communicate the original narrative. Thus, they were optimal for a computational linguistic approach. However, it is less clear whether such an approach can generalize to other, more variable and naturalistic language

contexts, in which there may be no objective gold standard. Arguably, though, these naturalistic studies are more ecologically valid, and also constitute the discourse context posing the most serious challenges to individuals with ASD.

1.1 Goals

The primary goal of the present work is to investigate whether this computational approach could be applied in a more open-ended conversational setting, in which there is no objective gold standard. The primary contributions of this work are as follows:

- We show that language from individuals with ASD can be distinguished from that of typically developing individuals, by applying vector semantic models, *even on semi-structured conversational data.*

- We demonstrate that semantic similarity metrics are affected by transcript length, raising the question of whether such metrics can yield valid conclusions with very small language samples, such as often occur with children or lower functioning populations.

- We present a method for adapting semantic similarity analyses to accommodate possibly-small language samples from younger or lower functioning populations who have more limited language abilities.

To do this, we analyzed semi-structured conversational interactions, consisting of relatively free ranging conversation in a number of somewhat consistent situations. We construct an approximate gold standard of comparison from the transcripts of a few individuals with typical development who had similar and typical language and cognitive abilities.

We focus on conversational interactions because this language context is among the most challenging for individuals with ASD, since lack of structure and high interpersonal demands pose serious barriers to effective communication (as opposed to picturebook narratives, for example) (Losh & Capps, 2003). Furthermore, prior studies of computational linguistic approaches to characterizing discourse in ASD have focused on more structured contexts. This study is the first to apply this technique to conversational interaction in ASD. If this technique can successfully differentiate neurotypical individuals and individuals with ASD, based on semi-structured conversation, it would suggest that the semantic differences in the language of individuals with ASD are quite widespread, and detectable across a range of everyday tasks. Finally, because the semi-structured interactions we analyze come from a standard ASD diagnosis task (the ADOS, see below), such a computational model has the potential to help with diagnosis.

The remainder of this paper is structured as follows. The following section describes our transcript dataset. Following that, Section 3 describes how we use word embeddings to quantify distances to gold standards. Section 4 describes our first experiment applying this method to conversation data. Section 5 points out that this similarity metric is confounded by transcript length and presents a method to remove this confound. Section 6 concludes.

2 Interaction session transcripts

2.1 Participants

We selected 109 participants, in three groups: (1) (younger) typically developing children used as a control due to comparable cognitive ability to the clinical groups (TD); (2) school aged children with idiopathic ASD, unrelated to any other known genetic disorders (ASD); and (3) children with ASD comorbid with fragile X syndrome (FXS-ASD). For all three groups, children were selected based upon the nonverbal mental age from the Leiter International Performance Scale (Wechsler, 2008). For typically developing children, mental age should on average match chronological age. However, for children with developmental impairments, mental age is often lower than chronological age.

Fragile X syndrome (FXS) is the most common heritable intellectual disability, and has common comorbidity with ASD (Rogers, Wehner, & Hagerman, 2001; Kaufmann et al., 2004; Martin et al., 2017; *inter alia*). Like ASD, fragile X syndrome often shows pragmatic deficits as well. Evidence also exists that language impairment within fragile X syndrome affects males with FXS more than it affects females with FXS (Abbeduto, McDuffie, & Thurman, 2014). For this reason, all selected participants were male. This also eliminates sex as a possible confound.

All participants were selected based on a mental age of approximately 5;0. All participants had a mean length of utterance (MLU) of at least three words per utterance and were L1 English speakers. Participants were drawn from a larger longitudinal study reported in Martin et al. (2017). Additionally, individuals with idiopathic ASD were required to have a previous clinical diagnosis, confirmed by administration of the Autism Diagnostic Observation Schedule (ADOS) (Lord et al., 2000) and/or the Autism Diagnostic Interview - Revised (Lord, Rutter, & Le Couteur, 1994). Individuals with FXS-ASD were confirmed based only on the ADOS. The average chronological and mental age for each group are provided in Table 1.

2.2 Procedure

Language samples were derived from the ADOS and/or ADOS-2, gold standard diagnostic tools for ASD. The ADOS includes several structured activities as well as opportunities for naturalistic interaction, in order to probe for social-communication skills and the presence of restricted and repetitive behaviors. Play-based activities included the opportunity to play with action figures and other toys. Non-play based activities included conversation between tasks, describing a picture, or telling a story from a book.

2.3 Transcription

Subsections of entire language samples were transcribed from high quality audio recordings by trained transcribers. The transcripts were based on a subset of the full assessment: specifically, 55 intelligible play based turns and 55 non-play based turns were transcribed (or fewer in the rare case that there were not 55 intelligible turns).

2.4 Processing

All child utterances were extracted from the transcripts, including filled pauses and stop words. Although stop word removal is common practice in distributional semantics and NLP (Levy, Goldberg, & Dagan, 2015), this class of words can be psychologically informative (Chung & Pennebaker, 2007). This also seems especially relevant to ASD, where incorrect pronoun usage is common, e.g. using the second-person *you* when referring to oneself, instead of the correct first-person *I* (Naigles et al., 2016).

Diagnostic Group	n	Chronological Age (SD)	Mental Age Equivalent (SD)
Typically developing (TD)	22	4.7 (1.1)	5.1 (1.2)
Autism spectrum disorder (ASD)	39	8.7 (2.9)	6.9 (3.4)
Fragile X syndrome + ASD (FXS-ASD)	48	10.6 (2.6)	5.0 (0.6)

Table 1: Participant chronological age and mental age equivalent for each diagnostic group.

2.5 Gold standard transcripts

Two of the transcripts from children with typical development were designated gold standard transcripts. This designation was performed by two researchers who were both familiar with the tasks in the interactions. Gold standards were selected based on detailed clinical-behavioral ratings. We selected TD participants who, based on this coding, demonstrated minimal pragmatic language deficits and highly-rated core features of conversation, such as contingency, reciprocity, and initiation. For the purposes of analyses conducted below, these two transcripts were excluded from the TD group, so as not to bias the results.

3 Word embeddings

A number of previous studies have used word embeddings (vector semantics) to study language transcripts of people with autism (Rouhizadeh et al., 2013; Rouhizadeh, 2015). A vector semantic model specifies an embedding, or mapping, from each word in the vocabulary to a point in a continuous vector space. A document in such models typically consists of an unordered collection of words. A vector semantic representation of a document can be obtained by combining the embeddings of the words it contains in some way, such as summing.

For the present study, each word in the transcript was converted to a vector using the `word2vec` model, via the pretrained Google News embeddings (Mikolov, Sutskever, Chen, Corrado, & Dean, 2013), which are 400-dimensional. A vector semantic representation of each document was created by summing the vectors for each of its words, and then normalizing to have unit length.

The gold standard vector was calculated as the mean of the two gold standard transcript vectors, and used as the basis of comparison for semantic similarity.[1] The transcripts identified to be the gold standard

were excluded from the TD group for all analyses.

Semantic distance of a transcript vector to the gold standard was measured as the cosine distance between them. That is, for a given transcript vector $\vec{v}_i$ and the gold standard vector $\vec{g}$, the distance was then calculated as

$$d(\vec{v}_i, \vec{g}) = \frac{\vec{v}_i \cdot \vec{g}}{\|\vec{v}_i\|_2 \|\vec{g}\|_2} \tag{1}$$

Because the transcript vectors are all normalized to have unit length, this reduces to a simple dot product.

A lower cosine distance means that the vectors being compared have more similar dimensions. Given this, we then defined the semantic similarity of a vector to the gold standard as one minus the cosine distance $(1 - d(\vec{v}, \vec{g}))$, so that a lower distance resulted in a higher semantic similarity score.

The code for converting transcripts to vectors and computing similarities is freely available on an open-source repository[2]. Although our transcripts themselves cannot be shared because of privacy concerns, we used a standard format for transcription, making our tools readily usable by other investigators.

4 Experiment 1

We performed three sets of analyses to compare TD individuals to the two populations with ASD.

4.1 Similarity to gold standard

For each transcript, we calculated the cosine distance between its vector embedding and the gold standard, yielding a single similarity score for each transcript. Figure 1 illustrates the mean semantic

---

[1]Other bases for comparison were also considered, including using the mean vector from all transcripts as well as the mean vector of all of the typically developing transcripts. Future studies will compare and contrast the utility of selecting different bases for comparison.

[2]`https://github.com/langcomp/vectoraut`

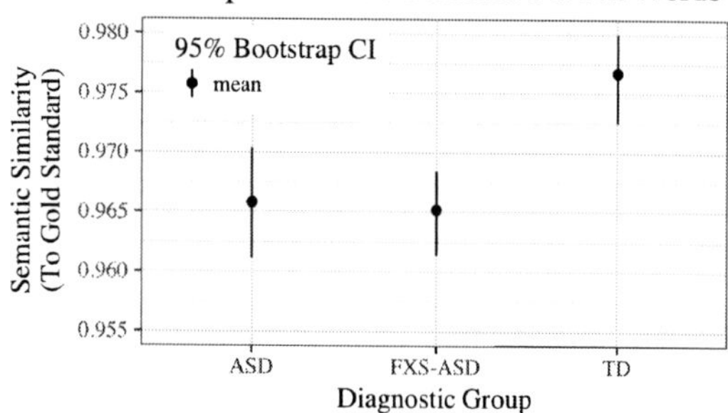

Figure 1: Semantic similarity for each diagnostic group as compared to the semantic content of Gold Standard transcripts

Comparison	All Words	Word Sampling
TD vs ASD	$p < 0.001$	$p < 0.05$
TD vs FXS-ASD	$p < 0.00001$	$p < 0.001$

Table 2: Significance levels for differences in semantic similarity between diagnostic groups and a gold standard. Both full transcripts as well as random word sampling from transcripts are reported.

similarity for each group, as well as the 95% bootstrapped confidence intervals. We then ran nonparametric Wilcoxon tests comparing the semantic similarity scores across groups, specifically comparing the TD group to the ASD group, and the TD group to FXS-ASD, the results of which are shown in Table 2, middle column. The results show reliable differences between TD and each of the two other groups, with the TD group being more semantically similar to the gold standard transcripts than the groups with ASD. The two groups with ASD appear very similar to each other.

4.2 Visualizing semantic space

To try to visualize the semantic space these transcripts are embedded in, we used Principal Component Analysis (Jolliffe, 2011) to reduce the 400-dimensional vectors to two dimensions. The results are visualized in Figure 2, where each transcript is identified by its group, and the two transcripts from which the gold standard was constructed have also been added. As can be seen, the ASD and FXS-ASD groups are much more dispersed than the typically developing group, which is relatively tightly clus-

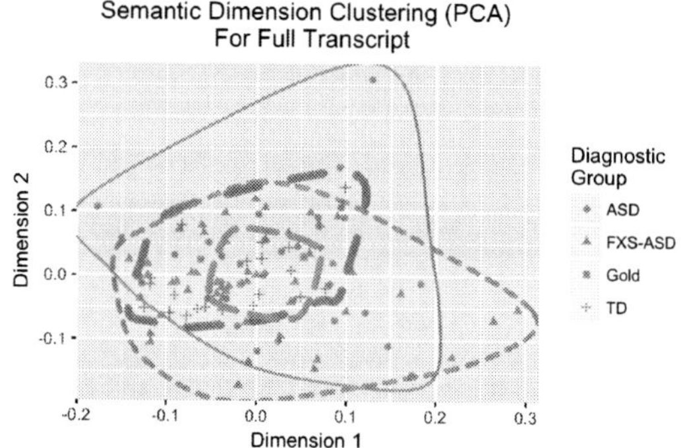

Figure 2: Most informative dimensions using full transcripts, as selected by PCA, for different diagnostic groups. Clusters for children with autism are more diffuse.

Diagnostic Group	Manhattan Distance (mean)
TD	3.44
FXS-ASD	4.42
ASD	4.49

Table 3: Manhattan distance between all pairs of word vectors within each diagnostic group, for full transcripts.

tered around the gold standard. This suggests a possible reason why the two groups with ASD were less similar to the gold standard than was the TD group: because they are more semantically variable.

4.3 Within-group variability

Finally, to test this hypothesis that variability within groups is higher for groups with ASD as opposed to the TD group, we measured the Manhattan distance between all pairs of transcript vectors within each group, using the full 400-dimensional transcript vectors. This distance is an indication of how far apart semantically two transcript are. We elected to use Manhattan distance rather than Euclidean distance because of the former's robustness in high-dimensional space (Aggarwal, Hinneburg, & Keim, 2001). The average distance between each vector pair in each group is reported in Table 3. The results show that the TD group is much more homogeneous, while the two groups with ASD exhibit larger variability. Interestingly, the two groups with ASD again appear very similar to each other.

5   Experiment 2

The results of Expt. 1 showed strong evidence that individuals in the ASD and FXS-ASD groups were on average less semantically similar to a gold standard than TD individuals were, and that individuals from both groups with ASD were more semantically variable. However, it is also a feature of this dataset that there is a systematic relationship between the word count of a particular individual's transcript and their semantic similarity. This is shown in Figure 3, where transcripts with a higher word count on average have higher similarity scores to the gold standard, within each of the three groups (although there is some suggestion for the ASD group that this effect may reverse for especially high word counts). There are multiple, non-exclusive hypotheses for where this relationship arises. It may be an objective feature of language production that individuals with more language impairment talk less on average. Alternatively, it may be that the semantic similarity metric becomes noisier and thus lower with smaller language samples.

There are also systematic differences between groups in transcript length, visualized in Figure 4. On the hypothesis that differences in transcript length are an artifact of the measure, not necessarily related to language proficiency, this raises the possibility that the reason the TD group had more semantic similarity to the gold standard on average was that it had longer transcripts on average. To rule out this possibility, and gain some insight into the relationship between semantic similarity and transcript length, we developed a simple method to remove the variance in transcript length.

5.1   Word sampling

To remove this variance in transcript length, we performed a random sampling algorithm. Specifically, we selected a target transcript length of 300 words, which was lower than the majority of transcript lengths in every diagnostic group. Then, we sampled, without replacement, 300 words from every transcript. For the 2 transcripts that fell below the 300-word threshold, we selected the entire transcript. With this new set of transcripts of a uniform length, we performed the same analyses as in Expt. 1. To leave in tact full information about the

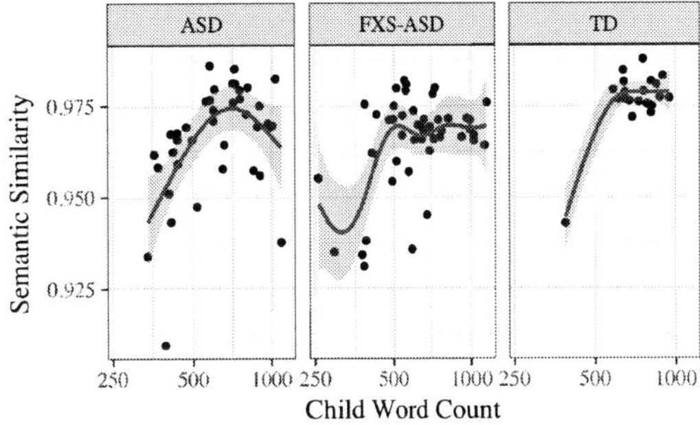

Figure 3: Child word counts versus semantic similarity to gold standard. As children produce more words, similarity to the gold standard also increases. Smoothing lines were calculated using a generalized additive model (GAM).

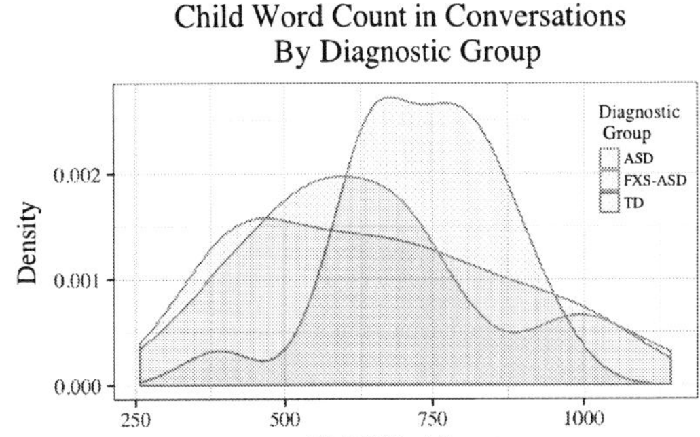

Figure 4: Child words counts for different diagnostic groups. Different diagnostic groups have markedly divergent distributions.

gold standard, we left it unchanged from Expt. 1.

5.2   Similarity to gold standard

The similarity of these uniform-length transcripts to the gold standard are shown in Figure 5. As can be seen, even without transcript length differences, semantic similarity is still lower for the ASD and FXS-ASD groups than for the TD group. The results of a Wilcoxon test are given in the rightmost column of Table 2, showing that these differences are still significant, suggesting that the group differences obtained in Expt. 1 were not merely an artifact of shorter transcript lengths.

Comparing the values in Figure 5 to those in Figure 1 from Expt. 1, however, we can see that the similarity values here are a bit lower, especially those

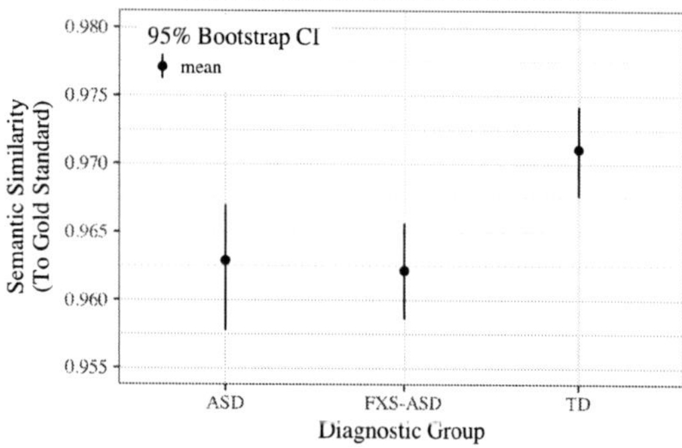

Figure 5: Semantic similarity for each diagnostic group as compared to the semantic content of Gold Standard transcripts, using a 300 word random sample

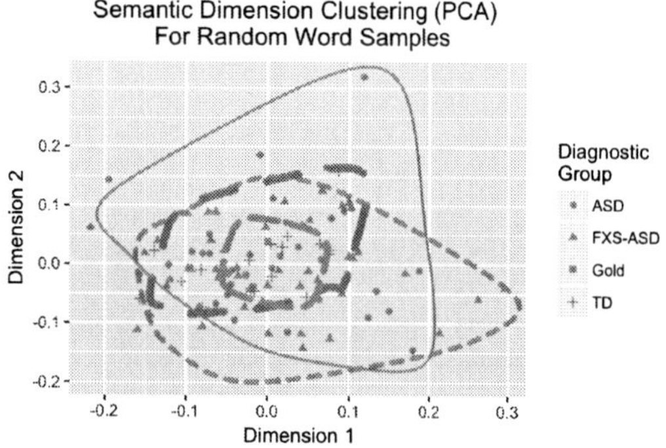

Figure 6: Most informative dimensions using random word sampling, as selected by PCA, for different diagnostic groups. Clusters for children with autism are more diffuse.

from the TD group. That suggests that these semantic similarity metrics are indeed somewhat biased lower by the smaller samples. For work such as this applying vector semantic similarity metrics to transcripts from younger and/or lower functioning individuals, analyses like this may be a useful tool.

5.3 Visualizing semantic space

As in Expt. 1, we reduced all of the transcript vectors to two dimensions using PCA. Even when randomly selecting words, the same spatial relationships seen in Expt. 1 still hold, with greater dispersion for the ASD and FXS-ASD groups, and more concentration for the TD and gold standard groups.

Diagnostic Group	Manhattan Distance (mean)
TD	3.76
FXS-ASD	4.54
ASD	4.67

Table 4: Manhattan distance between all pairs of word vectors within each diagnostic group, for random word samples.

5.4 Within-group variability

We aimed to understand whether the transcript vectors from randomly sampled words still had a very short distance between them, or whether the random word sampling obfuscated the similarities seen in Expt. 1. As seen in Table 4, the uniform-length transcripts still had the same qualitative distance relationships, with the vectors in the TD group being closer together than those within either of the two groups with ASD.

Comparing Table 4 to its Expt. 1 equivalent, Table 3, we see that the mean distance between TD group transcripts is about 0.3 units higher here, whereas the ASD and FXS-ASD group distances are only 0.1–0.2 units higher. This result suggests again, however, that there is some evidence that the variability within groups seen in Expt. 1 was biased to be somewhat higher for the groups with shorter transcript, and that this method can correct for that bias.

6 Discussion

In this study, we used vector semantics to show that semi-structured conversations produced by individuals with ASD were semantically further from a gold standard conversational sample by children with typical development, and that there was more variability within the groups with ASD than within the typically developing group. We also presented evidence that these semantic similarity and distance measures were moderately biased by transcript length, with low transcript lengths yielding larger semantic distances from a gold standard as well as yielding more within-group variability. Finally, we showed that this bias could not explain the differences in semantic similarity and distance across groups.

Many previous studies applying vector semantics to the language of autism relied upon narratives (Losh & Capps, 2003; Prud'hommeaux et al.,

2011; Rouhizadeh, Prud'hommeaux, van Santen, & Sproat, 2014; Losh & Gordon, 2014; Lee et al., 2017; *inter alia*), for which there is an objective gold standard of semantic evaluation, i.e., the original narrative. The present study demonstrates that such methods can be extended to the more naturalistic context of semi-structured conversation. This is important because narrative retellings are expected to use a more constrained vocabulary; thus, unexpected words are even more surprising when the vocabulary is expected to be more minimal. On the other hand, it is easy to assume that a naturalistic conversation would have a large variety of vocabulary, making unexpected words less surprising and less telling, since a conversation can have a more wide array of topic areas to discuss. Nonetheless, even when participating in a more unconstrained conversation, our study still picked up semantic differences for the ASD groups, despite the more freewheeling dialogue.

The results of this study of semi-structured conversation parallel those of Losh and Gordon (2014) and Lee et al. (2017) on narratives. All studies showed that individuals with ASD produced language semantically further from a gold standard of typical development. All studies also showed that language produced by typically developing children clustered together more closely in semantic space, whereas that from children with ASD was more variable and diffuse in semantic space (cf. Rouhizadeh et al., 2014). These findings suggest that greater semantic variability may be a general property of the language of ASD not confined to narrative retellings.

To our knowledge, this is the first study to present a method for analyzing semantic similarities in the presence of strong differences in word length of transcripts across individuals and groups, which may be a common occurrence in work analyzing populations that differ in conversation length. Since MLU has been commonly found to be strongly correlated to (chronological) age (Miller & Chapman, 1981), and would lead to more words in a conversation, this may be a common issue for younger populations, as well as those that are lower functioning.

Interestingly, even when reducing the lengths of the transcripts by a substantial amount (often more than 50%) via random sampling, the transcripts of individuals with ASD were still significantly se-mantically further from the gold standard than were those of typically developing individuals. This suggests that the language of ASD may be pervasive in speech and detectable from even shorter samples.

The question remains, though *What exactly are we detecting through different mean semantic similarities for each group?* Are we picking up different *styles* of language use, or are we picking up the same type of language, just describing different topics? Either of those differences could affect semantic similarity in a similar fashion.

To test this, we looked at the transcripts' connections to type-token ratio, which measures lexical diversity. We ran both Pearson and Spearman correlations between semantic similarity and type-token ratio (TTR). TTR is the ratio of the number of word types to the number of word tokens If lexical diversity was significantly different between groups in the same way that semantic similarity was different between groups, this would be a strong indicator that the difference in group semantic similarity was due to the use of different types of language, or at least different levels of lexical diversity. However, this correlation was very low and neither individual groups nor overall correlations approached statistical significance.

This results suggests that linguistic style (at least as indexed by the type-token ratio) is not a driving factor. Instead, we are left with the most glaring differences being due to using the same type of language while discussing different topics, and thereby using different words to describe different topics.

Perhaps this underscores the idiosyncratic nature of utterances from both the ASD and FXS-ASD groups. In other words, even though conversational language is more unconstrained than narrative retellings, Figures 2 and 6 still seem to illustrate that TD participants use a more confined vocabulary. This may seem counter-intuitive, as a more natural conversation can be assumed to be diverse, with a less constrained vocabulary. This seems to point to the robustness of word vectors, since they can still capture the diversity of the uncommon words often selected by children with ASD and FXS-ASD, while downplaying the natural diversity that is expected from conversations with typically-developing children.

6.1 Conclusion

The primary contribution of this study is to show that vector semantics distinguishes language of individuals with ASD from language of individuals who are typically developing, even when that language was produced in a semi-structured conversational setting with no objective semantic standard – the language context where individuals with ASD exhibit most severe impairments. It also presented evidence that such semantic metrics can be applied to populations who yield smaller word counts (such as younger, lower functioning children with intellectual disability) – despite short transcripts biasing the semantic metrics – and presented a simple method to help quantify and control this bias that can be implemented across age and ability levels.

This work represents a step toward developing a metric of language impairment in ASD that is empirically quantifiable, objective, and automatically generated, which has the potential to improve clinical assessments, offer objective quantitative indices of language impairment that could be used to stratify groups in biological studies, and possibly serve as sensitive measures of response to clinical interventions. The results here were based on conversational data from the ADOS assessment, a standard assessment for ASD including semi-structured conversational samples. This is a more generalized form of dialogue than the narrative retellings used in many previous studies. This finding, then, opens the door to investigate further diverse discourse settings where semantic similarity tests might be effectively implemented. For instance, if a classroom or family dinnertime setting could be used as a reliable source, then a child would not need to be removed from their typical daily activities in order to perform testing. Such assessments would also capture pragmatic impairments in more naturalistic settings, affording more generalizable findings.

Future investigations will investigate the seeming disparity between extremely uncommon word choice and word choice that is *too* identical to that employed by a conversation partner. Perhaps these phenomena cancel each other out when an entire conversation is considered, leaving both of these idiosyncrasies diluted by averaging. We plan on investigating this alongside semantic similarity as a means to predict, not merely quantify, ASD.

We also have data collected from the same participants at subsequent time points, which will allow us to test the rate of change for individuals. For example, if language production did not advance at an expected rate over a period of time, this could also be a sign of developmental deficits.

Finally, by quantifying the language of ASD in a continuous way, this method has possible applications to genetic studies of ASD, where quantitative as opposed to categorical phenotypic measures afford greater power to detect molecular genetic associations for complex traits and disorders such as ASD. For example, it could be used to quantify the extent to which family members of individuals with ASD, who are themselves typically developing, nevertheless exhibit values of this continuous measure that more closely resemble the language of ASD. More generally, these findings suggest that the linguistic signatures of ASD pervade child speech, and may be automatically detectable under wider conditions than previously demonstrated.

Acknowledgements

This research was supported by NIDCD R01DC010191 (to Losh), NICHD R01 HD038819 (to Martin), and a Northwestern Data Science Institute grant (to Bicknell and Losh).

References

Abbeduto, L., McDuffie, A., & Thurman, A. J. (2014). The fragile x syndrome–autism comorbidity: what do we really know? *Frontiers in genetics*, *5*.

Aggarwal, C. C., Hinneburg, A., & Keim, D. A. (2001). On the surprising behavior of distance metrics in high dimensional spaces. In *Icdt* (Vol. 1, pp. 420–434).

American Psychiatric Association. (2000). Task force on DSM-IV. diagnostic and statistical manual of mental disorders: DSM-IV-TR. *Washington, DC: American Psychiatric Association*, *4*.

American Psychiatric Association. (2013). Diagnostic and statistical manual of mental disorders: DSM-5. *Washington, DC: American Psychiatric Association*.

Capps, L., Kehres, J., & Sigman, M. (1998). Conversational abilities among children with autism and children with developmental delays. *Autism, 2*(4), 325–344.

Chung, C., & Pennebaker, J. W. (2007). The psychological functions of function words. *Social communication*, 343–359.

Deerwester, S., Dumais, S. T., Furnas, G. W., Landauer, T. K., & Harshman, R. (1990). Indexing by latent semantic analysis. *Journal of the American society for information science, 41*(6), 391.

Jolliffe, I. T. (2011). Principal component analysis. In *International encyclopedia of statistical science.*

Kanner, L. (1943). Autistic disturbances of affective contact. *Nervous child, 2*(3), 217–250.

Kaufmann, W. E., Cortell, R., Kau, A. S., Bukelis, I., Tierney, E., Gray, R. M., ... Stanard, P. (2004). Autism spectrum disorder in fragile x syndrome: communication, social interaction, and specific behaviors. *American Journal of Medical Genetics Part A, 129*(3), 225–234.

Lee, M., Martin, G. E., Hogan, A., Hano, D., Gordon, P. C., & Losh, M. (2017). Whats the story? A computational analysis of narrative competence in autism. *Autism*, 1362361316677957.

Levy, O., Goldberg, Y., & Dagan, I. (2015). Improving distributional similarity with lessons learned from word embeddings. *TACL, 3*, 211-225.

Lord, C., Risi, S., Lambrecht, L., Cook, E. H., Leventhal, B. L., DiLavore, P. C., ... Rutter, M. (2000). The autism diagnostic observation schedule-generic: A standard measure of social and communication deficits associated with the spectrum of autism. *Journal of autism and developmental disorders, 30*(3), 205–223.

Lord, C., Rutter, M., & Le Couteur, A. (1994). Autism diagnostic interview-revised: a revised version of a diagnostic interview for caregivers of individuals with possible pervasive developmental disorders. *Journal of autism and developmental disorders, 24*(5), 659–685.

Losh, M., & Capps, L. (2003). Narrative ability in high-functioning children with autism or asperger's syndrome. *Journal of autism and developmental disorders, 33*(3), 239–251.

Losh, M., & Capps, L. (2006). Understanding of emotional experience in autism: insights from the personal accounts of high-functioning children with autism. *Developmental psychology, 42*(5), 809.

Losh, M., & Gordon, P. C. (2014). Quantifying narrative ability in autism spectrum disorder: A computational linguistic analysis of narrative coherence. *Journal of autism and developmental disorders, 44*(12), 3016–3025.

Losh, M., Sullivan, P. F., Trembath, D., & Piven, J. (2008). Current developments in the genetics of autism: from phenome to genome. *Journal of Neuropathology & Experimental Neurology, 67*(9), 829–837.

Martin, G. E., Barstein, J., Hornickel, J., Matherly, S., Durante, G., & Losh, M. (2017). Signaling of noncomprehension in communication breakdowns in fragile x syndrome, down syndrome, and autism spectrum disorder. *Journal of Communication Disorders, 65*, 22–34.

Mikolov, T., Sutskever, I., Chen, K., Corrado, G. S., & Dean, J. (2013). Distributed representations of words and phrases and their compositionality. In *Advances in neural information processing systems* (pp. 3111–3119).

Miller, J. F., & Chapman, R. S. (1981). The relation between age and mean length of utterance in morphemes. *Journal of Speech, Language, and Hearing Research, 24*(2), 154–161.

Naigles, L. R., Cheng, M., Rattanasone, N. X., Tek, S., Khetrapal, N., Fein, D., & Demuth, K. (2016). "You're telling me!" The prevalence and predictors of pronoun reversals in children with autism spectrum disorders and typical development. *Research in autism spectrum disorders, 27*, 11–20.

Nazeer, A., & Ghaziuddin, M. (2012). Autism spectrum disorders: clinical features and diagnosis. *Pediatric Clinics of North America, 59*(1), 19–25.

Prud'hommeaux, E. T., Roark, B., Black, L. M., & Van Santen, J. (2011). Classification of atypical language in autism. In *Proceedings of the 2nd workshop on cognitive modeling and computational linguistics* (pp. 88–96).

Rogers, S. J., Wehner, E. A., & Hagerman, R. (2001). The behavioral phenotype in fragile x: symptoms of autism in very young children with fragile x syndrome, idiopathic autism, and other developmental disorders. *Journal of developmental & behavioral pediatrics*, *22*(6), 409–417.

Rouhizadeh, M. (2015). Computational analysis of language use in autism. *Oregon Health & Science University*.

Rouhizadeh, M., Prud'hommeaux, E., Roark, B., & Van Santen, J. (2013). Distributional semantic models for the evaluation of disordered language. In *Proceedings of the conference. association for computational linguistics. north american chapter. meeting* (Vol. 2013, p. 709).

Rouhizadeh, M., Prud'hommeaux, E., van Santen, J., & Sproat, R. (2014). Detecting linguistic idiosyncratic interests in autism using distributional semantic models. In *The workshop on computational linguistics and clinical psychology: From linguistic signal to clinical reality2014* (pp. 46–50).

Tager-Flusberg, H., & Sullivan, K. (1995). Attributing mental states to story characters: A comparison of narratives produced by autistic and mentally retarded individuals. *Applied Psycholinguistics*, *16*(3), 241–256.

Wechsler, D. (2008). Wechsler adult intelligence scale–fourth edition (WAIS–IV). *San Antonio, TX: NCS Pearson*, *22*, 498.

Grammar Size and Quantitative Restrictions on Movement

Thomas Graf
Stony Brook University
Stony Brook, NY 11794-4376
`mail@thomasgraf.net`

Abstract

Recently is has been proved that every Minimalist grammar can be converted into a strongly equivalent *single movement normal form* such that every phrase moves at most once in every derivation. The normal form conversion greatly simplifies the formalism and reduces the complexity of movement dependencies, but it also runs the risk of greatly increasing the size of the grammar. I show that no such blow-up obtains with linguistically plausible grammars that respect common constraints on movement. This establishes not only the cost-free nature of this normal form for realistic grammars, but also that the known restrictions on movement greatly reduce the range of licit movement configurations relative to what unconstrained Minimalist grammars are capable of. Moreover, this work constitutes a first step towards a quantitatively grounded view of movement.

1   Introduction

One of the defining properties of syntax is that phrases do not surface in their base position, also known as the *displacement property*. For example, the topicalized phrase in (1a) acts as an object and thus its base position is to the right of the verb as in (1b).

(1)   a. This guy, John really hates.

         b. John really hates this guy.

While displacement phenomena can be analyzed in numerous ways, movement as a generalization of Chomskyan transformations is the most commonly chosen option.

The last sixty years of generative research have unearthed numerous properties of movement (Ross 1967; Chomsky 1973; Chomsky 1986; Chomsky 2001; Chomsky 2013; Rizzi 1990; Fox and Pesetsky 2005, a.o.), but one of the most central is that movement produces "punctuated paths" (Abels, 2003). This means that phrases do not immediately move to their target position but may temporarily occupy intermediate landing positions on the way there. The nature of punctuated paths was recently studied in Graf et al. (2016), using *Minimalist grammars* (MGs; Stabler 1997; Stabler 2011a) as a formal model of syntax. Graf et al. (2016) prove a *single movement normal form* (SMNF) theorem for MGs. This theorem describes an encoding of MGs where all movement steps of a phrase are triggered by a single feature at the final target position. SMNF has the advantage of reducing the computational complexity of movement dependencies, making it a particularly parsimonious encoding of MGs. At the same time, it comes at the potential cost of a large blow-up in the size of the grammar. Since parsing and learning algorithms tend to scale badly with large grammars, this endangers the viability of SMNF for practical purposes.

In this paper, I show that such a blow-up is primarily observed with grammars that allow unnatural movement patterns — in realistic grammars, the set of licit movement configurations is greatly limited by locality conditions so that SMNF induces only a minimal blow-up. This is a welcome result for real-world applications, but it also points the direction

Proceedings of the Society for Computation in Linguistics (SCiL) 2018, pages 23-33.
Salt Lake City, Utah, January 4-7, 2018

towards a novel, quantitative perspective on movement. SMNF can distinguish some natural and unnatural movement patterns on quantitative grounds, and it allows us to evaluate constraints on movement in a more global fashion that considers not only their effect on individual derivations but the grammar as a whole.

The paper is laid out as follows: I first give an intuitive introduction to MGs (2.1), how every MG can be translated into SMNF, and why this may increase the size of the grammar (2.2). I also explain in detail why SMNF is not at odds with current syntactic assumptions and what advantages it may provide on a practical, theoretical, and cognitive level (2.3). I then discuss what kind of movement configurations may increase the size of an SMNF grammar (3.1), and how such configurations are blocked by the ban against improper movement (3.2), the ungrammaticality of superraising (3.3), freezing effects (3.4), and the wh-island constraint (3.5). This leaves only a handful of constructions as potentially problematic, foremost multiple wh-movement and scrambling (3.6). The relevance of these empirical phenomena greatly depends on the choice of syntactic analysis, though, so that the blow-up with SMNF grammars is still likely to be remarkably limited. I conclude with a brief discussion of the linguistic implications of these findings (3.7).

2 Formal Background

2.1 Minimalist Grammars

MGs are a rigorous formalization of Minimalist syntax (Chomsky, 1995). MGs can be decomposed into two components: a set of well-formed derivation trees, and a mapping from those derivation trees to phrase structure trees. Derivation trees are very similar to phrase structure trees, except that interior nodes are labeled *Merge* or *Move* and, more importantly, moving phrases remain in their base position (Fig. 1). The main role of the mapping to phrase structure trees thus is to move phrases into their surface position and insert traces in all intermediate landing sites.

While this general picture is largely sufficient for this paper, SMNF requires a deeper understanding of the MG feature calculus and how it controls movement. Every MG is a finite set *Lex* (the *lexicon*) of

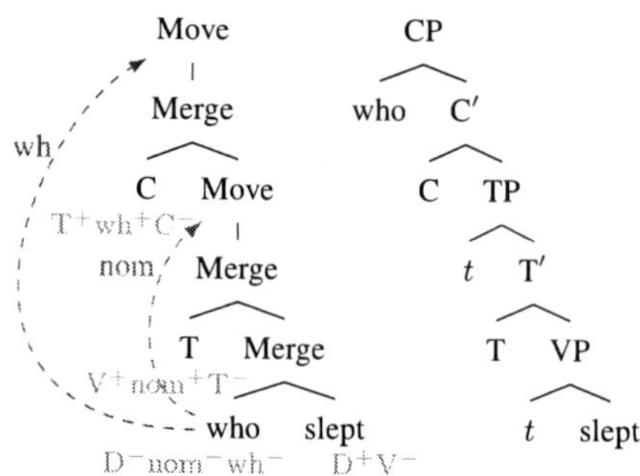

Figure 1: MG derivation tree (left) and corresponding phrase structure tree (right); for the sake of exposition, movement is indicated by arrows

lexical items (LIs), each one of which is annotated with finitely many features. Features come in two polarities, $+$ and $-$, and they trigger either Merge operations or Move operations. This paper adapts the terminology and notation shown in Tab. 1. An

	Merge	Move
$+$	selector F^+	licensor f^+
$-$	category F^-	licensee f^-

Table 1: Terminology and notation for MG feature calculus

MG derivation proceeds by combining LIs until all features have been checked (except the final C^--feature). Two features f° and $g^\bullet$ ($\circ, \bullet \in \{+, -\}$) can be checked iff $f = g$ and $\circ \neq \bullet$. In addition, the features on LIs have a linear order that encodes the sequence in which they must be checked.

Consider the derivation tree in Fig. 1. It represents a derivation that starts with the LIs who :: D^- nom$^-$ wh$^-$ and slept :: D^+ V^-. Their first unchecked features are, respectively, D^- and D^+. Since they have the same feature name but opposite polarity, they can be checked and trigger an application of Merge. The Merge node in the derivation tree is merely a record of this application, the actual result is only seen in the phrase structure tree where *who* and *slept* are combined into a VP.

After feature checking, the remaining feature strings for *who* and *slept* are nom$^-$ wh$^-$ and V^-. Since *who* only has licensee features left, it has to wait for matching licensor features to be introduced into the derivation. Until then, *who* is not available for further operations. But *slept* still has a category feature V^-. This feature can be checked by adding a new LI, the unpronounced T-head T :: $V^+\text{nom}^+T^-$. Once again this licenses an application of Merge with a corresponding structure-building step in the phrase structure tree.

All features of *slept* have now been checked, whereas the T-head still carries the feature string nom^+T^-. Recall that the remaining feature sequence of *who* is nom^-wh^-. So *who* has been waiting for a licensor feature nom^+ to check it licensee feature nom^-, and this licensor feature is exactly what the T-head provides at this point. Since nom^- and nom^+ are Move features rather than Merge features, their checking triggers an application of Move. Just as with Merge, the derivation tree only contains a record of the Move operation rather than its actual result. In the phrase structure tree, on the other hand, *who* has now been moved from its base position to the specifier of TP. After move, *who* only has the licensee feature wh^- left, and the T-head only has its category feature T^-. At this point, the unpronounced C-head C :: $T^+\text{wh}^+C^-$ enters the derivation. The reader is invited to verify for himself that the feature calculus enforces two more feature checking operations that license one instance each of Merge and Move, at which point the only remaining feature is C^- and the derivation can end.

The feature calculus employed in the example above is one of two core mechanisms of all MG derivations. A derivation tree over lexicon Lex is well-formed only if all its LIs are members of Lex and the features on those LIs can be checked in the manner described above. In addition, the derivation tree must also satisfy the Shortest Move Constraint (SMC): at no point during the derivation are there two distinct LIs with the same licensee feature as their first unchecked feature. Figure 2 shows an example of an SMC-violation. Note that the SMC makes Move a deterministic operation — the feature calculus completely determines which phrase moves where.

The determinism of Move means that the mapping from derivation trees to phrase structure trees is also deterministic. Hence derivation trees already contain all structural information and are MG's primary data structure for syntax (Kobele et al., 2007; Graf, 2012). The set of well-formed derivation trees, in turn, can be computed in a fully automatic fashion for any given lexicon Lex (and therefore any given

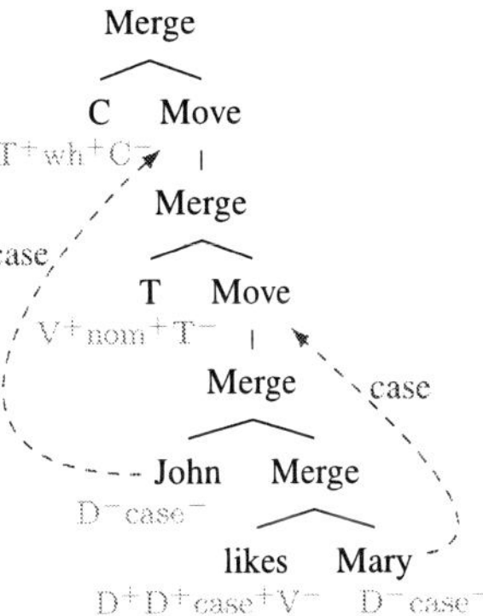

Figure 2: This derivation tree violates the SMC because the case^- features on the subject and the object are both active once the subject has been merged.

MG). In line with this well-established insight, I will also use derivation trees rather than phrase structure trees throughout this paper.

2.2 Single Movement Normal Form

The split between derivation trees and phrase structure trees makes it possible to disentangle movement steps and the feature checking operations that trigger them. In particular, a single feature checking operation can be taken to license multiple movement steps in the phrase structure tree.

This idea was used by Kobele (2006) to solve long-standing problems with successive cyclic movement. Consider a sentence like (2).

(2) [CP Who does Bill think [CP that John thinks [CP Mary thinks … [CP that Sue likes.] …]]]

Minimalist syntax posits that the wh-phrase *who* starts out as the object of *likes* and then moves through Spec,CP of each embedded clause until it finally reaches its final landing site in Spec,CP of the matrix clause (Chomsky, 1973; McCloskey, 2000; Abels, 2003). This analysis has been criticized because it requires every embedded C-head to carry the feature wh^+, yet only the matrix clause takes the form of an interrogative. MGs, however, face a much more severe issue: every intermediate landing site requires an extra wh^- to be present on *who*, but this is impossible because an LI can only have finitely many features whereas the number of intermediate landing sites is assumed to be unbounded.

Kobele (2006) addresses both problems by pushing successive cyclic movement out of the feature-controlled derivation trees into the mapping to derivation trees. Under this analysis, *who* carries a single wh$^-$ feature, which is checked by a wh$^+$ feature on the C-head of the matrix clause. The embedded C-heads do not carry any wh$^+$ features at all. They are landing sites for the wh-phrase not because of some feature checking mechanism, but rather because they occur along the movement path of the wh-phrase (Fig. 3).

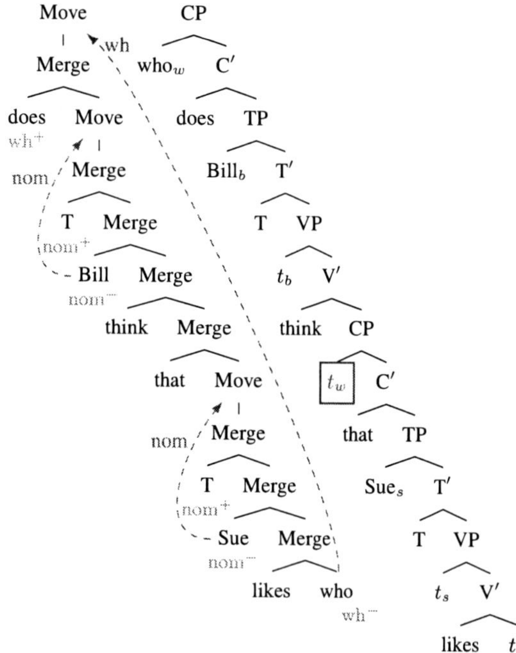

Figure 3: Intermediate landing sites do not need a feature trigger and are instead inserted by the mapping from derivation trees to derived trees. For greater clarity, I indicate only movement features and I highlight the trace that does not directly correspond to any feature-triggered movement operation.

Graf et al. (2016) take this approach and generalize it to a single movement normal form theorem. An MG is in SMNF iff there is no LI in *Lex* with more than one licensee feature. They prove that for every MG G there is an MG G' in SMNF such that G and G' generate the same phrase structure tree language *modulo* intermediate landing sites. In fact, G' can even be coupled with a modified mapping to phrase structure trees that correctly inserts all in-termediate landing sites, so that G and G' are fully equivalent with respect to the tree languages they generate.

The idea behind SMNF is very simple. As for successive cyclic movement, one deletes all feature triggers for intermediate movement from the derivation. Thus the derivation tree in Fig. 1 becomes the one in Fig. 4.

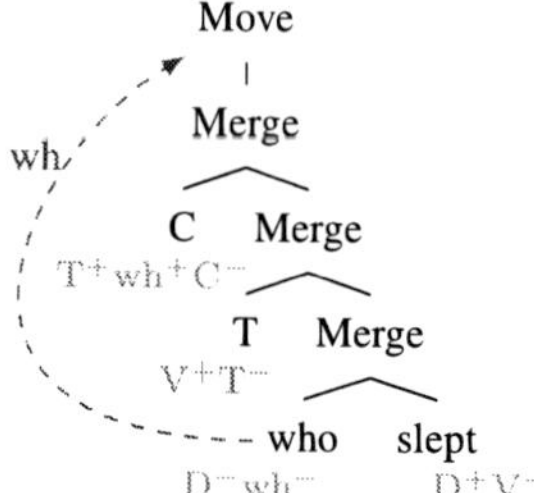

Figure 4: Every phrase moves at most once in an SMNF derivation. Intermediate landing sites can still be inserted by a modified mapping to phrase structure trees.

The SMNF-conversion becomes more complicated, however, if the removal of licensee features would induce an SMC violation. This occurs whenever the derivation contains n LIs ($n \geq 2$) that have the same final licensee feature f$^-$ and whose movement paths overlap at some point in the derivation. In these cases, the only solution is to split f$^-$ into multiple variants f$_1^-$, f$_2^-$, ..., f$_m^-$ ($2 \leq m \leq n$); see Fig. 5 for an abstract example of the relevant configuration.

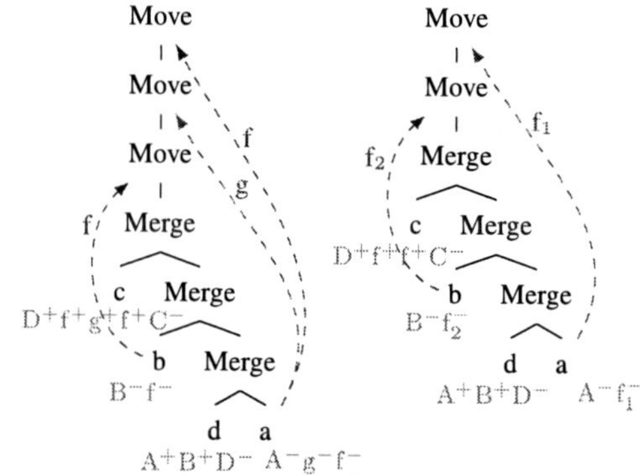

Figure 5: When the derivation tree to the left is brought into SMNF (right), the feature f$^-$ must be split into f$_1^-$ and f$_2^-$ to avoid SMC violations.

Graf et al. (2016) provide an algorithm that keeps

m as small as possible, but the blow-up in Lex may nonetheless be large: for every occurrence of f^- on some LI, m new variants must be added to Lex that only differ in the subscript on f^-. The size of Lex greatly increases as a result. Given an MG G with lexicon Lex, the lexicon size of its SMNF counterpart is linearly bounded by

$$\sum_{l \in Lex} \mu^{\gamma(l) + \delta(l)}$$

where μ is the number of distinct licensee features used by the SMNF grammar, $\gamma(l)$ is the number of licensor features of l, and $\delta(l)$ is 1 if l contains a licensee feature and 0 otherwise.[1]

A noticeable blow-up can be observed even with small toy grammars that generate only finite languages:

$$(3) \quad
\begin{array}{ll}
\text{T} :: \text{M}^+\text{M}^+\text{M}^+\text{T}^- & \text{C} :: \text{T}^+\text{C}^- \\
\text{a} :: \text{M}^-\text{a}^-\text{f}^- & \text{C} :: \text{C}^+\text{a}^+\text{f}^+\text{C}^- \\
\text{b} :: \text{M}^-\text{b}^-\text{f}^- & \text{C} :: \text{C}^+\text{b}^+\text{f}^+\text{C}^- \\
\text{d} :: \text{M}^-\text{d}^-\text{f}^- & \text{C} :: \text{C}^+\text{d}^+\text{f}^+\text{C}^-
\end{array}$$

Conversion to single movement normal form splits each one of a, b, and c into three variants with the feature string $\text{M}^-\,f_i^-$, $1 \leq i \leq 3$. It also replaces the three C-heads with licensor features by C-heads with feature string $\text{C}^+\,f_i^+\,\text{C}^-$. The total size of Lex thus grows from 8 to 14.

The worst-case scenario does not seem to obtain with realistic grammars, however. Multiple LIs in the same derivation rarely have the same f^- as their last feature, and in cases where they do their movement paths do not overlap. Section 3 looks at several cases where attempts to construct such configurations are thwarted by independent constraints on

movement. First, however, a few conceptual remarks on the linguistic plausibility of SMNF are in order.

2.3 Linguistic Plausibility of SMNF

It may seem that SMNF is at best of little relevance to linguistics, and at worst in direct conflict with some of the field's core findings. Numerous empirical arguments have been offered in support of intermediate movement and thus, presumably, against SMNF grammars. However, SMNF does not preclude the existence of intermediate movement, only that such movement is triggered by separate features. To the best of my knowledge there are no widely accepted tests to determine whether certain movement steps are feature-driven, so the status of SMNF is not diminished by current empirical observations.

At the same time, SMNF has several advantages that are of linguistic interest. First of all, the derivation trees of SMNF MG are very similar to dependency graphs, which might be leveraged to develop new learning algorithms for MGs. As dependency parsing has made major inroads in NLP, SMNF is also a first step towards corpus-based MG research.

On a more abstract level, Graf and Heinz (2015) show that SMNF lowers the complexity of Minimalist derivation trees so that they fit into a tree analogue of the subregular string class TSL (Heinz et al., 2011). This class has been found to play a major role in phonology (McMullin, 2016) and morphology (Aksënova et al., 2016; Graf, 2017). SMNF MGs as a model of syntax thus display an unexpected computational parallel to these other language domains, a parallel that disappears with standard MGs where intermediate movement is located in the derivation trees rather than the mapping to phrase structure trees.

There is tentative evidence that SMNF may in fact enjoy some degree of cognitive reality. If one subscribes to the idea that the grammar is not distinct from the parser but both describe the same object at different levels of granularity (cf. Marr 1982 and Neeleman and van de Koot 2010), then one cannot rule out that SMNF MGs are simply yet another level of description, situated between the highly compact grammars with intermediate movement and whatever optimized encoding is used in the

---

[1] Strictly speaking SMNF induces two kinds of lexical blow-up. The first is due to the refinement of movement features described above. But as described in Graf et al. (2016), the final step of the translation also involves the construction of a bottom-up tree automaton, which is then compiled directly into the category features of the grammar using the algorithm from Graf (2011) and Graf (2013). This final step can induce a blow-up that is polynominal in the size of the automaton. However, one can also incorporate the automaton into the grammar as a constraint definable in monadic second-order logic or simply run it in parallel to the grammar, avoiding the polynomial blow-up of the compilation step. The refinement of movement features, on the other hand, is unavoidable for SMNF MGs. Hence I limit myself to that specific kind of blow-up in this paper.

parser. It is interesting in this connection that intermediate movement is handled very differently from final movement in MG parsers (Stabler, 2011b; Stabler, 2013); whereas final movement directly effects the parser's predictions about the structure of the tree and the order in which it explores these predictions, intermediate movement is just a feature checking step for book keeping purposes. Moreover, recent attempts to use MGs as a model of human sentence processing also see an improvement in empirical coverage when intermediate movement steps are ignored (see e.g. Graf et al. 2017 and Ch. 5 of Zhang 2017). Similarly, Kotek (2017) presents an analysis of wh-intervention effects where at least some instances of intermediate movement must be absent in the syntactic representation.

In sum, SMNF is a useful encoding format of MGs for various practical purposes, and it can also facilitate linguistic research. There are no conclusive empirical arguments at this point to dismiss SMNF at the level of derivation trees, so it is an option worth entertaining. Future work may discover a number of robust arguments for an SMNF-like level of representation, but for the purposes of this paper it suffices that SMNF MGs are linguistically defensible while sporting a few computational advantages.

The major downside of SMNF MGs, on the other hand, is the risk of a blow-up in the number of LIs and hence grammar size. The performance of parsers and learning algorithms depends heavily on grammar size in real-world tasks (because average string length is very low in natural language). Consequently, large SMNF MGs would probably lead to worse performance than their counterparts with intermediate movement. In the next section, however, I argue that large blow-ups are unlikely to arise with realistic grammars because the movement configurations that would cause such a blow-up are disallowed anyways. There is no logical reason as to why languages should be this way, which raises the intriguing possibility that constraints on movement are at least partially motivated by a desire to keep grammars small, compact, and redundancy-free. The paper does not provide a conclusive answer to this larger issue and focuses instead on establishing the low risk of lexical blow-up with SMNF MGs. But in doing so it provides a glimpse of how these linguistic questions could be addressed in follow-up work.

3 Constraints and Grammar Size

3.1 General Observations

As discussed in Sec. 2.2, SMNF increases the size of the lexicon whenever removal of intermediate landing sites would induce SMC violations in some derivations. In this case, a licensee feature has to be split into multiple subscripted variants. This still does not necessarily induce a blow-up, though.

Suppose that the toy grammar in (3) only had a single C-head $C :: T^+a^+f^+b^+f^+d^+f^+C^-$. In contrast to (3) this now fixes the surface order of a, b, and c with respect to each other. Then the corresponding SMNF grammar would just have a C-head $C :: T^+f_1^+f_2^+f_3^+C^-$, and the LIs a, b, and c could be replaced by $a :: M^-f_1^-$, $b :: M^-f_2^-$, and $c :: M^-f_3^-$. Since the relative movement configurations of a, b, and c are fixed across all derivations, the feature refinement does not cause a multiplication of LIs.

Therefore the configurations where SMNF necessarily causes a blow-up involve multiple LIs that

1. have the same final licensee feature, and

2. have overlapping movement paths in some derivations, and

3. are flexible in the sense that the arrangement of the overlapping movement paths varies across derivations.

Let us briefly reflect on what kind of movement patterns in natural languages could possibly fit this description.

If one assumes that the different case positions for A-movement are associated with different features (nom, acc, and so on), and that every clause provides exactly one position for each type of case (Spec,TP, Spec,vP, and so on), then the first two conditions above cannot be met unless an LI A-moves to a case position outside its own clause. But this kind of movement is known to be heavily constrained, so overlapping paths are hard to construct.

With A′-movement, movement across clause boundaries is much less restricted, as it witnessed by unbounded wh-movement and topicalization. However, A′-movement is still subject to various principles that penalize overlapping movement paths. This again makes it difficult to design well-formed case of A′-movement that are problematic with SMNF.

The next few sections give concrete examples of how the desired movement configurations violate various well-known constraints on movement.

3.2 Improper movement

One option to create overlapping A-movement paths for LIs l and l' is to have l' first A′-move over the A-mover l, followed by l' undergoing the same kind of A-movement as l. But this requires l' to A-move from an A′-position, which is forbidden by the Ban on Improper Movement, illustrated in (4).

(4) a. John wonders who$_{wh}$ Bill$_{nom}$ t_{nom} saw t_{wh}.   (Proper movement)

     b. * who$_{wh,nom}$ wonders t_{nom} Bill$_{nom}$ t_{nom} saw t_{wh}. (Improper movement)

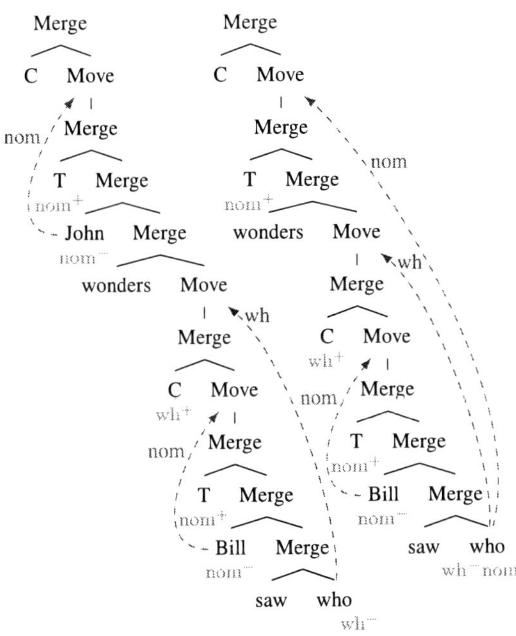

Figure 6: Since standard MGs do not impose any movement constraints besides the SMC, one can construct derivations like the one to the right that violates the ban on improper movement.

A standard MG with intermediate movement has no problem generating both the licit (4a) and the illicit (4b), as is shown in Fig. 6. Suppose for the sake of argument that (4b) were actually well-formed in English, so that the grammar would actually have to allow movement configurations like in Fig. 6. Then in the corresponding SMNF MG, the only licensee feature of *who* would be nom⁻, triggering direct movement from the object position to the subject position of the matrix clause. But since *Bill* also has nom⁻ as its last licensee feature and the two phrases have overlapping paths, this would trigger an SMC violation. Hence the SMNF MG must refine nom⁻ into two features nom$_1^-$ and nom$_2^-$.

(5) a. T$_{nom}$ wonders T$_{nom}$ Bill$_{nom}$ saw who$_{nom}$ (SMC violation)

     b. T$_{nom2}$ wonders T$_{nom1}$ Bill$_{nom1}$ saw who$_{nom2}$ (SMNF derivation tree)

     c. who$_{nom2}$ wonders Bill$_{nom1}$ t_{nom1} saw t_{nom2}.   (SMNF phrase structure tree)

Once nom⁻ has been replaced by nom$_1^-$ and nom$_2^-$, some LIs need to be duplicated. Every LI with nom⁺ now is split into two variants as it may serve as the landing site for a nom$_1^-$ mover (standard subjects) or a nom$_2^-$ mover (improperly moving wh-phrases). In addition, verbs like *wonder* that select a subject and a CP object now also have a variant that only selects an object CP. This is the result of the improper mover assuming the subject role for the clause containing *wonder*.

For the actual movers, however, duplication can be avoided. While the feature nom⁻ must be refined into nom$_1^-$ and nom$_2^-$, each type of licensee feature occurs with a specific type of phrase. The licensee feature nom$_2^-$ is limited to improper movers, which are wh-phrases. The licensee feature nom$_1^-$, on the other hand, occurs on DP that does not move improperly to a subject position. Note that the latter cannot be wh-movers: I) if a DP wh-moves before undergoing subject movement, it violates the ban against improper movement, contrary to our initial assumption; II) if a DP wh-moves after undergoing subject movement, then its final feature is not nom⁻ so that neither nom$_1^-$ nor nom$_2^-$ would presented on the DP's counterpart in an SMNF MG.

All these points jointly imply that nom⁻ is replaced by nom$_1^-$ for non-wh subjects and by nom$_2^-$ for wh-phrases whose final landing site is a subject position. Overall, then, the lexical blow-up is not as large as one would initially suspect. But the size of an SMNF grammar still increases by $2 \times |T| + 2 \times |V|$, where $|T|$ is the number of LIs that carry nom⁺ and $|V|$ indicates the number of LIs that select both a subject and a CP object.

3.3 Superraising

Another option to A-move a DP out of a finite clause is superraising, which looks very similar to improper movement from the perspective of SMNF MGs.

Prototypical cases of superraising are irrelevant for SMNF because they only involve a single mover.

(6) a. John seems [$_{TP}$ t to [$_{VP}$ t like Mary.]]

  b. * John seems [$_{TP}$ t likes [$_{VP}$ Mary.]]

However, analogous cases with two movers can be imagined.

(7) a. It seems Bill believes John likes Mary.

  b. * John seems [$_{CP}$ Bill believes t likes Mary.] (Superraising)

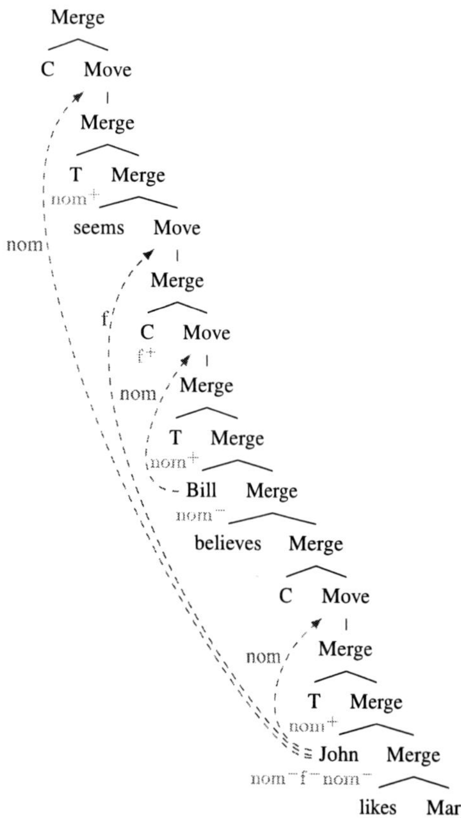

Figure 7: Standard MGs also allow for superraising configurations, the derivations of which look very similar to the improper movement derivations.

Again an MG analysis of (7b) is readily available. Due to the SMC, *John* cannot directly undergo nom-movement to the matrix clause because *Bill* is also undergoing nom-movement. Instead, some feature f$^-$ first moves *John* over *Bill* into Spec,CP of the highest embedded clause, from where *John* then moves on to the matrix subject position via nom$^-$. The role of f$^-$ is almost identical to wh$^-$ in the improper movement case in Fig .6, except that f$^-$ has no independent motivation beyond avoiding an SMC violation.

In a SMNF grammar, *John* would only possess the licensee feature nom$^-$. But *Bill* carries the same feature, so that once again nom$^-$ would have to be split into multiple features. As before, though, we can tie specific variants of nom$^-$ to specific LIs: nom$_1^-$ is chosen for normal subject movers, whereas nom$_2^-$ is for superraising subject movers, identified by their peculiar feature string nom$^-$f$^-$nom$^-$. We also preserve the usual split into nom$_1^+$ and nom$_2^+$ for LIs that carry nom$^+$, so that the SMNF-induced blow-up is $2 \times |T|$.

However, banning superraising configurations not only avoids this size increase, but shrinks the size of the lexicon even in comparison to the original MG. Where the original MG contained the LIs John :: D$^-$nom$^-$ and John :: D$^-$nom$^-$f$^-$nom$^-$, the SMNF MG contains John :: D$^-$nom$_1^-$ and John :: D$^-$nom$_2^-$, but the SMNF MG without superraising only needs John :: D$^-$nom$^-$. In other words, banning superraising cuts the number of subject movers listed in the lexicon in half.

3.4 Freezing Effects

One more attempt at using A-movement to induce lexical blow-up with SMNF centers around A-moving a phrase out of another A-moving phrase.

(8) a. It seems your comment about John annoys Sue.

  b. * John seems your comment about t annoys Sue. (Freezing effect)

Here *your comment about John* undergoes nom-movement before *John* nom-moves to the matrix subject position (presumably preceded by some kind of f-movement to avoid an SMC violation). The ungrammaticality of such configurations is known as *freezing effects*, but as far as the SMNF conversion is concerned the logic works exactly as for superraising (and hence improper movement).

That said, freezing effects are more general in that they also pertain to A'-movement as in the example below.

(9)   * Who don't you know [which pictures of t] Mary bought.   (Freezing effect)

Given standard Minimalist assumptions the sentence above would be generated by *which pictures of who* moving from the object position to Spec,CP, at which point *who* undergoes wh-movement to Spec,CP of the matrix clause. For MGs, the need to avoid an SMC violation would complicate the derivation somewhat in that *who* first f-moves to Spec,CP and then wh-moves to the next higher specifier. Nonetheless we would once again see SMNF induce a split for wh-movers into wh_1^- and wh_2^-, with one for normal wh-movement and one for wh-movement out of a freezing configuration. As for superraising, then, a SMNF MG that obeys freezing effects not only avoids a blow-up in grammar size but even sees a decrease compared to standard MGs.

3.5 Wh-Islands

Freezing effects make it impossible to create overlapping wh-movement paths by extracting a wh-mover from a wh-mover. But even if the wh-movers are independent of each other, overlapping movement paths are difficult to produce, due to the wh-island constraint. Consider first the simple paradigm below.

(10)   a.   What$_{wh}$ did John say Mary gave t_{wh} to Bill?

        b.   * What$_{wh0}$ did John say who$_{wh1}$ Mary gave t_{wh0} to t_{wh1}?   (Wh-island violation)

As before, sentences like (10b) would require refinement of the licensee and licensor features and thus increase grammar size. But in contrast to the previous constructions, wh-island violations easily allow for much more elaborate patterns that require even more indices. With each index, the SMNF grammar would gain more and more LIs.

(11)   a.   * What$_{wh0}$ did Bill think which$_{wh1}$ man t_{wh1} says who$_{wh1}$ Mary gave t_{wh0} to t_{wh1}?

        b.   * What$_{wh0}$ did Sue claim who$_{wh1}$ Bill thinks which$_{wh2}$ man t_{wh2} says Mary gave t_{wh0} to t_{wh1}?

3.6 Potential Cases of Blow-Up

The list of examples here is not exhaustive, but a wider sampling of the literature still confirms the general tendency that potential sources of lexical blow-up are blocked for independent reasons. One notable exception is the availability of superraising in some languages like Standard Arabic, but it is unclear whether this involves multiple movers of the same type (Ura, 2007).

Besides that, there is one more class of constructions that seem to be problematic. Like the toy grammar in (3), they involve configurations where many movers are drawn to the same target position. This is the case for multiple wh-movement, quantifier raising under certain movement-based analyses (May 1977; May 1985), and scrambling. However, all of them are already known to be problematic for standard MGs anyways, and alternative analyses have been proposed at least for the former two (Gärtner and Michaelis, 2010). With these analyses, SMNF is entirely unproblematic. Scrambling, on the other hand, is known to differ from other movement types in several respects and is also computationally challenging (Becker et al., 1996; Joshi et al., 2000)). Therefore a movement-based account may not be the best choice (see also Frey and Gärtner 2002). Overall, then, the few empirical cases that are problematic with SMNF MGs may not be adequately analyzed in terms of standard movement anyways.

Of course this does not guarantee that a wide-coverage MG can be safely translated into SMNF without a significant increase in grammar size. The constructions surveyed for this paper are noteworthy in that they only looked at movement with a clear function — wh-movement and case movement. These features are distributed in a principled manner and are usually tied to specific functional heads. But MGs, just like the Minimalist literature they are modeled after, also posit more abstract features like f, g, h whose only purpose is to produce the observed surface order. These features were completely ignored in this paper because it seems unlikely that manual analysis can reveal much about them. Instead, it seems more promising to run simulations where realistic MGs are automatically converted to SMNF. While such realistic MGs are currently being worked on (Torr, 2017), they are still in a highly preliminary stage. Hopefully some simulations will be feasible in the near future. If these features should turn out to be problematic for SMNF, this might suggest that there is a real difference between "functionally grounded" kinds of movement and the more stipulative word-order movement.

3.7 Linguistic Evaluation

The central claim of this paper is that SMNF is relatively safe for realistic grammars because most of the configurations that might induce a large blow-up in grammar size are ungrammatical anyways. It is tempting to couple this descriptive observation with a more speculative linguistic proposal: constraints on movement are (at least partially) motivated by the desire to keep grammars small and compact. This would be similar to a minimum-description-length approach and would provide a third-factor explanation (Chomsky, 2005) that could tie together seemingly unrelated phenomena such as freezing effects, wh-islands, superiority conditions, and the ban against improper movement. As we have already seen, however, these constraints are usually more general than necessary for grammar succinctness. Improper movement is a problem for SMNF only if the A-movement is of a type that was crossed by the A'-movement, superraising is fine unless one subject-raises over another subject, and so on. Hence one must not be too eager, at this point, to posit a causal link between grammar compactness and movement constraints. That said, the possibility is certainly intriguing, and the SMNF-perspective will be useful in exploring the idea to its fullest.

4 Conclusion

Single movement normal form is a useful encoding of MGs that greatly simplifies mathematical proofs and has potential applications in the design of new parsers and learning algorithms for MGs. While it comes with the risk of greatly increasing the size of the grammar, this seems to be less of an issue with natural languages because movement has to obey numerous constraints that greatly limit the set of possible movement configurations. In particular, it is very difficult for two lexical items to have overlapping movement paths while also sharing final landing sites of the same type. From an applied perspective, this result increases the confidence in SMNF as a useful MG encoding. But there is also linguistic potential: studying movement configurations with respect to their effect on grammar size may unearth entirely new generalizations about natural language.

References

Klaus Abels. 2003. *Successive Cyclicity, Anti-locality, and Adposition Stranding*. Ph.D. thesis, University of Connecticut.

Alëna Aksënova, Thomas Graf, and Sedigheh Moradi. 2016. Morphotactics as tier-based strictly local dependencies. In *Proceedings of the 14th SIGMORPHON Workshop on Computational Research in Phonetics, Phonology, and Morphology*, pages 121–130.

Tilman Becker, Owen Rambow, and Michael Niv. 1996. The derivational generative power of formal systems, or scrambling is beyond LCFRS. Technical Report IRCS 92-38, Institute for Research in Cognitive Science, University of Pennsylvania.

Noam Chomsky. 1973. Conditions on transformations. In Stephen Anderson and Paul Kiparsky, editors, *A Festschrift for Morris Halle*, pages 232–286. Holt, Rinehart, and Winston, New York.

Noam Chomsky. 1986. *Barriers*. MIT Press, Cambridge, MA.

Noam Chomsky. 1995. *The Minimalist Program*. MIT Press, Cambridge, MA.

Noam Chomsky. 2001. Derivation by phase. In Michael J. Kenstowicz, editor, *Ken Hale: A Life in Language*, pages 1–52. MIT Press, Cambridge, MA.

Noam Chomsky. 2005. Three factors in language design. *Linguistic Inquiry*, 36(1):1–22.

Noam Chomsky. 2013. Problems of projection. *Lingua*, 130:33–49.

Danny Fox and David Pesetsky. 2005. Cyclic linearization of syntactic structure. *Theoretical Linguistics*, 31:1–45.

Werner Frey and Hans-Martin Gärtner. 2002. On the treatment of scrambling and adjunction in Minimalist grammars. In Gerhard Jäger, Paola Monachesi, Gerald Penn, and Shuly Wintner, editors, *Proceedings of the Conference on Formal Grammar*, pages 41–52.

Hans-Martin Gärtner and Jens Michaelis. 2010. On the treatment of multiple-wh-interrogatives in Minimalist grammars. In Thomas Hanneforth and Gisbert Fanselow, editors, *Language and Logos*, pages 339–366. Akademie Verlag, Berlin.

Thomas Graf and Jeffrey Heinz. 2015. Commonality in disparity: The computational view of syntax and phonology. Slides of a talk given at GLOW 2015, April 18, Paris, France.

Thomas Graf, Alëna Aksënova, and Aniello De Santo. 2016. A single movement normal form for Minimalist grammars. In Annie Foret, Glyn Morrill, Reinhard Muskens, Rainer Osswald, and Sylvain Pogodalla, editors, *Formal Grammar : 20th and 21st International Conferences, FG 2015, Barcelona, Spain, August 2015, Revised Selected Papers. FG 2016, Bozen, Italy, August 2016*, pages 200–215, Berlin, Heidelberg. Springer.

Thomas Graf, James Monette, and Chong Zhang. 2017. Relative clauses as a benchmark for Minimalist parsing. *Journal of Language Modelling*, 5:57–106.

Thomas Graf. 2011. Closure properties of Minimalist derivation tree languages. In Sylvain Pogodalla and Jean-Philippe Prost, editors, *LACL 2011*, volume 6736 of *Lecture Notes in Artificial Intelligence*, pages 96–111, Heidelberg. Springer.

Thomas Graf. 2012. Locality and the complexity of Minimalist derivation tree languages. In Philippe de Groot and Mark-Jan Nederhof, editors, *Formal Grammar 2010/2011*, volume 7395 of *Lecture Notes in Computer Science*, pages 208–227, Heidelberg. Springer.

Thomas Graf. 2013. *Local and Transderivational Constraints in Syntax and Semantics*. Ph.D. thesis, UCLA.

Thomas Graf. 2017. Graph transductions and typological gaps in morphological paradigms. In *Proceedings of the 15th Meeting on the Mathematics of Language*, pages 114–126.

Jeffrey Heinz, Chetan Rawal, and Herbert G. Tanner. 2011. Tier-based strictly local constraints in phonology. In *Proceedings of the 49th Annual Meeting of the Association for Computational Linguistics*, pages 58–64.

Aravind Joshi, Tilman Becker, and Owen Rambow. 2000. Complexity of scrambling: A new twist to the competence-performance distinction. In Anne Abeill and Owen Rambow, editors, *Tree Adjoining Grammars: Formalisms, Linguistic Analysis and Processing*, pages 167–181. CSLI, Stanford.

Gregory M. Kobele, Christian Retoré, and Sylvain Salvati. 2007. An automata-theoretic approach to Minimalism. In James Rogers and Stephan Kepser, editors, *Model Theoretic Syntax at 10*, pages 71–80.

Gregory M. Kobele. 2006. *Generating Copies: An Investigation into Structural Identity in Language and Grammar*. Ph.D. thesis, UCLA.

Hadas Kotek. 2017. Movement and alternatives don't mix: A new look at wh-intervention effects. Handout for an invited talk presented on October 20 at Stony Brook University, Stony Brook, NY.

David Marr. 1982. *Vision: A Computational Investigation into the Human Representation and Processing of Visual Information*. Freeman, New York. Reprinted in 2010 by MIT Press.

Robert May. 1977. *The Grammar of Quantification*. Ph.D. thesis, MIT.

Robert May. 1985. *Logical Form: Its Structure and Derivation*. MIT Press, Cambridge, MA.

James McCloskey. 2000. Quantifier float and wh-movement in an Irish English. *Linguistic Inquiry*, 31:57–84.

Kevin McMullin. 2016. *Tier-Based Locality in Long-Distance Phonotactics: Learnability and Typology*. Ph.D. thesis, Uniersity of British Columbia.

Ad Neeleman and Hans van de Koot. 2010. Theoretical validity and psychological reality of grammatical code. In Martin Everaert, Tom Lentz, Hannah de Mulder, Oystein Nilsen, and Arjen Zondervan, editors, *The Linguistic Enterprise: From Knowledge of Language to Knowledge of Linguistics*, pages 183–212. John Benjamins, Amsterdam.

Luigi Rizzi. 1990. *Relativized Minimality*. MIT Press, Cambridge, MA.

John R. Ross. 1967. *Constraints on Variables in Syntax*. Ph.D. thesis, MIT.

Edward P. Stabler. 1997. Derivational Minimalism. In Christian Retoré, editor, *Logical Aspects of Computational Linguistics*, volume 1328 of *Lecture Notes in Computer Science*, pages 68–95. Springer, Berlin.

Edward P. Stabler. 2011a. Computational perspectives on Minimalism. In Cedric Boeckx, editor, *Oxford Handbook of Linguistic Minimalism*, pages 617–643. Oxford University Press, Oxford.

Edward P. Stabler. 2011b. Top-down recognizers for MCFGs and MGs. In *Proceedings of the 2011 Workshop on Cognitive Modeling and Computational Linguistics*. to appear.

Edward P. Stabler. 2013. Two models of minimalist, incremental syntactic analysis. *Topics in Cognitive Science*, 5:611–633.

John Torr. 2017. Autobank: a semi-automatic annotation tool for developing deep Minimalist grammar treebanks. In *Proceedings of the Demonstrations at the 15th Conference of the European Chapter of the Association for Computational Linguistics*, pages 81–86.

Hiroyuki Ura. 2007. Returning to superraising. *Departmental Bulletin Paper*, 56:59–74.

Chong Zhang. 2017. *Stacked Relatives: Their Structure, Processing, and Computation*. Ph.D. thesis, Stony Brook University.

Modeling the Decline in English Passivization

Liwen Hou
College of Computer and
Information Science
Northeastern University
lhou@ccs.neu.edu

David A. Smith
College of Computer and
Information Science
Northeastern University
dasmith@ccs.neu.edu

Abstract

Evidence from the Hansard corpus shows that
the passive voice in British English has declined in relative frequency over the last two
centuries. We investigate which factors are
predictive of whether transitive verb phrases
are passivized. We show the increasing importance of the person-hierarchy effects observed by Bresnan et al. (2001), with increasing strength of the constraint against passivizing clauses with local agents, as well as the rising prevalence of such agents. Moreover, our
ablation experiments on the Wall Street Journal and Hansard corpora provide support for
the unmarked information structure of 'given'
before 'new' noted by Halliday (1967).

1 Introduction

From the Hansard corpus of British parliamentary
proceedings (Alexander and Davies, 2015), we observe that the passive voice has declined in usage
frequency over the last two centuries. The early
19th century saw more frequent usage of this voice
compared to the late 20th century: As shown in Figure 1, while the passive was used in approximately
8% of two-argument clauses in the 1830s for example, it was used in less than 6% of such clauses in
the 1990s. Following Bresnan et al. (2001), we exclude short passives that contain no "by" phrase to
focus on those two-argument clauses where active
and passive voices are in direct competition.

Four corpora (LOB, F-LOB, Brown, and Frown)
are used by Mair and Leech (2006) to argue that the
passive decreased in frequency in written English
between the 1960s and the 1990s to match the norms

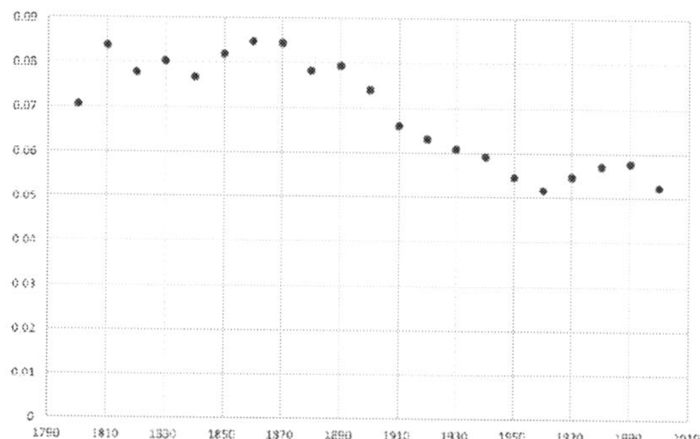

Figure 1: Proportions of passivized two-argument finite verb
phrases in the British Hansard over 200 years

of spoken English. While our analysis does not rule
out this effect of converging registers, we provide
evidence for additional factors in the evolution of the
English passive.

In this paper, we investigate the causes of the passive's decline as follows: First, we identify features
that are predictive of whether a verb phrase is passivized by building a logistic regression model using
features suggested in the literature. After identifying
important explanatory variables for predicting passivization, we use the British Hansard corpus to investigate the change in average value of each feature
over time to find explanations for the decline in passivization and then discuss the changes undergone
by feature weights over time. We show the rising importance of person-hierarchy effects in English passivization noted by Bresnan et al. (2001), with increasing strength of the constraint against passivizing clauses with local (i.e. first- or second-person)
agents and the increasing prevalence of such agents.

The majority of work on diachronic syntax has relied on manual annotations, and computational techniques in historical linguistics have mostly focused on phonology, morphology, and the lexicon (Lieberman et al., 2007; Ellison and Kirby, 2006; Bouchard-Côté et al., 2013, for example). One additional goal of this paper, therefore, is to employ automated methods to analyze the factors that affect passivization and that explain its decreasing frequency in English over the last two centuries.

2 Data

2.1 The British Hansard

To identify diachronic trends, we use the Hansard corpus (Alexander and Davies, 2015), which is a digitized version of two centuries of debates that took place in the British Parliament starting from 1803. We divide the data according to the decade in which each speech was given. When fitting models, we discard the decades prior to 1830 due to the small amount of data from those years.

The number of two-argument constructions and the number of words in each decade from 1830 to 1999 is shown in Table 1.

Decade	Words	Transitive Verbs
1830s	16,427,918	404,685
1840s	15,464,589	403,245
1850s	16,838,010	392,244
1860s	16,850,076	428,572
1870s	19,922,209	460,881
1880s	30,082,916	698,427
1890s	22,489,078	546,254
1900s	24,835,231	719,629
1910s	29,375,435	1,028,534
1920s	20,501,261	818,339
1930s	35,428,497	1,598,164
1940s	32,802,372	1,565,450
1950s	31,907,582	2,091,740
1960s	36,915,775	2,668,257
1970s	37,551,800	3,015,740
1980s	40,065,521	3,516,300
1990s	33,978,717	3,396,495

Table 1: The number of words and the number of two-argument actives/passives per decade

After parsing the text of the parliamentary debates using version 3.6.0 of the Stanford dependency parser (Manning et al., 2014; De Marneffe et al., 2006), we detect passive verb phrases by screening for two dependency relation types: those labeled with "auxpass" and with "nsubjpass". (In transitive constructions, passives can also be detected by screening relations that have the label "nmod:agent".) To identify the agent in a passive construction, we focus on the labels ending with "agent". To identify the subject of each verb, we use the labels "nsubjpass" and "nsubj". Finally, to identify the object in an active construction, we make use of the "dobj" relation. Although not all demoted subjects in passive constructions are agents, and not all promoted objects are patients, we use the terms "agent" and "patient" to refer to the former and the latter respectively. The aforementioned identification process yields approximately 26 million two-argument verb phrases in total, of which roughly 1.5 million are passives.

2.2 Evaluating Parser Accuracy

We have verified 300 clauses to ensure that the Stanford parser is sufficiently reliable for processing language from the Hansard corpus despite the time period covered by this corpus. The results of our manual verification process are listed in Table 2.

verb valency & voice	argument acc.	accuracy
2-argument actives	84%	95%
2-argument passives	88%	94%
active intransitives	86%	90%
short passives	92%	94%

Table 2: Manual evaluation of parser accuracy: In the middle column, a parse was considered accurate only when all arguments and the voice were correctly identified. In the last column, only valency and voice had to be correct.

We randomly sampled 100 verb phrases that were identified by the parser as being two-argument actives; of those, it correctly identified the voice and valency in 95 cases, but in only 84 cases were both arguments correctly identified as well. We also randomly sampled 100 verb phrases from the pool identified by the parser as two-argument passives; of those, it correctly identified the voice and valency in 94 cases (and both of the arguments in 88 samples). Finally, we sampled 100 verbs (50 actives and

50 passives) identified by the parser as having only one argument; it was correct 92% of the time on this sample for voice plus valency (and 89% of the time for identifying the argument).

In clauses with two arguments, the most common type of parser error was incorrectly identifying some argument of the verb. In addition, there were cases where the parser decided that a transitive verb phrase had only one argument and vice versa (e.g. treating copular constructions as transitive; classifying instrumental prepositional phrases as agentive); such valency errors were more common than voice identification errors. From our sample, we have observed that the parser rarely decides on an incorrect voice, which means that passives are correctly identified as such by the parser in the vast majority of cases.

2.3 Wall Street Journal

In addition, we report our model's performance on the Wall Street Journal corpus from the Penn Treebank Project (Marcus et al., 1993; Marcus et al., 1994) and use the latter to test the significance of explanatory variables. Even though accurate constituency trees are provided in the Wall Street Journal corpus, we parsed the text with a dependency parser and processed it in a manner similar to the aforementioned procedure for the Hansard so that results from the two corpora would be comparable.

3 Modeling Passivization

We fit a logistic regression model to predict the passivization of two-argument verbs. Similar to earlier models inspired by Harmonic Grammar (Legendre et al., 1990), we start with only the constraints on the locality of agent and patient.

Obtaining better predictions (on our task of interest of predicting whether a given verb phrase is passive or active) would help us identify the most important explanatory variables for why a speaker might choose to use the passive over the active voice.

3.1 Features

The features in our model were inspired by several previous studies of English passivization.

Person Features In our simplest model, inspired by the work of Bresnan et al. (2001) on person-hierarchy effects (see §5.1), each data point consists of two binary features. The first indicates whether or not the agent is a local (i.e. first or second) person, and the other corresponds to whether or not the patient is a local person.

Pronoun Features Because the existence of person-hierarchy effects would be confounded by the fact that local persons happen to be pronouns and thus more likely to be "given" information (see below), we add two features to denote whether the agent is a pronoun and whether the patient is a pronoun. In addition to personal pronouns, we include demonstrative pronouns (i.e. "this", "that" when the part-of-speech tag is "DT") as pronouns.

Length Features The length of a constituent was reported by Wolk et al. (2013) to have an effect on predicting the dative alternation. Specifically, a double object dative has a greater likelihood of being realized in British English as well as American English (and especially the latter) when the length of the patient is longer. We therefore also consider the length of the agent and that of the patient when predicting passivization.

Taking square roots of the lengths led to better performance on development data compared to using the raw lengths, so our two length features consist of the square root of the agent's length and that of the patient's length.

Given or New Information As a proxy for given information, we add a feature corresponding to whether the agent begins with the lemma "the", "this", "that" or a pronoun, as well as another feature indicating whether the patient begins with one such word.

Relative Clauses and Wh-words We add two features indicating whether the current verb is part of a relative clause and whether it is part of a clause beginning with a wh-word.

Preceding Passives Parallel structure among successive sentences was reported by Weiner and Labov (1983) to have a significant effect on whether a sentence contains a passivized verb. In the same vein, we add two features representing preceding passives: the first indicates whether or not any of the previous five verbs was passivized, and the second indicates whether there was a passive in any of the previous five sentences.

Lemma Features Finally, we add 1,000 features representing the 1,000 most common verb lemmas, with one additional feature to catch the remaining less common verbs. In order to see the effects of having different agent and patient head words, we also add 2,002 binary features corresponding to the 1,000 most common agents and the 1,000 most common patients (along with two features to catch the remainder) from across all years.

3.2 Performance

Since, as noted above, a little over 5% of two-argument transitive clauses in the Hansard as a whole are passive, a classifier that always predicts 'active' can achieve quite high token-level accuracy. For each test set, we report the proportion of active clauses as the "baseline" accuracy. We also, therefore, report not just the raw classifier accuracy on test data but also the precision, recall, and F1 for correctly detecting passive clauses. All evaluations are the result of five-fold cross validation.

Hansard Table 3 shows the full model's performance on different decades of the Hansard corpus, with each decade treated independently.

Decade	Acc.	F1	Prec.	Recall	Baseline
1830	0.962	0.745	0.772	0.721	0.923
1850	0.959	0.736	0.767	0.707	0.920
1870	0.957	0.734	0.765	0.705	0.917
1890	0.961	0.744	0.771	0.719	0.921
1910	0.969	0.754	0.782	0.729	0.935
1930	0.970	0.740	0.775	0.708	0.939
1950	0.970	0.712	0.759	0.671	0.945
1970	0.970	0.702	0.761	0.652	0.945
1990	0.966	0.673	0.755	0.608	0.942

Table 3: the full model's performance on every other decade of the British Hansard corpus since 1830

Sorting the features in each decade by the magnitude of their coefficients, the top four features are the same in every decade of the Hansard from the 1830s to the 2000s: whether the agent is given (instead of new), the agent lemma "who", the agent lemma "which", and the verb lemma "have". (The coefficients in these four cases are all negative, which means that these features suppress passivization.)

Wall Street Journal Table 4 shows the performance of the full model on the WSJ corpus.

Accuracy	F1	Prec.	Recall	Baseline
0.964	0.395	0.733	0.270	0.957

Table 4: Performance on the Wall Street Journal

The top ten features sorted by the magnitude of their coefficients are shown in Table 5. Positive weights correspond to passivization being more likely; for example, our results show that the verb "have" is rarely passivized, while the verb "offset" is passivized relatively often.

Top Feature	Weight
Given Agent	-5.039
Lemma "which" (Agent)	-3.257
Lemma "Tenders" (Patient)	3.130
Lemma "who" (Agent)	-3.126
Lemma "have" (Verb)	-2.851
Lemma "offset" (Verb)	2.815
Lemma "rate" (Verb)	2.334
Lemma "who" (Patient)	2.168
Lemma "affect" (Verb)	2.100
Lemma "cover" (Verb)	2.027

Table 5: Top Features for the WSJ Corpus

3.3 Effects from Feature Classes

We measure the effects on performance of removing classes of features from the full model and making predictions with five-fold cross-validation. Table 6 shows the predictive accuracy and F1 score achieved on the Wall Street Journal corpus by each ablated model.

Removed Features	Accuracy	F1	p-value
Pronouns	0.964	0.393	0.196
Lengths	0.961	0.283	< 0.005
Given	0.962	0.299	< 0.005
Rel.&Wh-Clauses	0.964	0.395	0.391
Preceding Passives	0.964	0.382	0.006
Persons	0.964	0.394	0.243
Lemma Features	0.958	0.122	< 0.005

Table 6: Effects on the WSJ of removing one group of features at a time

Compared to the performance reported in Table

4, the lemmas were the feature category whose removal caused the biggest impact on performance.

We have also found that the lemma features are extremely important for predicting passivization on the Hansard corpus. For example, if we use only the top 10 instead of the top 1,000 lemma features of each type, the F1 score for the full model drops from 0.745 to 0.514 for the 1830s and similarly drops from 0.673 to 0.391 for the 1990s.

To see the effects of the other features on the F1 score more clearly, we trained the model using only the top 10 lemmas of each type and then removed each of the other feature categories in turn to measure the decrease in performance. We did this separately for different decades of the Hansard; the results obtained for the 1830s and 1990s are shown in Table 7 and Table 8.

Removed Features	Accuracy	F1	p-value
(None)	0.936	0.514	
Persons	0.936	0.512	0.380
Pronouns	0.936	0.504	< 0.005
Lengths	0.934	0.461	< 0.005
Given	0.926	0.183	< 0.005
Rel.&Wh-Clauses	0.936	0.512	0.445
Preceding Passives	0.936	0.504	< 0.005
Lemma Features	0.927	0.313	< 0.005

Table 7: Effects on the 1830s of removing individual features (with the top 10 lemmas of each type in the full model)

Removed Features	Accuracy	F1	p-value
(None)	0.949	0.391	
Persons	0.949	0.391	0.245
Pronouns	0.949	0.386	< 0.005
Lengths	0.948	0.368	< 0.005
Given	0.946	0.218	< 0.005
Rel.&Wh-Clauses	0.949	0.372	< 0.005
Preceding Passives	0.949	0.373	< 0.005
Lemma Features	0.944	0.231	< 0.005

Table 8: Effects on the 1990s of removing individual features (with the top 10 lemmas of each type in the full model)

3.4 Statistical Significance

To test the statistical significance of the contribution of individual features, we compare the full model to each smaller model from Section 3.3 using a permutation test.

To test whether one model outperforms another in a statistically significant way, we swap or keep each pair of outputs with equal probability and, in this way, generate two new series of outputs. We then measure the difference in F1 scores between these two series of predictions and repeat this procedure 200 times to generate 200 such differences. Next, we compare the true difference in F1 scores of the original models to the 200 randomly generated differences. The reported p-values are the proportions of the randomly generated differences that are as large as or larger than the true difference.

For the Wall Street Journal, we see from Table 6 that the features whose removal caused a statistically significant decrease in the F1 score were the features representing the lengths of the agent and patient, the features indicating whether the agent and patient were given (instead of new) information, the features indicating whether the preceding five verb phrases and the preceding five sentences contained passives, and finally the lemma features.

For the Hansard corpus, after using only the top 10 lemmas of each type, we see from Table 7 and Table 8 that the removal of any feature category other than the person features (and relative/wh-clause features in the 1830s) causes a statistically significant decrease in the F1 score. In particular, removing the given/new information features causes the F1 to suffer the biggest drop.

4 Changes in Feature Values

We have thus far identified some features that affect whether or not a speaker chooses to passivize a verb phrase. We now examine how the average value of each feature changed over time. Note that these are not the estimated coefficients of these features in a model but the observed frequencies of features in the data without considering passivization.

For each decade of the Hansard corpus from 1830, we calculate the average value of each explanatory variable; except for the length features whose values are not Boolean, this average is between zero and one. Figure 2, for example, plots the average value in each decade of the feature indicating whether the agent is local.

Figure 2: The frequency of local agents has increased over time.

Feature	Change in Value
Local Agent	0.193
Local Patient	0.014
Pronoun Agent	-0.001 *
Pronoun Patient	-0.042
Agent Length	0.013 *
Patient Length	0.136
Given Agent	-0.004 *
Given Patient	-0.107
Relative Clauses	-0.049
Wh-Clauses	-0.061
Preceding Verbs	-0.182
Preceding Sentences	-0.184

Table 9: Change in average value of each feature between the 1830s and the 2000s (* indicates a statistically insignificant change)

The observed average value of the local agent feature increases over time as shown in Figure 2, and this increase is statistically significant ($p = 0.0003$) if we apply an F-test to the slope of the line of best fit. We apply this test to all the explanatory variables described in Section 3.1. As shown in Table 9, the only ones whose slopes are not significantly different from zero are the agent length feature, the pronoun agent feature, and the indicator for whether the agent is given or new information.

However, not every feature whose slope is significantly different from zero underwent a change as big as the one undergone by the agent feature depicted in Figure 2. In the 1830s, this feature had an average value of 0.069, which means that 6.9% of two-argument verb phrases had a local agent; in contrast, in the 2000s, this same feature had an average value of 0.262, indicating that over 26% of data points had a local agent. The magnitude of this change is thus more than 19 percentage points. For each feature, the raw change in average value from the 1830s to the 2000s is listed in Table 9. (Because agent length and patient length are not binary features, the increase of 0.013 and 0.136 in their average values should not be interpreted on the same scale as the others.)

The indicators for the presence of passives in the preceding verbs and preceding sentences cannot be used to explain the observed decrease in passivization frequency because it is unsurprising that these features decreased in value on average over time as a result of the general declining trend of the rate of passivization.

The relative and wh-clauses are not reliable predictors of passivization according to Table 6 and Table 7; therefore, although their average values exhibit a modest change over time, they are unlikely to be important for explaining the decline of passives.

This leaves the locality of the agent, the locality of the patient, the pronoun status of the patient, and the length of the patient as potential explanatory variables for the declining frequency of passivization. (Although the features for local agent and local patient both increased in average value, the change undergone by the latter is a small fraction of that undergone by the former between the 1830s and the 2000s.) To estimate the impact of these explanatory variables, we measure the overall passivization rate when each (binary) feature value is 0 and when it is 1; these rates are listed in Table 10.

Feature	Rate at 0	Rate at 1	Diff.
Local Agent	0.086	0.001	-0.085
Local Patient	0.062	0.125	0.063
Pronoun Patient	0.053	0.153	0.100

Table 10: Passivization rate at different feature values

The passivization rates in the 1830s and 2000s are respectively 8% and 5.2% as illustrated in Figure 1. This means we seek to explain a difference of 2.8% percentage points.

To get an estimate of the contribution to the decline in passivization that can be explained by each feature, we multiply the last column of Table 10 by the changes listed in Table 9. For example, the pronoun status of the patient contributes an estimated 0.42 percentage points to the decline.

We note that the local patient feature actually predicts a slight *increase* in passivization rate, meaning the change is going the wrong way. However, this predicted increase is very small: only about 0.09 percentage points (in comparison, agent locality predicts a 1.64 percentage point decline in the rate).

For the patient length feature, we measure the passivization rate when the value of the feature is 1 and when it is 2 (i.e. when the length is 4, since the feature value is a square root of the actual length). Across all decades, the passivization rate is 0.107 when the value of this feature is 1 and 0.039 when the feature value is 2. This difference of -0.068 should overestimate the effect on passivization rate of increasing the feature value by 1. Multiplying this difference by the change in the average value of this feature gives -0.009, which means that the change in this feature value can explain at most 0.9 percentage points of the declining passivization rate.

If we summed up the effects of the aforementioned contributions, we would seemingly explain the entire 2.8% percentage points. However, because these features correlate with each other, we cannot sum up the estimated effects. In particular, the patient locality, pronoun patient, and patient length features contain overlapping information. However, because one feature alone explains 1.64 percentage points, these features explain well over half of the difference.

5 Changes in Grammar

The significant increase in the frequency of local agents is suggestive, but is the decline in passivization mostly attributable to this lexical choice or, as Mair and Leech (2006) suggested, to increasing convergence with informal speech? We now turn from changes in the average values of features to evidence of changes in grammatical constraints' weights.

5.1 Person Hierarchy

Some languages have a person hierarchy (Aissen, 1999; Bresnan et al., 2001) in which "local" first and second persons outrank "nonlocal" third persons. In one such language, Lummi (Bresnan et al., 2001), the person hierarchy affects passivization in a way such that speakers avoid a construction at all times if the subject is the less prominent argument on the person hierarchy. While no such categorical effects are observed in English, Bresnan et al. use the Switchboard corpus to conclude that statistical preferences for harmonic person-argument associations do exist in English. Our findings are consistent with theirs; moreover, we find that the aforementioned person hierarchy preferences have become stronger in English over time.

The descriptive statistics from two centuries of the British Hansard show the following: With a third-person agent, the passive (instead of the active) is used approximately twice as much with a local patient than with a nonlocal one as shown in Table 11, which is consistent with the explanation that English speakers perceive it to be disharmonic when the subject is less prominent than the object and therefore use the passive to avoid having a nonlocal agent with a local patient in an active construction.

passive percentages	
1/2 acting on 1/2:	0.16%
1/2 acting on 3:	0.1%
3 acting on 3:	7.95%
3 acting on 1/2:	13.94%

Table 11: Descriptive statistics on argument locality

In addition, we find that this gap in frequency has become wider over time: As shown in Figure 3, although this ratio is 1.75 when we consider the entire corpus, it is 1.19 if we focus on the earliest decade.

When we consider a local agent and a third-person patient, the passive is used instead of the active 0.1% of the time across the entire corpus. (This is a weighted average of all the time periods, where a weight is the number of two-argument clauses in a time period.) However, throughout the 1800s, this statistic remained between 0.21% and 0.29%. In contrast, since 1950, this same measure has never been above 0.1%. Moreover, it has dropped from one decade to the next since 1940 without exception. Although the downward trend could be attributed to an overall decline in passive constructions over time, the trend is fairly constant if we instead consider the proportion of passives used with both third-person agent and patient. When we divide the former proportion by the latter, we still observe a clear de-

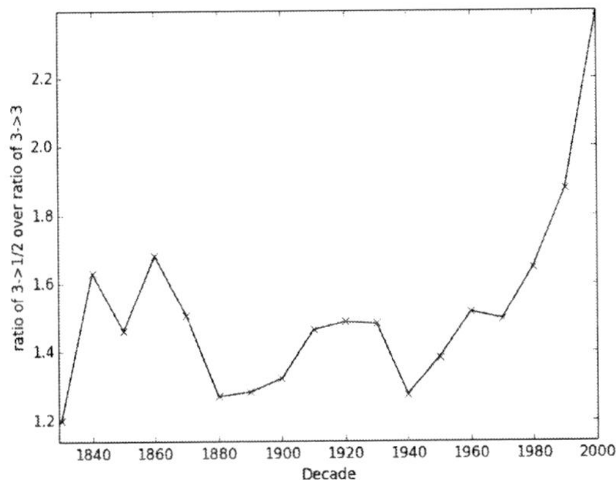

Figure 3: Between years 1830 and 2004: the passive proportion of 3rd-person agents with local patients over the proportion of passives used to express two 3rd-person arguments

cline (as shown in Figure 4), suggesting that English speakers have developed a stronger preference for harmonic person-argument associations over time.

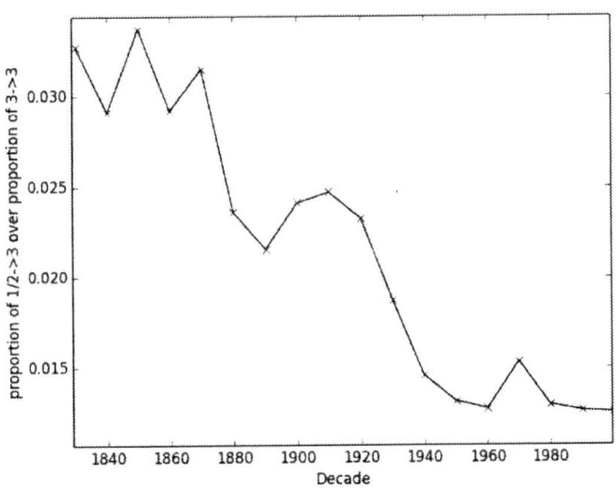

Figure 4: the passive proportion of 1st/2nd-person agent and 3rd person patient over the passive proportion of 3rd-person agent and 3rd-person patient

5.2 Logistic Regression

For each decade starting from 1830, we have created a balanced dataset in which each decade contains 64,000 data points, 50% of which are two-argument passive verb phrases and the other 50% are actives.

We fit a logistic regression model to the data from each decade (independently of the other decades).

We learn a different set of coefficients per decade while keeping the features the same across decades.

For the model containing only the person features and no other explanatory variables, the trajectories of the coefficients are consistent with our earlier observations that disharmonic person-argument associations are becoming less preferred over time.

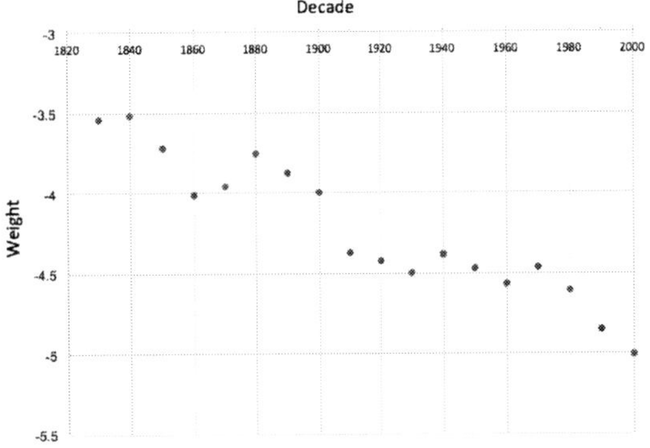

Figure 5: The coefficient of the local agent feature decreases over time.

For example, when the agent is local, we would expect speakers to make it the subject of an utterance by employing the active voice more frequently (and the passive less frequently) over time. Indeed, we observe in Figure 5 that the corresponding person feature's coefficient is decreasing over time.

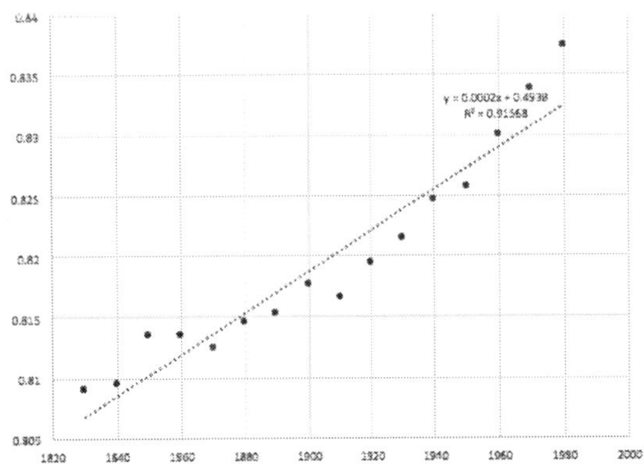

Figure 6: Accuracy of the model with person plus lemma features when trained on various decades and tested on the 1990s (the y-axis was truncated to focus on the change over time)

Figure 6 shows the accuracy achieved by a model with person features and lemma features. The task is predicting passivization for 1990–1999 when trained on data from the decades preceding it. (On the test set, employing the strategy of always guessing the same label achieves an accuracy of 50%.) We see from Figure 6 that performance improves when the training data is from later time periods and that the best performance is obtained by training on the time period immediately preceding the 1990s (i.e. closest to the decade used for testing).

5.3 Hierarchical Model

We have thus far fitted one model per decade assuming different decades are independent. In this section, we instead consider a linear hierarchical model:

$$
\begin{aligned}
a_i &\sim \text{normal}(0, \sigma_a^2) \\
b_i &\sim \text{normal}(0, \sigma_b^2) \\
\theta_i(t) &\sim \text{normal}\left(a_i t + b_i, \sigma^2\right) \\
Y_n &\sim \text{logistic}(X_n \cdot \theta(t))
\end{aligned}
$$

The coefficient vector for the period t is denoted by $\theta(t)$. The labels are denoted by Y_n. Each feature vector is denoted by X_n. Lastly, a_i and b_i are respectively the slope and intercept for the line describing the trajectory over time displayed by feature i. We set σ_a to be 0.1, σ_b to be 5, and σ to be 0.5.

Considering only the two person features, we obtain the following values for a and b using the Stan modeling language (Carpenter et al., 2017; Stan Development Team, 2017) on a dataset of 100,000 two-argument verb phrases consisting of an equal number of data points (sampled at random) per class and per time period (with 2,000 iterations and 4 chains):

$$
\begin{aligned}
a_{localA} &= -0.05, & a_{localP} &= 0.003, \\
b_{localA} &= -6.22, & b_{localP} &= -1.9
\end{aligned}
$$

This model corroborates the findings in earlier sections of the changing constraints against passivizing local agents: In Figure 7, we see that local agent displays a decreasing trend over time, which is consistent with the earlier Figure 5.

6 Conclusions and Future Directions

In this paper, we examined possible causes of the decline in the rate of passivization in English over time. We found that some explanatory variables predict passivization and are themselves changing in value over time; they can therefore be used to explain part of the decline. In particular, the local agent feature increased in average value, and this

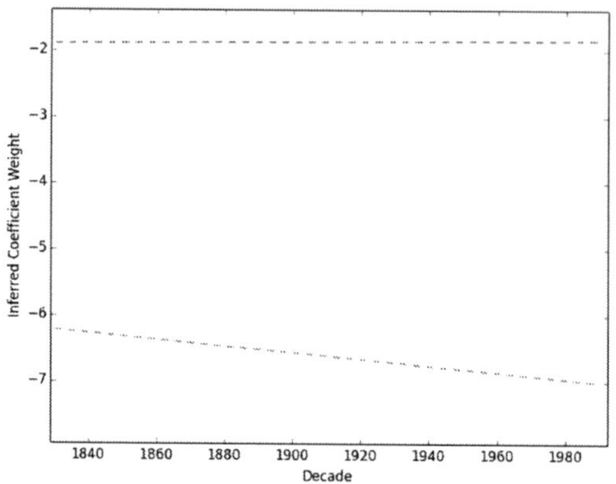

Figure 7: Parameters inferred by the linear model: red corresponds to agents, blue to patients

alone can explain at least half of the decline in passivization. We also found that the person-hierarchy effects noted by Bresnan et al. (2001) became more important over time; the constraint against passivizing clauses containing a local agent gained strength. Moreover, our ablation experiments on the Wall Street Journal and Hansard corpora showed support for the effect on passivization of the structural parallelism observed by Weiner and Labov (1983) and also for the unmarked information structure noted by Halliday (1967) of given information before new information.

Future directions include examining animacy as an explanatory variable, which affects passivization in other languages (De Cuypere et al., 2014; Sasaki and Yamazaki, 2006); however, animacy poses difficulties for automated methods as noted by Roland et al. (2007). Prescriptivism is another potential explanatory factor for the changing rate of passivization (Anderwald, 2012). While the prescriptive literature does not directly address the person-hierarchy features and their effect on the passivization rate change, an examination of "awkward" passives in that literature may yield a collection of examples in which first-person agents form the majority. Finally, cohort effects and other speaker variables that might be gleaned from corpora such as the Hansard offer opportunities for sociolinguistic modeling of syntactic change.

References

Judith Aissen. 1999. Agent focus and inverse in Tzotzil. *Language*, 75:451–485.

Marc Alexander and Mark Davies. 2015. Hansard corpus 1803-2005. `http://www.hansard-corpus.org`. Accessed: 2016-03-12.

Lieselotte Anderwald. 2012. Clumsy, awkward or having a peculiar propriety? Prescriptive judgements and language change in the 19th century. *Language Sciences*, 34(1):28–53.

Alexandre Bouchard-Côté, David Hall, Thomas L Griffiths, and Dan Klein. 2013. Automated reconstruction of ancient languages using probabilistic models of sound change. *Proceedings of the National Academy of Sciences*, 110(11):4224–4229.

Joan Bresnan, Shipra Dingare, and Christopher D. Manning. 2001. Soft constraints mirror hard constraints: Voice and person in English and Lummi. In *Proceedings of LFG 01*, pages 13–32.

Bob Carpenter, Daniel Lee, Marcus A Brubaker, Allen Riddell, Andrew Gelman, Ben Goodrich, Jiqiang Guo, Matt Hoffman, Michael Betancourt, and Peter Li. 2017. Stan: A probabilistic programming language. *Journal of Statistical Software*, 76(1).

Ludovic De Cuypere, Kristof Baten, and Gudrun Rawoens. 2014. A corpus-based analysis of the Swedish passive alternation. *Nordic Journal of Linguistics*, 37(2):199–223.

Marie-Catherine De Marneffe, Bill MacCartney, Christopher D Manning, et al. 2006. Generating typed dependency parses from phrase structure parses. In *Proceedings of LREC*, volume 6, pages 449–454. Genoa Italy.

T Mark Ellison and Simon Kirby. 2006. Measuring language divergence by intra-lexical comparison. In *Proceedings of the 21st International Conference on Computational Linguistics and the 44th annual meeting of the Association for Computational Linguistics*, pages 273–280. Association for Computational Linguistics.

Michael AK Halliday. 1967. Notes on transitivity and theme in English: Part 2. *Journal of linguistics*, 3(2):199–244.

Geraldine Legendre, Yoshiro Miyata, and Paul Smolensky. 1990. Harmonic grammar – a formal multi-level connectionist theory of linguistic well-formedness: Theoretical foundations. In *Proceedings of the Twelfth Annual Conference of the Cognitive Science Society*, pages 388–395.

Erez Lieberman, Jean-Baptiste Michel, Joe Jackson, Tina Tang, and Martin A Nowak. 2007. Quantifying the evolutionary dynamics of language. *Nature*, 449(7163):713–716.

Christian Mair and Geoffrey Leech. 2006. Current changes in English syntax. *The handbook of English linguistics*, 36.

Christopher D. Manning, Mihai Surdeanu, John Bauer, Jenny Finkel, Steven J. Bethard, and David McClosky. 2014. The Stanford CoreNLP natural language processing toolkit. In *Association for Computational Linguistics (ACL) System Demonstrations*, pages 55–60.

Mitchell P. Marcus, Beatrice Santorini, and Mary Ann Marcinkiewicz. 1993. Building a large annotated corpus of English: The Penn treebank. *Computational Linguistics*, 19(2):313–330.

Mitchell Marcus, Grace Kim, Mary Ann Marcinkiewicz, Robert MacIntyre, Ann Bies, Mark Ferguson, Karen Katz, and Britta Schasberger. 1994. The Penn treebank: annotating predicate argument structure. In *Proceedings of the workshop on Human Language Technology*, pages 114–119. Association for Computational Linguistics.

Douglas Roland, Frederic Dick, and Jeffrey L Elman. 2007. Frequency of basic English grammatical structures: A corpus analysis. *Journal of memory and language*, 57(3):348–379.

Kan Sasaki and Akie Yamazaki. 2006. Two types of detransitive constructions in the Hokkaido dialect of Japanese. *Passivization and typology: Form and function*, 68.

Stan Development Team. 2017. Pystan: the python interface to stan, version 2.16.0.0. `http://mc-stan.org`.

E Judith Weiner and William Labov. 1983. Constraints on the agentless passive. *Journal of Linguistics*, 19(1):29–58.

Christoph Wolk, Joan Bresnan, Anette Rosenbach, and Benedikt Szmrecsnyi. 2013. Dative and genitive variability in Late Modern English: Exploring cross-constructional variation and change. *Diachronica*, 30(3):382–419.

Syntactic Category Learning as Iterative Prototype-Driven Clustering

Jordan Kodner

University of Pennsylvania

Department of Linguistics

Department of Computer and Information Science

jkodner@sas.upenn.edu

Abstract

We lay out a model for minimally supervised syntactic category acquisition which combines psychologically plausible concepts from standard NLP part-of-speech tagging applications with simple cognitively motivated distributional statistics. The model assumes a small set of seed words (Haghighi and Klein, 2006), an approach with motivation in (Pinker, 1984)'s *semantic bootstrapping* hypothesis, and repeatedly constructs hierarchical agglomerative clusterings over a growing lexicon. Clustering is performed on the basis of word-adjacent syntactic frames alone (Mintz, 2003) with no reference to word-internal features, which has been shown to yield qualitatively coherent POS clusters (Redington et al., 1998). A prototype-driven labeling process based on tree-distance yields results comparable to unsupervised algorithms based on complex statistical optimization while maintaining its cognitive underpinnings.

1 Introduction

Supervised part-of-speech (POS) tagging is one of statistical NLP's classic problems (Meteer et al., 1991), but its reliance on large POS-annotated corpora makes it impractical to extend to new domains and unsuitable for low-resource languages without pre-existing annotation. Unsupervised tagging presents an interesting alternative because it does not require labelled training data, but it is a more difficult problem, and typical performance is substantially lower. The fundamental problem of training without examples aside, unsupervised tagging algorithms induce some number of clusters which must be mapped onto a desired tag set. This mapping need not be one-to-one, so error may be introduced going from algorithm output to final results.

Within NLP, unsupervised POS tagging is typically approached as a statistical optimization problem, though implementations vary widely. Brown et al. (1992) and Clark (2003) induce clusters via class-based n-gram models, the latter including morphological information. While these perform reasonably well, more recent approaches have instead been centered around HMMs. Goldwater and Griffiths (2007) and Johnson (2007) both place Dirichlet priors over the multinomial parameters of roughly typical HMM POS taggers. Berg-Kirkpatrick et al. (2010) define a feature-based HMM instead which allows the inclusion of discriminative orthographic information.[1] Haghighi and Klein (2006) implement a model based on Markov random fields (MRFs), an undirected generalization of HMMs.

Haghighi & Klein (H&K) also differs from the above models in that it is minimally supervised with *prototypes*. In their implementation, three words per tag are defined as prototypes or seeds and labelled with their correct tags, and the MRF sorts out which prototypes unknown words are most similar to. They choose the most frequent words per tag imposing the requirement that each seed must only support a single tag, so given the 45-tag Penn Treebank tag set, this yields 135 seeds, a tiny fraction of the tens of thousands of types in the Wall Street Journal corpus. Their MRF is trained on both distributional features and orthographic features follow-

---

[1]See Christodoulopoulos et al. (2010) for a fuller summary of such models.

ing Smith and Eisner (2005). This achieves impressive results on English, but their reliance on orthographic features curtails the model's performance on Chinese.

H&K's and the other computational models above are engineered primarily with performance in mind rather than cognitive plausibility. The complex optimization models in particular are slow, taking tens of hours to complete, while the simpler n-gram based models run in tens of minutes (Christodoulopoulos et al., 2010). But fundamentally, they are all tools which take advantage of statistical, especially distributional information.

For well over half a century now, it has been understood that children make use of distributional cues in the process of *syntactic category* (roughly POS) assignment as well. For example, Brown (1957)'s classic study found that children recognize a nonce word "sib" as a noun when if it is introduced to them in a sentence like "This is a sib," but prefer to label it as a verb if it is introduced in "It is sibbing." Along similar lines, Shi and Melançon (2010) present nonce words to year-old children and watch whether they then tend to focus on an image depicting an object or an action. They find that children presented with "the mige" prefer to look at the object image over the action image, consistent with them understanding that the word should be a noun. These experiments demonstrate that learners make use of distributional information (e.g., "a/the ___") even with limited exposure. Studies of child-directed corpora suggest the presence of distributional cues as well in a more naturalistic setting (Maratsos, 1979; Redington et al., 1998).

Children's sensitivity to such distributional information has been operationalized through the notion of *frequent frames*, single-word contexts on either side of an item (Mintz, 2003). Experimental evidence demonstrates that children who are exposed to items within the same frame, (e.g, "the ___ is") treat those items as members of the same class. However, the large number classes induced from frequent frames do not provide a clean one-to-one mapping to syntactic categories (Chemla et al., 2009). Syntactic frames can be seen as a purely structural cue, but semantic information play a role as well. As described by the *semantic bootstrapping* hypothesis (Pinker, 1984), children have innate rules for mapping real-world semantic onto syntactic categories. For example, actions should be verbs, objects should be nouns, and so on. These then serve as anchors in the input to provide early distributional context. The validity of semantic bootstrapping's claims of innateness and the exact nature and number of syntactic classes are not critical for the present work, rather it is sufficient that bootstrapping guides children to some kind of categorization. Experimental work has long confirmed that semantic bootstrapping basic prediction holds and that children really do associate actions and concrete objects with verbs and nouns (Gleitman et al., 2005; Pinker, 1984; Rondal et al., 1987).

We develop a computational implementation for semantic bootstrapping in syntactic frames which draws inspiration from hierarchical clustering and from Haghighi and Klein (2006)'s prototype-driven model for POS tagging. Since we know that children do not wait patiently to build up large vocabularies replete with distributional information before attempting to assign syntactic categories, our algorithm runs iteratively on the lexicon as it grows, revising category assignments as more evidence comes in. Additionally, we discard all word-internal morphological and phonological information to test the distributional cues on their own. The rest of this paper is organized as follows: section 2 introduces the iterative prototype-driven clustering model for tagging along with the basic insights behind it. Section 3 discusses the problem of evaluation for unsupervised POS tagging, provides results for child-directed English under various conditions, comparative results across nine other languages, and a comparison with H&K on English and Chinese. Section 4 reviews the model's cognitive plausibility and discusses possible extensions to the algorithm.

2   The Model

The primary insight for this work comes from the observation that words may be grouped into rough part-of-speech clusters on the basis of their single-word contexts. This is an implicit assumption of n-gram tagging models (Clark, 2003; Brown et al., 1992) for POS tagging, and the feasibility of distributional contexts for distinguishing between syntactic categories has been explicitly studied in cognitive

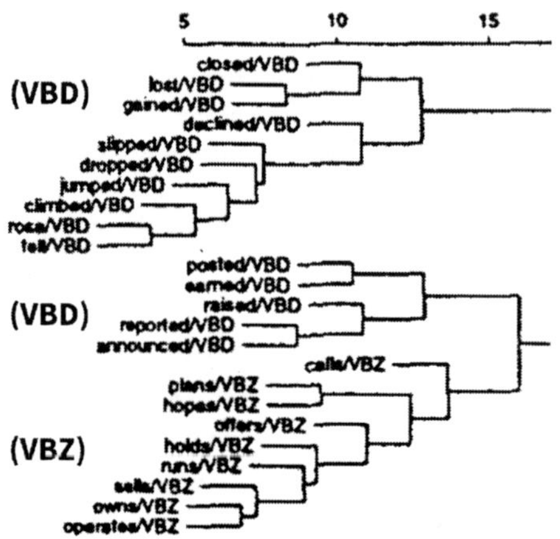

Figure 1: Example of the cutting problem from Parkes et al., (1998) with additional markup for readability

literature as well (Redington et al., 1998).

Parkes et al. (1998) provide a straightforward implementation for simple agglomerative clustering without orthographic input that serves to highlight the benefits and drawbacks of the approach. For each of the 400 most frequent words in the Wall Street Journal corpus, Parkes et al. tabulate the frequencies of left and right-context types. Using symmetricized KL-divergence ($\mathrm{KL}(p||q) + \mathrm{KL}(q||p)$) as a distance metric, they perform agglomerative clustering on those 400 types and note the qualitative purity of the resulting clusters. The immediately obvious problem is that there is no perfect mapping from clusters to tags. Figure 1 demonstrates this. Here, there are two pure VBD (past tense verb) clusters, but they cannot be joined without including a cluster of VBZ (present tense verb). Any simple cutting algorithm fails by either incorrectly postulating two VBD classes (VBD$_1$, VBD$_2$, VBZ), or postulating a mixed VBD/VBZ class. This is a general problem, independent of the choice of tag set, so while the WSJ VBD and VBZ should probably be collapsed into a single V class from a cognitive point of view, that alone does not solve it.

The simple counts over single-word contexts which Parkes et al. (1998) employ are equivalent to the syntactic frames described in the acquisition literature. So while the Parkes et al. study is neither presented as nor performs as a tagging algorithm, it holds promise from a cognitive perspective and pro-

vides clusters similar to those in the cognitive literature. The next two sections describe a prototype-driven labeling algorithm built on top of these clusters. The algorithm is described in two parts, first the inner loop basic algorithm which operates on a vocabulary of fixed size, then the outer loop, an iterative extension that operates on a growing lexicon.

2.1 Prototype-Driven labeling

Prototype-driven labeling operates over the trees created by hierarchical clustering and makes up the inner loop of the category labeling algorithm. Two vectors, one each of immediate left and right context type counts, are tabulated for the top k most frequent words in a corpus. Next, these k types are grouped by agglomerative clustering. This is slow ($O(k^2 \log(k))$ in a naïve implementation, but that can be mitigated with incremental clustering or other approaches. KL-divergence over the concatenated left and right context vectors serves as the distance metric. KL is not symmetric, so for each pair of vectors v and w, the sum of the KL-divergence between v and w and w and v is used as in Equation 1, where a and b are two words, and v and w are their corresponding context vectors.[2]

$$\mathrm{d}(a,b) = \mathrm{KL}(v||w) + \mathrm{KL}(w||v) \qquad (1)$$
$$= \sum_i v_i \log \frac{v_i}{w_i} + w_i \log \frac{w_i}{v_i}$$

In agglomerative clustering, it is necessary to define a *linkage criterion* that allows the constructed subtrees to be compared to each other along with individual words. The distance between the subtrees here is taken as the average distances between their members. This only performs slightly better than taking the minimum distance between any two members of the subtrees, and it can be updated on the fly as new members are added to the tree. Equation 2 gives a formal description of the average distance criterion. Clustering greedily joins whatever pair of words or subtrees has the smallest distance between them at each step. As a result, the final tree

---

[2]This is symmetric and is equivalent to Jenson-Shannon-divergence for the purpose of rank ordering, but it is marginally easier to compute.

can be thought of as a rank ordering of word similarities. There is no need to track the actual vector values of individual leaves once they have been joined into subtrees.

$$\mathrm{D}(A, B) = \frac{1}{|A||B|} \sum_{a \in A} \sum_{b \in B} \mathrm{d}(a, b) \qquad (2)$$

Before beginning the category labeling process, seed words are labelled in the tree to simulate semantic bootstrapping. This can be done by picking the three most frequent words per actual label as in H&K, or seeds can be chosen by contextual saliency. For a set of n tags, there is a *maximum* of $3n$ seeds in the tree. But if k is small, the actual number will usually be smaller. It is easy to see why when looking at the WSJ corpus and tag set, but the same is true of smaller cognitively-motivated tag sets as well. The three seeds with the FW "foreign word" tag are *perestroika*, *de*, and *kanji*.[3] None of these is in the top thousand most frequent words, so for $k = 1000$, there must be fewer than $3n$ seeds.

Once the seeds are assigned, the labeling can proceed for the remaining words. This can be equivalently implemented during the join steps of agglomerative clustering itself or on the completed agglomerative tree. Initially, the leaves of the tree are treated as labelled if they are seeds and unlabelled otherwise. Iterating over joins in the order that they occur from the leaves upward, if an unlabelled subtree is joined with a labelled one, each of its leaves is assigned the most common label from the labelled subtree. This is easiest to explain by example. In the simplest case, a seed is joined with an unlabelled word, and that word is assigned the same label as the seed (Figure 2 (left)). In the general case, when a labelled subtree (containing $\geq$ 1 seed) is joined with an unlabelled subtree, every word in the unlabelled subtree is assigned the most common label from the labelled subtree. For example, if a subtree that is 90% nouns and 10% verbs is joined with an unlabelled tree, every word in the unlabelled tree is tagged as a noun (Figure 2 (right)). This approach provides a solution to the cutting problem: it is not an issue if multiple clusters map to the same part-of-speech because what matters is the clusters' proxim-

---

[3] The frequent FW words effectively date this corpus.

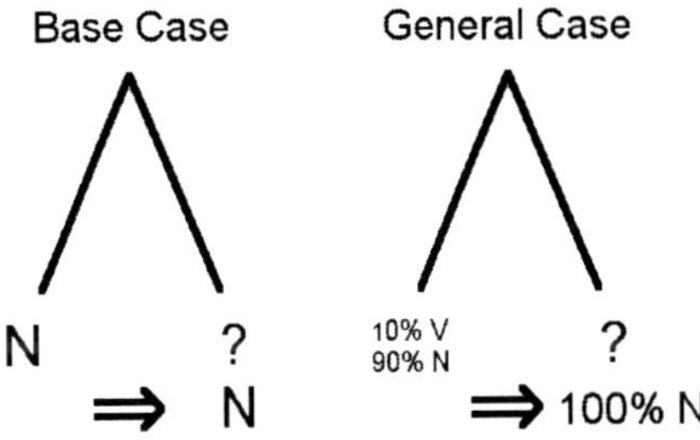

Figure 2: Visual depiction of assignment. (Left) leaves. (Right) subtrees.

ity to the seeds, not to each other. Referring back to the Parkes et al. example in Figure 1, the model will label the tree perfectly as long as each small cluster is centered around a seed.

2.2 Iterative Prototype-Driven labeling

The basic prototype-driven labeling algorithm operates on a hierarchical clustering of fixed size k. The labeling step itself is fast, but for large k, computing the pairwise distance function becomes becomes slow. It also runs afoul of experimental evidence on category learning. Children do not wait patiently to build a large vocabulary complete with distributional information before even attempting to assign syntactic categories. Rather, they assign what they can when they can, potentially revising their assignments as they go along (Pinker, 1984; Gleitman et al., 2005).

An iterative extension to the labeling algorithm solves both the practical and empirical problems. Instead of running once on a fixed large k, the algorithm is run multiple times on a sequence of lexicons with monotonically increasing sizes $K = (k_0, k_1, \ldots, k_m)$ where each lexicon contains the top k_i most frequent types in the corpus of study. This is meant to approximate which words a learner is statistically most likely to have heard early in development. The algorithm begins by labeling a small k_i, which is always quick to compute. Then it has working hypotheses for the first k_i words while it re-evaluates those words and learns new words up to k_{i+1}. While not purely online (Hewitt, 2017), this provides the sort of incremental advancement seen in the literature and is amenable to online implementation (Guedalia et al., 1999). Additionally, once a partial tree has been built, it becomes unnecessary to compute pairwise distance between every new vocabulary item and existing item. Once it is discovered which seeds are close to a new word, it is sufficient to only compute distances between the new words and those words which are close to its nearest seeds to achieve a kind of clustering. This dovetails nicely with some efficient agglomerative clustering implementations, e.g., (McCallum et al., 2000)'s canopies.

The algorithm attempts classification on frequent words multiple times, so it has the opportunity to use evidence from early classification to inform later attempts before picking its best guess in the end. To accomplish this, a *confidence* value is set for each subtree assignment operation. This is defined as the purity of the assigning tree, so a subtree that is 100% adjectives assigns members of an unlabelled subtree with a confidence of 1.0, while a 40% adjective, 30% noun, 30% verb subtree only assigns with a confidence of 0.4. Intuitively, a pure subtree is likely to represent an actual category cluster, while an impure tree is either a higher-level clustering of category clusters or garbage. Then at the end of each iteration, all words assigned with a confidence above some fixed threshold are added to the seed set and become prototypes for the next iteration. All other words are reassigned in subsequent iterations until they become prototypes themselves or the experiment finishes. At the end, all words which were never added to the prototype set are assigned the highest confidence label that they encountered during any iteration.

This iterative extension greatly improves performance because it expands the seed set as the size of the trees increase. This guarantees that the ratio of seeds to non-seeds is always relatively high, which improves assignment performance as long as the augmented seed set remains high accuracy. The ratio of seeds to non-seeds is always high for small k, but without this process, the ratio is prohibitively low at large k. Cognitively, this corresponds to the fact that children build up a lexicon of known words as they are available to them as evidence when categorizing words learned later.

3 Evaluation and Results

In this section, the iterative prototype-driven labeling model is evaluated on corpora from a wide range of languages. First, we discuss results on the English Brown (Harvard) corpus within the CHILDES corpus of child-directed speech (MacWhinney, 2000), since this serves as an in-domain application. Performance is compared on a range of tag sets, seed set sizes, and seed selection procedures. Next, we test on a range of languages from the Universal Dependency Treebank (McDonald et al., 2013) in order to gain insight into how language specific factors influence results while keeping extra-linguistic factors constant to the extent possible. Finally, we run on the WSJ portion of the Penn Treebank (Marcus et al., 1993) and on the Penn Chinese Treebank (Xue et al., 2005) in order to compare against H&K's prototype-driven model and ground this work in the wider field.

3.1 Evaluation Metrics

Evaluation for supervised POS tagging is straightforward. Sentences from a test corpus are labelled, then for each token, the proposed label is compared to the human annotated label. The simplest of such metrics is *one-to-one token accuracy*. On the other hand, the problem of evaluation is more complicated for unsupervised algorithms. Results are broadly not comparable across experiments because a wide of evaluation metrics are employed.[4]

Token-based metrics are an excellent option when the task is to automatically annotate running text with part-of-speech tags, but they have undesirable traits when applied to syntactic category learning. If syntactic category learning is analogous to labeling types in a dictionary or lexicon, then labeling sequences of text just obfuscates results. Type frequencies are not uniform across a corpus, so token-based metrics weight assignments to frequent types higher than assignments to infrequent types. For example, an algorithm which labels the pronoun "you" incorrectly will be punished more severely than one which labels the pronoun "whomever" incorrectly simply because "you" is more common than "whomever" in most corpora. This is particularly problematic because word frequencies follow

---

[4]See (Christodoulopoulos et al., 2010).

a distribution where just a few types are hundreds of times more frequent than most others. Mislabeling any pronoun is hundreds of times more damaging than labeling almost any noun from our daily lives (like "table" or "bug") incorrectly. Mislabeling any common noun is much more damaging than mislabeling a rare noun, and noun frequencies can be highly corpus specific. This makes it difficult to gauge the relative performance of different models.

A *one-to-many type accuracy* is a better choice for scoring syntactic category learning because each item is weighted the same for scoring. In natural language, types can potentially support multiple labels, so a one-to-many metric is needed to account for this. For example, "bat" could be a noun or a verb, so an algorithm which classifies it as either should be correct. The *many-to-one* accuracy used in some unsupervised models does not make sense here because the model does not output clusters which need to be mapped. The algorithm never demarcates clusters and instead assigns labels to individual items.

The difference between token and type-based metrics becomes clear when calculating the baselines for our model. Scoring by type accuracy, the baseline is arrived at by scoring the initial seeds as correct and marking everything else wrong. This typically yields a score of under 10%, often under 1%, and corresponds directly to the proportion of types which are selected as seeds. However, this tends to correspond to a $> 50\%$ token accuracy because seeds are drawn from the most frequent types. A final type score of, say, 70% is more meaningful than a final token score of 70% because the improvement over the baseline is greater.

3.2 Experiments on English CHILDES

The CHILDES corpus contains transcriptions of naturalistic child-directed speech. The English subset studied here consists of all caregiver text extracted from Adam, Eve, and Sarah of the Harvard (Brown) corpus, yielding 8,307 types and 588,888 tokens. The tag set used in the Brown corpus consists of 55 idiosyncratic tags, and this is tested along with a mapping that reduces these to an 8-tag (+SKIP[5]) set (DT, IN, JJ, NN, PRP, RB, VB, SKIP). Table 1 reports

k	# Seeds	Baseline %	Type Acc.
100	58	58.0	94.0
1000	100	10.0	81.2
8307	130	1.6	62.8

Table 1: CHILDES type accuracy by tree size. Baseline indicates the contribution from the seeds alone. Accuracy presented as percents

the impact of k on performance and indicates the best achieved type accuracy results training on the full Brown tag set then mapping to the reduced set (Brown-to-Reduced) for scoring for final $k = 100$, $k = 1000$, and $k = 8307$.[6] As expected, percent correct decreases for higher k because infrequent words which occur only once or twice in the corpus provide weaker distributional information than frequent words do. The number of seeds used never reaches 55*3 because some tags do not appear in the top k words. This is the same as the WSJ corpus FW-problem described earlier.

To determine what impact the choice of tag set and number of seeds have on the results, the experiment was run and evaluated directly on the Brown tag set as well as the reduced tag set. Reduced tag set experiments were run with 3 seeds per tag and 11 per tag. The Brown-to-reduced tests smooth out the difference between related tags when computing accuracy scores. The difference between B-to-R and straight Brown in Table 2 implies that the model struggles to differentiate some of the Brown tags. This could be because some of the more eccentric Brown tags do not actually distinguish distributionally coherent classes. The difference between the 3-seed and 11-seed results indicates that performance largely depends on the number of seeds. Note, however, that the baseline is still quite low even with 11 seeds per tag.

The point of syntactic frames is that they are available as primary evidence early on, and nobody who works on them would argue that they are the only source of evidence, so it is unsurprising that performance declines using frames alone for large k. If syntactic frames are indeed useful, then we would expect their application on early vocabulary to carry benefits downstream, and this this is what Table 3

---

[5]Tags which do not correspond to any of the 8 are mapped to SKIP and not scored.

[6]k sequence $K = (100, 500, 900, 1000, 2000, 4000, 6000, 8307)$ was used.

k	Tag Set	# Seeds	Baseline	Type Acc.
1000	B-to-R	100	10.0	**81.2**
1000	Brown	100	10.0	70.3
1000	Reduced	24	2.4	51.8
1000	Reduced	85	8.5	80.6
8307	B-to-R	130	1.6	**62.8**
8307	Brown	130	1.6	44.0
8307	Reduced	24	0.3	25.3
8307	Reduced	85	1.0	53.3

Table 2: CHILDES type accuracy by tag set and seed set size

Tag Set	# Seeds	Basic Acc.	Iter. Acc.
B-to-R	130	44.2	**62.8**
Brown	130	27.7	**44.0**
Reduced	24	9.3	**25.3**
Reduced	85	44.0	**53.3**

Table 3: Comparison between CHILDES basic and iterative prototype-driven labeling performance

Tag Set	# Seeds	Baseline	Token Acc.
B-to-R	130	50.2	82.7
Brown	130	48.0	73.4
Reduced	24	28.8	60.0
Reduced	85	52.3	**83.5**

Table 4: CHILDES one-to-one token accuracy performance

k	# Seeds	Baseline	Type Acc.
1000	74	7.4	73.4
8307	82	1.0	49.5

Table 5: CHILDES type accuracy with salient seeds

Language	# Seeds	k=1,000	k=10,000
French	28	77.92	62.07
German	30	79.04	26.52
Indonesian	30	75.84	65.21
Italian	26	54.26	37.08
Japanese	24	47.78	48.31
Korean	26	33.47	39.19
Portuguese	28	65.40	49.44
Spanish	29	63.41	46.14
Swedish	37	51.10	33.96

Table 6: UTB type accuracy by language

shows. It compares the results of iterative application from $k = 100$ to $k = 8307$ used for the previous experiments to a single non-iterative application $k = 8307$. The iterative results are 9 to 18 points higher, demonstrating that syntactic frames applied to early vocabulary set up better performance later. The iterative application of the algorithm which expands the seed set as the lexicon grows is critical to model performance.

Up to this point, seeds have been selected post hoc by corpus frequency, which cannot possibly be how children use semantic bootstrapping. To correct for this, a set of 82 lower frequency but high saliency seed words was selected for comparison based on studies of salience in child-directed speech (Carlson et al., 2014). Tables 5 lays out the result achieved with salient seeds on the reduced tag set, which can be compared to the 11 frequent seed results from Table 2. The type accuracy is lower and roughly what is to be expected given the size of the seed set even though the seeds themsleves are of lower frequency on average.

3.3 Experiments on Other Languages

The CHILDES results suggest that information from syntactic frames is useful for assigning syntactic categories from English child-directed speech. In order to compare performance across other languages as well, we apply the algorithm to nine languages from the Universal Dependency Treebank: German, Spanish, French, Indonesian, Italian, Japanese, Korean, Brazilian Portuguese, and Swedish. These corpora share a 10-tag tag set (excluding punctuation and non-word tags) and were compiled for the same task, which means that different performances reflect differences in the languages themselves to the extent possible. In order to more closely align these experiments to syntactic category learning, no seeds were provided for the punctuation (␣, MAD, MID, PAD) or non-word (X) tags, and punctuation and non-words were not scored.[7]

Performance varies substantially across languages. At $k = 1000$, type accuracy ranges from the low 30s (Korean), to the high 70s (German, French, Indonesian), and at $k = 10000$ from the mid 20s (German) to the 60s (French, Indonesian). Much of this variation can be explained linguistically with the important caveat that extra-linguistic factors in the corpora must still be at play.

Languages with complicated inflection are at a

---

[7]Each language was tested with $confidence = 0.3$, 0.5, 0.7, 0.9, and 1.0. Only the best confidence for each language is reported. The same k sequence $K = (100, 500, 900, 1000, 2000, 5000, 9000, 10000)$ was used each time.

disadvantage because the distributional context information of their roots is spread across inflectional forms, and without reference to word-internal features, it is impossible to group these forms by root to pool that information. For example, while all the distributional information for English BLUE is collected in the contexts for the word "blue," German spreads its distributional information across the contexts for its six inflected forms, "blau," "blauer," "blauen," "blauem," "blaue," and "blaues," and our algorithm has no way to combine them.

Another way to think about this is to compare token/type ratios between languages, which are equivalent to how many syntactic frames on average contribute to the context vectors for each type. A low ratio indicates that the typical context vector is sparser because it accounts for information from fewer frames. Languages with complex inflection naturally have more types and a lower token/type ratio.

The particularly poor performance for Korean and Japanese is at least partially due to the UTB corpus tokenization which attaches phrase final syntactic clitics to the preceding word as opposed to standalone tokens. This is in line with the traditional conception of "word" boundaries in these languages (called *bunsetsu* in Japanese and *eojeol* in Korean), but is not an obviously correct choice from a cognitive standpoint, and would be equivalent to not segmenting the possessive *'s* clitic in English. As shown in Table 7, *bunsetsu* tokenization creates multiple words for APPLE and PEAR and two example clitics, each with disjoint right contexts, while standalone tokenization would yield one word each for APPLE and PEAR with both clitics as right contexts. This technical choice effectively renders the clitics as inflections like in German rather than as useful syntactic context information. Also, it is unclear why Korean and Japanese perform better at high k than low k at the reported confidences.[8]

Languages with freer word order are also at a disadvantage because the entire premise of syntactic frames assumes that the syntax forces categories to appear adjacent to certain other categories. A freer word order means more violations of this assump-

Tokenization	Text Strings	Right Frames
Bunsetsu	ringo-ga X	ringo-ga: {X}
	ringo-wo Y	ringo-wo: {Y}
	nashi-ga Z	nashi-ga: {Z}
	nashi-wo W	nashi-wo: {W}
Standalone	ringo ga X	ringo: {ga, wo}
	ringo wo Y	nashi: {ga, wo}
	nashi ga Z	ga: {X, Z}
	nashi wo W	wo: {Y, W}

Table 7: Right frames for *apple-NOM X, apple-ACC Y, pear-NOM Z,* and *pear-ACC W*

tion relative to the number of frames attested, which manifests as more uniform and less discriminable context vectors.

3.4 Comparison with Haghighi & Klein

In order to ground the performance of this algorithm in the broader research context, we compare results with Haghighi and Klein (2006) since it is similarly semi-supervised. The H&K PROTO model represents the fairest comparison because they were calculated on atypically small datasets, fractions of the English Wall Street Journal and Mandarin Chinese Treebank. They report *one-to-one token* accuracy, so we follow suit.

The WSJ dataset contains 16,839 types across 193,000 tokens[9], capitalization removed.[10] The model takes 3 seeds for each of the 45 tags in the Penn Treebank tag set. Table 8 presents WSJ type accuracy at $k = 1000$ and $k = 10000$. The 1000-type model takes about five minutes to train, while the 10,000-type model takes just over eight hours under a naïve clustering implementation. The performance is overall worse than for CHILDES, likely because the type diversity is much higher than what would be expected in child-directed speech. CHILDES has a token/type ratio of 71.4, and the WSJ's ratio is almost three times lower at 27.8.

The CTB dataset contains 8,842 types across only 60,000 tokens and is annotated with a 33-tag set similar to the Penn Treebank tag set. Table 8 compares the Chinese type results to English. The WSJ model outperforms the CTB model, which, among factors like corpus size, is probably related to the number of seeds present and the token/type ratio.

---

[8]This only happens for Japanese and Korean, and only at $c = 0.7, 0.9$ for both.

[9]Starting from section 2. H&K report 18,423 types.

[10]H&K retain capitalization as a model feature.

Corpus	k	# Seeds	Baseline	Type Acc.
WSJ	1000	95	9.5	57.9
WSJ	10000	95	1.0	30.2
CTB	1000	74	7.4	50.4
CTB	8842	74	0.8	27.5

Table 8: Wall Street Journal and Chinese Treebank Type Accuracy

Model	# Seeds	Base	Top k	All	All+
k=1000	95	40.5	74.3	54.7	60.2
k=10000	95	40.5	63.2	60.9	61.4
H&K06	135	41.3	-	**68.8**	-

Table 9: Wall Street Journal token accuracy and comparison

The CTB model was trained on all types, but the WSJ model was only trained up to $k = 10000$ (accounting for 96.46% of tokens) because of time considerations, which makes token accuracy less straightforward to compute. Three numbers are provided: *Top k* only scores words appearing in the top k by frequency, *All* scores the top k as before and marks all other tokens incorrect, and *All+* instead assigns tokens outside the top k the type of their nearest seed by symmetricized KL-distance. Table 9 compares WSJ results with H&K. Overall performance is lower but still above 60.

Table 10 compares against H&K's CTB results. Here, the iterative prototype-driven labeling model is clearly superior. Even the $k = 1000$ *All* score is 8 points higher than H&K's MRF model, and the best $k = 10000$ *All+* score is over 15 points higher. That large discrepancy is due to H&K's reliance on orthographic features. Since suffix n-grams are meaningless in Chinese, they were forced to discard them from their model. It seems that the reason why H&K outperformed our model by over 7 points on English was that their model made reference to the word-internal features which ours discards. Chinese represents a more level playing field which demonstrates how our model makes good use of sparse distributional information.

Model	# Seeds	Base	Top k	All	All+
k=1000	74	29.5	62.80	46.9	50.4
k=8841	74	29.5	-	**54.1**	-
H&K06	99	34.4	-	39.0	-

Table 10: Chinese Treebank token accuracy and comparison

4 Discussion and Future Work

The minimally supervised iterative prototype-driven labeling algorithm laid out in this paper leverages only simple distributional statistics over adjacent word-forms to perform syntactic category labeling. Nevertheless it achieves English and Chinese results comparable to and surpassing the more complex H&K model respectively, and similar performance on French and Indonesian, though it struggles on other languages.

The most glaring deficiency in the model is that it lacks any notion of word-internal features. Throwing away this critical information prevents it from identifying and utilizing affixes as cues for syntactic categories and from pooling evidence from word-forms that share common roots. One promising avenue of research therefore, is determining how to cleanly incorporate morphological information into the clustering algorithm. This will be helpful for languages like Japanese under *bunsetsu* tokenization or German, and absolutely critical for language families with complex agglutinative or polysynthetic morphology like Turkic, Eskimo-Aleut, or Bantu.

Perhaps less obviously, the model is missing out on an important generalization by only training on lexical syntactic frames. Children are not only sensitive to the specific lexical items surrounding a word, but also the syntactic category of those items (Reeder et al., 2013). For example, a word preceded by a determiner and followed by a noun (DT __ N) is almost certainly an adjective, regardless of which determiner and which noun it is, so even though the adjectives in "the shiny ball" and "a scary cube" have different lexical contexts, they share the same category context. Relevant to our algorithm, category contexts reveal distributional similarities that are hidden by lexical contexts alone.

Acknowledgments

We would like to thank Charles Yang and Mitch Marcus for their helpful insights along with the rest of the Penn LORELEI team. This work was funded by the DARPA LORELEI program under Agreement No. HR0011-15-2-0023 and by the U.S. Army Research Office (ARO) through an NDSEG fellowship awarded to the author.

References

Taylor Berg-Kirkpatrick, Alexandre Bouchard-Côté, John DeNero, and Dan Klein. 2010. Painless unsupervised learning with features. In *Human Language Technologies: The 2010 Annual Conference of the North American Chapter of the Association for Computational Linguistics*, pages 582–590. Association for Computational Linguistics.

Peter F Brown, Peter V Desouza, Robert L Mercer, Vincent J Della Pietra, and Jenifer C Lai. 1992. Class-based n-gram models of natural language. *Computational linguistics*, 18(4):467–479.

Roger W Brown. 1957. Linguistic determinism and the part of speech. *The Journal of Abnormal and Social Psychology*, 55(1):1.

Matthew T Carlson, Morgan Sonderegger, and Max Bane. 2014. How children explore the phonological network in child-directed speech: A survival analysis of childrens first word productions. *Journal of memory and language*, 75:159–180.

Emmanuel Chemla, Toben H Mintz, Savita Bernal, and Anne Christophe. 2009. Categorizing words using frequent frames: what cross-linguistic analyses reveal about distributional acquisition strategies. *Developmental science*, 12(3):396–406.

Christos Christodoulopoulos, Sharon Goldwater, and Mark Steedman. 2010. Two decades of unsupervised pos induction: How far have we come? In *Proceedings of the 2010 Conference on Empirical Methods in Natural Language Processing*, pages 575–584. Association for Computational Linguistics.

Alexander Clark. 2003. Combining distributional and morphological information for part of speech induction. In *Proceedings of the tenth conference on European chapter of the Association for Computational Linguistics-Volume 1*, pages 59–66. Association for Computational Linguistics.

Lila R Gleitman, Kimberly Cassidy, Rebecca Nappa, Anna Papafragou, and John C Trueswell. 2005. Hard words. *Language Learning and Development*, 1(1):23–64.

Sharon Goldwater and Tom Griffiths. 2007. A fully bayesian approach to unsupervised part-of-speech tagging. In *Annual meeting-association for computational linguistics*, volume 45, page 744.

Isaac David Guedalia, Mickey London, and Michael Werman. 1999. An on-line agglomerative clustering method for nonstationary data. *Neural computation*, 11(2):521–540.

Aria Haghighi and Dan Klein. 2006. Prototype-driven learning for sequence models. In *Proceedings of the main conference on Human Language Technology Conference of the North American Chapter of the Association of Computational Linguistics*, pages 320–327. Association for Computational Linguistics.

Yang Charles Hewitt, John. 2017. Bootstrapping for syntactic categories. In *Cognitive Science Society*, London, UK.

Mark Johnson. 2007. Why doesn't em find good hmm pos-taggers? In *EMNLP-CoNLL*, pages 296–305.

Brian MacWhinney. 2000. *The CHILDES project: The database*, volume 2. Psychology Press.

Michael Maratsos. 1979. How to get from words to sentences. *Perspectives in Psycholinguistics*.

Mitchell P Marcus, Mary Ann Marcinkiewicz, and Beatrice Santorini. 1993. Building a large annotated corpus of english: The penn treebank. *Computational linguistics*, 19(2):313–330.

Andrew McCallum, Kamal Nigam, and Lyle H Ungar. 2000. Efficient clustering of high-dimensional data sets with application to reference matching. In *Proceedings of the sixth ACM SIGKDD international conference on Knowledge discovery and data mining*, pages 169–178. ACM.

Ryan T McDonald, Joakim Nivre, Yvonne Quirmbach-Brundage, Yoav Goldberg, Dipanjan Das, Kuzman Ganchev, Keith B Hall, Slav Petrov, Hao Zhang, Oscar Täckström, et al. 2013. Universal dependency annotation for multilingual parsing. In *ACL (2)*, pages 92–97.

Marie Meteer, Richard Schwartz, and Ralph Weischedel. 1991. Studies in part of speech labelling. In *Proceedings of the workshop on Speech and Natural Language*, pages 331–336. Association for Computational Linguistics.

Toben H Mintz. 2003. Frequent frames as a cue for grammatical categories in child directed speech. *Cognition*, 90(1):91–117.

Cornelia Parkes, Alexander Malek, Er M Malek, and Mitchell Marcus. 1998. Towards unsupervised extraction of verb paradigms from large corpora.

Steven Pinker. 1984. Language learnability and language development.

Martin Redington, Nick Chater, and Steven Finch. 1998. Distributional information: A powerful cue for acquiring syntactic categories. *Cognitive science*, 22(4):425–469.

Patricia A Reeder, Elissa L Newport, and Richard N Aslin. 2013. From shared contexts to syntactic categories: The role of distributional information in learning linguistic form-classes. *Cognitive psychology*, 66(1):30–54.

Jean A Rondal, Martine Ghiotto, Serge Brédart, and Jean-François Bachelet. 1987. Age-relation, reliability and grammatical validity of measures of utterance length. *Journal of child language*, 14(3):433–446.

Rushen Shi and Andréane Melançon. 2010. Syntactic categorization in french-learning infants. *Infancy*, 15(5):517–533.

Noah A Smith and Jason Eisner. 2005. Contrastive estimation: Training log-linear models on unlabeled data. In *Proceedings of the 43rd Annual Meeting on Association for Computational Linguistics*, pages 354–362. Association for Computational Linguistics.

Naiwen Xue, Fei Xia, Fu-Dong Chiou, and Marta Palmer. 2005. The penn chinese treebank: Phrase structure annotation of a large corpus. *Natural language engineering*, 11(2):207–238.

A bidirectional mapping between English and CNF-based reasoners

Steven Abney
University of Michigan
abney@umich.edu

Abstract

If language is a transduction between sound and meaning, the target of semantic interpretation should be the meaning representation expected by general cognition. Automated reasoners provide the best available fully-explicit proxies for general cognition, and they commonly expect Clause Normal Form (CNF) as input. There is a well-known algorithm for converting from unrestricted predicate calculus to CNF, but it is not invertible, leaving us without a means to transduce CNF back to English. I present a solution, with possible repercussions for the overall framework of semantic interpretation.

1 Overview

1.1 The problem

I would like to address a problem that illustrates how considerations of the place of semantic interpretation in the larger cognitive system, even very schematic considerations, can have consequences for the manner and target of interpretation.

Let us take seriously the idea that language is a mapping between sound and meaning—which is to say, essentially, an input-output device for general cognition—and let us provisionally accept current automated reasoners as the best available *fully explicit* models of general cognition. Then an important goal for a semantics of English is to define an invertible transduction between English sentences and a meaning representation that is suitable for use with an automated reasoner. Model-theoretic interpretation is good and useful, but it does not provide us with a transducer.

Standard accounts are easily recast as defining a mapping f from English sentences to predicate calculus. However, the mapping does not appear to be invertible. For one thing, not every predicate-calculus expression is in the range of f. If general cognition produces an arbitrary predicate-calculus expression ϕ to render into English, we must find a logically equivalent expression ϕ' such that $f^{-1}(\phi')$ is defined, but logical equivalence is undecideable, a problem pointed out by Shieber (1993). Even if $f^{-1}(\phi)$ is defined, it is unclear how to compute it.

In addition, the most common choice of meaning representation for automated reasoners is not general predicate calculus, but a normal form known as Clause Normal Form (CNF). Reasoners that require CNF input include systems based on resolution (McCune, 2003b), some model-building algorithms (McCune, 2003a), probabilistic reasoners using weighted model-counting (Gogate and Domingos, 2011), and more general cognitive architectures that incorporate such reasoners.

CNF is a genuine normal form, in the sense that for every expression of first-order predicate calculus (FOPC), there is a unique logically-equivalent CNF expression. Fortuitously, by mapping to CNF, we eliminate a significant part of the variation that leads to Shieber's logical-equivalence problem. But there is a catch. There is a well-known algorithm that converts FOPC expressions to CNF, but it is not invertible. That is the problem: once we have interpreted a sentence, converted the meaning to CNF, and passed it to an automated reasoner, we do not have a way of taking the CNF expressions that the reasoner produces as output and mapping them to English.

Proceedings of the Society for Computation in Linguistics (SCiL) 2018, pages 55-63.
Salt Lake City, Utah, January 4-7, 2018

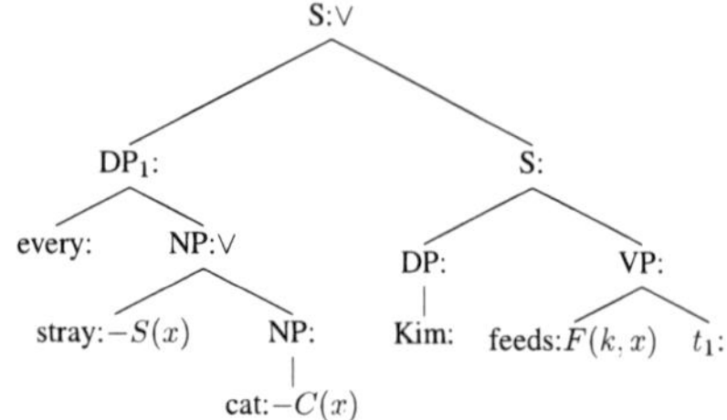

Figure 1: A tree that serves simultaneously as English LF and parse tree for the CNF translation $-S(x) \vee -C(x) \vee F(k, x)$.

1.2 A solution

The solution I propose can be stated briefly as follows. (1) Use CNF as the target of semantic translation. (2) Instead of assembling the translation in a bottom-up pass through the parse tree, creating larger and larger partial translations at each step, let us label selected nodes in the parse tree with CNF operators. In other words, take the English parse tree *to be* the CNF parse tree, albeit with some extraneous nodes and labels. The resulting tree is symmetric between English and CNF (e.g., Figure 1). In particular, the leaf nodes are labeled symmetrically with English words and CNF literals. Define a standard grammar with features to generate such trees. (3) Given a CNF expression as input from general cognition, use the grammar to parse the sequence of literals, constructing an English/CNF parse tree, and read off the English sentence.

Figure 1 provides an illustration of a combined English/CNF parse tree. The English portion is the LF for the sentence *Kim feeds every stray cat,* and the CNF portion represents the translation $-S(x) \vee -C(x) \vee F(k, x)$. Each node has a label pair $\alpha{:}\beta$. For the purposes of the grammar, the label pairs are simply complex categories; we construct a single grammar that generates the pairs. When parsing English, the input consists of the English labels of leaf nodes (*Kim feeds every stray cat*) and when parsing CNF, the input consists of the CNF labels $-S(x), -C(x), F(k, x)$.

A few complications must be addressed, but they have known solutions. We must convert the tree from LF to SS before parsing English, creating a necessity for two different versions of the grammar, one for LF and one for SS. However, both versions generate the same labels, and the two-step process of parsing and converting to LF is standard and fa-

miliar. In the CNF-to-English direction, the CNF input will actually be partially parsed input: for example, $[_\vee -S(x), -C(x), F(k, x)]$. We do not pass the nonterminal nodes directly as input to the parser, but rather use them to constrain the operation of the parser. In our example, the constraint prevents the parser from constructing a node whose right label is not $\vee$. Further, CNF is a "free word order" language. Unordered inputs make for less efficient parsing, but they are manageable, and the partial-parse constraints actually ameliorate the problem. There are also more empty nodes in the CNF-to-English direction than in the other direction—for example, in Figure 1, the nodes labeled "every:," "Kim:," and "t_1:" are all empty nodes in the CNF-to-English direction—but parsers routinely deal with empty nodes, and dealing with many of them is no harder than dealing with a few. In short, handling these issues requires some care in implementation but no novel parsing techniques.

The main question I will address in the rest of the paper is how we systematically design the grammar, that is, how we determine what the CNF labels should be.

2 Direct translation constrained by feature propagation

2.1 Assigning FOPC labels

To assign CNF operators to LF nodes, I propose (at least conceptually) that we first label the tree with the usual FOPC translation, and then apply the standard conversion to CNF. I adopt the particularly direct form of translation sketched in the previous section. A key desideratum is that the assignment of semantic operators and atomic formulae to parse-tree nodes should be constrained by local feature constraints of the usual sort. The full power of feature grammars will not be required; features with atomic values will suffice.

Let us construct the LF tree for the sentence *Kim feeds every stray cat* and annotate it with the obvious FOPC translation (Figure 2). I have made one unusual assumption in the LF tree: the determiner *every* has been raised to become head of the quantifier-raising structure. This is not essential, but it will simplify the statement of certain constraints in what follows.

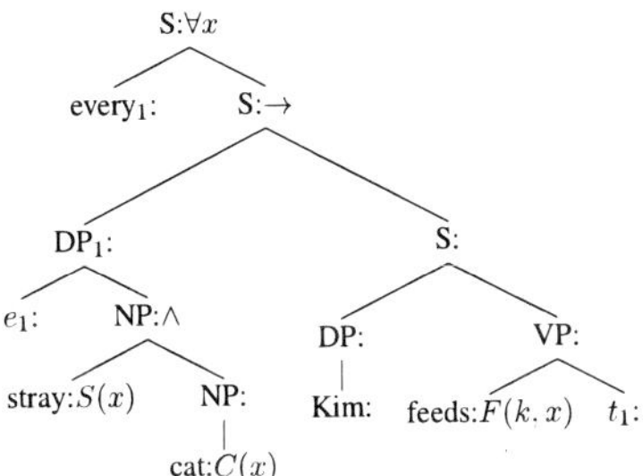

Figure 2: The LF tree labeled with the standard FOPC translation.

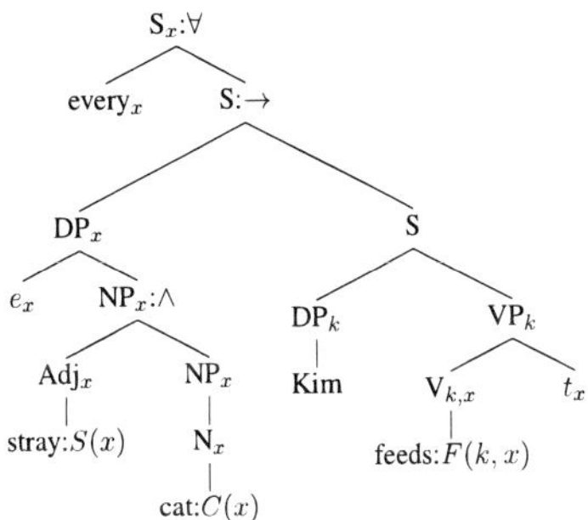

Figure 3: The results of index propagation.

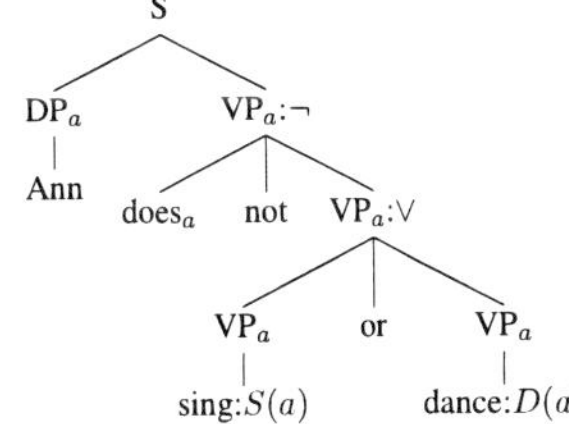

Figure 4: Negation and VP disjunction; the translation is $\neg(S(a) \vee D(a))$.

How do we specify this labeling within the grammar? Constraining the occurrence of semantic operators and predicates is generally straightforward and local. For our example, we may state as a general rule that an NP representing adjectival modification translates as $\wedge$, that an S headed by a (raised) universal determiner translates as $\forall$ (we return shortly to the question of the variable), and that an S that is sibling of a universal determiner translates as $\rightarrow$. In the leaf-node translations, the predicates obviously represent the lexical translations of the corresponding English words (S for *stray*, C for *cat*, F for *feed*). It is less obvious how to constrain the choice of variables.

2.2 Index propagation

The standard approach relies heavily on lambda expressions to specify which variable goes in which position. This is a major cause of difficulty in inversion: the inverse of beta-reduction is infinitely ambiguous. Instead of using lambda expressions, let us replace numeric syntactic indices with the semantic variables themselves and propagate them through the tree by syntactic feature-passing. We can then use the syntactic indices to determine the choice of variables in the atomic formulae.

In our example, let us use the variable k for the subject DP and x for the raised object DP. Let us propagate the DP index throughout the DP, and use it to determine the variables in the atomic formulae $S(x)$ and $C(x)$, as in Figure 3. (I give a more rigorous characterization of the spreading in Constraint 2 below.)

As for the variables in $F(k, x)$, let us assume a form of syntactic concord in which the subject's index k is shared with the VP and then, because V is

the head of VP, with the V. Let us also impose an object-agreement constraint on the verb, requiring its second subscript to match the object.

Only two minor items remain: traces obtain their indices from their antecedents in the usual way, and the variable associated with $\forall$ is now written as an index. Figure 3 shows the final result. Henceforth I omit colons when the semantic label is empty. I also usually omit preterminal nodes—Adj, N, V—to save space, but I include them when needed for clarity.

Let us consider some more examples (adapted from Heim and Kratzer (1997)). These will motivate additions to the index propagation rules, and will illustrate at least a small range of cases in which index propagation can be used in lieu of lambda expressions. The tree in Figure 4 illustrates negation and disjunction, and the trees in Figure 5 illustrate the handling of "case-marking" versus "lexical" prepositions. Relative clauses and multiple quantifiers are illustrated in later trees.

Note that Figure 4 includes an extension of the index propagation rules: the auxiliary (namely, *does*) shares its index with its complement (the disjunctive VP). In Figure 5 we have extended the object-agreement rule to apply to the two-place adjective *fond,* and we have treated *of* like an auxiliary in the

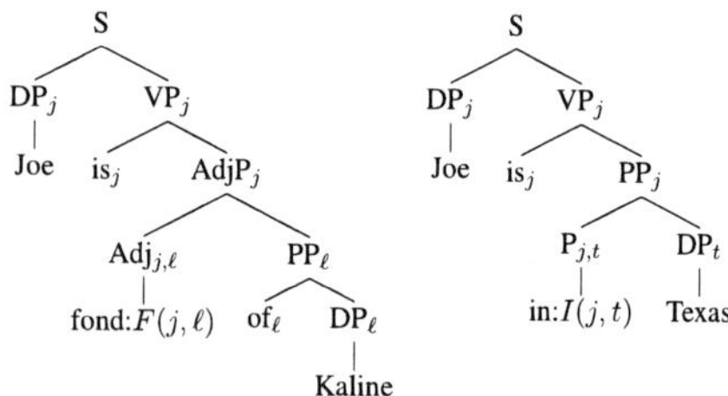

Figure 5: Differing treatments of case-marking (left) and lexical (right) prepositions.

sense that it shares its index with its complement. In the right-hand tree, *in* is treated like a transitive verb, sharing its first index with its parent and sharing its second index with its object.

2.3 Constraints on indices

Based on the examples we have considered, we may hazard a general statement of the index propagation rules. Indices are present only as required by the following two constraints.

Constraint 1 (Intrinsic Indices) *Every DP has an index (excluding pleonastics). A leaf node labeled with atomic formula $\pi(\alpha_1, \ldots, \alpha_n)$ must be child of a preterminal with syntactic indices $\alpha_1, \ldots, \alpha_n$.*

Constraint 2 (Index Propagation) *Syntactic indices are propagated as necessary to satisfy the following requirements.*

1. A trace has the same index as its antecedent.

2. A modifier has the same index as the node it modifies.

3. A function word (e.g., auxiliary, case marker) has the same index as its complement.

*4. An argument-taker's last index is the same as the argument's index. In this case and this case only, the index is **discharged**.*

5. A parent inherits its head's undischarged indices.

"Head" includes $\overline{X}$ heads, as well as the head in an adjunction structure, all heads in a coordination structure, and the relative pronoun in a relative clause.

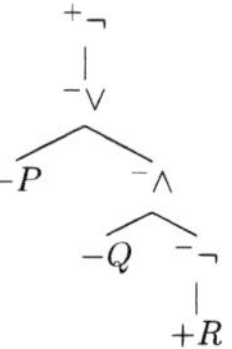

Figure 6: Local propagation of node polarity substitutes for negation lowering.

3 Conversion to CNF

The standard conversion from unrestricted FOPC to CNF involves a sequence of tree transformations: (1) rewriting conditionals, (2) lowering negation, (3) Skolemization, and (4) distribution (of disjunction over conjunction). We would like to consider how to implement the conversion via feature constraints, without altering the basic structure of our LF trees.

3.1 Negation lowering

Let us begin with negation lowering. Its effect is to eliminate the negation operator in favor of **literals**, consisting of an atomic formula and a sign (positive or negative). By adding polarity as an attribute of all nodes, not just terminal nodes, we can give a succinct characterization of negation lowering in the form of a local constraint that is readily implemented in a feature grammar.

Constraint 3 (Polarity) *(a) The polarity of the root node is positive. (b) The polarity of a child node is the same as the polarity of its parent, unless the parent node is labeled with an operator that is **polarity-reversing** for the child in question, in which case the child's polarity is the opposite of the parent's.*

For our purposes there are two polarity-reversing operators: negation and the conditional $\rightarrow$, which is polarity-reversing for its first child.

As an example, the FOPC expression $\neg(P \vee (Q \wedge \neg R))$ has the parse tree in Figure 6. Polarities have been added in accordance with Constraint 3. In particular, $\neg$ has inverse polarity to that of its child, but otherwise parent and child always have the same polarity. We achieve the effect of negation lowering by interpreting **signed operators** as specified in Table 1. Replacing the signed operators with their unsigned equivalents for readability, Figure 6 corresponds to the expression $-P \wedge (-Q \vee R)$, which

$$
\begin{array}{c|c}
{}^{+}\neg \;=\; \epsilon & {}^{-}\neg \;=\; \epsilon \\
{}^{+}\wedge \;=\; \wedge & {}^{-}\wedge \;=\; \vee \\
{}^{+}\vee \;=\; \vee & {}^{-}\vee \;=\; \wedge \\
{}^{+}\rightarrow \;=\; \vee & {}^{-}\rightarrow \;=\; \wedge \\
{}^{+}\forall \;=\; \epsilon & {}^{-}\forall \;=\; \epsilon \\
{}^{+}\exists \;=\; \epsilon & {}^{-}\exists \;=\; \epsilon
\end{array}
$$

Table 1: The interpretations of signed operators.

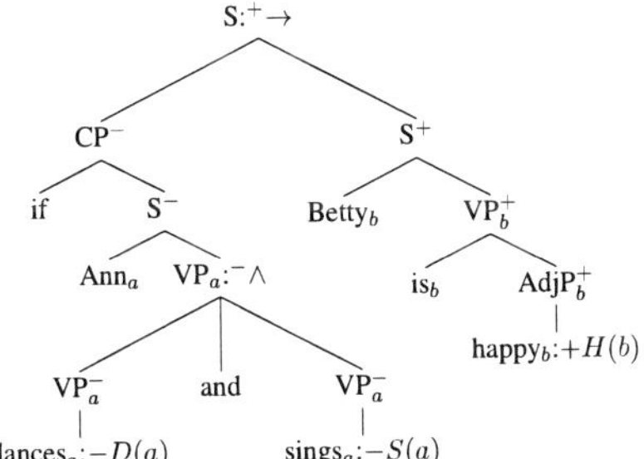

Figure 7: An LF tree illustrating polarity reversal under $\rightarrow$.

is indeed logically equivalent to $\neg(P \vee (Q \wedge \neg R))$. Note that ϵ indicates deletion of the operator.

3.2 Rewriting conditionals

In the standard conversion to CNF, rewriting conditionals precedes negation lowering. We can deal with conditionals as follows. We define the signed operator ${}^{+}\rightarrow$ to be a synonym for $\vee$ and ${}^{-}\rightarrow$ to be a synonym for $\wedge$. However, unlike $\vee$ or $\wedge$, ${}^{\pm}\rightarrow$ reverses the polarity of its first child. Consider the example of Figure 7. The $\rightarrow$ operator inverts the polarity of its first child, but otherwise polarities are passed unchanged from parent to child. Accordingly, Figure 7 is equivalent to $-D(a) \vee -S(a) \vee +H(b)$, which is indeed equivalent to $D(a) \wedge S(a) \rightarrow H(b)$, the natural translation for *if Ann dances and sings, Betty is happy.*

Note that Table 1 is used in the process of "reading off" the CNF expression for input to the reasoner; it is not used to eliminate signed operators from the LF tree. The signed operators do serve a purpose beyond the truth function they represent. For one thing, even though ${}^{+}\rightarrow$ is equivalent to $\vee$, the former reverses its first child's polarity whereas the latter does not. The signed operators also permit us to use local constraints to define the assignment of translations. An example of such a local constraint is the following: *a node has semantic operator $\rightarrow$ if*

it is headed by a CP headed by "if." Such a statement remains valid whether the polarity of the node is positive or negative, though in the former case the signed operator ${}^{+}\rightarrow$ is interpreted as $\vee$ and in the latter case the signed operator ${}^{-}\rightarrow$ is interpreted as $\wedge$.

3.3 Skolemization

The third step of the conversion to CNF is Skolemization. As usually formulated, one replaces existentially bound variables with Skolem terms consisting of a Skolem function applied to the list of outscoping universal variables, then one deletes all quantifiers. The deletion is already reflected in Table 1—though, as already mentioned, the signed operators remain in the LF tree and are not actually deleted until we read off the CNF expression for input to the reasoner.

I will use the term *variable* to refer loosely to both universal variables (that is, implicitly universally-bound variables) and Skolem terms. I write Skolem functions with a dot, e.g., $\dot{x}$, to make it easy to distinguish them from universal variables. Whether a variable should be a universal variable or a Skolem term is determined by the signed operator at the variable's **home**, which I define to be the node labeled with the quantifier that originally bound it. Specifically:

Constraint 4 (Variable type determination)
(a) The syntactic index of a node whose signed operator is ${}^{+}\forall$ or ${}^{-}\exists$ must be a universal variable, and (b) the syntactic index of a node whose signed operator is ${}^{+}\exists$ or ${}^{-}\forall$ must be a Skolem term.

This constraint determines the type of variable, and the variable is then propagated to other nodes by Constraint 2. See Figure 8 for an example.

The variable $\dot{y}$ in Figure 8 is a shorthand for the Skolem term $\dot{y}(x)$. To avoid clutter, I have suppressed the argument list, but it does need to be computed in a complete implementation. One may use a feature $\texttt{ouv}$ whose value for a given node ν is the list of **outscoping universal variables**, that is, the list of universal variables whose home position dominates ν. It is straightforward but tedious to write out the feature constraints that determine the correct value for $\texttt{ouv}$; I omit the details.

Figure 8 provides an example with two quantifiers. Note that there are two polarity reversals, both

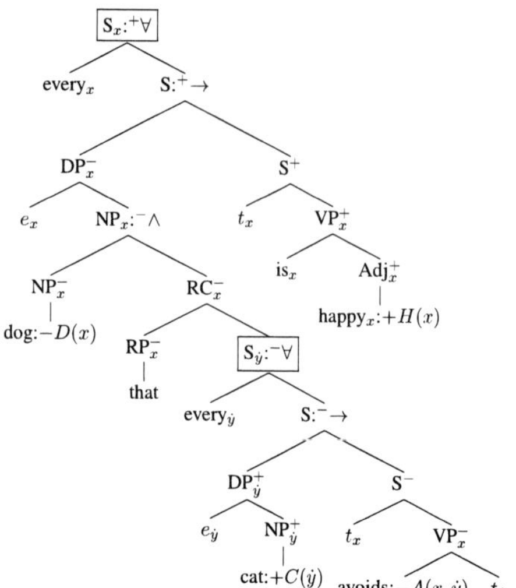

Figure 8: A complex example. The boxed nodes are the home nodes for the variables x and $\dot{y}$.

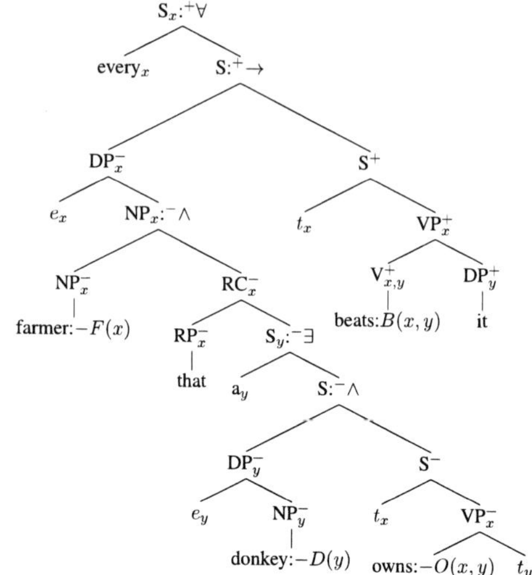

Figure 9: Donkey anaphora is covered without stipulation.

occurring at the first child of a node with operator $\rightarrow$. The boxed nodes are the homes of the two quantifiers. Because the upper one has signed operator $^+\forall$, the variable is a universal, and because the lower one has signed operator $^-\forall$, the variable is a Skolem term.

Reading off the CNF, we obtain the following. For readability, I have again replaced the signed operators with their more familiar unsigned equivalents; I also indicate the Skolem argument lists explicitly.

$$-D(x) \vee [C(\dot{y}(x)) \wedge -A(x, \dot{y}(x))] \vee H(x).$$

In words: either x is not a dog, or else x's $\dot{y}$ is a cat that x fails to avoid, or else x is happy. That is inferentially equivalent to the original sentence *every dog that avoids every cat is happy*.

3.4 Donkey anaphora

A pleasant side effect of the lack of explicit quantifiers in CNF is that donkey anaphora becomes available without any stipulations. The structure of *every farmer that owns a donkey beats it* is essentially the same as that in Figure 8 except for the choice of lower quantifier: see Figure 9. I assume that the pronoun *it* picks up the index of its antecedent *a donkey*. The resulting CNF translation is $-F(x) \vee -D(y) \vee -O(x, y) \vee B(x, y)$, which

correctly captures the strong reading.[1]

3.5 Distribution

The final step in the conversion to CNF is distribution of disjunction over conjunction. Distribution unavoidably involves a structural transformation of the tree, so we will not attempt to incorporate it into the LF structure. Although distribution is not uniquely invertible, the degree of ambiguity that arises in inversion is limited. When translating from CNF to English, let us assume the inverse of distribution, which we may call **consolidation**, as a preprocessing step.

To fix ideas, let us consider the following example:

$$\phi = P \vee (Q \wedge R)$$

The result of distribution is ψ:

$$\psi = (P \vee Q) \wedge (P \vee R)$$

In general, whenever distribution is non-trivial, it has the effect of introducing copies of existing atomic formulae, as with P in ψ. Hence inverting distribution (consolidation) involves recombining copies. Consolidation is ambiguous. For example, ϕ is not the only undistributed expression that

---

[1]I suggest that the weak reading is spurious; the use of the singular "a donkey" presupposes that the set of owned donkeys is a singleton, in which case the strong and weak readings are equivalent.

may give rise to ψ: ψ itself might have been the source. More generally, every way of combining copies produces a form that constitutes a possible undistributed source.

On the other hand, the amount of ambiguity is limited by the number of duplicates in the input (going from CNF to English). Moreover, each possible result of consolidation does give rise to a valid English sentence. The choice among them is not one of well-formedness but of stylistic preference. Since each duplicate atomic formula gives rise to duplicated words, it seems natural to prefer to do as much consolidation as possible, and we may adopt that as a heuristic.

In most cases, there is a unique most-consolidated form, though it is possible to construct examples with multiple distinct maximally-consolidated forms. For example, given the CNF expression $(P \vee Q) \wedge (Q \vee R) \wedge (R \vee P)$, we may eliminate any one of the three duplicate pairs, but only one, leaving us with three different maximally-consolidated forms. This is not likely to be a major problem in practice.

4 Discussion

4.1 Generalized quantifiers

Important questions remain. Perhaps the most urgent is how generalized quantifiers are to be accommodated in the proposed approach. Generalized quantifiers are relations between sets, so the question can be rephrased as accommodating phrases (namely, NPs) that define sets.

One can include sets in a first-order account by reification. That is, introduce a membership predicate M and define a set such as $\dot{s} = \lambda x . \phi[x]$ as:

$$M(x, \dot{s}) \leftrightarrow \phi[x].$$

The problem is that converting an LF tree that contains $\leftrightarrow$ to CNF involves a substantial structural change. For example, $M(x, \dot{s}) \leftrightarrow F(x) \wedge G(x)$, converted to CNF, expands out as:

$$\begin{aligned}
& [-M(x, \dot{s}) \vee F(x)] \wedge \\
& [-M(x, \dot{s}) \vee G(x)] \wedge \qquad (1) \\
& [-F(x) \vee -G(x) \vee M(x, \dot{s})].
\end{aligned}$$

My proposal relies crucially on the conversion to CNF being structure-preserving, but this is a case in which it emphatically does not preserve structure.

One possibility is to permit $\leftrightarrow$ in the LF tree as a primitive operator, and to handle it much as we handled distribution. Going from the LF tree to the reasoner, an expression containing $\leftrightarrow$ is expanded out as in (1). In the opposite direction, as a pre-processing step one seeks instances of the pattern illustrated in (1) and replaces them with $M(x, \dot{s}) \leftrightarrow F(x) \wedge G(x)$, much as we recognize the repetitions that may be consolidated. A more ambitious alternative is to incorporate the replacement into the reasoner as an inference rule, much as reasoners often include primitive support for an equality predicate and substitution of equals. I leave this as a question for future research.

4.2 Related work

There have been proposals in the literature for reversible grammars, which support both interpretation and generation (Appelt, 1987; de Kok et al, 2011; Copestake et al, 1996; Melamed, 2003; Shieber, 1988; Shieber and Schabes, 1990; Shieber et al, 1990; Strzalkowski, 1991; Strzalkowski, 1994). Reversibility was indeed one of the original motivations for unification grammars (Kay, 1975; Kay, 1996), though the translational target was predicate-argument structure rather than FOPC. The present paper can be seen as extending that work to map bidirectionally between English and CNF using a feature grammar.

For general unification grammars, it was proposed that one define an interpretation relation $I(s, \phi)$ in Prolog: to parse, provide the sentence s and solve for the meaning ϕ, and to generate, provide ϕ and solve for s (Shieber, 1988; Shieber et al, 1990). Unfortunately, solving for s proved to be beyond Prolog's abilities, and much work went into elaborate methods for helping Prolog along (Strzalkowski, 1991; Strzalkowski, 1994). In additional, the usual unification grammars were susceptible to the logical-equivalence problem that Shieber pointed out: the range of ϕ in $I(s, \phi)$ is typically not the entire space of FOPC expressions but only a subset of the space, and given an arbitrary input ψ one must seek a logically equivalent ψ' for which $I(s, \psi')$ is defined; but logical equivalence is not decideable (Shieber, 1993).

These difficulties led to an interest in flat semantic languages, which, one hoped, reduce the number of logically equivalent expressions corresponding to a given semantic input (Whitelock, 1992; Trujillo, 1995). Perhaps the best known current approach is Minimal Recursion Semantics (MRS) (Copestake et al, 2005). However, MRS expressions are not "flat" in the right way—an MRS expression is actually a meta-logical description of a standard FOPC parse tree—and the use of MRS does not ameliorate the logical equivalence problem. The main attraction of MRS is not that it addresses the problems of interest here, but that it supports a transparent and compact representation of certain ambiguities, particularly quantifier-scope ambiguities.

When genuinely flat semantic languages have been proposed (Whitelock, 1992; Trujillo, 1995), they usually have severely limited expressivity, permitting only conjunctions of ground clauses, and excluding disjunction and quantification. By contrast, CNF represents a flat semantic language with the full expressive power of FOPC. It is flat in the sense that no CNF expression has depth greater than three: the most complex CNF expression is a conjunction of clauses, each clause being a disjunction of literals. There are no explicit quantifiers, but their expressive capacity is preserved via the distinction between universal variables and Skolem terms. The use of CNF for semantic translations does ameliorate the logical equivalence problem. A CNF expression is the normal form for an (infinite) equivalence class of unrestricted FOPC expressions, and the commonest sorts of logically equivalent pairs fall together when we map to CNF.

I build also on a line of inquiry into reversibility that involves simultaneous grammars, in which a single derivation constructs two parse trees. Simultaneous grammars have been used both for machine translation (Melamed, 2003) and for translation between English and FOPC (Shieber and Schabes, 1990). However, previous work has not considered the further conversion from FOPC to CNF. Moreover, the simultaneous grammars considered in this paper are unusually simple: the two syntax trees are homomorphic, allowing them to be treated as a single tree with paired labels.

4.3 Conclusion

I have described a method of translating between English and CNF whose advantages are as follows:

it provides a direct connection to automated reasoners; it is fully invertible; it is arguably simpler than simultaneous-tree or standard direct-interpretation approaches; it ameliorates the logical-equivalence problem by virtue of CNF's status as normal form; it is computable using an atomic-valued feature grammar, enabling efficient parsing/generation; and it predicts the existence of donkey anaphora as a side effect of Skolemization, which is an essential step in the conversion to CNF. To the extent that the proposal has merit, it illustrates how considerations of the role of interpretation in the larger cognitive system can influence the form of the semantic account in fundamental ways.

Acknowledgements

I have benefited greatly from discussions with Ezra Keshet and joint work we have done on semantic consequences of using CNF as metalanguage. The paper has also benefited from the comments of anonymous reviewers. Obviously, they bear no responsibility for any remaining shortcomings of the work.

References

James Allen. 1995. *Natural Language Understanding* (Second edition). Benjamin Cummings, Menlo Park, CA.

Douglas E. Appelt. 1987. Bidirectional grammars and the design of natural language generation systems. In: *Theoretical Issues in NLP 3*.

Patrick Blackburn and Johan Bos. 2005. *Representation and Inference for Natural Language*. CSLI Publications, Stanford, CA.

Ann Copestake, Dan Flickinger, Robert Malouf, Susanne Riehemann, and Ivan Sag. 1996. Translation using minimal recursion semantics. *Proceedings of the Sixth International Conference on Theoretical and Methodological Issues in MT*.

Ann Copestake, Dan Flickinger, Carl Pollard, and Ivan Sag. 2005. Minimal Recursion Semantics: An introduction. *Research on Language and Computation* 3:281–332.

Daniël de Kok, Barbara Plank, and Gertjan van Noord. 2011. Reversible Stochastic Attribute-Value Grammars. *Proceedings of the Conference of the Association for Computational Linguistics (ACL)*.

Vibhav Gogate and Pedro Domingos. 2011. Probabilistic Theorem Proving, *Proceedings of UAI*.

Irene Heim and Angelika Kratzer. 1997. *Semantics in generative grammar.* Blackwell Publishers.

Daniel Jurafsky and James H. Martin. 2009. *Speech and Language Processing* (2nd edition). Prentice Hall, Upper Saddle River, NJ.

Martin Kay. 1975. Syntactic processing and functional sentence perspective. *Proceedings of TINLAP.*

Martin Kay. 1996. Chart generation. *Proceedings of the Conference of the Association for Computational Linguistcs (ACL).*

John E. Laird. 2012. *The Soar Cognitive Architecture.* The MIT Press, Cambridge, MA and London, England.

William McCune. 2003a. *Mace4 Reference Manual and Guide.* Tech. Memo ANL/MCS-TM-264, Mathematics and Computer Science Division, Argonne National Laboratory, Argonne, IL.

William McCune. 2003b. *Otter 3.3 Reference Manual.* Tech. Memo ANL/MCS-TM-263, Mathematics and Computer Science Division, Argonne National Laboratory, Argonne, IL.

Dan Melamed. 2003. Multitext Grammars and Synchronous Parsers, *Proceedings of NAACL.*

Robert C. Moore. 1989. Unification-based semantic interpretation. *Proceedings of the 27th Meeting of the Association for Computational Linguistics.*

Fernando Pereira and Yves Schabes. 1992. Inside-outside reestimation from partially bracketed corpora. *Proceedings of the Association for Computational Linguistics 30th Annual Meeting,* 128–135. Newark, Delaware.

Stuart J. Russell and Peter Norvig. 2002. *Artificial Intelligence: A Modern Approach* (2nd edition). Prentice Hall, Upper Saddle River, NJ.

Stuart Shieber. 1988. A uniform architecture for parsing and generation. *Proceedings of the 12th Conference on Computational Linguistics (COLING),* vol. 2, pp. 614–619.

Stuart Shieber. 1993. The problem of logical-form equivalence. *Computational Linguistics* 19(1), 179–190.

Stuart Shieber and Yves Schabes. 1990. Synchronous Tree-Adjoining Grammars. *Proceedings of the Conference on Computational Linguistics (COLING).*

Stuart Shieber, Gertjan van Noord, Fernando Pereira, and Robert Moore. 1990. Semantic head-driven generation. *Computational Linguistics* 16(1):30–42.

Tomek Strzalkowski. 1991. A general computational method for grammar inversion. *Proceedings of the ACL Workshop on Reversible Grammar in Natural Language Processing.*

Tomek Strzalkowski (ed.) 1994. *Reversible Grammar in Natural Language Processing.* Kluwer Academic Publishers.

Indalecio Arturo Trujillo. 1995. *Lexicalist Machine Translation of Spatial Prepositions.* PhD dissertation, University of Cambridge.

P. Whitelock. 1992. Shake-and-bake translation. *Proceedings of the Conference on Computational Linguistics (COLING).*

Formal Restrictions On Multiple Tiers

Alëna Aksënova and **Sanket Deshmukh**
Stony Brook University
{alena.aksenova,sanket.deshmukh}@stonybrook.edu

Abstract

In this paper, we use harmony systems with multiple feature spreadings as a litmus test for the possible configurations of items involved in certain dependence. The subregular language classes, and the class of tier-based strictly local (TSL) languages in particular, have shown themselves as a good fit for different aspects of natural language. It is also known that there are some patterns that cannot be captured by a single TSL grammar. However, no proposed limitations exist on tier alphabets of several cooperating TSL grammars. While theoretically possible relations among tier alphabets of several TSL grammars are containment, disjunction and intersection, the latter one appears to be unattested. Apart from presenting the typological overview, we discuss formal reasons that might explain such distribution.

1 Introduction

Recent investigations in the field of complexity of linguistic dependencies suggest that in different parts of language, well-formedness conditions are *subregular*, i.e. they do not require the full power of regular languages. For example, see (Heinz, 2010) for phonology, (Aksënova et al., 2016) for morphotactics, and (Graf and Heinz, 2015) for syntax among others.

A fruitful subregular class for natural languages is the class of *tier-based strictly local* (TSL) languages (Heinz et al., 2011). The core intuition behind this class is to capture long-distance dependencies locally by projecting elements relevant for a cer-

tain process on a tier, therefore "ignoring" all the intervening material that is irrelevant for this process. While the learner proposed in (Jardine and McMullin, 2017) is capable of inducing tier-based strictly local grammar in polynomial time using positive data only, there are numerous attested patterns that show that in some cases, one TSL grammar is not enough (McMullin, 2016). Extracting multiple cooperating grammars might become a problem if *any* type of relation is possible among *tier alphabets*, the sets of elements over which the TSL grammar operates.

In this paper, we explore possible relations among tier alphabets in natural languages, using harmonic systems with several spreadings as the litmus test. Theoretically possible relations between the two sets of harmonizing elements are containment ($\{a,b,c\}$ and $\{a,b\}$), disjunction ($\{a,b\}$ and $\{c,d\}$), and intersection ($\{a,b\}$ and $\{b,c\}$). Here, we show that the latter case in unattested. Surprising as it may seem, this restriction actually reduces the amount of tier alphabet configurations. For example, for a set of 10 elements, there are 511 ways to form two disjoint sets, 1022 ways to arrange them with respect to the containment relation, and 27990 ways to form two sets with a non-empty intersection. The difference is striking: in this case, by removing the intersection relations, the amount of possible tier arrangements will be reduced by 95%.

The importance of eliminating possibilities that are not related to natural language and how it makes learning easier was highlighted by (Keenan and Stavi, 1986; Szymanik, 2016). For a domain with n elements, there are 2^{4^n} possible generalized quantifiers. However, when we take into account such property of natural language quantifiers as conservativity, it reduces the number of options to 2^{3^n}. For example, for a domain with 2 elements, there are 65536 possible generalized quantifiers, but only 64 of them are conservative.

The range of these topics recalls the "gavagai" problem (Quine, 1969): the learner of a language converges on a meaning for a word even though there are infinitely many possibilities to assign interpretation to this word. There, as well as in the case of inducing several tier alphabets, the successful learning is achieved by eliminating multiple theoretically possible assumptions.

We introduce the subregular class of tier-based strictly local languages in Sec. 2. Sec. 3 provides typological overview of different types of systems that exhibit several feature spreadings. In Sec. 4, we give a formal explanation of why it is efficient to eliminate the intersection relation from the scope of possible relations among tier alphabets. Sec. 5 concludes the paper.

2 TSL grammars

Tier-based Strictly Local (TSL) grammars (Heinz, 2011; Heinz et al., 2011) capture non-local dependencies by projecting selected elements on a *tier* in order to achieve locality among remotely dependent units. This allows us to analyze long-distance processes and rule out illicit sequences locally over the tier, because all the intervening irrelevant material is ignored. A TSL grammar consists of a tier alphabet T – set of items to be projected on a tier, and the set of n-grams G_{TSL} that must not be presented in a tier representation of a well-formed string.

For example, consider vowel harmony in LOKAA (Niger-Congo). In this language, a non-high vowel agrees with the preceding non-high vowel in ATR, whereas other vowels and consonants are transparent for the harmony, see (1-4) from (Akinlabi, 2009).

(1) èsìsòn   'smoke'
(2) ɛ̀sísɔ̀n   'housefly'
(3) lèjìmə̀   'matriclan'
(4) ɛ́kílìkà   'kind of plant'

The agreeing items are not adjacent to each other, that makes this process long-distance. For strings in (1–3), 5-grams are needed to capture this pattern, because there are 3 intervening elements in-between the two agreeing non-high vowels. But for (4), this window size is not enough: there are 5 segments in-between ε and a. In this language, there is no upper bound on the amount of material separating two non-high vowels that agree with respect to the [tense] feature; therefore, only projecting a tier of non-high vowels will allow to create the required locality relation among agreeing vowels.

Tier of non-high vowels $T = \{\varepsilon, e, o, \partial, \mathrm{\textipa{O}}, a\}$	
1.	*[α tense] [β tense]$
	$H_{ATR} = \{$*ɛe, *eɛ, *ɛo, *oɛ, *ɛə, *əɛ, *ɔe, *eɔ, *ɔə, *əɔ, *ɔo, *oɔ, *aə, *əa, *ao, *oa, *ae, *ea$\}$

Table 1: TSL grammar for LOKAA harmony

In order to analyze this pattern with a TSL grammar, its tier alphabet T must include all non-high vowels presented in this language, and the ATR spreading is captured by blocking combinations of non-high vowels disagreeing in their [tense] specification, see H_{ATR} in Table 1. Figure 1 illustrates this analysis.

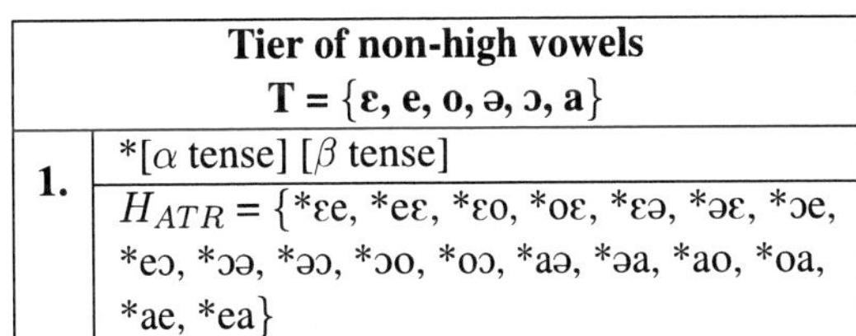

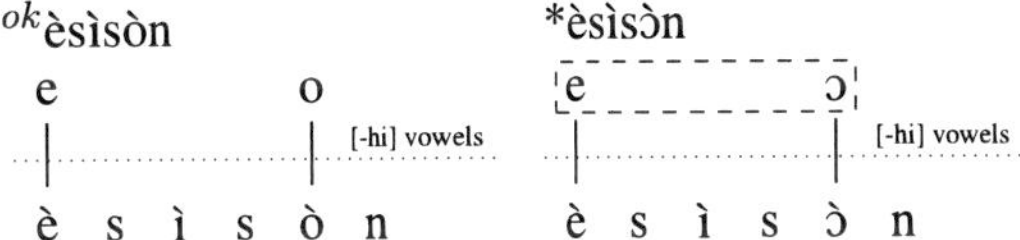

Figure 1: ATR harmony in LOKAA

The left subfigure shows the well-formed word *èsìsòn*. The only non-high vowels (*e* and *o*) are projected on the tier, and their combination *eo* is not among those that need to be ruled out, thus the word *èsìsòn* is considered acceptable. However, its ill-formed counterpart **èsìsɔ̀n* contains two non-high vowels *è* and *ɔ* that disagree in [tense]. These vowels are projected, and the bigram **eɔ* is banned over the tier by the grammar H_{ATR}. Therefore the word **èsìsɔ̀n* must be ruled out.

The LOKAA harmony involved spreading of a single feature, and one tier was enough to capture the pattern. In the following section we will exemplify harmonic processes that involve multiple feature spreadings.

3 Types of multiple feature spreadings

In many languages, long-distance agreement processes involve spreading of more than one feature. The choice of items involved in a harmonic process, as well as of the harmonizing feature, varies a lot from language to language. For example, in many systems, vowel harmony in a feature such as backness (TURKISH, FINNISH) or tongue root position (MONGOLIAN, BURYAT) co-exists with labial assimilation, see (Kaun, 1995) for numerous examples of such vowel harmonies. Or it can be sibilant harmony in two features such as anteriority and voicing (NAVAJO, TUAREG). Also, in several languages it is possible to find both consonantal and vowel harmonies in features such as nasality and height (KIKONGO, KIYAKA, BUKUSU).

Further we show that in some cases, one TSL grammar is enough (Case 1) – it is possible to enforce both harmonic spreadings over a single tier. Another possibility is containment, and it is attested as well (Case 2) – there are languages in which one spreading affects a subset of items involved in another spreading. In some languages, harmonies affect two separate sets of segments, and the intersection of these two sets is empty (Case 3) – such tier alphabets are disjoint. And the only relation that appears to be typologically unattested is non-empty intersection (Case 4): to the best of our knowledge, there are no harmonies that affect two sets of elements that only partially overlap.

For the details and properties of the class of Multiple TSL (MTSL) languages, see (De Santo, 2017). We would like to highlight that this current work is preliminary, and the provided data and generaliza-tions are drawn to the best of our knowledge.

3.1 Case 1: single tier

Many harmonies with multiple feature spreadings can be captured with a single tier-based strictly local grammar. This does not mean that undergoers and blockers are the same for both harmonies, it only means that none of the items taking part in one harmony is irrelevant for the other one.

Consider YAKUT (Turkic) as an example of such configuration. In this language, all vowels must agree in fronting. However, labial harmony spreads from low vowels onto both low and high ones, from high vowels to high ones, but it cannot spread from high vowels to low ones. The latter ones, in this case, function as *harmonizing blockers*: they inherit [round] specification from any preceding vowel, but block the rounding assimilation in [+high][–high] configuration, see (Sasa, 2001; Sasa, 2009).

The accusative affix *-(n)ü, -(n)u, -(n)i, -(n)ɨ* with a high vowel and the plural marker *-lor, -lör, -lar, -ler* with a non-high vowel demonstrate this pattern, see examples (5-12) below from (Kaun, 1995).

(5)	oɣo-lor	'child-PL'	*oɣo-lar
(6)	börö-lör	'wolf-PL'	*börö-ler
(7)	oɣo-nu	'child-ACC'	*oɣo-nɨ
(8)	börö-nü	'wolf-ACC'	*börö-ni
(9)	murum-u	'nose-ACC'	*murum-ɨ
(10)	tünnük-ü	'window-ACC'	*tünnük-i
(11)	ojum-lar	'shaman-PL'	*ojum-lor
(12)	tünnük-ler	'window-PL'	*tünnük-lör

Within a word, all vowels must share the same [tense] specification (5-12). High suffixal vowels agree with any preceding vowel in rounding (7-10), whereas low vowels can only inherit rounding feature from preceding low vowel (5,6), otherwise they are realized as non-rounded (11,12).

The tier alphabet T of TSL grammar that captures YAKUT pattern consists of all vowels presented in the language. H_{front} rules out sequences of vowels that disagree in fronting, whereas the part of the grammar responsible for the labial harmony ($H_{r1} \cup H_{r2} \cup H_{r3}$) blocks occurrence of a rounded low vowel if it is preceded by a high one, and also any other combination of vowels that disagree in their labial features. The obtained TSL grammar op-

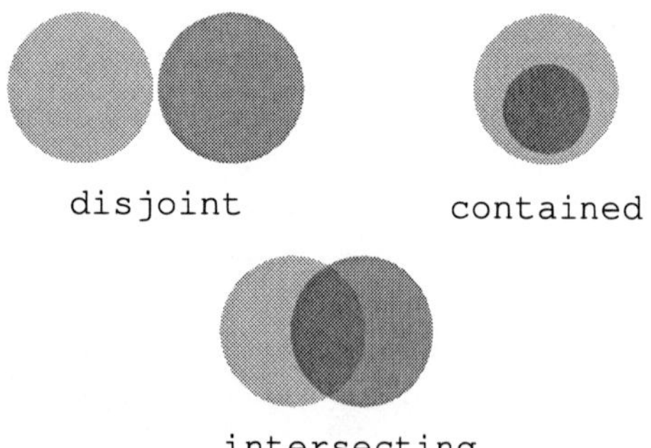

Figure 2: Theoretically possible tier alphabet relations

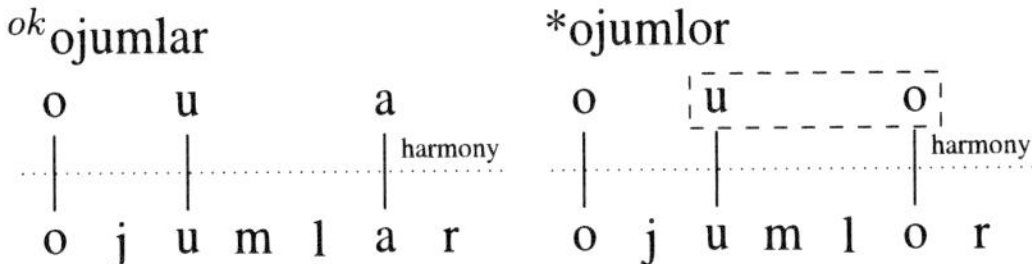

Figure 3: Fronting and labial harmony in YAKUT

erates over the tier alphabet T and its list of illicit substrings is $G_{TSL} = H_{front} \cup H_{r1} \cup H_{r2} \cup H_{r3}$.

Vowel tier $T = \{a, ɨ, e, i, o, ö, u, ü\}$		
1.	*$[\alpha$ front] $[\beta$ front]	
	$H_{front} = \{$*ai, *ae, *aö, *aü, *oi, *oe, *oö, *oü, *ii, *ie, *iö, *iü, *ui, *ue, *uö, *uü, *ia, *io, *ii, *iu, *ea, *eo, *ei, *eu, *öa, *öo, *öɨ, *öu, *üa, *üo, *üɨ, *üu$\}$		
2.	*[+ high, α round] [+ high, β round]	
	$H_{r1} = \{$*ui, *üi, *iü, *iu, *iu, *iü, *ui, *üi$\}$		
3.	*[+ high, α round] [− high, + round]	
	$H_{r2} = \{$*üö, *uo, *iö, *io, *io, *iö, *uö, *üö$\}$		
4.	*[− high, α round] [β round]	
	$H_{r3} = \{$*oa, *oi, *öi, *öe, *ao, *au, *eö, *eü, *aö, *aü, *eo, *eu, *oi, *oe, *öa, *öi$\}$		

Table 2: TSL grammar for YAKUT harmony

Figure 3 shows that such a grammar correctly predicts that the word *ojumlar* is well-formed with respect to the constructed TSL grammar, because the labial harmony spreads from the non-high vowel *o* to the following high vowel *u*. However, it cannot spread from a high vowel to a low one, therefore *ojumlor* is blocked as the illicit bigram *uo* is found on its vowel tier.

3.2 Case 2: tier and its sub-tier

Another possibility for the tier alphabets is to be in a set-subset relation. In this case, one harmony operates over a proper superset of items that are involved in another agreement.

In IMDLAWN TASHLHIYT[1] (Berber), affixal sibilants regressively harmonize with the stem in voicing and anteriority, see (Hansson, 2010b; McMullin, 2016). Whereas the anteriority harmony is not a subject for blockers of any kind, the voicing assimila-

<hr>

[1]The IMDLAWN TASHLHIYT generalization is presented here in a simplified way. Please refer to (McMullin, 2016) for the detailed description and discussion of the pattern.

tion is blocked by any intervening voiceless obstruents. If there are no sibilants in the stem, the underspecified affixal element is realized as the voiceless anterior sibilant [s]. The data in (13-22) from (Elmedlaoui, 1995; Hansson, 2010a) illustrate the harmonic pattern using the causative prefix *s-*.

(13) **s:-uga** 'CAUS-evacuate'
(14) **s-as:twa** 'CAUS-settle'
(15) **ʃ-fiaʃr** 'CAUS-be.full.of.straw'
(16) **z-bruz:a** 'CAUS-crumble'
(17) **ʒ-m:ʒdawl** 'CAUS-stumble'
(18) **s-ħuz** 'CAUS-annex'
(19) **s:-ukz** 'CAUS-recognize'
(20) **sˤ-rˤuˤfˤzˤ** 'CAUS-appear.resistant'
(21) **s-mχazaj** 'CAUS-loathe.each.other'
(22) **ʃ-quʒ:i** 'CAUS-be.dislocated'

In (13), there are no sibilants in the root, so the prefix appears in its by-default form *s-*. In all other examples, this prefix agrees with the sibilant in a root in its voicing and anteriority, therefore the possible feature specifications are [−voice, +ant] (14), [−voice, −ant] (15), [+voice, +ant] (16), and [+voice, −ant] (17). However, as mentioned before, the anteriority harmony in this language does not have blockers, whereas the voicing spreading is blocked by any intervening voiceless obstruent such as /ħ/, /k/, /f/, /χ/, or /q/. In (18-22), stem-internal sibilants are voiced, but the ones in the prefix are voiceless, because of the intervening voiceless obstruents in-between them that block the agreement relation. Note that even if the voicing harmony is blocked, the anteriority one is still obeyed.

Sibilant tier $T_{ant} = \{s, z, ʃ, ʒ\}$		
1.	*$[\alpha$ ant] $[\beta$ ant]	
	$H_{ant} = \{$*sʃ, *sʒ, *ʃs, *ʒs, *zʃ, *ʃz, *ʒz, *zʒ$\}$		
Tier of sibilants and voiceless obstruents $T_{voice} = \{s, z, ʃ, ʒ, ħ, k, f, χ, q\}$		
1.	*[+ cont, α voice] [+ cont, β voice]	
	$H_{v1} = \{$*sz, *zs, *ʃz, *ʃʒ, *ʒʃ, *sʒ, *ʒs, *zʃ$\}$		
2.	*[+ cont, + voice] [− sonor, − voice]	
	$H_{v2} = \{$*zh, *zk, *zf, *zχ, *zq, *ʒh, *ʒk, *ʒf, *ʒχ, *ʒq$\}$		

Table 3: TSL grammars for IMDLAWN TASHLHIYT harmony

One tier is not enough, because there is no limit on

the number of voiceless obstruents in-between the two sibilants agreeing in anteriority. This process is not local over a single tier – the locality required for the anteriority harmony cannot be achieved over a single tier, because both sibilants and voiceless obstruents are projected on the same tier.

The solution is to project two tiers. The first tier contains only sibilants (T_{ant}) and blocks their combinations that disagree in anteriority (H_{ant}): this tier enforces anteriority harmony. Both sibilants and voiceless obstruents must be projected on the second tier (T_{voice}), and the set of its illicit bigrams includes sibilants that disagree in anteriority (H_{v1}) and voiced sibilants followed by voiceless obstruents (H_{v2}). In this case, the second tier captures voicing assimilation.

Figure 4 illustrates this analysis. The word *sukz* is well-formed, because the anteriority grammar allows for the *sz* combination: they both agree in anteriority, and the voicing tier is satisfied with the bigrams *sk* and *kz*. However, **ʃukz* is ruled out because the **ʃz* combination is banned over the anteriority tier. Note that over the voicing tier, the sibilants *ʃ* and *z* are not adjacent. The word **zukz* is also out, because the voicing grammar prohibits voiced sibilants followed by the voiceless obstruents (**zk*). Note that even though this word is ruled out, there are no violations over the anteriority tier: the voiceless obstruent *k* is not seen there.

IMDLAWN TASHLHIYT pattern requires two tiers, because the set of the elements affected by the anteriority assimilation is the proper subset of the one

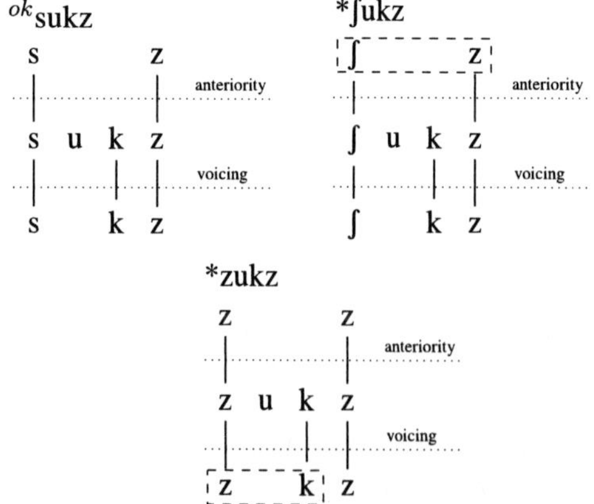

Figure 4: Sibilant harmony in IMDLAWN TASHLHIYT

taking part in the voicing harmony. One tier cannot provide the locality that is required in order to capture both spreadings.

3.3 Case 3: disjoint tiers

In some cases, two spreadings target absolutely different sets of elements: neither of the elements involved in one harmony takes a part in another agreement, and vice versa.

As an example of such a system, consider KIKONGO (Bantu). In this language, there are both consonant and vowel harmonies. Vowel harmony enforces vowels to agree in height, whereas nasal agreement turns both /d/ and /l/ into /n/ if preceded by a nasal in the stem, see (Ao, 1991; Hyman, 1998).

First, consider the height harmony that applies to vowel. In the examples below, the applicative suffix *-el, -il,* and the reversive transitive suffix *-ol, -ul* show that all vowels within a word must share the same height specification.

(23)	-somp-**el**-	'attach-APPL'
(24)	-leng-**el**-	'languish-APPL'
(25)	-tomb-**ol**-	'do-TRANS'
(26)	-lemb-**ol**-	'broom-TRANS'
(27)	-sik-**il**-	'support-APPL'
(28)	-vur-**il**-	'surpass-APPL'
(29)	-vil-**ul**-	'move-TRANS'
(30)	-bub-**ul**-	'bribe-TRANS'

In this language, suffixes are specified for rounding, and acquire their height specification depending on the stem vowel. In (23-26), both vowels in the stem and in the affix are non-high, whereas (27-30) contain only the high vowels.

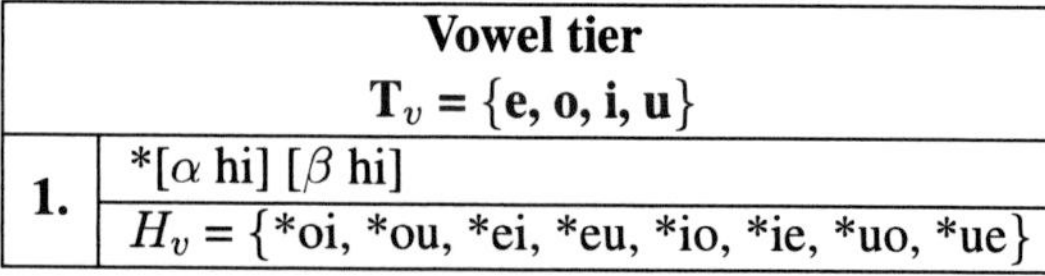

Table 4: TSL grammar for KIKONGO vowel harmony

This harmony operates over the tier of vowels T_v, and the grammar must rule out all combinations of vowels that disagree in height, see Table 4.

But along with vowel harmony, this language also has a consonantal one – nasal agreement. Segments /d/ and /l/ in the affix both become /n/ if nasal consonants such as /m/ or /n/ are found in the root. See examples below from (Ao, 1991), where *-idi* is the perfective active suffix, and *-ulu* is its passive counterpart.

(31)	-suk-idi-	'wash-PERF.ACT'
(32)	-nik-ini-	'ground-PERF.ACT'
(33)	-meng-ene-	'hate-PERF.ACT'
(34)	-suk-ulu-	'wash-PERF.PASS'
(35)	-nik-unu-	'ground-PERF.PASS'
(36)	-meng-ono-	'hate-PERF.PASS'

In (31, 34), there are no nasals in the root, so the consonant in the affix is unchanged – it remains /d/ and /l/ respectively. However, when there are nasals /n/ or /m/ in the stem, both affixal /d/ and /l/ assimilate to /n/, see (32, 35) and (33, 36) for *-idi-* and *-ulu-* respectively.

$T_n = \{n, m, d, l\}$	
1.	*d [+ nasal], *l [+ nasal]
	$H_n = \{$*nd, *nl, *md, *ml$\}$

Table 5: TSL grammar for KIKONGO consonant harmony

Only /d/, /l/, and nasals are involved in the process, therefore those are the items that must be projected on the tier. Then the grammar H_n blocks occurrence of /d/ and /l/ after the nasals.

The two TSL grammars that capture vowel and consonantal harmonies have absolutely different tier alphabets T_v and T_n, and cannot be combined together, because nasals can occur in-between vowels, as well as vowels in-between nasals. The tier alphabets are disjoint: their intersection is empty.

As the illustration, see Figure 5. Two tiers are necessary for the description of KIKONGO pattern, because only they can provide the needed locality relations among the vowels for vowel harmony, and /d/, /l/ and nasals for the nasal assimilation. The well-formed word *nikunu* is permitted because its vowel tier representation *iuu* does not violate the vowel harmony rule, and the nasal tier *nn* also satisfies the nasal assimilation. The ill-formed combinations of segments such as *io, *uo, and *nl are ruled out by the two TSL grammars H_v and H_n, respectively. Note that the two vowels /i/ and /u/ are intervening between the two /n/ in the rightmost subfigure, and only the existence of the separate tier for the nasal harmony makes the two /n/ adjacent over the tier.

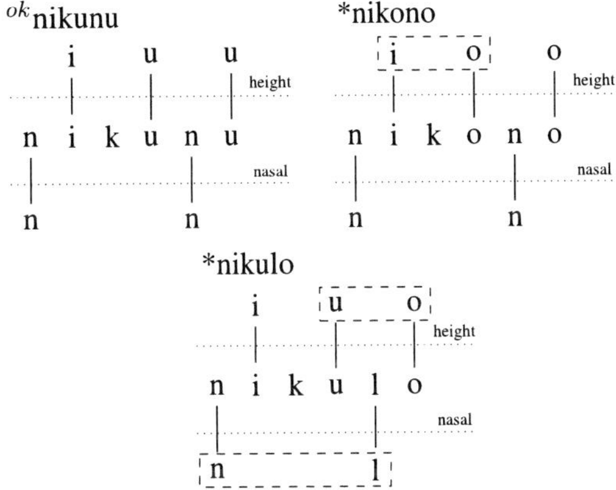

Figure 5: Vowel and nasal harmonies in KIKONGO

3.4 Case 4 (unattested): incomparable tiers

The following tier alphabet configurations were considered in this paper so far: single set (two harmonies operate over the same sets of elements), set-subset relation (one harmony operates over the proper subset of elements that are involved in another harmony), and disjoint sets (there is no item that is affected by both harmonies). The configuration that was not discussed yet is incomparable sets, i.e. a set in which the tiers are only partially overlapping. Going forward, such cases are unattested.

An example of such a system where the sets of segments that are involved in different harmonies will have non-empty intersection (excluding the proper subset case), would be the following. Imagine a pattern of a non-existent toy language YAKONGO that combines agreements from YAKUT and KIKONGO. Its alphabet includes *a, o, n,* and *d*. Vowels within a word agree in rounding, i.e. all of them are either /a/ or /o/, unless /n/ intervenes: only non-rounded vowels can follow /n/. The consonant /d/ assimilates to /n/ if it is preceded by /n/. Obviously, such pattern would require two TSL grammars, where the first one enforces the vowel harmony: $T_v = \{a, o, n\}$, $H_v = \{$*ao, *oa, *no$\}$. The second grammar captures the nasal assimilation: $T_n = \{n, d\}$, $H_n = \{$*nd$\}$. The intersection of the two tier alphabets is not empty and contains $\{n\}$.

However, to the best of our knowledge, there are no attested cases like this: if two TSL grammars are needed to capture two harmonies, their tier alphabets are either disjoint, or one is a proper subset of the other. This generalization might be surprising, but one of the possible reasons why it is the case is discussed in the following section.

4   Formal explanations of the typology

In this section, we are considering the problem of tier alphabet configurations from the formal point of view. Namely, we are discussing ways to partition sets in order to get each of the configurations discussed above. We show that if we consider all possible partitioning of a set into two subsets, then the vast majority of the resulting sets are incomparable, and it is exactly the configuration that seems to be absent from natural languages. Note that the partitioning considered here allows for replication, i.e. it allows for an item to be present in both sets obtained by partitioning of the initial set.

One of the reasons to think in this direction is related to learnability. It might be easier for a learner to converge on a particular hypothesis for the tiers if one does not need to consider all possible tier alphabet configurations. Eliminating the option of incomparable tier alphabets helps to remove the majority of guessing options from the set of hypotheses that a learner is considering. On a relevant note, (Keenan and Stavi, 1986; Szymanik, 2016) show that if we assume all possible generalized quantifiers, there are 2^{4^n} of them, where n is the size of the domain. However, if we take into account such property of all natural language quantifiers as conservativity (Barwise and Cooper, 1981), it reduces the amount of possible quantifiers to 2^{3^n}. For a domain of 2 elements, there are 65536 possible generalized quantifiers, but only 64 of them are conservative. The topic of tier alphabets and possible quantifiers share the same core idea: the importance of restricting the system in a way that natural languages restrict themselves.

The question that we are answering in the following subsections is the following: in how many ways it is possible to partition a set of n elements into 2 sets such that these sets will be in the set-subset relation, or disjoint, or incomparable.

Proper subset: if we have n elements in a set and we want to create a subset of k elements, this is equivalent to choosing k elements from a set of n, or $\binom{n}{k}$. Two of such subsets need to be excluded: $k = 0$, where one of the tier alphabets is empty, and

$k = n$, where the two tier alphabets are equivalent. The amount of all other proper subsets is given by the following formula:

$$\sum_{k=1}^{n-1} \binom{n}{k} = 2^n - 2 \tag{1}$$

For example, consider the set of 10 elements, i.e. $n = 10$. Then there are $2^{10} - 2 = 1022$ ways to form two sets that are in such containment relation.

Disjoint sets: the general case of partitioning a set of n elements into k disjoint subsets is given by Stirling Numbers of the Second Kind also denoted as $S(n, k)$, see (Knuth, 1968). It is evaluated as follows:

$$S(n, k) = \frac{1}{k!} \sum_{j=0}^{k} (-1)^{k-j} \binom{k}{j} j^n \tag{2}$$

If we want to partition the set of n elements into 2 disjoint sets, we can substitute the variable k in the expression (2) by 2, therefore getting the following formula:

$$S(n, 2) = \frac{1}{2} \sum_{j=0}^{2} (-1)^{2-j} \binom{2}{j} j^n \tag{3}$$

In this case, the number of partitions obtained from the set of 10 elements is 511, which is times less than the number of possibilities for the previous case.

Partition with intersection: in this case we want to partition a set of n elements into two sets with a non-empty intersection. This problem can be divided into two sub-problems: partitioning the set of n elements into 3 disjoint sets; and ordering the partitions to generate all possible intersections.

The solution to the first problem is the $S(n, 3)$, see (2) above. As for the second problem, let A_1, A_2 and A_3 be the three obtained partitions. Then we can create two sets with a non-empty intersection as follows: $A_1 A_2$ and $A_2 A_3$ where A_2 is the intersection, $A_2 A_1$ and $A_1 A_3$ where A_1 is the intersection, and $A_1 A_3$ and $A_3 A_2$ where A_3 is the intersection. Therefore for every partition, there are 3 combinations of sets that can be generated. The number of partitions given by $S(n, 3)$ needs to be multiplied by 3. The following expression calculates the number of 2 sets with incomparable intersection that can be obtained from a set with n elements:

$$3 * S(n, 3) = \frac{1}{2} \sum_{j=0}^{3} (-1)^{3-j} \binom{3}{j} j^n \qquad (4)$$

For $n = 10$, this would give 27990 ways to create two sets with a non-empty intersection. This number is 95% more than the previous two combined.

Looking at the numbers of possible ways to partition a set of n elements, it is easy to notice that the biggest contribution is always made by the sets with a non-empty intersection. This fact makes us suspect that the absence of such tier alphabet configuration is due to the limitation on the computational processes: much less options need to be considered when such limit is established.

In order to illustrate the growth, consider Figures 6 and 7 below. Figure 6 shows the normal scale of growth of the amount of partitions. The green dashed line shows the disjoint partitions, the blue dotted line represents the partitions with set-subset relation, and the solid red line is representing exponentially growing number of incomparable partitions. If the number of elements in the initial set is larger than 10, the two lowest lines become nearly indistinguishable, therefore for bigger numbers it is better to consider the growth on a loglog scale, see Figure 7.

5 Conclusion

In this paper, we studied various harmonic processes involving transmission of multiple features, and used such systems as a litmus test for detecting possible tier alphabet configurations. We found out that there are 3 typologically attested cases, namely: single tier, when both harmonies operate over the same set of elements, tier containment, where one harmony operates over the proper subset of items that are involved in another assimilation, and disjoint tiers, where no the items involved in one harmony are relevant for the other one. The fourth possibility, being incomparable tier alphabets, is unattested to the best of our knowledge.

Although it might seem unexpected, in fact this restriction limits the amount of possible tier configurations a lot, as it is shown in Sec. 4. For a set of 10 elements, this limitation excludes 95% of all possible tier alphabet organizations. With the increasing number of elements in the set of items relevant for harmonic processes, this percentage grows as well.

This is just preliminary research about the typology of long-distance processes and the math behind it, and, of course, a lot is still remained unexplored. For example, here we are investigating harmonic processes, but these generalization must be checked on a variety of dissimilation processes, see (Bennett, 2013). Another route will be to investigate the

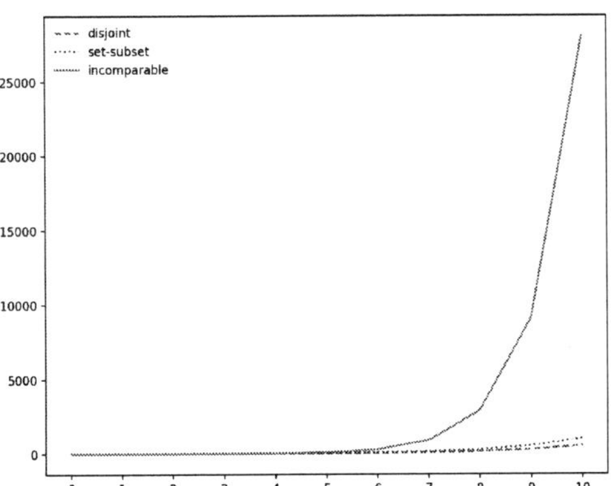

Figure 6: Growth of number of partitions of sets containing up to 10 elements (normal scale)

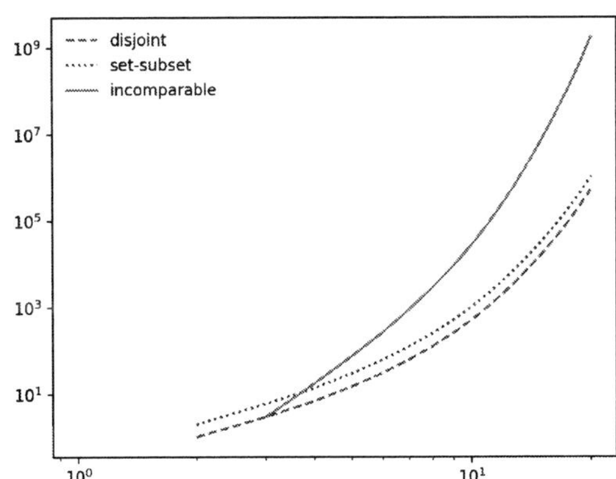

Figure 7: Growth of number of partitions of sets containing up to 20 elements (loglog scale)

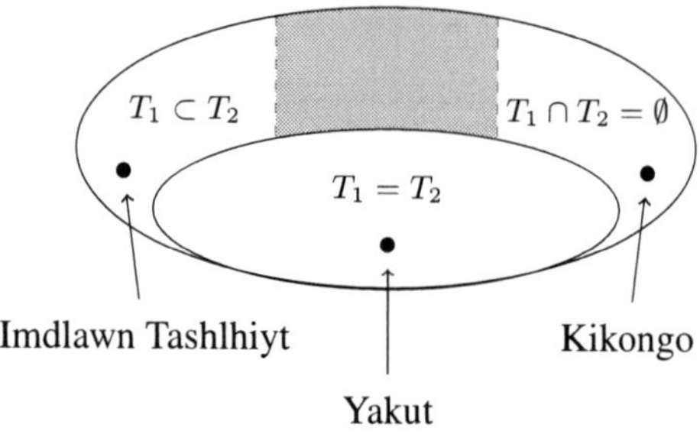

Figure 8: Attested tier alphabets relations

size n of tier alphabets that is relevant for natural languages, and check which tier alphabet configurations are available for each range of n. And, of course, more careful typological overview is needed.

However, this result can be interesting from several different perspectives. First, it reveals new typological generalization about harmonic systems and natural languages in general. Secondly, it might shed light on the issues related to the learnability of multiple tier-based strictly local grammars. And, lastly, it brings the desired naturalness to the theory of formal languages.

Acknowledgments

We thank the anonymous referees for their useful comments and suggestions. We are very grateful to our friends and colleagues at Stony Brook University, especially to Thomas Graf, Lori Repetti, Jeffrey Heinz, and Aniello De Santo for their unlimited knowledge and constant help. Also big thanks to Gary Mar, Jonathan Rawski, Sedigheh Moradi, and Yaobin Liu for valuable comments on the paper. All mistakes, of course, are our own.

References

Akinbiyi Akinlabi. 2009. Neutral vowels in lokaa harmony. *Canadian Journal of Linguistics*, 59(2):197–228.

Alëna Aksënova, Thomas Graf, and Sedigheh Moradi. 2016. Morphotactics as tier-based strictly local dependencies. In *Proceedings of the 14th SIGMORPHON Workshop on Computational Research in Phonetics, Phonology, and Morphology*, pages 121–130.

Benjamin Ao. 1991. Kikongo nasal harmony and context-sensitive underspecification. *Linguistic Inquiry*, 22(1):193–196.

Jon Barwise and Robin Cooper. 1981. Generalized quantifiers and natural language. *Linguistics and Philosophy*, 4:159–219.

William G. Bennett. 2013. *Dissimilation, Consonant Harmony, and Surface Correspondence*. Ph.D. thesis, Rutgers University.

Aniello De Santo. 2017. Pushing the boundaries of tsl languages. Manuscript. Stony Brook University.

Mohamed Elmedlaoui. 1995. *Aspects des représentations phonologiques dans certaines langues chamito-sémitiques*. Ph.D. thesis, Université Mohammed V.

Thomas Graf and Jeffrey Heinz. 2015. Commonality in disparity: The computational view of syntax and phonology. Slides of a talk given at GLOW 2015, April 18, Paris, France.

Gunnar Olafur Hansson. 2010a. *Consonant Harmony: Long-Distance Interaction in Phonology*. University of California Press, Los Angeles.

Gunnar Olafur Hansson. 2010b. Long-distance voicing assimilation in berber: spreading and/or agreement? In *Proceedings of the 2010 annual conference of the Canadian Linguistic Association*, Ottawa, Canada. Canadian Linguistic Association.

Jeffrey Heinz, Chetan Rawal, and Herbert G. Tanner. 2011. Tier-based strictly local constraints for phonology. In *Proceedings of the 49th Annual Meeting of the Association for Computational Linguistics*, pages 58–64, Portland, USA. Association for Computational Linguistics.

Jeffrey Heinz. 2010. Learning long-distance phonotactics. *Linguistic Inquiry*, 41(4):623–661.

Jeffrey Heinz. 2011. Computational phonology part II: Grammars, learning, and the future. *Language and Linguistics Compass*, 5(4):153–168.

Larry Hyman. 1998. Positional prominence and the 'prosodic trough' in yaka. *Phonology*, 15:14–75.

Adam Jardine and Kevin McMullin. 2017. Efficient learning of tier-based strictly k-local languages. *Lecture Notes in Computer Science*, 10168:64–76.

Abigail Rhoades Kaun. 1995. *The typology of rounding harmony: an optimality theoretic approach*. Ph.D. thesis, UCLA.

Edward L. Keenan and Jonathan Stavi. 1986. A semantic characterization of natural language determiners. *Linguistics and Philosophy*, 9:253–326.

Donald E. Knuth. 1968. *Fundamental Algorithms*. Addison-Wesley, Reading, MA.

Kevin James McMullin. 2016. *Tier-based locality in long-distance phonotactics: learnability and typology*. Ph.D. thesis, University of British Columbia.

Willard O. Quine. 1969. Ontological relativity. In *Ontological relativity and other essays*. Columbia University Press, New York.

Tomomasa Sasa. 2001. Yakut vowel harmony: an optimality theory account. *Turkic Languages*, 5:270–287.

Tomomasa Sasa. 2009. *Treatment of vowel harmony in optimality theory*. Ph.D. thesis, University of Iowa.

Jakub Szymanik. 2016. *Quantifiers and Cognition: Logical and Computational Perspectives*. Springer, Switzerland.

Differentiating Phrase Structure Parsing and Memory Retrieval in the Brain

Shohini Bhattasali
Cornell University
Ithaca, NY, USA
sb2295@cornell.edu

John Hale
Cornell University
Ithaca, NY, USA
jthale@cornell.edu

Christophe Pallier
INSERM-CEA
Paris-Saclay, France
christophe@pallier.org

Jonathan R. Brennan
University of Michigan
Ann Arbour, MI, USA
jobrenn@umich.edu

Wen-Ming Luh
Cornell University
Ithaca, NY, USA
wl358@cornell.edu

R. Nathan Spreng
McGill University
Montreal, Canada
nathan.spreng@mcgill.ca

Abstract

On some level, human sentence comprehension must involve both memory retrieval and structural composition. This study differentiates these two processes using neuroimaging data collected during naturalistic listening. Retrieval is formalized in terms of "multiword expressions" while structure-building is formalized in terms of bottom-up parsing. The results most strongly implicate Anterior Temporal regions for structure-building and Precuneus Cortex for memory retrieval.

1 Introduction

This study differentiates processes of structure-building and memory retrieval in the brain, as they occur during naturalistic language comprehension. We use multiword expressions to investigate this distinction. The term itself comes from computational linguistics; roughly it means expressions that are better treated non-compositionally (Sag et al., 2002). Figure 2 on page 2 highlights several examples.

MWEs raise an important theoretical question about language processing, namely the balance between productivity and reuse (Goldberg, 2006; Jackendoff, 2002; O'Donnell, 2015). If MWEs indeed lack internal structure, then perhaps their comprehension proceeds through a single, unitary memory retrieval operation, rather than some kind of multistep composition process. Proceeding from this hypothesis, the paper contributes a localization of these two cognitive processes in the brain through an analysis of fMRI timecourses collected during naturalistic listening.

2 Memory Retrieval vs. Structure-building

The name MWE loosely groups a wide variety of linguistic phenomena including idioms, perfunctory greetings and personal titles.

(1) *When I drew the baobabs, I was spurred on by a **sense of urgency***

(2) *"**Good morning**", said the **little prince** politely, who then turned around, but saw nothing.*

The syntactic or semantic properties of the bold-faced expressions cannot be derived just from their parts and in some way, they are conventionalized. They are plausibly stored, rather than built on the fly (Cacciari, 2014).

By contrast, other expressions are less likely to have been explicitly memorized and therefore call for some degree of structural composition, in comprehension. This sort of processing can be formalized using parsing algorithms (Hale, 2014). Figure 1 on page 2 indicates the number of reduce steps that a bottom-up parser would take, word-by-word, as it builds the depicted phrase structure. Our analysis of the neuroimaging data described in the next section takes this number as an index of structure-building effort.

3 fMRI Study

3.1 Method

We follow Brennan et al. (2012) in using a spoken narrative as a stimulus. Participants hear the story over headphones while they are in the scanner. The

Proceedings of the Society for Computation in Linguistics (SCiL) 2018, pages 74-80.
Salt Lake City, Utah, January 4-7, 2018

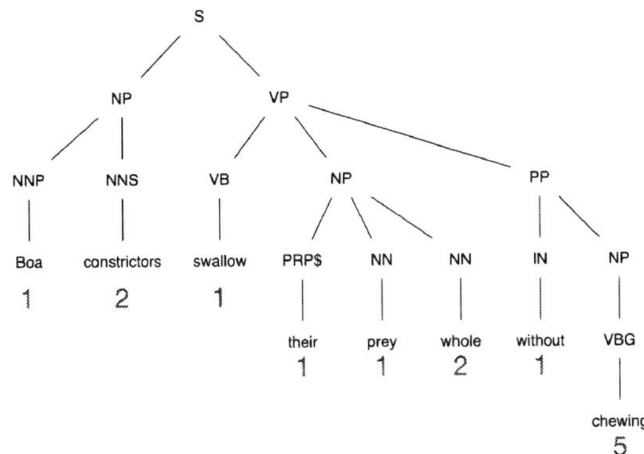

Figure 1: Phrase structure tree with bottom-up parser action counts in purple. For more on parsing algorithms see Hale (2014).

sequence of neuroimages collected during their session becomes the dependent variable in a regression against word-by-word predictors, derived from the text of the story.

3.2 Stimuli

The audio stimulus was Antoine de Saint-Exupéry's *The Little Prince*, translated by David Wilkinson and read by Nadine Eckert-Boulet.

Within this text, 1,274 MWEs were identified using a CRF tagger. This tagger was trained on examples from the English Universal Dependency treebank, in combination with external lexicons as suggested by Constant and Tellier (2012). The tagger used feature templates, as seen in Table 1 below, where w_t stands for the token at the relative position t from the current token and l_t is the label at the relative position t. The external lexicons included the Unitex lexicon (Paumier et al., 2009), SAID corpus (Kuiper et al., 2003), Cambridge International Dictionary of Idioms (White, 1998), and Dictionary of American Idioms (Makkai et al., 1995).

Among these MWEs, attestation rates for particular subtypes are given in Table 2.

121 my ₁ friend ₂ broke ₃ into ₄ another ₅ **peal ₆ of ₇ laughter ₈** : ₉ `` ₁₀ where ₁₁ do ₁₂ you ₁₃ think ₁₄ he ₁₅ 'd ₁₆ go ₁₇ ! ₁₈ '' ₁₉

122 `` ₁ anywhere ₂ . ₃

123 straight ₁ ahead ₂ ... ₃ '' ₄ then ₅ the ₆ **little ₇ prince ₈** said ₉ gravely ₁₀ : ₁₁ `` ₁₂ that ₁₃ does ₁₄ n't ₁₅ matter ₁₆ ; ₁₇ where ₁₈ i ₁₉ live ₂₀ , ₂₁ everything ₂₂ is ₂₃ so ₂₄ small ₂₅ ! ₂₆ '' ₂₇

124 and ₁ perhaps ₂ with ₃ a ₄ **hint ₅ of ₆ sadness ₇** , ₈ he ₉ added ₁₀ : ₁₁ `` ₁₂ straight ₁₃ ahead ₁₄ you ₁₅ ca ₁₆ n't ₁₇ go ₁₈ far ₁₉ ... ₂₀ '' ₂₁

125 i ₁ thus ₂ learned ₃ a ₄ second ₅ very ₆ **important ₇ thing ₈** : ₉ that ₁₀ his ₁₁ home ₁₂ planet ₁₃ was ₁₄ barely ₁₅ bigger ₁₆ than ₁₇ a ₁₈ house ₁₉ ! ₂₀

126 it ₁ did ₂ n't ₃ surprise ₄ me ₅ much ₆ . ₇

127 i ₁ knew ₂ that ₃ , ₄ **apart ₅ from ₆** the ₇ large ₈ planets ₉ like ₁₀ the ₁₁ earth ₁₂ , ₁₃ jupiter ₁₄ , ₁₅ mars ₁₆ , ₁₇ and ₁₈ venus ₁₉ , ₂₀ which ₂₁ have ₂₂ been ₂₃ given ₂₄ names ₂₅ , ₂₆ there ₂₇ are ₂₈ hundreds ₂₉ of ₃₀ others ₃₁ that ₃₂ are ₃₃ sometimes ₃₄ so ₃₅ small ₃₆ that ₃₇ one ₃₈ has ₃₉ **great ₄₀ difficulty ₄₁** in ₄₂ spotting ₄₃ them ₄₄

Figure 2: Samples MWEs in the English text, visualized with mwetoolkit (Ramisch et al., 2010)

$w_t = X, t \in \{2, 1, 0, 1, 2\}$	$\&l_0 = L$
Lowercase form of $w_0 = W$	$\&l_0 = L$
Prefix of $w_0 = P\,with\,|P|<5$	$\&l_0 = L$
Suffix of $w_0 = S\,with\,|S|<5$	$\&l_0 = L$
w_0 contains a hyphen	$\&l_0 = L$
w_0 contains a digit	$\&l_0 = L$
w_0 is capitalized	$\&l_0 = L$
w_0 is all in capital	$\&l_0 = L$
w_0 is capitalized and BOS	$\&l_0 = L$
w_0 is part of a multiword	$\&l_0 = L$
$w_i w_j = XY, (j, k) \in \{(1, 0), (0, 1), (1, 1)\}$	$\&l_0 = L$
$l_{-1} = L'$	$\&l_0 = L$

Table 1: Feature templates to detect MWEs

3.3 Participants

Participants were forty-two volunteers (26 women and 16 men, 18-37 years old) with no history of

MWE Category	Occurrence
Verb + Participle	145
Verb + Noun	37
Adj + Noun	285
Det + Noun	712
(Verb) + Noun + Prep + Noun	24
N-N Compounds	71

Table 2: MWE Attestation Rates

psychiatric, neurological, or other medical illness or history of drug or alcohol abuse that might compromise cognitive functions. All qualified as right-handed on the Edinburgh handedness inventory (Oldfield, 1971). They self-identified as native English speakers and gave their written informed consent prior to participation, in accordance with Cornell University IRB guidelines.

3.4 Presentation

After giving their informed consent, participants were familiarized with the MRI facility and assumed a supine position on the scanner gurney. The presentation script was written in PsychoPy (Peirce, 2007). Auditory stimuli were delivered through MRI-safe, high-fidelity headphones (Confon HP-VS01, MR Confon, Magdeburg, Germany) inside the head coil. The headphones were secured against the plastic frame of the coil using foam blocks. Using a spoken recitation of the US Constitution, an experimenter increased the volume until participants reported that they could hear clearly. Participants then listened passively to the audio storybook for 1 hour 38 minutes. The story had nine chapters and at the end of each chapter the participants were presented with a multiple-choice questionnaire with four questions (36 questions in total), concerning events and situations described in the story. These questions were used to confirm their comprehension and were viewed by the participants via a mirror attached to the head coil and they answered through a button box. The entire session lasted around 2.5 hours.

3.5 Data Collection

Imaging was performed using a 3T MRI scanner (Discovery MR750, GE Healthcare, Milwaukee, WI) with a 32-channel head coil at the Cornell MRI Facility. Blood Oxygen Level Dependent (BOLD) signals were collected using a T2-weighted echo planar imaging (EPI) sequence (repetition time: 2000 ms, echo time: 27 ms, flip angle: 77deg, image acceleration: 2X, field of view: 216 x 216 mm, matrix size 72 x 72, and 44 oblique slices, yielding 3 mm isotropic voxels). Anatomical images were collected with a high resolution T1-weighted (1 x 1 x 1 mm^3 voxel) with a Magnetization-Prepared RApid Gradient-Echo (MP-RAGE) pulse sequence.

4 Data Analysis

4.1 Preprocessing

fMRI data is acquired with physical, biological constraints and preprocessing allows us to make adjustments to improve the signal to noise ratio. Primary preprocessing steps were carried out in AFNI version 16 (Cox, 1996) and include motion correction, coregistration, and normalization to standard MNI space. After the previous steps were completed, ME-ICA (Kundu et al., 2012) was used to further preprocess the data. ME-ICA is a denoising method which uses Independent Components Analysis to split the T2*-signal into BOLD and non-BOLD components. Removing the non-BOLD components mitigates noise due to motion, physiology, and scanner artifacts (Kundu et al., 2017).

4.2 Statistical Analysis

The GLM typically used in fMRI is a hierarchical model with two levels (see Poldrack et al., 2011). At the first level, the data for each subject is modelled separately to calculate subject-specific parameter estimates and within-subject variance such that for each subject, a regression model is estimated for each voxel against the time series. The second-level model takes subject-specific parameter estimates as input. It uses the between-subject variance to make statistical inferences about the larger population.

The GLM analysis was performed using SPM12 (Penny et al., 2011). The following regressors were used. One regressor formalizes structure-building using a standard bottom-up parsing algorithm (see chapter 3 of Hale, 2014). We computed the number of parser actions that would be required, word-by-word, to build the correct phrase structure tree as determined by the Stanford parser (Klein and Manning, 2003). Another regressor formalizes memory retrieval, by marking multiword expressions (MWE; see section 3.2). Each word in the text was annotated with a 0 or 1, depending on whether it was the last word of a MWE. This coding scheme expresses the idea that a different process occurs at the end of multiword expressions, and this provisionally assumes a very conservative approach to the Configuration Hypothesis (Cacciari and Tabossi, 1988; Tabossi et al., 2009). We regressed the word-by-word predictors described above against fMRI timecourses recorded during passive story-listening in a whole-brain analysis. Along with the parsing and MWE regressors of theoretical interest, we entered four "nuisance" variables or regressors of non-interest into the GLM analysis using SPM12. One regressor simply marks the offset of each spoken word in time. Another gives the log-frequency of the individual word in movie subtitles (Brysbaert and New, 2009). The last two reflect the pitch (f0) and intensity (RMS) of the talker's voice. These nuisance regressors are added to the GLM analysis to improve sensitivity, specificity and validity of activation maps (Bullmore et al., 1999; Lund et al., 2006). In particular, we sought to ensure that any conclusions about parsing and memory retrieval would be specific to those processes, as opposed to more general aspects of speech perception.

5   Results

In the second-level group analysis, bottom-up parsing and multi-word expressions were analyzed separately. Results are presented below in Tables 3 and 4 using region names from the Harvard-Oxford Cortical Structure Atlas.

5.1   Group level results for bottom-up parsing

MNI Coordinates			Region	p-value	k-size	T-score
x	y	z		(corrected)	(cluster)	(peak-level)
52	8	-22	Temporal pole	0.000	2769	12.72
54	-40	12	Supramarginal Gyrus	0.000	2212	12.69
-34	18	-12	Frontal Orbital Cortex	0.000	2380	10.40
12	20	58	Superior Frontal Gyrus	0.000	7191	9.27
42	2	48	Middle Frontal Gyrus	0.000	286	9.19
-38	26	36	Middle Frontal Gyrus	0.000	382	8.47
-40	-78	6	Lateral Occipital Cortex	0.000	693	7.42
-52	-56	32	Angular Gyrus	0.000	802	7.12
28	-52	-8	Temporal Occipital Fusiform Cortex	0.001	83	6.74
-44	46	-12	Frontal Pole	0.000	176	6.28

Table 3: Significant clusters for bottom-up parser action count after FWE voxel correction.

The largest clusters (p < 0.05 FWE) were observed in Anterior Temporal regions (Temporal Pole) and Frontal regions.

Figure 3, plotted with nilearn (Abraham et al., 2014) is the T-score map for the bottom-up parser action count regressor. This regressor formalizes processing effort related to structural composition.

5.2   Group level results for MWE

MNI Coordinates			Region	p-value	k-size	T-score
x	y	z		(corrected)	(cluster)	(peak-level)
6	-60	52	Precuneus Cortex	0.000	559	7.62
24	10	56	Superior Frontal Gyrus	0.000	182	7.23
-40	42	26	Frontal Pole	0.000	158	6.94
66	-38	34	Supramarginal Gyrus	0.000	103	6.77
34	38	36	Frontal Pole	0.001	38	5.83

Table 4: Significant clusters for MWEs after FWE voxel correction

The largest clusters (p < 0.05 FWE) were observed in Precuneus Cortex and Frontal regions.

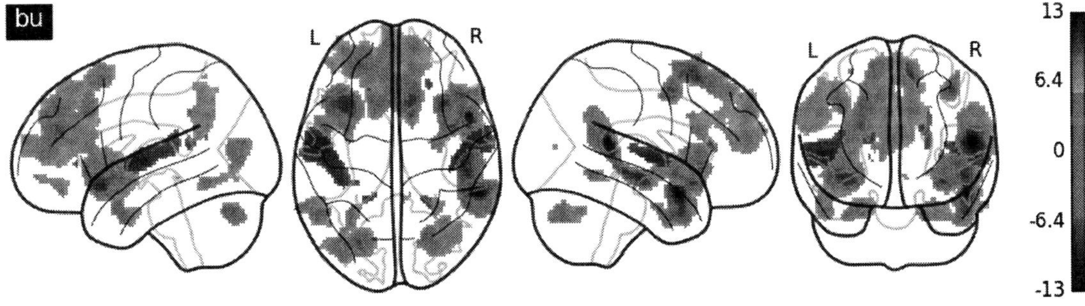

Figure 3: T-score map for the Bottom-up Parser action count regressor. Red represents the positive score while blue represents the negative score.

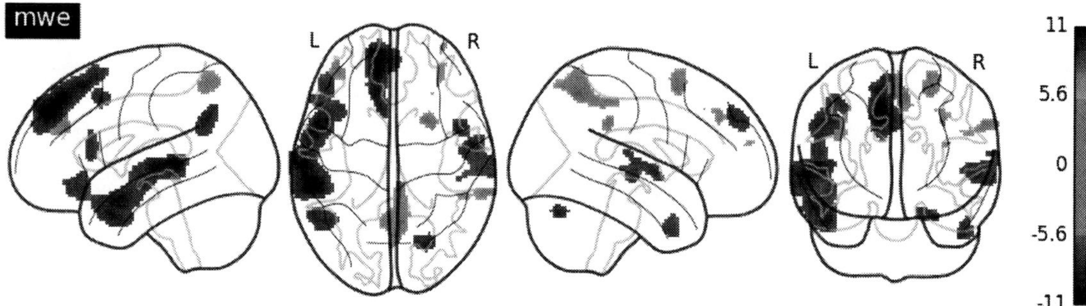

Figure 4: T-score map for the MWE status regressor. Red represents the positive score while blue represents the negative score.

Figure 4 (also plotted with nilearn) is the T-score map for the MWE status regressor, which is meant to formalize the retrieval of these noncompositional expressions.

6   Discussion

The operationalization of structure-building as bottom-up parsing highlights Anterior Temporal as well as Frontal regions. These results are consistent with earlier work including deficit-lesion data (Dronkers et al., 2004), fMRI studies of text comprehension (Ferstl et al., 2008), and magnetoencephalography studies of phrasal composition (Bemis and Pylkkänen, 2011). This literature also confirms the sensitivity of Anterior Temporal regions to parametric variation of phrase size (Pallier et al., 2011).

With respect to MWEs, significant activation was observed in the Precuneus. The Precuneus has not traditionally been viewed as part of the language network. However, it has been designated as part of the Protagonist's Perspective Interpreter Network (Mason and Just, 2006). This network in fact appears to be activated by many different sorts of story characters, not just the protagonist (Wehbe et al., 2014). Along these lines, the Precuneus activation in Figure 4 might be interpreted narrowly as an effect of reference to dramatis personae in the narrative stimulus. This restricted interpretation would be challenged by the fact that less than 25% of the MWEs in the stimulus text are references to story characters. To account for the full collection, including verbal MWEs, a more general characterization in terms of memory retrieval seems appropriate.

This more general characterization is bolstered by data that implicate the Precuneus in memory tasks:

- Verbal memory (Halsband et al., 2002)

- Spatial memory (Wallentin et al., 2008)

- Episodic memory (Andreasen et al., 1995)

- Memory-related imagery (Fletcher et al., 1995; Mashal et al., 2014)

As Spreng et al. (2009) suggest, the Precuneus could be part of a wider, task-general network that is also recruited in Theory-of-Mind, Prospection and Autobiographical memory tasks. These considerations strengthen the interpretation, based on MWEs, that the Precuneus mediates memory retrieval during naturalistic language comprehension.

The findings as a whole are broadly consistent with existing neurocognitive models of language. For example, within Hagoort's (2016) MUC model, MWE comprehension might tap memory resources, whereas bottom-up parsing might involve unification. With MUC, our analysis suggests a localization of these memory resources to the Parietal lobe. Within the Procedural/Declarative model (Ullman, 2001; 2004), rule-based linguistic knowledge would be localized to Frontal regions. This is consistent with the Frontal activations that we observe in response to the bottom-up parsing regressor.

7   Conclusion

These results point to a spatial differentiation between reuse and composition in language comprehension. Reuse, here operationalized with multiword expressions, seems to involve the Precuneus. Composition, in the sense of phrase-structure parsing, seems to call upon Anterior Temporal areas.

Acknowledgments

This material is based upon work supported by the National Science Foundation under Grant No. 1607441.

References

Alexandre Abraham, Fabian Pedregosa, Michael Eickenberg, Philippe Gervais, Andreas Mueller, Jean Kossaifi, Alexandre Gramfort, Bertrand Thirion, and Gaël Varoquaux. 2014. Machine learning for neuroimaging with scikit-learn. *Frontiers in neuroinformatics*, 8.

Nancy C Andreasen, Daniel SO Leary, Ted Cizadlo, Stephan Arndt, et al. 1995. Remembering the past: two facets of episodic memory explored with positron emission tomography. *The American journal of psychiatry*, 152(11):1576.

Douglas K Bemis and Liina Pylkkänen. 2011. Simple composition: A magnetoencephalography investigation into the comprehension of minimal linguistic phrases. *The Journal of Neuroscience*, 31(8):2801–2814.

Jonathan Brennan, Yuval Nir, Uri Hasson, Rafael Malach, David J Heeger, and Liina Pylkkänen. 2012. Syntactic structure building in the anterior temporal lobe during natural story listening. *Brain and language*, 120(2):163–173.

Marc Brysbaert and Boris New. 2009. Moving beyond kučera and francis: A critical evaluation of current word frequency norms and the introduction of a new and improved word frequency measure for american english. *Behavior research methods*, 41(4):977–990.

ET Bullmore, MJ Brammer, S Rabe-Hesketh, VA Curtis, RG Morris, SCR Williams, T Sharma, and PK McGuire. 1999. Methods for diagnosis and treatment of stimulus-correlated motion in generic brain activation studies using fmri. *Human brain mapping*, 7(1):38–48.

Cristina Cacciari and Patrizia Tabossi. 1988. The comprehension of idioms. *Journal of memory and language*, 27(6):668–683.

Cristina Cacciari. 2014. Processing multiword idiomatic strings: Many words in one? *The Mental Lexicon*, 9(2):267–293.

Matthieu Constant and Isabelle Tellier. 2012. Evaluating the impact of external lexical resources into a crf-based multiword segmenter and part-of-speech tagger. In *8th International Conference on Language Resources and Evaluation (LREC'12)*, pages 646–650.

Robert W. Cox. 1996. Afni: software for analysis and visualization of functional magnetic resonance neuroimages. *Computers and Biomedical research*, 29(3):162–173.

Nina F Dronkers, David P Wilkins, Robert D Van Valin, Brenda B Redfern, and Jeri J Jaeger. 2004. Lesion analysis of the brain areas involved in language comprehension. *Cognition*, 92(1):145–177.

Evelyn C Ferstl, Jane Neumann, Carsten Bogler, and D Yves Von Cramon. 2008. The extended language network: a meta-analysis of neuroimaging studies on text comprehension. *Human brain mapping*, 29(5):581–593.

PC Fletcher, CD Frith, SC Baker, T Shallice, RSJ Frackowiak, and RJ Dolan. 1995. The mind's eyeprecuneus activation in memory-related imagery. *Neuroimage*, 2(3):195–200.

Adele E. Goldberg. 2006. *Constructions at work: The nature of generalization in language*. Oxford University Press.

Peter Hagoort. 2016. MUC (memory, unification, control): A model on the neurobiology of language beyond single word processing. In *Neurobiology of language*, pages 339–347. Elsever.

John T Hale. 2014. *Automaton theories of human sentence comprehension*. CSLI Publications.

U Halsband, BJ Krause, H Sipilä, M Teräs, and A Laihinen. 2002. Pet studies on the memory processing of word pairs in bilingual finnish–english subjects. *Behavioural brain research*, 132(1):47–57.

Ray Jackendoff. 2002. Foundation of language: Brain, meaning, grammar. *Evolution*.

Dan Klein and Christopher D Manning. 2003. Accurate unlexicalized parsing. In *Proceedings of the 41st Annual Meeting on Association for Computational Linguistics-Volume 1*, pages 423–430. Association for Computational Linguistics.

Koenraad Kuiper, Heather McCann, Heidi Quinn, Therese Aitchison, and Kees van der Veer. 2003. Syntactically Annotated Idiom Dataset (SAID) LDC2003T10. In *Linguistic Data Consortium*, Philadelphia.

Prantik Kundu, Souheil J Inati, Jennifer W Evans, Wen-Ming Luh, and Peter A Bandettini. 2012. Differentiating bold and non-bold signals in fmri time series using multi-echo epi. *Neuroimage*, 60(3):1759–1770.

Prantik Kundu, Valerie Voon, Priti Balchandani, Michael V. Lombardo, Benedikt A. Poser, and Peter A. Bandettini. 2017. Multi-echo fmri: A review of applications in fmri denoising and analysis of bold signals. *NeuroImage*, 154:59 – 80. Cleaning up the fMRI time series: Mitigating noise with advanced acquisition and correction strategies.

Torben E Lund, Kristoffer H Madsen, Karam Sidaros, Wen-Lin Luo, and Thomas E Nichols. 2006. Non-white noise in fmri: does modelling have an impact? *Neuroimage*, 29(1):54–66.

Adam Makkai, M. T. Boatner, and J. E. Gates. 1995. *A Dictionary of American idioms*. ERIC.

Nira Mashal, Tali Vishne, and Nathaniel Laor. 2014. The role of the precuneus in metaphor comprehension: evidence from an fmri study in people with schizophrenia and healthy participants. *Frontiers in human neuroscience*, 8.

Robert A Mason and Marcel Adam Just. 2006. Neuroimaging contributions to the understanding of discourse processes. *Handbook of psycholinguistics*, 799.

Timothy J O'Donnell. 2015. *Productivity and reuse in language: A theory of linguistic computation and storage*. MIT Press.

Richard C Oldfield. 1971. The assessment and analysis of handedness: the edinburgh inventory. *Neuropsychologia*, 9(1):97–113.

Christophe Pallier, Anne-Dominique Devauchelle, and Stanislas Dehaene. 2011. Cortical representation of the constituent structure of sentences. *Proceedings of the National Academy of Sciences*, 108(6):2522–2527.

Sébastien Paumier, Takuya Nakamura, and Stavroula Voyatzi. 2009. Unitex, a corpus processing system with multi-lingual linguistic resources. *eLEX2009*, page 173.

Jonathan W Peirce. 2007. Psychopypsychophysics software in python. *Journal of neuroscience methods*, 162(1):8–13.

William D Penny, Karl J Friston, John T Ashburner, Stefan J Kiebel, and Thomas E Nichols. 2011. *Statistical parametric mapping: the analysis of functional brain images*. Academic press.

Ivan A Sag, Timothy Baldwin, Francis Bond, Ann Copestake, and Dan Flickinger. 2002. Multiword expressions: A pain in the neck for NLP. In *International Conference on Intelligent Text Processing and Computational Linguistics*, pages 1–15. Springer.

R Nathan Spreng, Raymond A Mar, and Alice SN Kim. 2009. The common neural basis of autobiographical memory, prospection, navigation, theory of mind, and the default mode: a quantitative meta-analysis. *Journal of cognitive neuroscience*, 21(3):489–510.

Patrizia Tabossi, Rachele Fanari, and Kinou Wolf. 2009. Why are idioms recognized fast? *Memory & Cognition*, 37(4):529–540.

Michael T Ullman. 2001. A neurocognitive perspective on language: The declarative/procedural model. *Nature reviews. Neuroscience*, 2(10):717.

Michael T Ullman. 2004. Contributions of memory circuits to language: The declarative/procedural model. *Cognition*, 92(1):231–270.

Mikkel Wallentin, Ethan Weed, Leif Østergaard, Kim Mouridsen, and Andreas Roepstorff. 2008. Accessing the mental spacespatial working memory processes for language and vision overlap in precuneus. *Human Brain Mapping*, 29(5):524–532.

Leila Wehbe, Brian Murphy, Partha Talukdar, Alona Fyshe, Aaditya Ramdas, and Tom Mitchell. 2014. Simultaneously uncovering the patterns of brain regions involved in different story reading subprocesses. *PloS one*, 9(11):e112575.

James Gordon White. 1998. *Cambridge International Dictionary of Idioms*. Cambridge University Press, New York.

Modeling the Complexity and Descriptive Adequacy
of Construction Grammars

Jonathan Dunn
Illinois Institute of Technology
Dept. of Computer Science
`jdunn8@iit.edu`

Abstract

This paper uses the Minimum Description Length paradigm to model the complexity of CxGs (operationalized as the encoding size of a grammar) alongside their descriptive adequacy (operationalized as the encoding size of a corpus given a grammar). These two quantities are combined to measure the quality of potential CxGs against unannotated corpora, supporting discovery-device CxGs for English, Spanish, French, German, and Italian. The results show (i) that these grammars provide significant generalizations as measured using compression and (ii) that more complex CxGs with access to multiple levels of representation provide greater generalizations than single-representation CxGs.

1 Complexity and Descriptive Adequacy

Construction Grammars (CxGs; Goldberg, 2006; Langacker, 2008) operate at multiple levels of representation (lexical, syntactic, and semantic) making them potentially much more complex than purely syntactic grammars. This paper models both (i) the computational complexity of CxGs and (ii) their descriptive adequacy against unannotated corpora using Minimum Description Length (MDL). These two measures, complexity and descriptive adequacy, can be used together as an objective function for measuring the quality of CxGs: the optimum grammar balances higher descriptive adequacy against lower complexity. Once we can measure the quality of a particular grammar in reference to a corpus of observed language use, we can search until we find the optimum grammar for that corpus. This paper uses measures of complexity and descriptive adequacy to learn CxGs for English, Spanish, French, German, and Italian.

The goal is not to examine the representational capacity of CxGs in general because CxG is a fundamentally usage-based paradigm (Hopper, 1987; Kay & Fillmore, 1999; Bybee, 2006). This means that the general capacity of its grammars must be weighted by their actual content: how can we model the complexity of a specific CxG used to describe a specific language, where that language is represented by a specific observable corpus?

Previous computational work on CxG (Steels, 2004; Bryant, 2004; Chang, et al., 2012; Steels, 2012) has relied on introspection-based representations that require a linguist to determine the optimum constructions by intuition. From a linguistic perspective, these representations are neither replicable nor falsifiable and are unable to test hypotheses about the mechanisms of emergence that map from observed usage to learned generalizations. From a computational perspective, these representations are not scalable across domains and languages and are subject to all the constraints of knowledge-based systems. Other data-driven approaches (Wible & Tsao, 2010; Forsberg, et al., 2014) generate potential constructions but do not evaluate the quality of competing CxGs as collections of constructions.

Section 2 discusses how CxGs are represented and Section 3 considers interactions between different levels of representation. Section 4 presents Minimum Description Length as a joint measure of complexity and descriptive adequacy suitable for measuring grammar quality while Section 5 operationalizes CxG encoding. Section 6 describes the search algorithm for optimizing grammar quality. Section 7 describes a multi-lingual experiment in measuring CxG complexity and descriptive adequacy and Appendix A discusses constructions learned from the corpus of English.

(1a) [SLOT 1 — SLOT 2 — SLOT 3 — SLOT 4]
(1b) [NOUN — "gave" — (*animate*) — "a hand"]
(1c) "Bill gave Peter a hand."
(1d) [NOUN — (*transfer*) — (*animate*) — NOUN]
(1e) "Bill sent Peter a package."

Table 1: Construction Notation and Examples

2 Representing CxGs

This section introduces the symbolic notation used to represent CxGs and describes how these representations are implemented. The algorithm recognizes three distinct types of representation as atomic units in its descriptions: Lexical representation consists of tokenized word-forms (in lowercase). Syntactic representation consists of part-of-speech categories (defined using the Universal POS tagset, Petrov, et al., 2012, and computed using RDRPosTagger, Nguyen, et al., 2016). Semantic representation consists of clusters of distributionally similar words that represent semantic domains and are computed using GenSim's implementation of word2vec (Rehurek & Sojka, 2010). The embedding model is trained using 1 billion words from web-crawled corpora for each language (from the WAC corpora: Baroni, et al., 2009; and Aranea corpora: Benko, 2014) using skip-grams with 500 dimensions. These embeddings are segmented into categorical domains using k-means clustering ($k = 100$). The idea behind these three types of representation is that a particular slot in a construction can be defined or constrained at the lexical, syntactic, or semantic level. These representations thus form the basic alphabet of the algorithm.

Constructions are sequences containing a certain number of slots, as in (1a) with four individual slots. Each construction is surrounded by brackets and each slot within a construction is separated by a dash ("—"). Each slot in a construction is represented or defined by constraints that govern which units can occupy that slot. Lexical constraints are indicated using single quotes (e.g.,"gave" in 1b). Syntactic constraints are indicated using part-of-speech tags in uppercase (e.g., NOUN in 1b). Semantic constraints are indicated within parentheses with the identifier for the semantic domain (e.g., *animate* in 1b). Thus, the construction in (1b) describes the utterance in (1c) but not the utterance in (1e); the construction in (1d) describes the utterances in both (1c) and (1e).

This provides a good example of the complexity problem: CxGs potentially have multiple overlapping representations for any given sentence. The sentence in (1e), for example, can be represented by the construction in (1d), in which slots are defined by both syntactic constraints (i.e., NOUN) and semantic constraints (i.e., *animate*). CxGs can distinguish between (1e) and its more idiomatic counterpart (1c) using representations such as (1d) and (1b). The question, however, is how many of these item-specific or idiomatic representations are needed in the grammar: each item-specific construction increases grammar complexity.

In this paper, the term *construction* refers to the grammatical description (e.g., 1b) and the term *construct* refers to a member of the set of utterances which that construction represents (e.g.,1c). For a given grammar, the set of constructions is closed but the set of constructs is open. A construct or utterance can be represented by multiple constructions: representations like (1b) that are more item-specific alongside representations like (1d) that are more schematic. This leads to relationships between constructions: an inheritance hierarchy in which (1b) is a child of (1d). The current implementation has three limitations in respect to the ideal CxG: First, constraints are limited to a single type of representation per slot. For example, if a slot is constrained to the semantic domain *animate*, any syntactic category could be used to fill that slot. Second, although constituents are able to fill construction slots (i.e., "a hand" can occupy a single slot as a single NOUN), larger constructions such as (1d) cannot fill slots in other constructions. Third, no relations are learned between constructions in the grammar (i.e., the inheritance hierarchy is not modeled).

In computational terms, each construction is an array of slots. Each slot is defined as a tuple that contains two pointers: first, a pointer to the alphabet constraining that slot (i.e., lexical or syntactic units) and, second, a pointer to a particular unit within that alphabet (i.e., "a hand" or NOUN). Constituents are allowed to fill slots. This is accomplished using a context-free phrase structure grammar containing rules such as

$$\text{DETERMINER} - \text{NOUN} \rightarrow \text{NOUN}$$

that is learned during a syntax-only iteration described in the next section. The syntactic alphabet, then, also supports pointers to complex sequences through this CFG: the construction points to a NOUN and the CFG allows larger constituents to be labeled as a single NOUN. The current implementation produces a context-free CxG.

3 Finding CxGs

In the experiments that follow, each language is represented by a large web-crawled corpus in that language. Its grammar is learned by searching across potential grammars, each of which is evaluated against the corpus until the optimum grammar is found (using a measure defined in Section 4). The search for the optimum grammar is conducting using a tabu search (Glover 1989, 1990a) with multi-unit association measures (Dunn, 2017) used to sample potential constructions. The main focus of this paper is on defining the objective function: how can we know that one grammar is better than another without evaluating them against gold-standard annotations?

Three levels of CxGs are learned: The first pass operates on only lexical representations, CxG_{LEX}. This identifies purely lexical constructions: sequences of lexical items that have been fused together so that their internal structure can be ignored. For example, "could be" and "will be" are identified as single units when the algorithm is applied to English. Later passes view these lexical constructions as a single lexical item with a single syntactic type.

The second pass operates on only syntactic representations, CxG_{SYN}. Syntactic constructions are later used as phrase structure rules. For example, when applied to English the sequence

$$[\text{VERB} - \text{NOUN}]$$

is identified as a purely syntactic construction. In later passes, these sequences are converted into constituents that can be treated as a single unit. The third pass operates on all levels of representation, CxG_{FULL}. The grammar accumulates struc-

ture across these iterations in the sense that constructions output from a previous pass become atomic units in the current pass. This set-up allows us to examine complexity and descriptive adequacy across CxGs with access to different levels of representation: do we actually benefit from more complex multi-level grammars?

4 Measuring Grammar Quality

This approach depends on the central insight of MDL (Rissanen, 1978, 1986; Grünwald & Rissanen, 2007): a grammar is a method for encoding observed linguistic utterances and the learner is searching for the smallest adequate encoding method. Explanation here is a matter of prediction: can the grammar produce the utterances observed in held-out test-sets? The optimum grammar balances model complexity (the number and type of constructions in the grammar) and the amount of compression achieved when the model is used to encode a test corpus (c.f., Goldsmith, 2001; 2006). The complexity of the grammar is balanced against its descriptive adequacy on a held-out corpus. This is formalized in MDL as

$$MDL = \min_{G}\{L_1(G) + L_2(D \mid G)\}$$

This defines the optimum grammar as the one which minimizes the model complexity, represented by the encoding size of the grammar, plus the size of the dataset encoded by means of the grammar. Encoding size in MDL (here based on the natural log) is further defined as

$$L_C(X^n) = -log_e P(X^n)$$

Methods for calculating the encoding size of CxGs are discussed below in Section 5. An additional term, $L_3(G)$, is sometimes used (Grünwald & Rissanen, 2007: 409) to control for the size of the encoding required for the universal code used to determine the size of G. This term is often not included in the MDL metric (it is not necessary when evaluating models against one another). It will be necessary here, however, when measuring grammar quality against the baseline of an unencoded test set. We are using the MDL principle as a metric for model selection. One aspect of model selection is confidence: to what degree is G_A better than G_B? This is given by

$$|MDL(G^A) - MDL(G^B)|$$

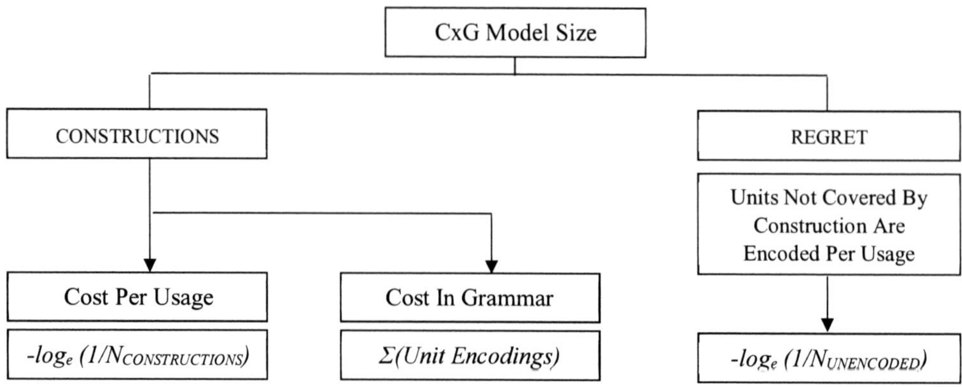

Figure 1: Encoding Model

Higher values indicate a more significant difference between G_A and G_B (c.f., Grünwald & Rissanen, 2007: 411). This measure of confidence will be useful for evaluating the quality of grammars against the baseline of an unencoded dataset. We can refine this measure of confidence further

$$1 - \frac{MDL(G^A)}{MDL(U)}$$

This is the relative degree of compression adjusted so that values close to 1 represent higher compression (U represents the size of the data without the grammar). Thus, if the MDL of G_A is 256 and the unencoded MDL, U, is 927, this gives a compression of 0.7239 over the unencoded baseline as a measure of grammar quality. Negative values indicate that the grammar makes the MDL metric worse, an unlikely but possible occurrence. This ratio measure is important because, without it, the MDL metric and the significance of the metric are both dependent on the encoding size of a specific test set.

We are searching for the grammar with the lowest MDL metric on a held-out test set, but we also need to measure the amount of variation across restarts. This provides a measure of stability: a restart is a search technique that restarts the search for the optimum grammar from scratch on a different portion of the corpus in order to determine if similar grammars are discovered. Let G_k be the optimum grammar across restarts and $G_{i...n}$ be the set of all output grammars across restarts regardless of whether they are optimal. The agreement between the two grammars is

$$A_i^k = \frac{(k \cap i)}{(k \cup i)}$$

The significance of the difference between the encoding quality of k and i relative to the encoding quality of the optimum grammar is

$$M_i^k = 1 - \frac{|MDL(k) - MDL(i)|}{MDL(k)}$$

This is adjusted to make large differences closer to 0 and small differences closer to 1. The stability measure, $STA(k)$, is

$$\frac{\sum_{i=0}^{n} A_i^k(M_i^k)}{n}$$

This is the mean agreement between the current grammar and the optimum grammar for all restarts n with each weighted so that more significant differences in the MDL metric lower the agreement. This is a joint measure of stability in grammar content and grammar quality, with higher scores (toward 1) indicating stable grammars and lower scores (toward 0) indicating unstable grammars.

This section has used the Minimum Description Length paradigm to develop measures of grammar complexity (i.e, L_1) and descriptive adequacy (i.e., L_2) that do not rely on gold-standard annotations. This is important for two reasons: First, we do not necessarily have gold-standard annotations for every language and language variety we are interested in (i.e., CxGs are also subject to variation).

Second, simply relying on gold-standard annotations ignores the question we are most interested in: how do we know empirically that one grammar is better than another?

5 Measuring the Encoding Size of CxGs

The MDL paradigm depends on the concept of encoding size to measure complexity and descriptive adequacy: how do we calculate this for CxGs? The MDL metric contains three terms: L_1, or the encoding size of the grammar; L_2, or the encoding size of the corpus given the grammar; and L_3, or the encoding size of the universal code necessary for encoding L_1. Additionally, we need to determine the uncompressed encoding size of the corpus to serve as a baseline for measuring the overall rate of compression of competing grammars.

The basic encoding model, shown in Figure 1, has two top level categories composing its alphabet: *Constructions* (representations within the current CxG), and *Regret* (units not described by known constructions). Each of these top-level categories is assigned the same probability, 0.5, and thus, because encoding size is equivalent to $-log_e P(X^n)$, each comes with an initial encoding size of 0.693 nats (where a *nat* is a *bit* based on the natural logarithm).

The reason for separating these top-level categories is that each has a different number of units, each of which is again assigned equal probability. For example, if there are 1,000 constructions in the grammar, then each usage of a construction costs 0.693 nats (for indicating a construction) and 6.907 nats (for pointing to a specific construction). Rather than assume that each construction in a given CxG is equally probable, an alternate approach is to assign probabilities to individual constructions and use these to determine the cost of encoding constructions on an individual basis. This problem is left for future work. Here, constructions are distinguished from one another only using (i) their relative complexity and (ii) the productivity of the particular grammar they belong to.

The *Regret* category holds units in the corpus that are not described by a construction in the current grammar. Each occurrence of a non-construction unit is encoded on-the-fly: as the number of undescribed units increases, the cost in nats of encoding each occurrence also increases. For example, if there are 1,000 undescribed units the cost per unit is 0.693 nats plus 6.907 nats; if there are 10,000 undescribed units the cost per unit is 0.693 nats plus 9.210 nats. This cost is specific to a given dataset, not to a given model, because the cost per undescribed unit depends on the total number of undescribed units. It is important to note that each instance of a unit not described by the grammar is stored in the *Regret* category independently: this is a measure of model error.

If the encoded dataset were transmitted, the model itself would need to be encoded and transmitted at the same time in order to decode the dataset; this is the information-theory rationale behind L_1, the encoding size of the grammar. In linguistic terms, grammars with larger encoding sizes are more complex. The *Regret* category has already been encoded with unique pointers for each undescribed unit; thus, it does not incur an additional model cost. The cost of encoding the model, then, consists entirely of the cost of encoding each construction it contains: the sum of all unit-encoding costs for each slot-filler representation in the construction,

$$\sum_{i}^{N_{SLOTS}} -log_e(\frac{1}{N_{R_i}}) + -log_e(\frac{1}{T_R})$$

N_{SLOTS} here is the number of slots in the construction being encoded, $N_{(R_i)}$ is the number of units available for a given representation type, and T_R is the number of representation types total for the current grammar. This is the total cost of encoding both (i) which representation type (alphabet) fills the slot and (ii) which unit of that alphabet fills the slot.

The full CxG has three representation types so that, for this grammar type, the encoding size for each slot is 1.098 nats (the cost of encoding a three-way distinction) plus $log_e(1/N)$ where N is the total vocabulary of that unit type. Thus, if there are 20,000 lexical items in the vocabulary, the cost of encoding a construction with three lexically-filled slots is 11.001 nats per slot or 33.003 nats total. This is a one-time encoding cost: each occurrence of a construction is a pointer that incurs the encoding cost described above.

The *Regret* category more properly belongs as an added term in L_2, the size of the dataset as encoded by the grammar. However, in this case it clarifies the discussion of grammar complexity to show the impact that each unencoded unit has on the MDL metric as a whole. Note that the complexity cost includes L_3 or the cost of encoding the

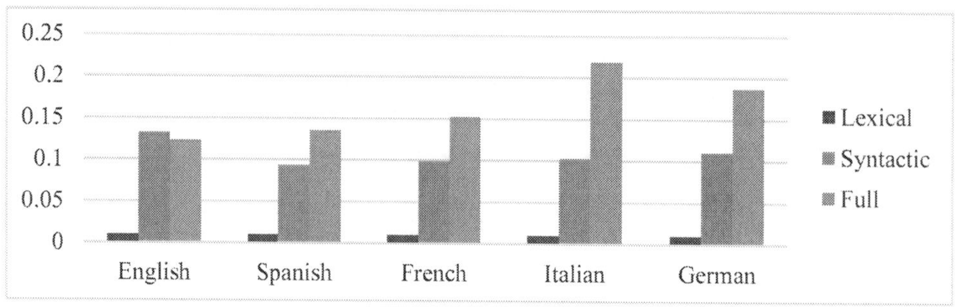

Figure 2: Compression Rates Across Grammar Types

encoding size of the grammar. In other words, in order for each construction to be encoded we also have to encode the lexicon of lexical, syntactic, and semantic units used in construction descriptions. This is included as part of the cost of each construction in the grammar.

5.1 Maintaining Lossless Encoding

The data consists of atomic units from three types of representation. In order to maintain the grammar as a lossless encoding of the corpus, we define the task for CxG_{FULL} as encoding one of these representations for each unit. Importantly, this means that each unit needs to be represented by only one type of representation in the decoded version of the dataset; part of the learning task for CxG_{FULL} is to choose the optimum type of representation for each slot. What lossless encoding means, in practice, depends on the type of CxG. For CxG_{LEX} lossless encoding means to return the same word-forms but for CxG_{SYN}, it means to return the original sequence of parts-of-speech.

It is important that CxG_{SYN} is evaluated while not in Chomsky normal form in order to correctly encode the complexity of the grammar. Consider the individual phrase structure rules in (2a) through (2c) which map from a particular sequence of part-of-speech tags to a single constituent type. For CxG_{SYN} internally each sequence is a construction (i.e., phrase structure rules are not typed). In the same way, for CxG_{LEX} internally, each sequence of word-forms is not typed (i.e., assigned to a part-of-speech category). Constructions from each of these passes need to be typed before filling slots in later passes. The part-of-speech tagger is used to assign lexical constructions to a single part-of-speech. An additional algorithm (outside the scope of this paper but available in the external resources) converts CxG_{SYN} sequences into phrase structure rules to support the CFG that allows longer sequences to fill individual slots.

(2a) DET — NOUN $\rightarrow$ NOUN

(2b) NOUN $\rightarrow$ NOUN

(2c) NOUN — NOUN $\rightarrow$ NOUN

The point is that, while the representations in (2a) through (2c) do not provide a lossless encoding of the observed utterances, the MDL metric is not applied to these representations but to their untyped forms (e.g., [DET — NOUN]). The CxG encoding system consists of *AtomicUnits* located within *Constructions*. As the level of abstraction increases (i.e., as we go through multiple iterations), members of the *Construction* repository for the current pass become members of the *AtomicUnits* repository for the next pass. Thus, lexical constructions are considered part of *Constructions* in CxG_{LEX} but part of *AtomicUnits* in CxG_{SYN}. The effect of this is to maintain lossless encoding at each level of abstraction while incorporating previously learned representations into the next level of abstraction.

This means that grammar complexity is not directly comparable across iterations because each iteration is encoding a different level of abstraction. For example, the task for CxG_{SYN} is to provide a lossless encoding of sequences of syntactic units (out of an inventory of 14 unit types). A relatively small number of syntactic sequences will be able to form phrase structure rules that, taken together, provide a high rate of compression. A full CxG, however, must do much more than predict sequences of syntactic units because it also incorporates lexical and semantic representations.

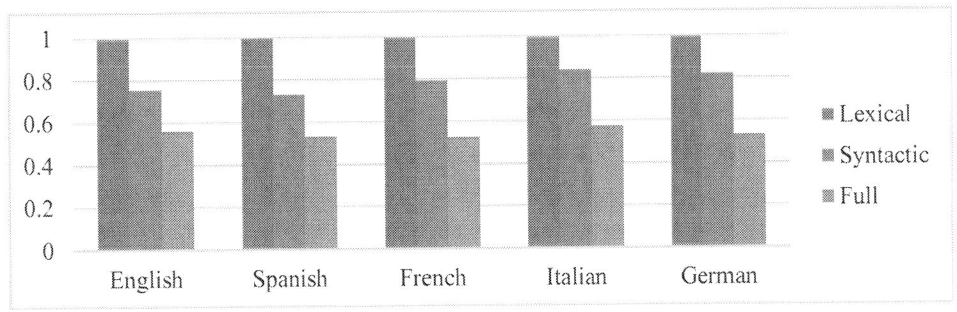

Figure 3: Stability Over Folds Across Grammar Types

On the other hand, though, the full MDL metric is comparable across iterations because it balances complexity and descriptive adequacy: does the more complex CxG_{FULL} provide enough descriptive adequacy to justify incorporating multiple types of representation?

6 Searching Over Potential CxGs

The search algorithm has three components: (i) randomly initializing the starting state, or what set of constructions belongs in the initial grammar; (ii) an indirect tabu search (Glover, 1989, 1990a) to move toward the optimum grammar by updating construction sampling parameters; and (iii) a direct tabu search across constructions to determine if small changes in the inventory of constructions improves the quality of the current CxG.

The first tabu search takes a randomly initialized starting state and searches for improved grammars by exploring different sampling parameters. These parameters take a number of association measures (c.f., Dunn, 2017) and use them to determine which constructions belong in the grammar. The essential idea of tabu search is (i) to define the set of possible moves from the current grammar state to a new grammar state and (ii) to combine tabu restrictions and aspiration criteria to move the search toward promising areas of the overall search space that are not directly reachable from the current state. We divide the parameter space into n discrete values for each of the 30 direction-specific association measures, with the maximum and minimum values defined empirically. This provides a finite set of possible moves from any given state.

For each turn, the algorithm generates a set of possible moves and, after evaluating each, takes the best available move even if it reduces the overall grammar quality. *Best* is defined using the MDL-metric: the best move is that which provides the smallest MDL-metric of all possible moves. *Available* is defined as a move that is either (i) not on the tabu list or (ii) satisfies an aspiration criteria that overrules the tabu list. The tabu list is a short-term memory item that contains the last n moves, each represented using the association measures that have been changed. For practical reasons, n is set at 7 (c.f., Glover, 1990b); this means that for any given turn the best move cannot involve a sampling parameter that has been changed over the last 7 turns. This prevents the algorithm from cycling between local optima in an endless loop. The aspiration criteria used is that the grammar produced by a move is not only the best available grammar but also the best observed grammar: a new global minimization of the MDL metric. Thus, the tabu against altering a recently changed sampling parameter can be overruled if that change creates a new best grammar. The use of such an aspiration criteria makes intuitive sense: the tabu search is designed to prevent cycling between previously visited states, but a grammar which reaches a new global minimum has not previously been visited.

Three types of moves are available at each turn: First, a parameter can be removed from the current sampler (i.e., OFF); this allows the tabu search to eliminate sampling parameters that reduce grammar quality. Second, a parameter can be grouped with n randomly chosen changes to other parameters (i.e., AND); this allows the tabu search to explore states similar to the current grammar. Third, a parameter can be allowed to overrule all other parameters (i.e., OR); this allows the tabu search to move toward better but more distant states.

Potential moves for each turn are generated as follows: for each association measure, one move is added with that measure removed from the sampler (OFF); two OR moves above and two below the feature's current threshold, serving as escape hatches; and 25 AND moves that include the current feature and $1...k$ other features ($k = 5$). The stopping criteria is that a new best grammar has not been observed for 14 turns, twice the size of the tabu list. This stopping criteria is an intermediate memory item that monitors the general direction of the search. The intuition is that, if a new optimum grammar has not been reached within two complete cycles of the short-term tabu list, such a grammar is unlikely to exist. It is important to keep in mind that each turn evaluates a wide range of possible moves. This means that a large number of potential grammars are evaluated in determining each move. Given the size of the space reachable from any given state and the number of states visited during the tabu search, it is unlikely at this point that a significantly better grammar exists.

7 Results and Discussion

The evaluation uses web-crawled corpora (from the WaC and Aranea projects) for English, Spanish, French, German, and Italian. The same data segmentation shown in Table 3 is used for each language. Each grammar type is evaluated using cross-validation with two folds; the training-testing split is randomly assigned. The search stage uses two restarts, each with a unique segment of the training data. This means that the learning algorithm makes four passes per iteration (two folds with two restarts) over which we can measure stability.

Used For	# Sentences
Candidates and Association	1 million
Test Sets for Restarts (Lex, Syn)	100k
Test Sets for Restarts ($Full$)	20k
Calculating Evaluation Metric	200k

Table 2: Data Segmentation Per Fold

The first measure of grammar quality, in Figure 2, is the compression achieved over the unencoded dataset on held-out testing data. Values close to 1 represent a large amount of compression while values close to 0 represent very little compression. We see across languages that lexical constructions (i.e., "because of") do not provide much compression. In part, this is because few such constructions are selected: an average of 22 per language.

Purely syntactic constructions, however, do provide compression (with an average of 120 identified per language). For all languages except English CxG_{FULL} has the highest rate of compression, with each grammar containing between 4k and 5k constructions.

This measure shows us three things: First, there is a balance between complexity and descriptive adequacy that is forced by MDL. In other words, the descriptive power of the purely lexical constructions are only able to justify 22 constructions as opposed to 4k - 5k for CxG_{FULL}. CxGs with multiple types of representations are allowed to produce more complex grammars because they produce better descriptions of the corpus. Second, the learned grammars provide meaningful generalizations. In other words, this compression metric shows that not only does the algorithm find the optimum grammar with respect to competing grammars but that it also finds grammars that offer above-the-baseline compression. Full compression is, of course, impossible and these results provide a benchmark for future work. Third, these results show that the addition of semantic representations provide improved descriptive adequacy. A representative sample of the output of CxG_{FULL} for English is shown in Appendix A.

How consistent are the grammars learned across different sub-sets of the corpora? This is shown in Figure 3 using the stability metric introduced in Section 4 over the grammars produced from different sub-sets of the corpora. We see that more complicated grammars are less stable. Thus, CxG_{LEX} has low compression but almost perfect stability because the same small number of lexical constructions are consistently identified. CxG_{FULL}, on the other hand, has a much larger number of constructions that provide much higher compression; but the inventory of these constructions is subject to more variation.

Lack of stability here is not necessarily caused by error: grammars are subject to variation. Some amount of this variation results from errors: tagging errors, parsing errors, and learning errors in which the search algorithm does not converge on the best grammar. Some amount of this variation, however, comes from differences in usage across different portions of the corpus: these large corpora contain many varieties, dialects, domains, and speakers, each introducing variant constructions. To what degree do these variations represent error and to what degree do they represent actual grammatical differences across the corpora? That is a question for future work because it requires testing grammars over data explicitly drawn from different varieties of a language.

This paper has shown that the MDL paradigm can be used to jointly model the complexity and descriptive adequacy of CxGs against unannotated corpora. This is important because methods that rely on gold-standard annotations to evaluate grammar quality ultimately depend on the introspections behind those annotations. How valid are these CxGs using external measures? One application-specific evaluation of a learned grammar is its ability to model dialectal variations. Separate work using these learned CxGs for dialectometry (Dunn, *Forthcoming*) shows that these grammars are able to model regional varieties with a high degree of accuracy.

Resources. Code and models for this work are available at jdunn.name and github.com/jonathandunn/c2xg

Acknowledgements. This research was supported in part by an appointment to the Visiting Scientist Fellowship at the National Geospatial-Intelligence Agency administered by the Oak Ridge Institute for Science and Education through an interagency agreement between the U.S. Department of Energy and NGA. The views expressed in this presentation are the author's and do not imply endorsement by the DoD or the NGA.

Appendix A: Representative Examples

[ADVERB — "about"]	*Modified Adverbs*
"at about"	This simple construction modifies adverbs
"how about"	to include information about vagueness.
"only about"	
"on about"	
["provide" — 25 — 25]	*Verb-Specific Direct Object*
"provide added value"	This verb-specific construction constrains
"provide an opportunity"	the object of "provide" to members of an
"provide general advice"	unlabeled semantic domain.
"provide information about"	
[25 — "to" — 14]	*Complex Verb Phrase*
"designed to ensure"	This construction represents a complex event
"want to improve"	phrase that contains both a main verb, "want,"
"made to ensure"	as well as an infinitive verb, "improve."
"able to understand"	
[VERB — "to" — 25 — ADVERB]	*Evaluative Verb Phrase*
"need to consider how"	This construction describes a basic verb phrase
"wish to consider how"	embedded within an evaluative verb describing
"want to be here"	how the speaker perceives the event.
"like to find out"	
[DETERMINER — NOUN — ADPOSITION — 14]	*Complex Noun Phrase*
"some experience in research"	This construction encodes a noun phrase that
"a need for research"	contains a modifying prepositional phrase.
"the process of planning"	
"a number of activities"	
[SUB-CONJ. — 25 — ADJECTIVE — NOUN]	*Subordinated Noun Phrase*
"whether small independent companies"	This construction provides sub-ordinated
"that the international community"	noun phrases that attach to main clause verbs
"because the current version"	and then act as the subject for additional
"while the other party"	modifying material that remains unspecified.
[PRON. — AUX. — VERB — PARTICLE — 25]	*Partial Main Clause*
"you should continue to receive"	This construction represents the largest
"i was told to make"	representations that are identified by the
"they were going to have"	algorithm; it specifies most of a main clause
"this was going to be"	with a pronominal subject.

References

Baroni, M., Bernardini, S., Ferraresi, A., and Zanchetta, E. 2009. The WaCky Wide Web: A Collection of Very Large Linguistically Processed Web-crawled Corpora. *Language Resources and Evaluation*, 43: 209-226.

Benko, V. 2014. Aranea: Yet Another Family of (Comparable) Web Corpora. In *Proceedings of Text, Speech and Dialogue. 17th International Conference*. 257-264.

Bryant, J. 2004. Scalable Construction-based Parsing and Semantic Analysis. In *Proceedings of the Workshop on Scalable Natural Language Understanding (HLT-NAACL)*: 33-40.

Bybee, J. 2006. From Usage to Grammar: The Mind's Response to Repetition. *Language*, 82(4): 711-733.

Chang, N.; De Beule, J.; and Micelli, V. 2012. Computational construction grammar: Comparing ECG and FCG. In Steels, L. (ed.), *Computational Issues in Fluid Construction Grammar*. Berlin: Springer. 259-288.

Dunn, J. 2017. Computational Learning of Construction Grammars. *Language & Cognition*, 9(2): 254-292.

Dunn, J. Forthcoming. Finding Variants for Construction-Based Dialectometry: A Corpus-Based Approach to Regional CxGs. *Cognitive Linguistics*.

Forsberg, M.; Johansson, R.; Bckstrm, L.; Borin, L.; Lyngfelt, B.; Olofsson, J.; and Prentice, J. 2014. From Construction Candidates to Constructicon Entries: An experiment using semi-automatic methods for identifying constructions in corpora. *Constructions and Frames*, 6(1): 114-135.

Glover, F. 1989. Tabu Search, Part 1. *ORSA Journal on Computing*, 1(3): 190-206.

Glover. F. 1990a. Tabu Search, Part 2. *ORSA Journal on Computing*, 2(1): 4-32.

Glover. F. 1990b. Tabu Search: A Tutorial. *Interfaces*, 20(4): 74-94.

Goldberg, A. 2006. *Constructions at Work: The Nature of Generalization in Language*. Oxford: Oxford University Press.

Goldsmith, J. 2001. Unsupervised Learning of the Morphology of a Natural Language. *Computational Linguistics*, 27(2): 153-198.

Goldsmith, J. 2006. An Algorithm for the Unsupervised Learning of Morphology. *Natural Language Engineering*, 12(4): 353-371.

Grünwald, P. and Rissanen, J. 2007. *The Minimum Description Length Principle*. Cambridge, MA: The MIT Press.

Hopper, P. 1987. Emergent Grammar. In *Proceedings of the 13th Annual Meeting of the Berkeley Linguistics Society*, 139-157.

Kay, P. and Fillmore, C. 1999. Grammatical Constructions and Linguistic Generalizations: The Whats X Doing Y? Construction. *Language*, 75(1): 1-33.

Langacker, R. 2008. *Cognitive Grammar: A Basic Introduction*. Oxford: Oxford University Press.

Nguyen, Dat Quoc; Nguyen, Dai Quoc; Pham, Dang Duc; and Pham, Son Bao. 2016. A Robust Transformation-Based Learning Approach Using Ripple Down Rules for Part-Of-Speech Tagging. *AI Communications*, 29(3): 409-422.

Petrov, S.; Das, D.; and McDonald, R. 2012. A Universal Part-of-Speech Tagset. In *Proceedings of the Eight International Conference on Language Resources and Evaluation*.

Rehurek, R. and Sojka, P. 2010. Software Framework for Topic Modelling with Large Corpora. In *Proceedings of the LREC 2010 Workshop on New Challenges for NLP Frameworks*.

Rissanen, J. 1978. Modeling by the Shortest Data Description. *Automatica*, 14: 465-471.

Rissanen, J. 1986. Stochastic Complexity and Modeling. *Annals of Statistics*, 14: 1,080-1,100.

Steels, L. 2004. Constructivist development of grounded construction grammar. In *Proceedings of the 42nd Meeting of the Association for Computational Linguistics*: 9-16.

Steels, L. 2012. Design methods for fluid construction grammar. In Steels, L. (ed), *Computational Issues in Fluid Construction Grammar*. Berlin: Springer. 3-36.

Wible, D. and Tsao, N. 2010. StringNet as a Computational Resource for Discovering and Investigating Linguistic Constructions. In *Proceedings of the Workshop on Extracting and Using Constructions in Computational Linguistics (NAACL-HTL)*: 25-31.

Decomposing phonological transformations in serial derivations

Andrew Lamont
University of Massachusetts, Amherst
alamont@linguist.umass.edu

Abstract

While most phonological transformations have been shown to be subsequential, there are tonal processes that do not belong to any subregular class, thereby making it difficult to identify a tighter bound on the complexity of phonological processes than the regular languages. This paper argues that a tighter bound obtains from examining the way transformations are computed: when derived in serial, phonological processes can be decomposed into iterated subsequential maps.

1 Introduction

Phonological transformations map underlying representations (UR) onto surface forms (SF). The maps between UR and SF are known to be REGULAR (Johnson, 1972; Kaplan and Kay, 1994), meaning they can be modeled with finite state transducers (FST). This generalization is stated as the Regular Hypothesis (1).

(1) **Regular Hypothesis**: Phonological transformations are regular.

The Regular Hypothesis is not strong enough. There are many regular maps that are phonologically implausible, and most UR↦SF maps belong to the SUBREGULAR classes shown in Figure 1. The majority are in the SUBSEQUENTIAL classes in gray. Bidirectional long-distance processes like stem-controlled vowel harmony belong to the more powerful WEAKLY DETERMINISTIC class (Heinz and Lai, 2013). Only two tonal processes, unbounded tonal plateauing and conditional rightward

spreading (in bold), have been shown to not belong to any subregular class (Jardine, 2016a).

Because of their wide empirical coverage and computational properties, the union of the subsequential classes was an early candidate for a tighter bound on the complexity of phonological processes than the regular class (Chandlee and Heinz, 2012; Gainor et al., 2012). Heinz (forthcoming) states this as the Subsequential Hypothesis (2). The Subsequential Hypothesis is stronger than the Regular Hypothesis, while maintaining its uniform generalization over all phonological transformations.

(2) **Subsequential Hypothesis**: Phonological transformations are left- or right-subsequential.

In light of the weakly deterministic and regular processes, the Subsequential Hypothesis is too strong. Because there are phonological transformations that are not subregular, there is not a uniform revision of the Subsequential Hypothesis stronger than the Regular Hypothesis. Jardine (2016a) argues that only tonal processes exceed the weakly deterministic class, so a possible revision states that segmental processes are weakly deterministic and tonal processes are regular.[1] In short, from examining the UR↦SF maps on their own, there is no subregular class that subsumes all phonological transformations.

This paper argues that a uniform revision of the Subsequential Hypothesis obtains by examining not only the UR↦SF maps, but also how their derivations are computed. There is an open question in

---

[1] Tutrugbu vowel harmony challenges this generalization (McCollum et al., 2017).

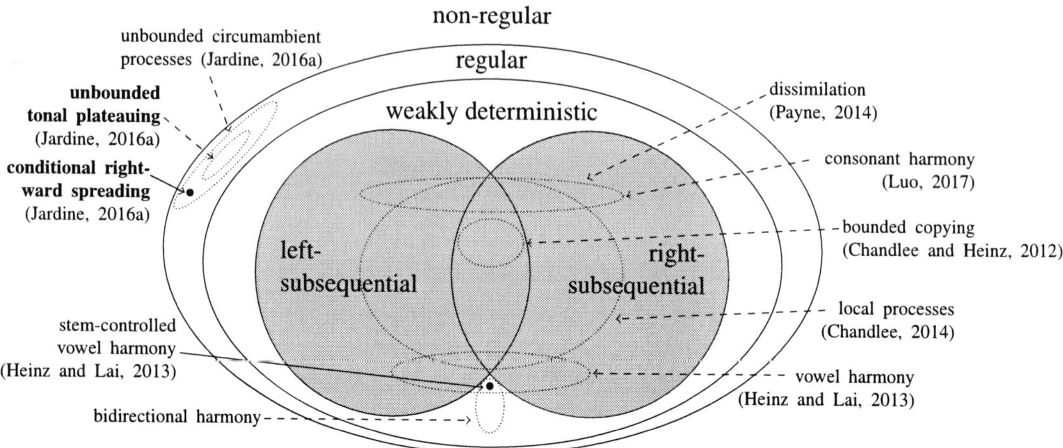

Figure 1: Subregular hierarchy of phonological transformations (based on Jardine's Figure 1 (2016, 263))

phonological theory whether UR↦SF maps are derived in one fell swoop, or whether they are broken down into sub-derivations. For example, consider the sibilant harmony process that transforms the UR /sasasaʃ/ into the SF [ʃaʃaʃaʃ] in Figure 2. The dashed line directly from the UR to the SF shows the PARALLEL derivation, where every /s/ changes at the same time. The solid lines from UR to SF via two intermediate forms show the SERIAL derivation, where only one /s/ changes at a time. Each line represents one computation made by the phonology. Both derivations yield the same SF, the parallel derivation in one step and the serial in three.

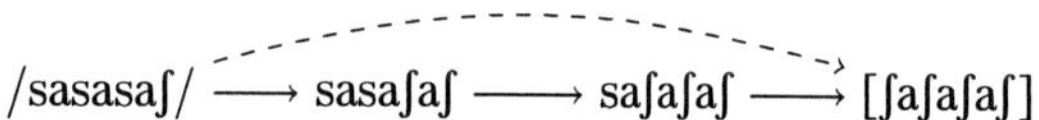

$$/\text{sasasaʃ}/ \longrightarrow \text{sasaʃaʃ} \longrightarrow \text{saʃaʃaʃ} \longrightarrow [\text{ʃaʃaʃaʃ}]$$

Figure 2: Serial and parallel sibilant harmony

In a parallel derivation, the SF is derived directly from the UR, so the derivation is exactly the UR↦SF map. Because they are identical, parallel derivations have the same computational complexity as UR↦SF maps. This paper argues that in a serial derivation, where the SF is derived gradually over a number of steps, each step is subsequential. This is stated as the Serial Subsequential Hypothesis (3). Restricting each step to making a single change requires iterating processes. The solid lines in Figure 2, represent a process that changes one /s/, which applies three times to gradually yield the

SF. As Section 4 argues, this restriction also predicts that some regular maps are not possible phonological processes.

(3) **Serial Subsequential Hypothesis**: Phonological transformations are decomposable into iterated left- or right-subsequential maps.

The paper is organized as follows. Section 2 reviews the characterization of the classes in Figure 1 in terms of FSTs, providing empirical examples, and discusses the serial counterparts of the subregular classes. Section 3 demonstrates that the regular tonal processes can be broken down into subsequential steps in a serial derivation. Sections 4 and 5 discuss the predictions of the Serial Subsequential Hypothesis and conclude.

2 Phonological transformations and FSTs

2.1 Subsequential transformations

Subsequential transformations include local processes like place assimilation, and unidirectional long-distance processes like regressive sibilant harmony. They can be computed by SUBSEQUENTIAL FSTs (Mohri, 1997). These are deterministic FSTs where every state is accepting. When the end of the input is reached, an additional string is appended to the output, determined by the current state the machine is in. This can be thought of as standing in for transitions on boundary symbols (Chomsky and Halle, 1968). LEFT-SUBSEQUENTIAL

FSTs (L-SFST) read inputs left-to-right; RIGHT-SUBSEQUENTIAL FSTs (R-SFST) read inputs right-to-left.

Example subsequential FSTs are given in Figures 3 and 4 for a toy sibilant harmony system. The machines remember the identity of the first sibilant they read. If the first sibilant is /s/, they transition to state q_1; if /ʃ/, state q_2. That information and the current position in the input determine what is written to the output. In the diagrams, the end-of-input string is shown after states' labels. λ stands for the empty string, so neither machine appends to the output when the input is exhausted.

The L-SFST in Figure 3 reads inputs left-to-right. The leftmost sibilant controls harmony, yielding progressive sibilant harmony, such as that in Aari (Hansson, 2010, 51). Table 1 gives sample derivations; the I row gives the current symbol in the input read by the FST, Q the state the machine is in, and O the string written to the output.

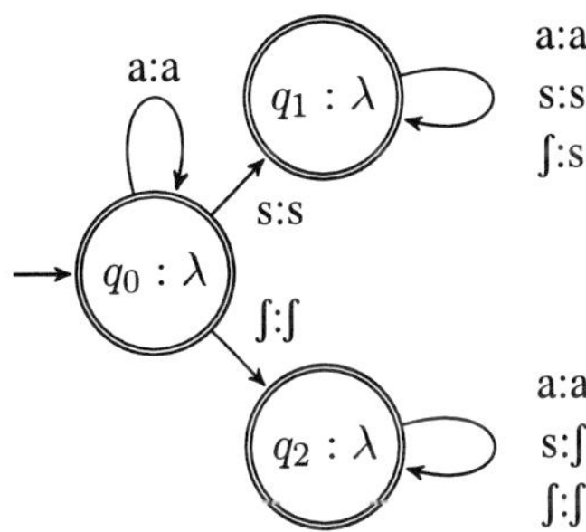

Figure 3: L-SFST for progressive sibilant harmony

/saʃaʃa/↦[sasasa]

I	s	a	ʃ	a	ʃ	a	
Q	$q_0 \rightarrow$	$q_1 \rightarrow$	$q_1 \rightarrow$	$q_1 \rightarrow$	$q_1 \rightarrow$	$q_1 \rightarrow$	q_1
O	s	a	s	a	s	a	λ

/ʃasasa/↦[ʃaʃaʃa]

I	ʃ	a	s	a	s	a	
Q	$q_0 \rightarrow$	$q_2 \rightarrow$	$q_2 \rightarrow$	$q_2 \rightarrow$	$q_2 \rightarrow$	$q_2 \rightarrow$	q_2
O	ʃ	a	ʃ	a	ʃ	a	λ

Table 1: Sample derivations for the L-SFST in Figure 3

The R-SFST in Figure 4 is the mirror image of the L-SFST in Figure 3. It reads inputs right-to-left, so the rightmost sibilant controls harmony, yielding regressive harmony, such as that in Navajo (Hansson, 2010, 43). For the URs in Table 1, this machine pro-

duces SFs with the opposite direction of harmony: /saʃaʃa/↦[ʃaʃaʃa]; /ʃasasa/↦[sasasa].

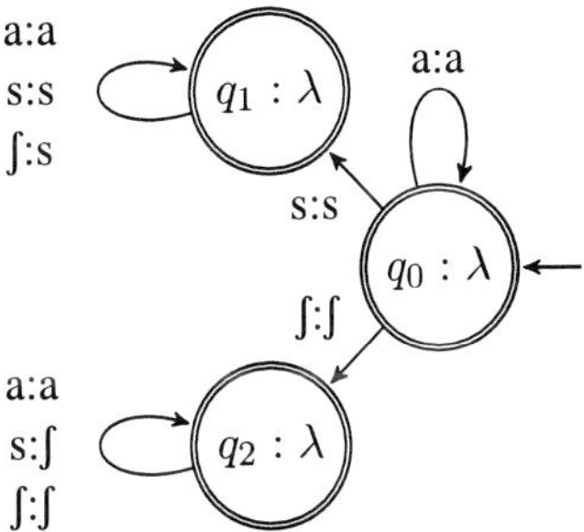

Figure 4: R-SFST for regressive sibilant harmony

The direction in which subsequential FSTs read inputs determines whether a long-distance process is regressive or progressive. That is, R-SFSTs model regressive harmony, but L-SFSTs cannot. The R-SFST in Figure 4 first identifies a trigger and remembers its identity. This is enough information to write the correct output for every target in the input. A L-SFST would read the targets first, and face the insurmountable problem of anticipating the identity of the trigger. Until it finds the trigger, a L-SFST does not have enough information to write the correct output for a target. Because the trigger may be arbitrarily far away, the L-SFST would have to wait until the end of the input to correctly output the targets. Because FSTs cannot remember arbitrarily long sequences, this strategy fails.

The FSTs in Figures 3 and 4 compute the UR↦SF maps and, equivalently, the parallel derivations of these processes. Once the machines transition into a harmonizing state, q_1 or q_2, they remain in that state until the input is exhausted, because the only transitions from these states are self-loops. The machines therefore apply harmony to every focus in an UR.[2]

In the corresponding serial derivation, each computation applies harmony to only one sibilant in the input. Compare the L-SFST in Figure 3 to its serial counterpart in Figure 5. In the latter, the unfaithful transitions, i.e. the arcs leaving q_1 on ʃ and q_2 on s, lead to a state q_3, where the input is copied faithfully to the output. Thus, once this machine makes a sin-

---

[2]In a phonological rule of the form A → B / C_D, A is called the *focus*, B the *structural change*, C_D the *context*, and CAD the *structural description*.

gle change, it transitions to a state where it is unable to make any further changes. Restricted to making one change at a time, inputs with multiple foci must pass through the machine a number of times before the final SF is computed.

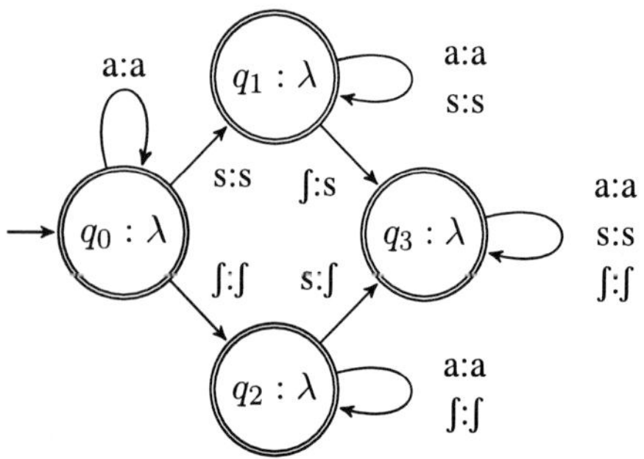

Figure 5: L-SFST for serial progressive sibilant harmony

Subsequential FSTs have enough memory to compute long-distance processes like sibilant harmony. To satisfy the restriction that they make only one change, they simply have to remember whether they have already made a change. In the L-SFST in Figure 5, this is implemented by transitioning into the faithful state q_3 on the unfaithful arcs leaving q_1 and q_2. This modification does not require any additional computational power, so the serial FST is still left-subsequential.

2.2 Weakly deterministic transformations

Weakly deterministic maps are defined as length- and alphabet-preserving[3] compositions of a left-subsequential and a right-subsequential map (Heinz and Lai, 2013), and include long-distance bidirectional processes like stem-controlled vowel harmony. Because SFSTs are limited to unidirectional long-distance processes, they are not powerful enough to compute these maps on their own. Characterizing these maps in terms of independent unidirectional processes is empirically sound, as blocking and other restrictions can vary with directionality (Rose and Walker, 2011).

Emphasis spreading in South Palestinian Arabic is an illustrative example. Emphasis spreads bidirectionally from a pharyngealized segment. Examples are given in (4-6) (Al Khatib, 2008; Jardine,

---

[3]These restrictions are necessary to define a subregular class. Without them, composing a left- and right-subsequential map can produce any regular map (Elgot and Mezei, 1965).

2016a); targeted segments are underlined in the SFs. Regressive spreading is unrestricted; the final obstruent in (4) triggers pharyngealization of the entire word. Progressive spreading is blocked by /i, ʃ, j, dʒ/; pharyngealization in (5) affects one vowel and is stopped by the /j/. In (6), there are no blockers, and the medial stop triggers pharyngealization of the entire word.

(4) /χajːaːtˤ/ ↦ [χˤaˤjˤːaˤːtˤ] 'tailor'

(5) /sˤajːaːd/ ↦ [sˤaˤjːaːd] 'hunter'

(6) /ʔatˤfaːl/ ↦ [ʔˤaˤtˤfˤaˤːlˤ] 'children'

While this process is beyond the capability of a subsequential FST, it can be computed by feeding a UR into a left-subsequential FST and its output into a right-subsequential FST. Table 2 makes this explicit, showing emphasis spreading as the outcome of ordering progressive spreading before regressive spreading. Though the SFSTs are not shown here, these processes can be computed by a left- and right-subsequential FST, respectively. As with sibilant harmony, these SFSTs can be restricted to making only one change without affecting their computational complexity. Thus, because weakly deterministic maps can be decomposed into subsequential maps, they can be further decomposed into iterated subsequential maps in a serial derivation.

UR	/χajːaːtˤ/	/sˤajːaːd/	/ʔatˤfaːl/
L→R	—	sˤaˤjːaːd	ʔatˤfˤaˤːlˤ
R→L	χˤaˤjˤːaˤːtˤ	—	ʔˤaˤtˤfˤaˤːlˤ
SF	[χˤaˤjˤːaˤːtˤ]	[sˤaˤjːaːd]	[ʔˤaˤtˤfˤaˤːlˤ]

Table 2: Emphasis spreading as two directional processes

2.3 Regular transformations

Weakly deterministic maps can be decomposed into two unidirectional processes because each process has a single trigger. Thus, even though crucial information may be at a distance from a target, a subsequential FST can identify the trigger before it encounters a target. This is not the case with regular transformations that are UNBOUNDED CIRCUMAMBIENT, meaning crucial information lies both to the left and to the right of a target and may be arbitrarily far away in both directions (Jardine, 2016a). This property means that a subsequential FST will not have enough information when it reaches a target to write the correct output (see Jardine (2016a) for a formal account). In the attested unbounded circumambient processes, the crucial information consists of a trigger and a blocker, as in conditional rightward spreading, or two triggers, as in unbounded tonal plateauing.

Conditional rightward spreading (CRS) is a process in Copperbelt Bemba that exemplifies the combination of a trigger and a blocker. Tone bearing units (TBU) surface with high tones if there is a high tone to the left and there is no high tone at the right edge of the prosodic word; examples are given in (7-8) (Bickmore and Kula, 2013; Kula and Bickmore, 2015; Jardine, 2016a). High tones are indicated with an acute accent (V́) and low tones with a grave accent (V̀). When no underlying high tones are present, words surface with all low tones (7a). In words with high tones and underlyingly toneless final vowels, the rightmost high tone spreads all the way to the right edge; in (7b-c), the subject marker /bá-/ provides the high tone. Word-final high-tones block conditional rightward spreading, and high tones only spread across two TBUs; in (8), the locative enclitic /=kó/ provides the blocker.

(7)   a. /u-ku-tul-a/ ↦ [ùkùtùlà] 'to pierce'

       b. /bá-ka-fik-a/ ↦ [bák<u>áfík</u>á] 'they will arrive'

       c. /bá-ka-mu-londolol-a/ ↦ [bák<u>ámúlóóndólól</u>á] 'they will introduce him/her'

(8)   a. /bá-ka-pat-a=kó/ ↦ [bák<u>ápàt</u>àkó] 'they will hate'

       b. /bá-mu-luk-il-a=kó/ ↦ [bám<u>úlúkìl</u>àkó] 'they will plait a bit for him'

       c. /bá-ka-londolol-a=kó/ ↦ [bák<u>álóóndòlòl</u>àkó] 'they will introduce'

CRS cannot be decomposed into two unidirectional processes because a subsequential FST will not have enough information once it encounters a target TBU. Reading inputs left-to-right, a L-SFST remembers whether a triggering high tone is present, but cannot anticipate whether a blocking high tone is present word-finally. Likewise, reading right-to-left, a R-SFST remembers whether a blocker is present, but cannot anticipate the presence of a trigger.

Unbounded tonal plateauing (UTP) exemplifies the combination of two triggers. TBUs surface with high tones if there is a high tone to the left and a high tone to the right; examples from Luganda are given in (9-10) (Hyman and Katamba, 2010; Jardine, 2016a). Underlyingly toneless TBUs in phrases without high tones (9a) and in phrases with only one high tone span (9b) surface with low tones. In words with multiple high tone spans, underlyingly toneless TBUs flanked by two high tones surface with high tones (10).

(9)   a. /mu-tund-a/ ↦ [mùtùndà] 'seller'
       b. /mu-tém-a/ ↦ [mùtémà] 'chopper'

(10)   a. /mu-tém-a-bi-sikí/ ↦ [mùtém<u>ábísí</u>kí] 'log-chopper'

       b. /tw-áa-láb-w-a walúsimbi/ ↦ [twáálábwá w<u>álúsìmbì</u>] 'we were seen by Walusimbi'

       c. /tw-áa-génd-a na=byaa=ba=walúsimbi/ ↦ [twá<u>ágéndá nábyáábáwálúsìmbì</u>] 'we went with those of Walusimbi'

Like CRS, UTP cannot be decomposed into two unidirectional processes. A SFST reading the input in either direction will have only seen one trigger when it identifies a target. Because both triggers must be present for an underlyingly toneless TBU to surface with high tone, the SFST will not have enough information to write the correct output.

Jardine (2016a) argues that CRS and UTP must be modeled by non-deterministic FSTs. Unlike finite state acceptors, non-deterministic FSTs cannot in general be determinized (Lothaire, 2013), and can compute regular maps that deterministic FSTs cannot. The FST for UTP is given in Figure 6 (Jardine, 2016a, 268). Following Jardine (2016a), tonal FSTs read inputs in TBU-sized chunks; U indicates a TBU unspecified for tone and H a high-toned TBU. Anticipating Section 3, while the circumambient processes cannot be decomposed into two subsequential maps like weakly deterministic processes, they can be decomposed into arbitrarily many iterated subsequential maps in a serial derivation.

Non-determinism allows the FST to anticipate the presence of a second trigger, effectively granting it

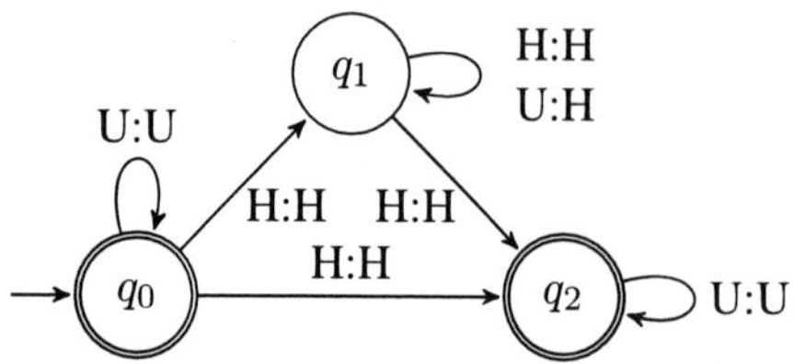

Figure 6: Non-deterministic FST for UTP (based on Jardine's Figure 5 (2016, 268))

unbounded lookahead. The FST in Figure 6 accepts an input with exactly one high tone only if it takes the lower path, transitioning to q_2 on its high tone. Inputs with more than one high tone must take the upper path, transitioning to q_1 on the first high tone. In this state, high tones are written for unspecified TBUs. Reading inputs without high tones, the FST does not transition out of q_0, and faithfully maps the input string. Table 3 gives sample derivations.

/UUHUU/↦[UUHUU]

I	U		U		H		U		U
Q	q_0	$\to$	q_0	$\to$	q_0	$\to$	q_2	$\to$	q_2	$\to$	q_2
O	U		U		H		U		U

/HUUUH/↦[HHHHH]

I	H		U		U		U		H
Q	q_0	$\to$	q_1	$\to$	q_1	$\to$	q_1	$\to$	q_1	$\to$	q_2
O	H		H		H		H		H

Table 3: Sample derivations for the FST in Figure 6

Unlike weakly deterministic maps, which can be decomposed into two independently attested subsequential processes, Jardine (2016a) argues that unbounded circumambient processes are different. Taking a derivational perspective, Section 3 argues that in a serial derivation, the regular tonal maps can be decomposed into empirically-motivated subsequential processes that are iterated.

3 Decomposing regular transformations in serial derivations

This section presents the main contribution of this paper, that, under a serial derivation, the computation of the unbounded circumambient processes can be decomposed into iterated subsequential maps which are empirically motivated. In a serial derivation, the left high tone trigger is always adjacent to the target, so no step depends on non-local informa-

tion on both sides. By exploiting this locality, FSTs in serial do not require unbounded lookahead, obviating nondeterminism. In parallel, this connection is not obvious, and the computation requires non-determinism just like the UR↦SF map.

The tonal processes discussed in §2.3 have been characterized as spreading (Kisseberth and Odden, 2003; Kula and Bickmore, 2015). Spreading involves associating a tone onto a TBU adjacent to a TBU already associated with that tone. This is represented visually in Figure 7 for UTP; solid lines indicate associations between tones and TBUs (here syllables) in the UR and dashed lines indicate new associations. The high tones of the UR /HUUUH/ trigger spreading, which is assumed to be progressive (Hyman, 2011), yielding the SF [HHHHH].

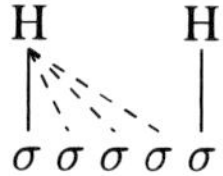

Figure 7: UTP as high tone spreading

Evidence supporting a spreading analysis comes from inhibitory effects by blockers, which produce partial spreading. A clear example of this is found in Digo, where voiced obstruents impede high tone spreading; examples are given in (11-12) (Kisseberth, 1984). In these examples, UTP is fed by a process that displaces a high tone to the word-final vowel, which realizes as a final rise-fall contour (V̌V̂). The displaced high tone of the subject prefix /á-/ realizes as this final rise-fall in isolation (11a). In (11b-c), the object prefix /á-/ provides a second high tone, creating the context for UTP. Verb stems with initial voiceless obstruents show rightward spreading (11b), but stems with initial voiced obstruents do not (11c).

The words in (12) have verb stems with initial high tones that interact with the displaced high tone of the tense/aspect prefix /ká-/, creating the context for UTP. The high tone on the verb stem spreads rightwards until it reaches a voiced obstruent. In (12a), rightward spreading is blocked entirely, because the voiced obstruent is adjacent to the left high tone. In (12b), the voiced obstruent is further away, so the high tone spreads, but only across one syllable before it is blocked.

(11) a. /á-na-tsukur-a/ ↦ [ànàtsùkǔrâ] 'he/she is
taking'

b. /á-na-á-tsukur-a/ ↦ [ànàátsúkúrâ] 'he/she
is taking them'

c. /á-na-á-demurir-a/ ↦ [ànàádèmùrǐrâ]
'he/she is scolding them'

(12) a. /a-ká-ézeker-a/ ↦ [àkàézèkěrâ] 'he/she
has thatched with/for'

b. /a-ká-súrubik-a/ ↦ [àkàsúrúbǐk-â]
'he/she is strong/firm'

The pattern in Digo reveals a local relation between the target and left high tone trigger in UTP. TBUs to the right of a voiced obstruent do not surface with high tones because the left high tone cannot spread across voiced obstruents to establish adjacency. These facts receive a natural explanation under a spreading analysis.

Further evidence for UTP being sensitive to locality comes from Saramaccan Creole. Saramaccan Creole has an underlying three-way contrast between high-toned TBUs, low-toned TBUs, and TBUs unspecified for tone. UTP only targets unspecified TBUs. When a low tone intervenes between either high tone and a span of toneless TBUs, plateauing is blocked; examples are given in (13-14) (Good, 2004; McWhorter and Good, 2012). When toneless TBU spans contact only one high tone, they surface with default low tone (13a). When toneless TBUs are flanked by two high tones, as with the subject and verb in (13b), they surface with high tones. The high tones must be adjacent to the toneless span as the examples in (14) show. In (14a), two low tones intervene between the left high tone and the toneless span, and in (14b), the intervention is between the toneless span and the right high tone. In both cases, spreading is blocked and the unspecified TBUs surface with low tones.

(13) a. /páulu lègèdè/ ↦ [páúlù lègèdè] 'Paul
lies'

b. /dí wómi kulé alá/ ↦ [dí wómí kúlé àlá]
'the man runs there'

(14) a. /dí káìmà kulé alá/ ↦ [dí káìmà kùlé àlá]
'the alligator runs there'

b. /dí wómi bà wáta/ ↦ [dí wómì bà wátà]
'the man carried water' (Good, p.c.)

The Saramaccan Creole pattern supports the generalization drawn from Digo that the left high tone trigger must be adjacent to a target TBU. Further, it also shows that the right high tone trigger must be adjacent to the span of toneless TBU targets. This indicates that the structural description is subject to locality constraints defined over the tonal tier rather than being unbounded over the timing tier (Jardine, 2016b; Jardine, 2017).

The locality between the left high tone trigger and the target may be implicit in the UR↦SF map, but it is made explicit in a serial derivation. Consider Figure 8, which gives the serial derivation of the UR↦SF map in Figure 7. In each step, the target is adjacent to the left high tone trigger, but may be at a distance from the right trigger. Because only the triggering high tone to the right is ever at a distance, no single step is unbounded circumambient.

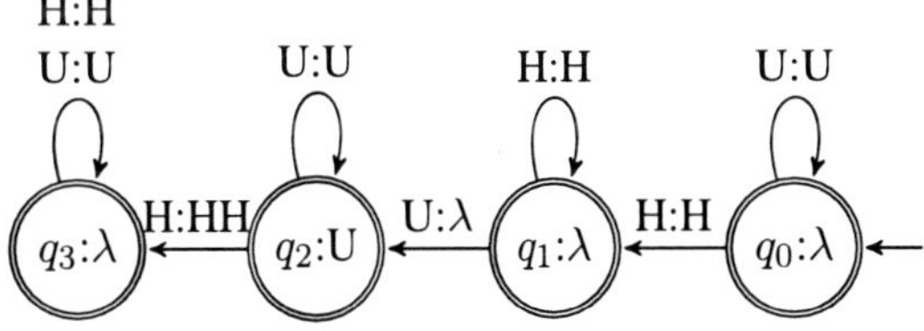

Figure 8: UTP as high tone spreading in a serial derivation

Each step in the serial derivation of UTP is right-subsequential and can be computed by the R-SFST in Figure 9. Reading an input without a high tone, the R-SFST does not transition out of q_0, and faithfully outputs the input. Likewise, inputs with one high tone span do not trigger any changes (e.g. /UUHUU/ in Table 4). On inputs with U...H sequences, the R-SFST transitions to q_2, where it waits to identify a HU string. If it does, it writes two high tones to the output and makes no more changes (e.g. /HUUUH/ in Table 4). If the input ends before another high tone trigger is identified, the end-of-input function writes a toneless TBU to the output.

Figure 9: R-SFST for serial UTP

Looking for a string of a bounded length obviates the need for non-determinism. The R-SFST only needs to lookahead one segment at a time once it finds the right high tone trigger and a toneless TBU. State q_2 enables lookahead. Transitioning to q_2, the R-SFST writes nothing onto the output; instead it remembers that it has seen one U. Rather than having to memorize an arbitrarily long sequence of toneless TBUs, the self-loop on q_2 allows it to keep one in memory. If the input ends in q_2, the memorized U is written to the output. Otherwise, if a second high tone is found, the memorized U is forgotten, and a second high tone is written to the output.

/UUHUU/↦[UUHUU]

U		U		H		U		U		I
q_2	←	q_2	←	q_1	←	q_0	←	q_0	← q_0	Q
U U		λ		H		U		U		O

/HUUUH/↦[HHUUH]

H		U		U		U		H		I
q_3	←	q_2	←	q_2	←	q_2	←	q_1	← q_0	Q
λ	HH	U		U		λ		H		O

Table 4: Sample derivations for the FST in Figure 9

CRS can be similarly broken down. The R-SFST in Figure 10 computes each step in a serial derivation, using exactly the same lookahead strategy as the R-SFST for UTP in Figure 9. The only difference is that it checks for a blocker rather than a trigger. Reading an input right-to-left, if the first TBU is high-toned, the machine transitions directly from the starting state to the faithful state q_2 (bounded spreading is assumed to be a separate process). Otherwise, it looks for a HU sequence and spreads the high tone.

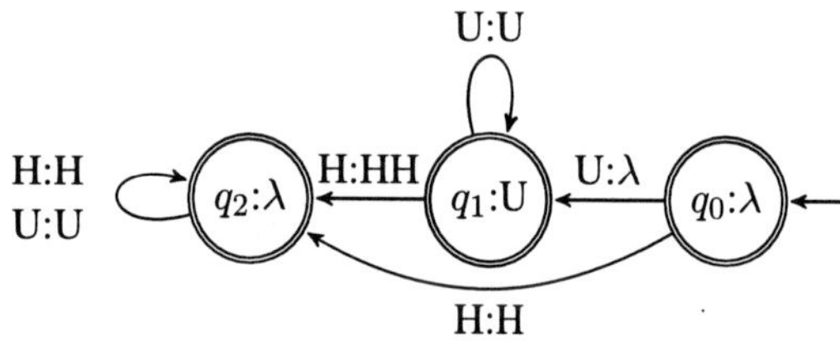

Figure 10: R-SFST for serial CRS

4 Discussion

Phonologists have long debated whether to describe phonological processes as applying in parallel or in serial. In rule-based models, the debate is whether a rule applies simultaneously to a string with multiple foci (Chomsky and Halle, 1968; Anderson, 1974) or whether rules apply to each focus one-by-one (Howard, 1972; Johnson, 1972; Lightner, 1972; Kenstowicz and Kisseberth, 1977). In constraint-based models, the debate is whether competing possible outputs may differ from inputs in unlimited ways, as in parallel Optimality Theory (Prince and Smolensky, 1993/2004), or whether they can only differ from the input by only one change, as in Harmonic Serialism (McCarthy, 2000, et seq.), where the derivation iterates until converging. This is a fundamental question in phonological theory.

This paper has argued that serial phonological models, where only one focus is changed at a time, are advantageous to characterizing the class of UR↦SF maps. Parallel models of phonology, where derivations are identical to UR↦SF maps, do not offer stronger generalizations than the Regular Hypothesis. Serial models, on the other hand, allow for the decomposition of UR↦SF maps, yielding the Serial Subsequential Hypothesis. The Serial Subsequential Hypothesis is stated as a uniform generalization over phonological transformations and does not need to distinguish between segmental and tonal processes. This is desirable as a general, restrictive characterization.

As a general characterization, it can reduce the computational differences between related phonological processes. Consider the case of UTP, which avoids sequences of H...U...H from surfacing (Yip, 2002). Cross-linguistically, this sequence is also avoided by deleting the second high tone, giving maps like /HUH/↦[HUU]. Examples of this progressive lowering process in Barasana are given in (15-16) (Gomez-Imbert and Kenstowicz, 2000; Gomez-Imbert, 2001; Hyman, 2010); the tilde ∼ marks nasalized stems. This is also attested in Yongning Na (Michaud, 2017). The high tone of the diminutive suffix /-áka/ surfaces when attached to stems with all high-toned TBUs (15a) and stems with UH contours (15b). Attaching the suffix to stems with HU contours creates a H...U...H sequence, triggering the diminutive high tone to lower (16). Progressive lowering also targets the underlying high tone on the suffix /-ɾi/ (16c). This process is left-subsequential; the L-SFST in Figure 11 computes the UR↦SF map.

(15)   a. /∼kúbú-áka/ ↦ [∼kúbúákà] 'small shaman'

b. /gohé-áka/ ↦ [gòhéákà] 'small hole'

(16) a. /∼céda-áka/ ↦ [∼cédàa̱kà] 'a bit of pineapple'

b. /∼céda-a-áka/ ↦ [∼cédàa̱a̱kà] 'a small pineapple'

c. /∼céda-a-íri-áka-re/ ↦ [∼cédàa̱rìa̱kàrè] 'small pineapples-OBJ'

Progressive lowering and UTP target the same marked structure. In a parallel derivation, languages like Luganda use a regular process to repair H…U…H sequences, while languages like Barasana use a subsequential repair. This computational gap disappears in a serial derivation, where both repairs comprise iterated subsequential maps.

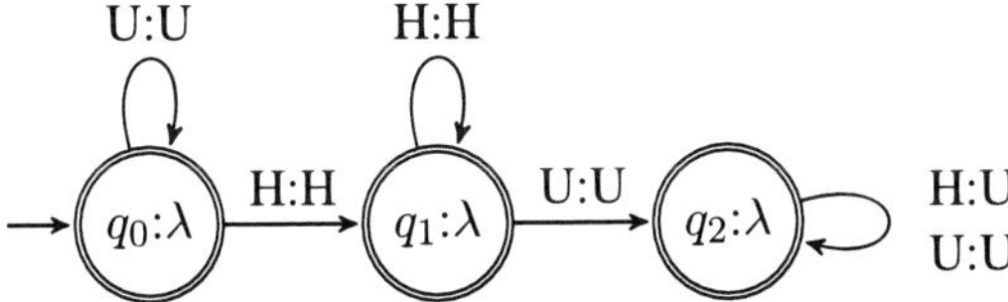

Figure 11: L-SFST for progressive lowering

As a restrictive characterization, the Serial Subsequential Hypothesis predicts that certain regular maps are not possible phonological transformations. For example, consider a variant of Saramaccan Creole, Saramaccan′, in which low tones do not act as blockers. In Saramaccan′, arbitrarily many low tones may intervene between a toneless TBU and the two triggering high tones, yielding maps such as $/HL^m UL^n H/ \mapsto [HL^m \underline{H}L^n H]$, where L indicates a low-toned TBU. This cannot be modeled by an iterated subsequential map, as there is no guarantee that a SFST will identify the second high tone trigger within a bounded distance from the target. Besides its larger alphabet, the non-deterministic FST for Saramaccan′ in Figure 12 is indistinguishable from that for UTP in Figure 6. Without considering the derivation, it is not clear how to predict the non-existence of Saramaccan′, or for that matter, any regular map in a principled way.

While the Serial Subsequential Hypothesis excludes some regular maps like Saramaccan′, it also overgenerates. Consider the phonological rule $\emptyset \rightarrow$ ab / a_b. Kaplan and Kay (1994) demonstrate that iteratively applying this rule $n \geq 1$ times to an input /ab/ produces the context-free string set $a^n b^n$. Such a derivation is within the scope of the Serial Subse-

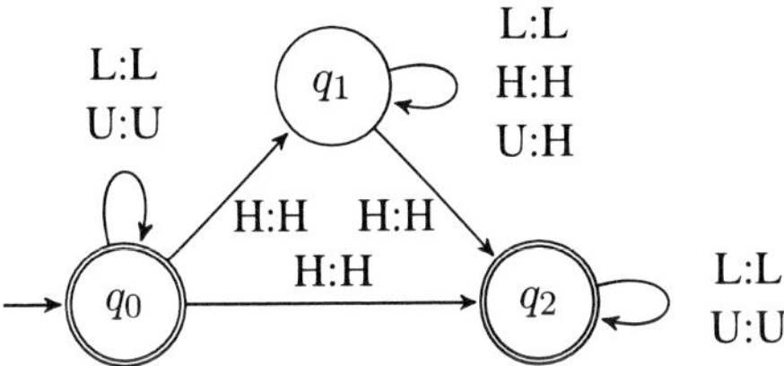

Figure 12: Non-deterministic FST for Saramaccan′

quential Hypothesis, because the rule can be computed subsequentially. The overgeneration caused by this particular rule stems from its ability to apply without motivation. Moreton (2004) argues that constraint-based frameworks like Optimality Theory, which limit processes to apply only if motivated by marked structures, avoid circular processes and infinite augmentation. In the case of inserting [ab] into the string, there is no clear improvement in these terms. Imposing restrictions of this sort from formal phonological analyses is a promising direction to take to characterize the class of serial SFSTs.

5 Conclusion

This paper argued that a phonologically uniform characterization of UR↦SF maps obtains under a serial model of phonology. Phonological transformations can be decomposed into iterated left- or right-subsequential maps, when computed in serial. Combined with restrictions already imposed on phonological computations, the Serial Subsequential Hypothesis was argued to make restrictive typological predictions. This demands a precise characterization of the class of maps produced by iterating subsequential maps, and is left to future work.

The result of this paper draws on the interaction between formal language theory and traditional phonology. The decision to examine whether UR↦SF maps are computed in parallel or serial is not arbitrary, but has been an important question in phonological research for decades. A formal language understanding of phonological transformations is enriched by an appreciation for the models that compute them. Likewise, the models should be restricted by a knowledge of the formal language landscape. The interface between these two disciplines can produce interesting generalizations and should continue to be probed.

Acknowledgments

This work has greatly benefited from discussions with Carolyn Anderson, Thomas Graf, Jeff Heinz, Adam Jardine, Gaja Jarosz, John McCarthy, Joe Pater, Brandon Prickett, Kristine Yu, participants in the Phonology Reading Group and Sound Workshop at the University of Massachusetts, Amherst, and the audience at NECPHON 11, as well as comments from three anonymous reviewers for SCiL 2018. This work was supported by the National Science Foundation through grant BCS-424077. All remaining errors are of course my own.

References

Sam Al Khatib. 2008. On the directionality of emphasis spread. In Susie Jones, editor, *Proceedings of the 2008 annual conference of the Canadian Linguistic Association*.

Stephen R. Anderson. 1974. *The Organization of Phonology*. Academic Press, New York.

Lee S. Bickmore and Nancy C. Kula. 2013. Ternary spreading and the OCP in Copperbelt Bemba. *Studies in African Linguistics*, 42:101–132.

Jane Chandlee and Jeffrey Heinz. 2012. Bounded copying is subsequential: Implications for metathesis and reduplication. In *Proceedings of SIGMORPHON 2012*, pages 42–51.

Jane Chandlee. 2014. *Strictly local phonological processes*. Ph.D. thesis, University of Delaware.

Noam Chomsky and Morris Halle. 1968. *The Sound Pattern of English*. Harper & Row, New York.

C. C. Elgot and J. E. Mezei. 1965. On relations defined by generalized finite automata. *IBM Journal of Research and Development*, 9:47–68.

Brian Gainor, Regine Lai, and Jeffrey Heinz. 2012. Computational characterizations of vowel harmony patterns and pathologies. In *Proceedings of the 29th West Coast Conference on Formal Linguistics*, pages 63–71.

Elsa Gomez-Imbert and Michael Kenstowicz. 2000. Barasana tone and accent. *International Journal of American Linguistics*, 66:419–463.

Elsa Gomez-Imbert. 2001. More on the tone versus pitch accent typology: Evidence from Barasana and other Eastern Tukanoan languages. In Shigeki Kaji, editor, *Proceedings of Symposium Cross-Linguistic Studies of Tonal Phenomena: Tonogenesis, Japanese Accentology, and Other Topics*, pages 369–412.

Jeff Good. 2004. Tone and accent in Saramaccan: charting a deep split in the phonology of a language. *Lingua*, 114:575–619.

Gunnar Ólafur Hansson. 2010. *Consonant Harmony: Long-Distance Interactions in Phonology*. University of California Press, Berkeley, CA.

Jeffrey Heinz and Regine Lai. 2013. Vowel harmony and subsequentiality. In *Proceedings of the 13th Meeting on the Mathematics of Language*, pages 52–63.

Jeffrey Heinz. forthcoming. The computational nature of phonological generalizations. In Larry Hyman and Frans Plank, editors, *Phonological Typology*. Mouton.

Irwin Howard. 1972. *A Directional Theory of Rule Application*. Ph.D. thesis, Massachusetts Institute of Technology.

Larry M. Hyman and Francis Katamba. 2010. Tone, syntax and prosodic domains in Luganda. *ZAS Papers in Linguistics*, 53:69–98.

Larry M. Hyman. 2010. Amazonia and the typology of tone systems. Technical report, UC Berkeley Phonology Lab Annual Reports.

Larry M. Hyman. 2011. Tone: Is it different? In John Goldsmith, Jason Riggle, and Alan C. L. Yu, editors, *The Handbook of Phonological Theory*, pages 197–239. Blackwell Publishing, Malden, MA, 2 edition.

Adam Jardine. 2016a. Computationally, tone is different. *Phonology*, 33:247–283.

Adam Jardine. 2016b. *Locality and Non-Linear Representations in Tonal Phonology*. Ph.D. thesis, University of Delaware.

Adam Jardine. 2017. The expressivity of autosegmental grammars. Unpublished manuscript.

C. Douglas Johnson. 1972. *Formal Aspects of Phonological Description*. Mouton, The Hague.

Ronald Kaplan and Martin Kay. 1994. Regular models of phonological rule systems. *Computational Linguistics*, 20:331–378.

Michael Kenstowicz and Charles Kisseberth. 1977. *Topics in Phonological Theory*. Academic Press, New York.

Charles W. Kisseberth and David Odden. 2003. Tone. In Derek Nurse and Gérald Philippson, editors, *The Bantu languages*, pages 59–70. Routledge, London.

Charles W. Kisseberth. 1984. Digo tonology. In George N. Clements and John Goldsmith, editors, *Autosegmental Studies in Bantu Tone*, pages 105–182. Foris Publications, Dordrecht.

Nancy C. Kula and Lee S. Bickmore. 2015. Phrasal phonology in Copperbelt Bemba. *Phonology*, 32:147–176.

Theodore M. Lightner. 1972. *Problems in the Theory of Phonology*. Linguistic Research, Inc., Edmonton.

M. Lothaire. 2013. *Applied Combinatorics on Words*. Cambridge University Press, Cambridge.

Huan Luo. 2017. Long-distance consonant agreement and subsequentiality. *Glossa*, 2(52).

John J. McCarthy. 2000. Harmonic serialism and parallelism. In Masako Hirotani, Andries Coetzee, Nancy Hall, and Ji-Yung Kim, editors, *Proceedings of the North East Linguistics Society 30*, pages 501–524. GLSA, Amherst, MA.

Adam McCollum, Eric Baković, Anna Mai, and Eric Meinhardt. 2017. Conditional blocking in Tutrugbu requires non-determinism: implications for the subregular hypothesis. Presentation at NELS 48.

John H. McWhorter and Jeff Good. 2012. *A Grammar of Saramaccan Creole*. De Gruyter Mouton, Berlin.

Alexis Michaud. 2017. *Tone in Yongning Na*. Language Science Press, Berlin.

Mehryar Mohri. 1997. Finite-state transducers in language and speech processing. *Computational Linguistics*, 23:269–311.

Elliott Moreton. 2004. Non-computable functions in Optimality Theory. In John J. McCarthy, editor, *Optimality Theory in Phonology: A Reader*, pages 141–163. Blackwell Publishing, Malden, MA.

Amanda Payne. 2014. Dissimilation as a subsequential process. In Jyoti Iyer and Leland Kusmer, editors, *NELS 44*, volume 2, pages 79–90.

Alan Prince and Paul Smolensky. 1993/2004. *Optimality Theory: Constraint Interaction in Generative Grammar*. Blackwell Publishing, Malden, MA.

Sharon Rose and Rachel Walker. 2011. Harmony systems. In John Goldsmith, Jason Riggle, and Alan C. L. Yu, editors, *The Handbook of Phonological Theory*, pages 240–290. Wiley-Blackwell, Malden, MA, 2 edition.

Moira Yip. 2002. *Tone*. Cambridge University Press, Cambridge.

Phonologically Informed Edit Distance Algorithms for Word Alignment with Low-Resource Languages

R. Thomas McCoy[*]
Department of Cognitive Science
Johns Hopkins University
tom.mccoy@jhu.edu

Robert Frank
Department of Linguistics
Yale University
robert.frank@yale.edu

Abstract

Edit distance is commonly used to relate cognates across languages. This technique is particularly relevant for the processing of low-resource languages because the sparse data from such a language can be significantly bolstered by connecting words in the low-resource language with cognates in a related, higher-resource language. We present three methods for weighting edit distance algorithms based on linguistic information. These methods base their penalties on (i) phonological features, (ii) distributional character embeddings, or (iii) differences between cognate words. We also introduce a novel method for evaluating edit distance through the task of low-resource word alignment by using edit-distance neighbors in a high-resource pivot language to inform alignments from the low-resource language. At this task, the cognate-based scheme outperforms our other methods and the Levenshtein edit distance baseline, showing that NLP applications can benefit from information about cross-linguistic phonological patterns.

1 Introduction

Many NLP techniques require large quantities of training data, which is a problem for low-resource languages (languages with little available data). Work on low-resource languages often focuses on tackling this low-data problem, such as by creating more data (Marton et al., 2009), collecting more data from the Internet (Mendels et al., 2015) or from

scholarly papers (Xia et al., 2016), efficiently eliciting informative data (Probst et al., 2002), or crowdsourcing the collection of corpora (Post et al., 2012). One promising approach is to supplement the available data for a low-resource language with data from higher-resource languages, an approach which has been applied to tasks ranging from speech recognition (Thomas et al., 2012) to machine translation (Dholakia and Sarkar, 2014).

An open problem within this approach is finding the best way to map information from one language to another. When connecting related languages, a natural place to start is with cognates, and many works use edit distance for cognate detection (Simard et al., 1993; Barker and Sutcliffe, 2000; Koehn and Knight, 2000; Mann and Yarowsky, 2001; Inkpen et al., 2005; Bergsma and Kondrak, 2007; Munro and Manning, 2012). Edit distance refers to the difference between two strings, and this paper explores several techniques for determining edit distance. Our baseline is the Levenshtein edit distance algorithm (Levenshtein, 1966; Wagner and Fischer, 1974), and we introduce three novel edit distance algorithms, namely feature-based edit distance, char2vec-based edit distance, and cognate-based edit distance, and assess their performance at transferring information across languages using the task of low-resource cognate identification. Finally, we introduce a novel method for evaluating edit distance algorithms through the task of word alignment.

2 Related work

Ristad and Yianilos (1998) first presented schemes for training weighted edit distances, and others such

---

[*]Work done while at Yale University.

Proceedings of the Society for Computation in Linguistics (SCiL) 2018, pages 102-112.
Salt Lake City, Utah, January 4-7, 2018

as Cotterell et al. (2014) have proposed modifications to this method. Weighted edit distance and other weighted schemes for computing string similarity such as point-wise mutual information have been used by several authors for cognate detection (Kondrak, 2001; Ciobanu and Dinu, 2014; Jäger and Sofroniev, 2016; Jäger et al., 2017).

This paper's novel contribution is to extend this technique to a low-resource setting. The prior work in edit-distance-based cognate detection has relied on phonetic transcriptions, information about word meaning, or hand-created lists of cognates on which to train a system. Here we investigate how to assign edit distance weights when no such information is available for one of the languages in question. Several prior systems have used word similarity to assess historical linguistic claims about language phylogeny (Kondrak, 2002; Jäger, 2013; List, 2013), but here we follow the inverse strategy of using knowledge about language phylogeny to inform the determination of string similarity by compensating for the lack of resources about a language with information from closely related and better-resourced languages. An additional novel contribution of this paper is to propose a new technique for assessing string similarity metrics based on how much a given metric can improve performance on a practical NLP task.

3 Edit distance algorithms

We use four basic approaches to calculating edit distance, detailed in the following subsections.

3.1 Levenshtein edit distance

As a baseline, we use Levenshtein edit distance (Levenshtein, 1966; Wagner and Fischer, 1974). Levenshtein edit distance focuses on three operations that can be performed on a string of characters:

1. **Insertion:** The insertion of a new character into the string.

2. **Deletion:** The deletion of a character already present in the string.

3. **Substitution:** The substitution of some new character for a character already in the string.

The Levenshtein edit distance between two words w_1 and w_2 is defined as the minimum number of insertions and/or deletions and/or substitutions that must be made to transform w_1 into w_2. Table 1 contains some examples of word pairs and the Levenshtein edit distance ($dist_L(w_1, w_2)$) between them.

3.2 Feature-based edit distance

This section details two approaches to edit distance in which the basic aim is to alter the Levenshtein penalties based on the phonological properties of the characters involved. The assumption underlying this method is that, when two cognates differ in some of the phonemes they contain, they are likely to differ in phonologically sensible ways. For example, it is more likely that one cognate will contain a d where its partner contains a t than it is for one cognate to contain a d where the other contains a u. If this assumption is true, an edit distance algorithm that encodes some phonological information may be more successful at identifying cognates than the basic Levenshtein algorithm. Indeed, Kondrak (2002) showed that the ALINE system, which computes string similarity based on a sophisticated set of phonological features, performed better at cognate identification than the basic Levenshtein method did; however, this success does not necessarily extend to our current situation because, due to our assumption that we are in a low-resource environment, we use only orthographic representations of words, not phonetic transcriptions.

3.2.1 Vowel/consonant approach

In this model, the penalty for substituting a vowel for a consonant, or for substituting a consonant for a vowel, is greater than that for substituting a vowel for a vowel or for substituting a consonant for a consonant. Specifically, this model works almost exactly like the basic Levenshtein—with a penalty of 1 for an insertion or a deletion or for a substitution that does not change a vowel to a consonant or vice versa—but the penalty for substituting a vowel for a consonant (or vice versa) is 2.

3.2.2 More features

For this model, we assign a set of phonological features to each character and make the penalty for any operation equal to the number of features that change when that operation occurs. For example, substituting a d for a t incurs a penalty of 1 because a

w_1	w_2	$dist_L(w_1, w_2)$	Operations performed
stephen king	stephen hawking	3	insert(h), insert(a), insert(w)
lemony snicket	jiminy cricket	5	sub(l, j), sub(e, i), sub(o, i), sub(s, c), sub(n, r)
jim carrey	john kerry	6	sub(i,o), insert(h), sub(m, n), sub(c, k), sub(a, e), del(e)

Table 1: Examples of Levenshtein edit distance.

single feature (namely, voicing) has changed, while substituting a b for a t incurs a penalty of 2 because two features (voicing and place) have changed. In practice, it is impossible to enact this approach rigorously because orthography does not map cleanly to phonology and does not have consistent phonological properties across languages. Therefore, many of the weights used for this method are by necessity somewhat arbitrary because the set of phonological features that we assign to each character does not necessarily match that character's true features in all contexts and across all languages.

3.3 Char2vec edit distance

The word2vec algorithm from Mikolov et al. (2013a) uses word distributions to train representations of words as vectors in high-dimensional vector space; such vector representations are called embeddings. Inspired by word2vec's success at creating semantically sensible embeddings for words, we apply the word2vec algorithm to characters in an attempt to create phonologically sensible embeddings for characters. We refer to this technique as *char2vec*. The char2vec algorithm begins by considering a window of a fixed size around every instance of character c in the training corpus (which, in this case, was the monolingual Portuguese data from the Europarl corpus; see Section 4 for more details). We tested windows of size 3 and 5. For word2vec, larger windows are typically used, but since there are far fewer characters than words, a smaller window size seemed sensible for the char2vec experiments because, unlike with word2vec, the cooccurrence vectors for char2vec are not at all sparse, so there is little need to look farther away from the target character to populate the cooccurrence vector.

Once the desired windows around different occurrences of c were established, a neural network was used to generate the vector embedding for c. The neural network used was a simple feed-forward network with an input layer and an output layer both having dimensionality equal to the number of characters in the character set, and with a single hidden layer of dimensionality 16. The network was then trained using either the continuous bag of words (CBOW) method or the skip-gram method, both described in Mikolov et al. (2013a). Once the network finished training, the trained weight matrix used to transition from the input layer to the hidden layer was used to generate the embeddings for all of the characters. Specifically, for the character at index i in the input vector, its embedding was row i of the weight matrix. An embedding was also created for the empty string ϵ by pretending that there was an ϵ between every two letters in the training data.

Once these embeddings were trained, the char2vec edit distance between any two characters was defined as one divided by the cosine distance between the embeddings for those two characters, which is given by the following equation:

$$(cosdist(c_1, c_2))^{-1} = \frac{||\vec{c_1}|| \, ||\vec{c_2}||}{\vec{c_1} \cdot \vec{c_2}} \qquad (1)$$

where $\vec{c_1}$ and $\vec{c_2}$ are the vector embeddings of c_1 and c_2. The negative exponent is there because the cosine is greater for more similar vectors, whereas we want a smaller penalty for more similar vectors. For insertions and deletions, the same equation is used, except that either c_1 (for insertions) or c_2 (for deletions) is ϵ because deleting a character can be thought of as replacing it with the empty string, and inserting a character can be thought of as replacing the empty string with that character.

These embedding-based edit distances are founded upon two assumptions: First, as with the feature-based edit distance methods in Section 3.2, these methods assume that, across a pair of cognates, it is more likely for one character to substitute for a character phonologically similar to it than for a character that is not very phonologically similar to it. Secondly, the embedding-based methods make the further assumption that the distribution of a character can give an accurate portrayal of the character's phonological nature. Distributional facts certainly can shed light on the phonological properties of a speech sound; for example, Peperkamp et al. (2006) created an algorithm that was highly effective at determining which sounds were allophones vs. distinct phonemes based on the distributions of those sounds. Despite this success, it is not necessarily the case that distributional evidence is useful for cognate determination, since identifying allophones within a language might entail significantly different types of evidence than identifying cognates across languages.

3.4   Cognate-based edit distance

The embedding-based methods in the previous section all derive their embeddings from a single training language (in this case Portuguese). We now try to utilize cross-linguistic information from three Romance languages, namely Portuguese, Italian, and French. The idea behind this approach is to identify cognates amongst Portuguese, Italian, and French and to use those cognates to determine which phonological differences are likely to be present in Romance cognate pairs and which are not and to apply this information to the test language of Spanish (which is not used as a training language).

The following criteria were used to generate training examples for this experiment; positive examples were identified by finding any pairs (w_1, w_2) that satisfied criteria (1), (2), (3), and (4a), while negative examples were identified by finding any pairs (w_1, w_2) that satisfied criteria (1), (2), (3), and (4b):

1. w_1 and w_2 are from different languages.

2. The Levenshtein edit distance between w_1 and w_2 is greater than 0 but less than some specified amount d.

3. Both w_1 and w_2 are at least 4 characters long.

4. (a) The most likely English translation of w_1 is the same as the most likely English translation of w_2.

   (b) The cosine similarity between the GloVe embeddings (Pennington et al., 2014) of the most likely English translation of w_1 and w_2 is less than 0.5.

For criterion (1), the languages considered were Portuguese, French, and Italian, which are all of the Romance languages (besides the test language of Spanish) considered in this paper. For criterion (2), we ran the experiments both with $d = 1$ and with $d = 2$. Criterion (3) is included because a low Levenshtein edit distance does not mean much for very short words—for example, any two two-letter words will have an edit distance of at most 2, but this by no means implies that all two-letter words are cognates of each other. For criterion (4), the most likely English translation of a word is identified based on the IBM Model 1 (Brown et al., 1993) translation probabilities generated by running the mgiza word alignment program (Gao and Vogel, 2008) on the bilingual Portuguese/English, French/English, and Italian/English training sets. Finally, for criterion (4b), we used the GloVe embeddings from Pennington et al. (2014) as a metric for determining semantic similarity; words with a cosine similarity less than 0.5 tend not to be very semantically similar, so this criterion is intended to ensure that the negative examples are not cognates despite being phonologically similar, while criterion (4a) is meant to find positive examples by identifying words that appear phonologically similar and have similar meanings.

When d from criterion (2) was specified to be 1, this criteria generated 8,718 positive examples and 25,440 negative examples, while having $d = 2$ generated 27,744 positive examples and 448,746 negative examples. We restricted the number of negative examples to be equal to the number of positive examples in each case, so that there ended up being both 8,718 positive examples and 8,718 negative examples when $d = 1$ and 27,744 positive examples and 27,744 negative examples when $d = 2$. Table 2 shows some of the positive and negative example pairs generated when $d = 1$.

These examples were used to train weights for each possible operation of insertion, deletion, or substitution. There are 27 characters for which to learn weights (the 26 letter plus an OTHER character[1]); thus there are $\binom{27}{2}$ possible substitutions that can be made. Because it makes sense for these edit distances to be symmetrical, it was deemed that the

---

[1] A character with a diacritic is represented as 2 characters, the base character plus a diacritic character that is collapsed into the OTHER category.

Word 1	Word 2	Word 1	Word 2
afgane (It.)	afghane (Fr.)	colmando (It.)	comando (Port.)
"afghan"	"afghan"	"closing"	"command"
stupide (Fr.)	stupido (It.)	eternamente (It.)	externamente (Port.)
"stupid"	"stupid"	"eternally"	"externally"
serviu (Port.)	servi (Fr.)	monge (Port.)	ronge (Fr.)
"served"	"served"	"monk"	"plaguing"
discriminata (It.)	discriminada (Port.)	paute (Port.)	faute (Fr.)
"against"	"against"	"transparent"	"fault"
finali (It.)	finale (Fr.)	mentis (It.)	mentir (Fr.)
"final"	"final"	"mindset"	"lie"

Table 2: Some of the examples used for training the cognate-based edit distance. The table on the left shows positive examples (pairs deemed to be cognates), while the table on the right shows negative examples (pairs deemed not to be cognates).

penalty for inserting a character should be the same as the penalty for deleting that character, so there were also 27 possible insertion/deletion operations. Thus, there are a total of $\binom{27}{2} + 27 = 378$ operations for which to learn weights. We used logistic regression to find the weights that performed best at classifying the training items as cognates or non-cognates.

The success of this approach depends on the assumption that the types of sound changes that occur between some pairs of languages within a language family are similar to the types of sound changes that occur between other pairs of languages in that language family. This assumption is not necessarily true; a language pair could easily have some systematic sound changes between its members that are not represented in any other language pairs. However, perhaps it is the case that there will be some broader trends that cut across many members of a family.

4 Experimental setups

For all experiments, Spanish is treated as if it is a low-resource language for which we wish to gain information based on its high-resource relatives of Portuguese, Italian, and French. Although Spanish is a very high-resource language in real life, for these experiments we simulate low-resourcedness by not providing the computer with any Spanish training data; thus, the test data is the computer's only exposure to Spanish. We chose this path rather than using a truly low-resource language because it is much easier to create gold standards for evaluation for a high-resource language. As in real life, Portuguese, Italian, and French are treated as high-resource (that

is, there is ample training data for these languages), as is English, which is used in the word alignment experiments. Thus, the char2vec embeddings are trained on Portuguese data, and the cognate-based edit distances are trained on Portuguese, French, and Italian data. All experiments used the Europarl parallel corpus (Koehn, 2005) as sources of text in the languages of interest. This corpus comes from the proceedings of the European Parliament, a governing body of the European Union.

4.1 Cognate identification

Cognate identification was used as a direct method of testing how well each edit distance algorithm performed. To do this, a set of pairs of likely Spanish/Portuguese cognates was formed in the same way as the likely cognates were chosen for the cognate-based embeddings (see Section 3.4). Call such a Spanish/Portuguese pair (s, p). For each such pair, each edit distance algorithm was used to identify the Portuguese word $p_{closest}$ with the smallest edit distance from s (with ties being broken randomly). It was then checked whether $p = p_{closest}$. A total of 12,198 cognate pairs were tested in this manner for each edit distance algorithm.

4.2 Word alignment

4.2.1 Background

Though cognate identification is the most direct method for evaluating each edit distance algorithm, it has several flaws. First, it requires the selection of exactly one Portuguese word as the cognate for a given Spanish word, when in reality there may be many valid Portuguese choices (such as other inflected forms of the intended Portuguese word). More generally, cognacy only really makes sense at the lemma level, but the low-resource setting of our task means that we do not have access to lemmatization and must use words instead of lemmas, making the cognate detection task ill-defined in this context. In addition, the fact that the method of selecting cognates so closely mirrors the steps for training cognate-based edit distance may unfairly advantage the cognate-based edit distance algorithm[2]. Therefore, as a fairer and more definitely quantifiable assessment, we use the task of word alignment.

Word alignment is the task of, given two sentences that are translations of each other, determining which words correspond to each other semantically across the two languages. Word alignment is an important step in many machine translation systems, such as the popular Moses software system (Koehn et al., 2007), and effective word alignment depends heavily upon the size of the alignment algorithm's training corpus. Therefore, success at word alignment (and, by extension, machine translation programs based on word alignment) suffers greatly under a data shortage. Cognate information can be used to combat this data shortage because, if a low-resource language is related to a high-resource language, educated guesses about the meanings of words in the low-resource language may be formed based on similar-looking words in the high-resource language. Presumably, an edit distance algorithm that more accurately identifies cognates will perform better at this sort of pivoting than an edit distance algorithm that does not perform as well at cognate identification. Multiple authors in the past have worked on exploiting language relatedness to assist in machine translation (Mikolov et al., 2013b; Zoph et al., 2016; Cheng et al., 2016), including via a focus on using this information to improve word alignment performance (Xiang et al., 2010).

4.2.2 Pivot-based alignment algorithm

All word alignment experiments aim to align Spanish sentences with their English translations, with no Spanish-English training data available. Instead, a bilingual Portuguese-English training set of 1 million lowercased and tokenized sentences from the Europarl corpus is used to train Portuguese-English translation probabilities of the form $t(e|p)$, where $t(e|p)$ is the probability that a given Portuguese word p will be translated as the English word e. The training of these translation probabilities was accomplished using mgiza (Gao and Vogel, 2008), which is an implementation of the IBM models of word alignment (Brown et al., 1993). The test set for the word alignment experiments is a set of 1,000 lowercased and tokenized parallel Spanish/English sentences from the Europarl corpus. The test set also contains a gold standard set of alignments from the NAACL 2006 shared task on statistical machine translation, available at http://www.statmt.org/wmt06/shared-task/. These gold standard alignments were generated using automatic methods (the exact methods are not stated), so they can be expected to contain some errors, but for the purposes of low-resource NLP these errors are expected to be negligible.

In order to pivot from Portuguese (the pivot language used for training) to Spanish (the low-resource language used for testing), we define the translation score[3] $t(e|s)$ between English word e and Spanish word s as

$$t(e|s) = \arg\max_{p \in P} \frac{t(c|p)}{ed(s, p) + \lambda n} \qquad (2)$$

where P is the set of all Portuguese words, $ed(s, p)$ is the edit distance between s and p, and λn is the product of a smoothing factor λ and the number of edit operations n, where λ was optimized for each edit distance algorithm to scale the relative importance of t and ed. This definition encodes our assumption that similar-looking Spanish and Portuguese words (i.e., Spanish and Portuguese words with low edit distances) will have similar meanings.

The Spanish and English sentences are then aligned based solely on this translation score (as in IBM Model 1), without reference to any of the properties such as distortion or fertility used in higher IBM models. The choice to only use translation

---

[2]An anonymous reviewer notes that this second problem could be overcome by testing on human-generated cognate lists, which would be a useful metric to compute in future work. However, the other problem with the cognate task remains.

[3]We call it a score rather than a probability because we do not normalize, so the scores do not sum to 1.

probability was made for simplicity; since the focus of these experiments is on edit distance algorithms, not on alignment algorithms, it was simplest to use the most basic alignment algorithm.

In the typical instantiation of IBM Model 1, the choice of which target word to align with source word a is made by iterating through all words in the target sentence and finding which has the greatest translation probability for a. This pivot-based formalism adds another step: Now, for each Spanish word s, the choice of which word to align with is made by iterating through all of s's closest Portuguese edit distance neighbors, and for each of those iterating through all words in the English sentence, to find which pair of a Portuguese neighbor and an English word yields the highest translation probability, and then aligning with that English word. Because IBM Model 1 treats all word alignments as independent, the probability of a set **a** of word alignments that align English sentence **e** and Spanish sentence **s** can be maximized simply by maximizing the probabilities of each individual alignment between a Spanish word s and some English word e—that is, by aligning each Spanish word s with the English word e that maximizes $t(e|s)$.

5 Evaluation

An advantage of the word alignment task is that we can straightforwardly quantify the results via the Alignment Error Rate (AER), defined as

$$\text{AER} = 1 - \frac{2P}{p + c} \tag{3}$$

where P is the number of predicted alignments that are correct, c is the number of alignments in the gold standard, and p is the number of predicted alignments (where an alignment is defined as a connection between one Spanish word and one English word). AER falls within the range of 0 to 1, where it is best to be as close to 0 as possible.

6 Results and discussion

6.1 Cognate identification

The results at the cognate identification task are reported in Table 3. The cognate-based results are reported with $d = 2$, where d is the maximum edit distance between French/Italian, French/Portuguese,

Algorithm	Accuracy
Levenshtein	0.314
Vowel-Consonant	0.316
More Features	0.320
Char2vec	0.312
Cognate	**0.330**

Table 3: Results on cognate identification.

and Italian/Portuguese cognate pairs used to train the weights for edit distance operations, since $d = 2$ performed better than $d = 1$. This is likely because increasing the maximum edit distance between cognate pairs creates more pairs for the training set.

6.2 Word alignment

Table 4 shows the results at the word alignment task. The first set of methods are included as baselines. Random refers to randomly aligning each Spanish word with one English word, while Diagonal refers to aligning the ith Spanish word with the ith English word for all i less than the minimum of the two sentences' lengths, so these two methods show how well an extremely naive model can perform. Meanwhile, fast-align is a state-of-the-art word alignment program from the cdec package (Dyer et al., 2010) and was trained directly on the Spanish-English section of Europarl; thus, its performance is indicative of the best performance that can reasonably be expected on this task in a high-resource setting.

The second part of the table compares the various edit distance algorithms. To scale each algorithm's set of penalties to a reasonable range of penalty ratios, all algorithms were tested with each smoothing factor λ in the set [0.01, 1, 5, 10, 50, 100], where the smoothing factor in question was added to each penalty used in the calculation of a word pair's overall edit distance. Results are reported with the best-performing smoothing factor for each algorithm.

The char2vec algorithm was tested both using the CBOW and the skip-gram methods from Mikolov et al. (2013a) as well as with window sizes of 3 and 5 (i.e., 1 character on either side of the target word and 2 characters on either side of the target word). CBOW and skip-gram performed comparably; because CBOW performed slightly better, results are reported with it. The window size of 3 performed significantly better than a window size of 5, so re-

Edit distance algorithm	λ	Alignment model	Pivot langauge	AER
-	-	Random	-	0.948
-	-	Diagonal	-	0.819
-	-	fast-align	-	0.288
Levenshtein	0.01	IBM M1	Portuguese	0.673
VC	100	IBM M1	Portuguese	0.670
More features	100	IBM M1	Portuguese	0.674
Char2vec	10	IBM M1	Portuguese	0.672
Cognate	1	IBM M1	Portuguese	**0.663**
Cognate	1	IBM M1	Portuguese	0.554
Cognate	1	HMM	Portuguese	0.504
Cognate	1	IBM M3	Portuguese	0.548
Cognate	1	IBM M4	Portuguese	**0.448**
Levenshtein	0.01	IBM M4	Spanish	0.360
Levenshtein	0.01	IBM M4	Portuguese	0.500
Levenshtein	0.01	IBM M4	Italian	0.571
Levenshtein	0.01	IBM M4	French	0.613
Levenshtein	0.01	IBM M4	German	0.722
Levenshtein	0.01	IBM M4	Danish	0.732
Levenshtein	0.01	IBM M4	Finnish	0.776

Table 4: Smoothed word alignment results for various experimental settings.

sults are reported with this window size. This difference is likely because there are so few characters in the alphabet that considering characters in a wider window ceases to uniquely characterize a given character, since pretty much any character can easily occur two letters away from pretty much any other character. For the cognate-based edit distance, as in Section 6.1, results are reported with $d = 2$.

Part 2 of this table only uses IBM Model 1. To see whether more advanced models can improve performance, the third section of Table 4 uses basic implementations of the higher IBM models from Brown et al. (1993) and the HMM model from Vogel et al. (1996). For each of these models, the parameters from training on Portuguese-English alignment were transferred directly to the Spanish-English case. Note that, in this section, IBM M1 really refers to using the IBM Model 1 algorithm with translation probabilities trained using IBM Model 4; this is why the IBM Model 1 performs better in part 3 of the table than in part 2, because part 2 only uses translation probabilities trained with IBM Model 1.

Finally, the fourth part of Table 4 shows results with various pivot languages that vary in their level of relatedness to Spanish. Spanish itself is included in this section as a baseline for the best possible performance under the pivot-based framework.

6.3 Discussion

For word alignment, feature-based edit distance did not beat the Levenshtein baseline, while the vowel-consonant based edit distance led to a modest improvement. These results may arise from the fact that the only edit distance neighbors being considered are the words that actually occur in the Portuguese corpus, which means that creating a more phonologically-informed model might not do much good because all candidates are already phonologically well-formed. For example, the feature-based edit distance algorithm would strongly indicate that *blanco* and *branco* are more likely to be cognates than *blanco* and *bkanco*; but there is no real need to make this distinction since no word like *bkanco* will occur in the Portuguese corpus anyway.

The char2vec method also led to modest improvements; its performance may have been hindered by its assumption that distributional similarity implies phonological similarity, when in fact there are some reasons to suppose the contrary. For example, a language might have voicing assimilation of all consonants in a cluster. This would mean that [t] and [d] would never appear next to the same consonants as each other and would thus have quite different distributions, despite only differing in voicing.

Cognate-based edit distance had the strongest performance. Since it was only trained on cognate pairs using Romance languages other than Spanish, while it was tested on Spanish words, this result justifies our assumption that facts about the phonological relatedness of Spanish's relatives can also be used to learn useful information about Spanish. The cognate identification task corroborates the word alignment results in indicating that cognate-based edit distance is the best-performing algorithm for bootstrapping information from a high-resource language to one of its low-resource relatives.

The second part of Table 4 shows that three more linguistically informed algorithms presented here (particularly cognate-based edit distance) outperform the less-informed basic Levenshtein algorithm. These results broadly suggest that incorporating linguistic information can be of significant benefit to NLP applications with low-resource languages, since it was helpful here to utilize information about the phonological relatedness between languages rather than using the flat distribution of the basic Levenshtein algorithm. Though the alignment results in the second part of Table 4 are not impressive at an absolute level, the results in the third part of the table show that alignment performance can be significantly improved by preserving the same pivot-based setup but using more advanced alignment algorithms, so there is hope that refining the alignment algorithms more could further improve performance. Finally, the bottom segment of Table 4 shows that alignment performance generally improves as the pivot language becomes more closely related to Spanish, corroborating the claim that it is language relatedness that fuels the success of the pivot-based alignment method. (Figure 1 shows a family tree of the pivot languages used.)

7   Conclusions and future work

We have presented three new techniques for computing edit distance. All of these make use of more linguistic information (specifically, cross-linguistic phonological information) than the baseline of Lev-

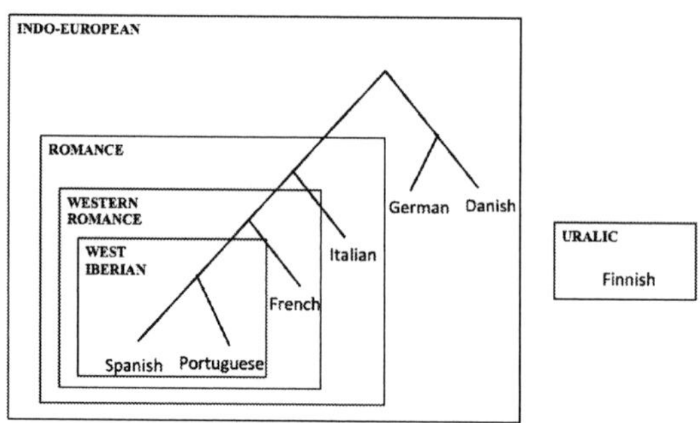

Figure 1: Family tree of the pivot languages used; language groups were derived from Ethnologue (Lewis et al., 2009).

enshtein edit distance, and all of them perform at least as well as Levenshtein edit distance at low-resource cognate identification and word alignment. In particular, cognate-based edit distance brings the greatest performance improvements in these tasks compared to Levenshtein edit distance. This work focuses on the IBM alignment models, so future work could explore more advanced algorithms relating to word alignment and machine translation, such as neural machine translation (Collobert and Weston, 2008; Cho et al., 2014; Bahdanau et al., 2015), or phrase-based machine translation (Koehn et al., 2003; Och and Ney, 2004) to bring alignment performance improvement. In addition, the edit distance algorithms could be refined to encode more phonological information. For example, separate penalties could be assigned based on the environment in which changes occur since environment is highly significant in phonological changes both within and across languages. Another refinement specific to the cognate-based algorithm would be training on a list of likely cognates to choose weights and then using those weights to choose an updated list of likely cognates, and iterating this process until the weights converge; the algorithm as presented here only represents one iteration of such a process, but further iterations might yield better weights.

Acknowledgments

We would like to thank the anonymous reviewers and the members of Yale's 2017 Senior Essay in Linguistics class for their helpful suggestions on this work. Any errors remain our own.

References

Dzmitry Bahdanau, KyungHyun Cho, and Yoshua Bengio. 2015. Neural machine translation by jointly learning to align and translate. *International Conference on Learning Representations (ICLR 2015)*.

Gosia Barker and Richard FE Sutcliffe. 2000. An experiment in the semi-automatic identification of false-cognates between english and polish. *Proceedings of the Irish Conference on Artificial Intelligence and Cognitive Science*.

Shane Bergsma and Grzegorz Kondrak. 2007. Alignment-based discriminative string similarity. *Annual meeting-Association for Computational Linguistics*, 45.

Peter F. Brown, Vincent J. Della Pietra, Stephen A. Della Pietra, and Robert L. Mercer. 1993. The mathematics of statistical machine translation: Parameter estimation. *Computational Linguistics*, 19:263–311.

Yong Cheng, Yang Liu, Qian Yang, Maosong Sun, and Wei Xu. 2016. Neural machine translation with pivot languages. *arXiv preprint arXiv:1604.02201*.

KyungHyun Cho, Bart van Merriënboer, Dzmitry Bahdanau, and Yoshua Bengio. 2014. On the properties of neural machine translation: Encoder-decoder approaches. *International Conference on Learning Representations (ICLR 2013)*.

Alina Maria Ciobanu and Liviu P. Dinu. 2014. Automatic detection of cognates using orthographic alignment. *Proceedings of the 52nd Annual Meeting of the Association for Computational Linguistics, volume 2: Short Papers, ACL 2014,*, pages 99–105.

Ronan Collobert and Jason Weston. 2008. A unified architecture for natural language processing: Deep neural networks with multitask learning. *Proceedings of the 25th International Conference on Machine Learning (ICML 2008)*.

Ryan Cotterell, Nanyun Peng, and Jason Eisner. 2014. Stochastic contextual edit distance and probabilistic fsts. *Proceedings of the 52nd Annual Meeting of the Association for Computational Linguistics, volume 2: Short Papers, ACL 2014,*, pages 625–630.

Rohit Dholakia and Anoop Sarkar. 2014. Pivot-based triangulation for low-resource languages. *Proc. AMTA*.

Chris Dyer, Jonathan Weese, Hendra Setiawan, Adam Lopez, Ferhan Ture, Vladimir Eidelman, Juri Ganitkevitch, Phil Blunsom, and Philip Resnik. 2010. cdec: A decoder, alignment, and learning framework for finite-state and context-free translation models. *Proceedings of the ACL 2010 System Demonstrations*.

Qin Gao and Stephan Vogel. 2008. Parallel implementations of word alignment tool. *Software engineering, testing, and quality assurance for natural language processing*, 5:49–57.

Diana Inkpen, Oana Frunza, and Grzegorz Kondrak. 2005. Automatic identification of cognates and false friends in french and english. *Proceedings of the International Conference Recent Advances in Natural Language Processing*, 9.

Gerhard Jäger and Pavel Sofroniev. 2016. Automatic cognate classification with a support vector machine. *Proceedings of the 13th Conference on Natural Language Processing*, 16:128–134.

Gerhard Jäger, Johann-Mattis List, and Pavel Sofroniev. 2017. Using support vector machines and state-of-the-art algorithms for phonetic alignment to identify cognates in multi-lingual wordlists. *Proceedings of the 15th Conference of the European Chapter of the Association for Computational Linguistics: Volume 1, Long Papers*, pages 1204–1215.

Gerhard Jäger. 2013. Phylogenetic inference from word lists using weighted alignment with empirically determined weights. *Language Dynamics and Change 3*, 2:245–291.

Philipp Koehn and Kevin Knight. 2000. Estimating word translation probabilities from unrelated monolingual corpora using the em algorithm. *AAAI/IAAI*.

Philipp Koehn, Franz Josef Och, and Daniel Marcu. 2003. Statistical phrase-based translation. *Proceedings of the 2003 Conference of the North American Chapter of the Association for Computational Linguistics on Human Language Technology*, 1:48–54.

Philipp Koehn, Hieu Hoang, Alexandra Birch, Chris Callison-Burch, Marcello Federico, Nicola Bertoldi, Brooke Cowan, Wade Shen, Christine Moran, Richard Zens, Chris Dyer, Ondrej Bojar, Alexandra Constantin, and Evan Herbst. 2007. Moses open source toolkit for statistical machine translation. *Proceedings of the 45th annual meeting of the ACL on interactive poster and demonstration sessions)*, pages 177–180.

Philipp Koehn. 2005. Europarl: A parallel corpus for statistical machine translation. *MT Summit*, 5:79–86.

Grzegorz Kondrak. 2001. Identifying cognates by phonetic and semantic similarity. *Proceedings of the Second Meeting of the North American Chapter of the Association for Computational Linguistics on Language Technologies*, pages 1–8.

Grzegorz Kondrak. 2002. *Algorithms for language reconstruction*. Ph.D. thesis, University of Toronto.

Vladimir I. Levenshtein. 1966. Binary codes capable of correcting deletions, insertions, and reversals. *Soviet Physics Doklady*, 10(8):707–710.

M. Paul Lewis, Gary F. Simons, and Charles D. Fennig. 2009. *Ethnologue: Languages of the world*, volume 16. SIL International, Dallas, TX.

Johann-Mattis List. 2013. *Sequence comparison in historical linguistics*. Ph.D. thesis, Heinrich-Heine-Universität Düsseldorf.

Gideon S. Mann and David Yarowsky. 2001. Multipath translation lexicon induction via bridge languages. *Proceedings of the second meeting of the North American Chapter of the Association for Computational Linguistics on Language technologies.*

Yuval Marton, Chris Callison-Burch, and Philip Resnik. 2009. Improved statistical machine translation using monolingually-derived paraphrases. *Proceedings of the 2009 Conference on Empirical Methods in Natural Language Processing*, 1.

Gideon Mendels, Erica Cooper, Victor Soto, Julia Hirschberg, Mark JF Gales, Kate M. Knill, Anton Ragni, and Haipeng Wang. 2015. Improving speech recognition and keyword search for low resource languages using web data. *Sixteenth Annual Conference of the International Speech Communication Association.*

Tomas Mikolov, Kai Chen, Greg Corrado, and Jeffrey Dean. 2013a. Efficient estimation of word representations in vector space. *International Conference on Learning Representations (ICLR 2013).*

Tomas Mikolov, Quoc V. Le, and Ilya Sutskever. 2013b. Exploiting similarities among languages for machine translation. *arXiv preprint arXiv:1309.4168.*

Robert Munro and Christopher D. Manning. 2012. Accurate unsupervised joint named-entity extraction from unaligned parallel text. *Proceedings of the 4th Named Entity Workshop.*

Franz Josef Och and Hermann Ney. 2004. The alignment template approach to statistical machine translation. *Computational Linguistics*, 30.4:417–449.

Jeffrey Pennington, Richard Socher, and Christopher D. Manning. 2014. GloVe: Global vectors for word representation.

Sharon Peperkamp, Rozenn Le Calvez, Jean-Pierre Nadal, and Emmanuel Dupoux. 2006. The acquisition of allophonic rules: Statistical learning with linguistic constraints. *Cognition*, 101.3:B31–B41.

Matt Post, Chris Callison-Burch, and Miles Osborne. 2012. Constructing parallel corpora for six indian languages via crowdsourcing. *Proceedings of the Seventh Workshop on Statistical Machine Translation.*

Katharina Probst, Jaime Carbonell, and Lori Levin. 2002. Semi-automatic learning of transfer rules for machine translation of low-density languages. *Proceedings of the Student Session at the 14th European Summer School in Logic, Language and Information (ESSLLI-02).*

Eric Sven Ristad and Peter N. Yianilos. 1998. Learning string-edit distance. *IEEE Transactions on Pattern Analysis and Machine Intelligence 20*, 5:522–532.

Michel Simard, George F. Foster, and Pierre Isabelle. 1993. Using cognates to align sentences in bilingual corpora. *Proceedings of the 1993 conference of the Centre for Advanced Studies on Collaborative research: distributed computing*, 2.

Samuel Thomas, Sriram Ganapathy, and Hynek Hermansky. 2012. Multilingual mlp features for low-resource lvcsr systems. *2012 IEEE International Conference on Acoustics, Speech and Signal Processing (ICASSP).*

Stephan Vogel, Hermann Ney, and Christoph Tillmann. 1996. Hmm-based word alignment in statistical translation. *Proceedings of the 16th conference on computational linguistics*, 2:836–841.

Robert Wagner and Michael J. Fischer. 1974. The string to string correction problem. *Journal of the ACM (JACM)*, 21.1:168–173.

Fei Xia, William D. Lewis, Michael Wayne Goodman, Glenn Slayden, Ryan Georgi, Joshua Crowgey, , and Emily M. Bender. 2016. Enriching a massively multilingual database of interlinear glossed text. *Language Resources and Evaluation*, 50:321–349.

Bing Xiang, Yonggang Deng, and Bowen Zhou. 2010. Diversify and combine: Improving word alignment for machine translation on low-resource languages. *Proceedings of the ACL 2010 Conference Short Papers.*

Barret Zoph, Deniz Yuret, Jonathan May, and Kevin Knight. 2016. Transfer learning for low-resource neural machine translation. *arXiv preprint arXiv:1604.02201.*

Conditions on abruptness in a gradient-ascent Maximum Entropy learner[*]

Elliott Moreton
University of North Carolina, Chapel Hill
moreton@unc.edu

Abstract

When does a gradual learning *rule* translate into gradual learning *performance*? This paper studies a gradient-ascent Maximum Entropy phonotactic learner, as applied to two-alternative forced-choice performance expressed as log-odds. The main result is that slow initial performance cannot accelerate later if the initial weights are near zero, but can if they are not. Stated another way, abruptness in this learner is an effect of transfer, either from Universal Grammar in the form of an initial weighting, or from previous learning in the form of an acquired weighting.

1 Introduction

An important class of constraint-based phonological learning models responds to training by making small changes in the weight or rank of constraints (reviewed in Jarosz 2016). The gradualness of the learning rule seems to suggest that performance ought to change gradually as well, resembling the first rather than the second panel in Figure 1. In work on non-linguistic pattern learning, abrupt improvement has been cited as diagnostic of an explicit, "rule-based" learning algorithm which serially tests hypotheses, as opposed to a "cue-based" one which slowly learns association weights (Ashby et al., 1998; Love, 2002; Maddox and Ashby, 2004; Smith et al., 2012; Kurtz et al., 2013). Abruptness

---

[*]The author is indebted to Jen Smith, Joe Pater, Katya Pertsova, and Chris Wiesen for comments and suggestions. Any errors are of the author's own making. The research was supported in part by NSF BCS 1651105, "Inside phonological learning", to E. Moreton and K. Pertsova.

has been found to correlate with other indicia of explicitness by humans learning artificial phonology (Moreton and Pertsova, 2016).

In fact, performance can change abruptly in gradual learners (Elman et al. 1996, Ch. 3–4; GLA examples in Boersma 1998, Figure 14.25; Boersma and Levelt 2000; Jesney 2016). When does a gradual learning rule entail gradual learning performance? Could the model spend many trials invisibly inching its way around to some point in weight space from which it can suddenly accelerate? Conversely, if we observe abrupt improvement in human learners, does that disconfirm the model?

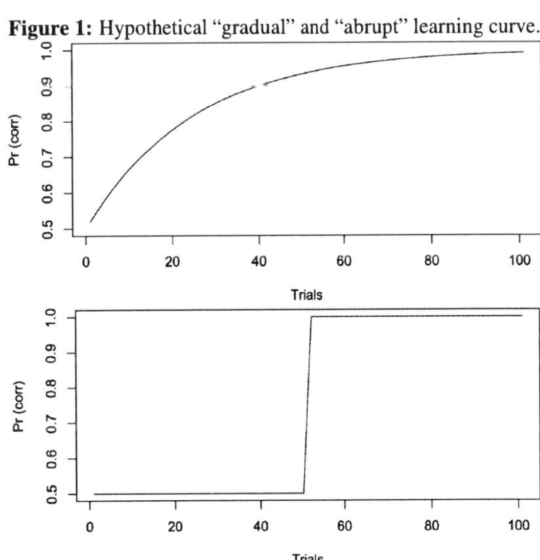

Figure 1: Hypothetical "gradual" and "abrupt" learning curve.

This paper addresses the question in a particularly basic case, that of a Maximum Entropy phonotactic learner with a fixed constraint set that uses gradient ascent on log-likelihood, no prior, and no restrictions on weights, and that makes two-alternative forced-choice (2AFC) decisions using the Luce choice rule. Gradient ascent Max-Ent is of interest not only in its own right, but because of its close relation to the Gradual Learning Algorithms for Stochastic Optimality Theory, Harmonic Grammar and Noisy Harmonic Grammar, and models of non-linguistic learning such as the Perceptron (Boersma and Hayes, 2001; Fischer, 2005; Jäger, 2007; Johnson, 2007; Pater, 2008; Pater and Moreton, 2012; Boersma and Pater, 2016; Moreton et al., 2017).

The results can be summarized as follows: Regardless of what the constraints actually are, if the initial weights are exactly zero then — provided that the training and test distributions are chosen in a particular way — 2AFC performance improves fastest at the outset of learning, making abrupt learning impossible. Even if, instead, the initial weights are only *near* zero, the 2AFC learning curve tracks that of a learner whose initial weights are *exactly* zero, in that the two learners' trajectories in weight space steadily converge, and the closer they are in weight space, the more similar their 2AFC performance is. An example is given to show that large *non*-zero initial weights can, but need not, lead to abrupt 2AFC performance.

2 Learner and experimental scenario

The universe of candidates is a finite set $X = \{x_1, \ldots, x_n\}$, known to the experimenter. The model uses an unobservable set of constraints $c_1, \ldots, c_m$ and an unobservable weight vector $\mathbf{w} = (w_1, \ldots, w_m)$ to assign unobservable probabilities $\mathbf{p} = (p_1, \ldots, p_n)$ to the candidate. This is done as follows (Goldwater and Johnson, 2003; Jäger, 2007; Hayes and Wilson, 2008):

The *harmony* of a candidate x_j is defined as the sum of its score vector, weighted by the current weights:

$$h_{\mathbf{w}}(x_j) = \sum_{i=1}^{m} w_i c_i(x_j) \qquad (1)$$

The model's estimate of the probability p_j of candidate x_j is the exponential of its harmony, divided by the summed exponentials of the harmonies of all representations:

$$Z_{\mathbf{w}} = \sum_{j=1}^{n} \exp h_{\mathbf{w}}(x_j) \qquad (2)$$

$$\Pr(X = x_j \mid \mathbf{w}) = \frac{\exp h_{\mathbf{w}}(x_j)}{Z_{\mathbf{w}}} \qquad (3)$$

The experimenter can at any time give the model a two-alternative forced-choice *test*, in which two candidates x_i and x_j are presented to the model, which chooses x_i with probability

$$\Pr(x_i|(x_i, x_j)) = \frac{p_i}{p_i + p_j} \qquad (4)$$

This is the Luce choice rule (Luce, 1959, 23). The test is assumed not to change the state of the model. At the beginning of the experiment, the experimenter chooses two probability distributions $\mathbf{r}^+$ and $\mathbf{r}^-$. On each test trial, one candidate is sampled from X with probabilities given by $\mathbf{r}^+$, and the other is sampled from X with probabilities given by $\mathbf{r}^-$.

The experimenter can also *train* the model by giving it a candidate x_i as an example of a legal word. Instead of training on individual candidates (stochastic gradient ascent), we instead run the learner in batch mode (gradient ascent); i.e., instead of a candidate on each trial, the learner receives a distribution $\mathbf{p}^+$, where p_i^+ corresponds to the probability of presenting x_i on a stochastic gradient ascent training trial.

The model updates its weights according to the following rule:

$$\Delta w_i = \theta \cdot (E_{\mathbf{p}^+}[c_i] - E_{\mathbf{w}}[c_i]) \qquad (5)$$

This the Maximum Entropy gradient-ascent update rule, as described by Jäger (2007). Its contribution to the update is independent of $\mathbf{p}^-$, the probabilities of the negative training candidates; i.e., the learner does "unsupervised" learning.

Below a continuous approximation to this discrete update rule is used, substituting dw_i/dt for Δw_i. The learning rate parameter η is omitted by setting it to 1; i.e., the training-time unit is defined to be how long it takes a constraint to change its weight by one weight unit when $E_{emp}[c_i] - E_{\mathbf{w}}[c_i] = 1$. The step size in weight space is thus fixed, rather than decreasing on a preset schedule (Boersma and Hayes,

2001) or adaptively (Boyd and Vandenberghe, 1999, Section 5.2.1).

In this paper, "abrupt" is used to mean that performance improves slowly at the outset of the experiment, then accelerates later (e.g., a sigmoid). Performance is expressed here as log-odds rather than proportion correct because (A) log-odds is more transparently related both to the learning model (Jäger, 2007) and to the statistical models fit to experimental results (Jaeger, 2008), and (B) proportion correct acts as a squashing function, reducing the visible influence of changing large weights and thus exaggerating the effect whose existence we are arguing for on other grounds.

3 Improvement in log-likelihood decelerates monotonically

We begin by establishing a result that is almost what we want:

Proposition 1. *Let* $L(t) = \sum_{j=1}^{n} p_j^+ \log p_j(t)$ *denote the model's expectation of the log-likelihood of the empirical distribution at time t (Berger et al., 1996). Then $L(t)$ is always increasing but never accelerating; i.e., for any $t \geq 0$, $dL/dt \geq 0$ and $d^2L/dt^2 \leq 0$.*

Proof. We convert the learner to its Replicator form (Moreton et al., 2017):

$$\frac{\mathrm{d}}{\mathrm{d}t} \log p_i = (C^T C \mathbf{e})_j - \mathbf{p}^T C^T C \mathbf{e} \qquad (6)$$

where C is the matrix[1] whose (i,j)-th entry is $c_i(x_j)$, and $\mathbf{e} = \mathbf{p}^+ - \mathbf{p}$. Differentiating the definition of $L(t)$ then yields

$$\begin{aligned}
\frac{\mathrm{d}L}{\mathrm{d}t} &= \sum_{j=1}^{n} p_j^+ \frac{\mathrm{d}}{\mathrm{d}t} \log p_j \\
&= \sum_{j=1}^{n} p_j^+ ((C^T C \mathbf{e})_j - \mathbf{p}^T C^T C \mathbf{e}) \\
&= (\mathbf{p}^+ - \mathbf{p})^T C^T C \mathbf{e} \\
&= \mathbf{e}^T C^T C \mathbf{e} \\
&= \|C\mathbf{e}\|^2
\end{aligned} \qquad (7)$$

---

[1]Note difference from familiar tableaus: *Rows* of C correspond to constraints, and *columns* to candidates.

(In this paper, $\| \cdot \|$ is the usual Euclidean norm.) Since $C^T C$ is positive semidefinite, $dL/dt \geq 0$. That confirms what we already know, since the learner does gradient ascent on L. The second derivative is

$$\begin{aligned}
\frac{\mathrm{d}^2 L}{\mathrm{d}t^2} &= \frac{\mathrm{d}}{\mathrm{d}t} \mathbf{e}^T C^T C \mathbf{e} \\
&= 2\mathbf{e} C^T C \left(\frac{\mathrm{d}}{\mathrm{d}t} \mathbf{e} \right) \\
&= -2 \left(\sum_j p_j (C^T C \mathbf{e})_j^2 - \sum_j (p_j (C^T C \mathbf{e})_j)^2 \right) \\
&= -2 \sum_j p_j (1 - p_j)(C^T C \mathbf{e})_j^2
\end{aligned}$$

$$(8)$$

Since $0 < p_j < 1$, the sum is positive unless $\mathbf{e} = \mathbf{0}$. Hence $d^2L/dt^2 \leq 0$ — the log-likelihood is always increasing, but always more and more slowly, until it stops. $\square$

Regardless of the constraint set, initial state, target pattern, or model parameters, learning, measured as log-likelihood, only ever slows down. Abrupt, sigmoidal, or U-shaped $L(t)$ curves are not possible. However, what the experiments measure is not log-likelihood, which depends only on the probability assigned by the model to the winners, but rather 2AFC performance, which depends in part on how it distributes probability among the losing candidates. The next section addresses that complication.

4 When initial weights are all zero, initial improvement bounds later improvement

In typical "artificial-language" experiments, the training and testing stimuli are, or approximate, random samples from the same distribution, and are presented to participants with equal frequency. We consider here a slightly more general possibility:

Proposition 2. *Suppose the experimenter chooses $\mathbf{p}^+$, $\mathbf{r}^+$, and $\mathbf{r}^-$ such that at time $t = 0$, we have*

$$\mathbf{p}^+ - \mathbf{p}(0) = \alpha(\mathbf{r}^+ - \mathbf{r}^-) \qquad (9)$$

for some $\alpha > 0$. Let $\lambda_{+,-}$ be the log-odds of a correct 2AFC response. Then at any time $t \geq 0$,

$$\left.\frac{d}{dt}E_{\mathbf{w}}[\lambda_{+,-}]\right|_t \leq \left.\frac{d}{dt}E_{\mathbf{w}}[\lambda_{+,-}]\right|_0 \qquad (10)$$

Proof. For a given weight vector $\mathbf{w}$, the expected harmony of a positive test candidate is

$$E_{\mathbf{w},\mathbf{r}^+}[h_{\mathbf{w}}(x^+)] = \sum_j r_j^+ h_{\mathbf{w}}(x_j)$$

$$= \sum_j r_j^+ \left(\sum_i w_i c_i(x_j)\right)$$

$$= \sum_i w_i \left(\sum_j r_j^+ c_i(x_j)\right) \qquad (11)$$

$$= \sum_i w_i E_{\mathbf{r}^+}[c_i]$$

i.e, the expected harmony of a positive test candidate is the weighted-by-the-weights sum of the average score on each constraint among positive test candidates. In terms of C, the matrix whose (i,j)-th entry is $c_i(x_j)$, we can write this as

$$E_{\mathbf{w},\mathbf{r}^+}[h_{\mathbf{w}}(x^+)] = \sum_i w_i(C\mathbf{r}^+)_i$$
$$= \mathbf{w}^T C\mathbf{r}^+ \qquad (12)$$

The same holds, *mutatis mutandis*, for negative test candidates. For any test pair (x_i, x_j), the log-odds $\lambda_{i,j}$ of choosing x_i is, by Equation 3, just the difference in harmony scores given the current weighting:

$$\lambda_{i,j} = h_{\mathbf{w}}(x_i) - h_{\mathbf{w}}(x_j) \qquad (13)$$

That gives us the following expression for the expected value of $\lambda_{+,-}$, the log-odds in favor of a correct test response:

$$E_{\mathbf{w}}[\lambda_{+,-}] = E_{\mathbf{w}}[h_{\mathbf{w}}(x^+) - h_{\mathbf{w}}(x^-)]$$
$$= \sum_i w_i(E_{\mathbf{r}^+}[c_i] - E_{\mathbf{r}^-}[c_i]) \qquad (14)$$
$$= \mathbf{w}^T C(\mathbf{r}^+ - \mathbf{r}^-)$$

We differentiate that to get

$$\frac{d}{dt}E_{\mathbf{w}}[\lambda_{+,-}] = \sum_i \left(\frac{d}{dt}w_i\right)(C(\mathbf{r}^+ - \mathbf{r}^-))_i$$
$$= \left(\frac{d}{dt}\mathbf{w}\right)^T C(\mathbf{r}^+ - \mathbf{r}^-) \qquad (15)$$

By the update rule in Equation 5, we have

$$\frac{d}{dt}w_i = (E_{\mathbf{p}^+}[c_i] - E_{\mathbf{w}}[c_i]) \qquad (16)$$

If $\mathbf{q}$ is any probability distribution over the candidates $X = \{x_1, \dots, x_n\}$, then $C\mathbf{q}$ is a vector with m elements in which the ith element is $E_{\mathbf{q}}[c_i]$, the expected score on Constraint c_i when a candidate is sampled from X under the distribution $\mathbf{q}$. Hence

$$\frac{d}{dt}\mathbf{w} = C(\mathbf{p}^+ - \mathbf{p}) \qquad (17)$$

Substituting back into Equation 15 then yields

$$\frac{d}{dt}E_{\mathbf{w}}[\lambda_{+,-}] = (C(\mathbf{p}^+ - \mathbf{p}))^T C(\mathbf{r}^+ - \mathbf{r}^-) \qquad (18)$$

Setting $\mathbf{e} = \mathbf{p}^+ - \mathbf{p}$, we have

$$\frac{d}{dt}E_{\mathbf{w}}[\lambda_{+,-}] = (C\mathbf{e})^T C(\mathbf{r}^+ - \mathbf{r}^-) \qquad (19)$$

Applying the Cauchy-Schwarz inequality to Equation 19 yields:

$$\left|\frac{d}{dt}E_{\mathbf{w}}[\lambda_{+,-}]\right| \leq \|C\mathbf{e}\| \cdot \|C(\mathbf{r}^+ - \mathbf{r}^-)\| \qquad (20)$$

with strict equality if and only if $C(\mathbf{r}^+ - \mathbf{r}^-)$ is a scalar multiple of $C\mathbf{e}$. Because the experimenter chose $\mathbf{p}^+, \mathbf{r}^+$, and $\mathbf{r}^-$ to satisfy the hypothesis in Equation 9, $C(\mathbf{r}^+ - \mathbf{r}^-)$ is a scalar multiple of $C\mathbf{e}(0)$, and so strict equality holds at $t = 0$:

$$\left|\frac{d}{dt}E_{\mathbf{w}}[\lambda_{+,-}]|_{t=0}\right| = \|C\mathbf{e}(0)\| \cdot \|C(\mathbf{r}^+ - \mathbf{r}^-)\| \qquad (21)$$

From Proposition 1, we know that $\|C\mathbf{e}\|$ decreases monotonically as t increases. Since $\|C(\mathbf{r}^+ - \mathbf{r}^-)\|$ is constant, the product is never bigger than at $t = 0$:

$$\left|\frac{d}{dt}E_{\mathbf{w}}[\lambda_{+,-}]\right| \leq \|C\mathbf{e}(0)\| \cdot \|C(\mathbf{r}^+ - \mathbf{r}^-)\|$$
$$\leq \left|\frac{d}{dt}E_{\mathbf{w}}[\lambda_{+,-}]|_{t=0}\right| \qquad (22)$$

$\square$

In other words, if the learner starts with $\mathbf{w} = \mathbf{0}$ at $t = 0$, then 2AFC performance can't later on improve (or deteriorate) any faster than it did at $t = 0$. In particular, the abrupt learning curve of Figure 1 is impossible for such a learner.[2]

This result was checked numerically by simulation. Each replication of the simulation was done as follows: m and n were sampled uniformly from $\{4, \ldots, 30\}$. A probability s was sampled uniformly from the interval $(0, 1)$, and an $m \times n$ constraint-by-candidate matrix C was generated by randomly setting each entry to 1 with probability s, else to 0. A random concept was generated by uniformly sampling an integer k from $\{1, \ldots, m\}$, and decreeing Candidates $\{x_1, \ldots, x_k\}$ to be positive. The training and test distributions were set thus: $\mathbf{p}^+ = \mathbf{r}^+ = (1/k, \ldots, 1/k, 0, \ldots, 0)^T$; $\mathbf{r}^- = (0, \ldots, 0, 1/(n - k), \ldots, 1/(n - k))^T$. The learning rate η was set to $1/100$, $\mathbf{w}(0)$ was set to $\mathbf{0}$, and the learner was run for 300 update cycles. The change in the model's log-likelihood on each cycle was measured, and the index of the largest increase was recorded. Ten thousand such replications were run. The largest increase always occurred on the first cycle, as predicted.

5 Adjacent learning trajectories converge in weight space

In this section, we show that learning erases small perturbations in the state of the model: Two learners that now have slightly different weights will in the future draw closer and closer together. This is not altogether unexpected; after all, the learners are climbing the same convex hill, and eventually they will both arrive at the summit. But what if a small initial difference somehow leads to paths that diverge before converging, or causes one to lag further and further behind the other for a while? Fortunately, this is not the case.

Proposition 3. *Consider two otherwise identical learning simulations such that at a given time t_1, one is in state $\mathbf{w}(t_1)$ and the other is in a nearby state $\mathbf{w}'(t_1)$. For any $t_2 > t_1$, we have $\|\mathbf{w}(t_2) - \mathbf{w}'(t_2)\| \leq \|\mathbf{w}(t_1) - \mathbf{w}'(t_1)\|$.*

[2]The rate of improvement is bounded above by a monotonically decreasing quantity (Equation 20), but that does not guarantee that the rate itself is monotonically decreasing. Hence, U-shaped curves are not excluded by this result. None were found in the simulations described on this page.

Proof. The rate of change in the squared distance between the two learners in weight space at any time t is

$$D = \frac{\mathrm{d}}{\mathrm{d}t}\|\mathbf{w} - \mathbf{w}'\|^2 = 2(\mathbf{w} - \mathbf{w}')^T \frac{\mathrm{d}}{\mathrm{d}t}(\mathbf{w} - \mathbf{w}')$$
$$= 2(\mathbf{w} - \mathbf{w}')^T (C\mathbf{e} - C\mathbf{e}')$$
$$= -2(\mathbf{w} - \mathbf{w}')^T C(\mathbf{p} - \mathbf{p}') \tag{23}$$

Since the harmonies of the candidates are the weighted sums of their constraint scores,

$$(\mathbf{w} - \mathbf{w}')^T C = (\mathbf{h} - \mathbf{h}')^T \tag{24}$$

It will be convenient to set $\boldsymbol{\gamma} = \mathbf{h}' - \mathbf{h}$ and write

$$D = 2\boldsymbol{\gamma}^T(\mathbf{p} - \mathbf{p}') \tag{25}$$

We will show that D attains a local maximum at $\boldsymbol{\gamma} = \mathbf{0}$, using the usual second-derivative test.

When $\mathbf{w} = \mathbf{w}'$, $\boldsymbol{\gamma} = \mathbf{0}$, and so of course $D = 0$. We now find the first and second partial derivatives of D with respect to the elements of $\boldsymbol{\gamma}$, evaluated at $\boldsymbol{\gamma} = \mathbf{0}$. From Equation 3, we have

$$p_i' = \frac{e^{h_i + \gamma_i}}{\sum_k e^{h_k + \gamma_k}} \tag{26}$$

The effect on $\mathbf{p}'$ of small changes in $\boldsymbol{\gamma}$ is given by the derivatives

$$\frac{\partial}{\partial \gamma_i} p_i' = p_i'(1 - p_i') \qquad \text{and} \qquad \frac{\partial}{\partial \gamma_i} p_{j \neq i}' = -p_i' p_j' \tag{27}$$

Hence the first-order partials of D are

$$\frac{\partial}{\partial \gamma_i} D = 2 \sum_k \frac{\partial}{\partial \gamma_i}\left(\gamma_k(p_k - p_k')\right)$$
$$= 2\left(p_i - p_i' - \gamma_i p_i' + p_i' \sum_k \gamma_k p_k'\right) \tag{28}$$

These are all zero at $\boldsymbol{\gamma} = \mathbf{0}$, since then $p_i = p_i'$. The second-order partials at $\boldsymbol{\gamma} = \mathbf{0}$ turn out (after considerable algebra, omitted here) to be

$$\frac{\partial^2}{\partial \gamma_i^2} D = -4p_i(1 - p_i) \tag{29}$$

and

$$\frac{\partial^2}{\partial\gamma_i\partial\gamma_j}D = 4p_ip_j \tag{30}$$

The Hessian matrix H of D at $\boldsymbol{\gamma} = \mathbf{0}$ is thus[3]

$$H = -4(\mathrm{diag}(\mathbf{p}) - \mathbf{p}\mathbf{p}^T) \tag{31}$$

The row sums of H are all zero, the diagonal entries are all negative, and the off-diagonal entries are positive, so by the Gershgorin circle theorem (Horn and Johnson, 1985, 344–345), none of the eigenvalues of H are positive. We now show that exactly one of the eigenvalues is zero: Suppose $H\mathbf{x} = \mathbf{0}$. Then $\mathrm{diag}(\mathbf{p})\mathbf{x} = \mathbf{p}(\mathbf{p}^T\mathbf{x})$, i.e., a scalar multiple of $\mathbf{p}$. Consequently, for every i, it is true that $p_ix_i = p_i\mathbf{p}^T\mathbf{x}$. We can cancel the p_is to get $x_i = \mathbf{p}^T\mathbf{x}$, so $\mathbf{x} = \mathbf{1}(\mathbf{p}^T\mathbf{x})$. Hence, $\mathbf{1}$ is the *only* eigenvector whose eigenvalue is zero. The other eigenvalues are all negative.

Thus the value that D attains at $\boldsymbol{\gamma} = \mathbf{0}$ is a local maximum in every direction except along the line where $\boldsymbol{\gamma}$ is a scalar multiple of $\mathbf{1}$. We now show that along this line, D is constantly zero: Let $\boldsymbol{\gamma} = t\mathbf{1}$. Then, from the original definition of D in Equation 25, $D = 2t\mathbf{1}^T(\mathbf{p} - \mathbf{p}') = 2t(\mathbf{1}^T\mathbf{p} - \mathbf{1}^T\mathbf{p}') = 0$. All derivatives of D along that line are therefore constantly zero.[4]

If $\mathbf{w}'$ differs by a small amount from $\mathbf{w}$, then $\boldsymbol{\gamma}$ differs by a small amount from $\mathbf{0}$. The component of the difference along the line $t\mathbf{1}$ has no effect on

---

[3]The Hessian H is -4 times the variance-covariance matrix of the multinomial distribution parametrized by $\mathbf{p}$ (Agresti 1990, 423; Chris Wiesen, p.c., 2017), i.e., the Max Ent distribution parametrized by $\mathbf{w}$. Hence D is approximately a scalar multiple of the variance in the difference between the two learners in harmony, sampled under the distribution of the original learner.

[4]Moving $\boldsymbol{\gamma}$ along the line $\mathbf{1}t$ has the effect of adding the same fixed amount t to the harmony of every candidate. Doing that does not change the model's candidate-probability estimates (e^t cancels in the numerator and denominator of Equation 3), and so it also does not change the model's expectations of the constraint scores, and so it also does not change the update to the weights. Two learners whose weights differ by a multiple of $\mathbf{1}$ are indistiguishable by any experiment. That is a special case of a general consequence of Max-Ent/Replicator equivalence, which is that if two learners assign the same probabilities to all candidates at some time t, they will continue to do so at all later times if exposed to identical training data.

D; all other components make D negative. Since D is the rate of change in the squared distance between $\mathbf{w}(t)$ and $\mathbf{w}'(t)$, that distance must be stable or decreasing over time. Thus for any $t_2 > t_1$, we have $\|\mathbf{w}(t_2) - \mathbf{w}'(t_2)\| \leq \|\mathbf{w}(t_1) - \mathbf{w}'(t_1)\|$, as claimed. $\qquad\square$

To check this result, the simulations from Section 4 were repeated, except this time the initial weights $\mathbf{w}(0)$ were not zero, but were sampled from a normal distribution (mean 0, s.d. 1). Then, for each of those 10,000 simulations, a perturbed mate was made by adding normally distributed noise (mean zero, s.d. 0.1) to $\mathbf{w}(0)$ to get $\mathbf{w}'(0)$. The second-order Taylor approximation to D around $\boldsymbol{\gamma} = \mathbf{0}$ is $D \approx (1/2)\boldsymbol{\gamma}^T H\boldsymbol{\gamma}$, where $\boldsymbol{\gamma} = C^T(\mathbf{w}' - \mathbf{w})$. This was used to predict D on each of the 300 update steps for each pair. Results, shown in Figure 2, verify the accuracy of the approximation (and hence corroborate the analysis), and show that D was in every case negative, i.e., that each learner consistently converged with its mate over time.

Figure 2: Actual vs. predicted rate of convergence between pairs in weight space. Values have been multiplied by -1 so that logarithmic axes can be used. Each streak is one of $N = 1000$ pairs (9,000 more omitted to reduce image size).

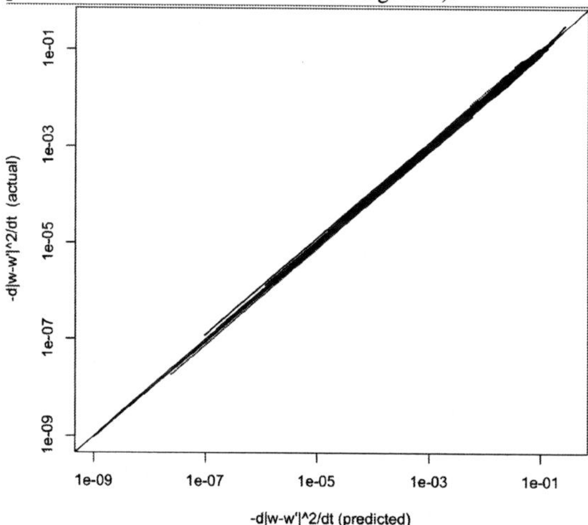

6 Similar initial weights imply similar 2AFC learning curves

A learner that starts with weights *near* 0 follows a trajectory that is close to, and convergent with, that of the learner that started *at* 0 (Proposition 3). 2AFC performance in a learner that starts at $\mathbf{0}$ never improves faster than it did at $t = 0$ (Proposition 2). Just how closely is the 2AFC learning curve of the near-$\mathbf{0}$ learner tethered to the bounded learning curve of the at-$\mathbf{0}$ learner?

Proposition 4. *For any $\mathbf{w}$ and $\mathbf{w}'$, the difference $\Delta\lambda(\mathbf{w}, \mathbf{w}') = E_{\mathbf{w}'}[\lambda_{+,-}] - E_{\mathbf{w}}[\lambda_{+,-}]$ is bounded by $|\Delta\lambda| \le \|\mathbf{w}' - \mathbf{w}\| \sqrt{m} c_{range}$, where c_{range} is the largest absolute difference between any two entries in C.*

Proof. From Equation 14, the difference between the two learners in the expected log-odds of a correct test response is given by $\Delta\lambda(\mathbf{w}, \mathbf{w}') = (\mathbf{w}' - \mathbf{w})^T C(\mathbf{r}^+ - \mathbf{r}^-)$. By Cauchy-Schwarz, this is no greater than $\|\mathbf{w}' - \mathbf{w}\| \|C(\mathbf{r}^+ - \mathbf{r}^-)\|$. Each entry in $C(\mathbf{r}^+ - \mathbf{r}^-)$ is the difference between the average scores of the positive versus negative test stimuli on one of the constraints, which is at most c_{range}. Thus $\|C(\mathbf{r}^+ - \mathbf{r}^-)\| \le \sqrt{m} c_{range}$. $\square$

Since $\|\mathbf{w}'(t) - \mathbf{w}(t)\| \le \|\mathbf{w}'(0) - \mathbf{w}(0)\|$ by Proposition 3, the 2AFC learning curve of a learner that started at $\mathbf{w}'(0) \ne \mathbf{0}$ cannot stray further than $\|\mathbf{w}'(0)\| \sqrt{m} c_{range}$ from one that started at $\mathbf{0}$.

In actual practice, the experimenter will often divide the candidates into positive and negative test sets in a controlled way, so that the two sets receive, on average, the same score from all but some small number $m^\star$ of the m constraints, which we can suppose are Constraints c_1 through $c_{m^\star}$. Since the ith entry of $C(\mathbf{r}^+ - \mathbf{r}^-)$ is the average difference between the positive and the negative test sets in their score on the ith constraint, all but the first $m^\star$ of the entries will be as close to zero as the experimenter is able to arrange. In that case, we can truncate $\mathbf{w}$, $\mathbf{w}'$, and C to their first $m^\star$ entries or rows, tightening the bound to $|\Delta\lambda| \le \|\mathbf{w}'^\star - \mathbf{w}^\star\| \sqrt{m^\star} c_{range}^\star$.

Proposition 5. *Let $M = \max_i \|C_{i,\cdot}\|$ be the norm of the row of C with the largest norm, and let $R = \max_i |C_{i,\cdot}\mathbf{1}|$ be the largest absolute row sum in C. Then the difference between the initial rate of 2AFC improvement of a learner that starts at $\mathbf{w} = \mathbf{0}$ and one that starts at $\mathbf{w}'$ near $\mathbf{0}$ is bounded by*

$$|d\Delta\lambda/dt|_{\mathbf{w}=\mathbf{0}} \le \|\mathbf{w}'\| \left(\frac{M^2}{n} + \frac{R^2}{n^2} \right) m\sqrt{m^\star} c_{range} \tag{32}$$

Proof. Use Equation 19, approximating $\mathbf{p}' - \mathbf{p} \approx JC^T(\mathbf{w}' - \mathbf{w})$, where $J_{i,j} = \partial p_i / \partial \gamma_j$ is the Jacobian of $\mathbf{p}'$ as a function of $\boldsymbol{\gamma}$. From Equation 27 it follows that $J = \text{diag}(\mathbf{p}) - \mathbf{p}\mathbf{p}^T$ (i.e., $J = -H/4$; see Eqn. 31). Then

$$
\begin{aligned}
|d\Delta\lambda/dt| &\approx |(\mathbf{w}' - \mathbf{w})^T CJC^T C(\mathbf{r}^+ - \mathbf{r}^-)| \\
&\le \|(\mathbf{w}' - \mathbf{w})^T\| \|CJC^T\| \|C(\mathbf{r}^+ - \mathbf{r}^-)\|
\end{aligned}
\tag{33}
$$

where $\| \cdot \|$, for matrices, is the operator norm, the maximum factor by which the matrix can stretch a vector (Strang, 1980, 284). Since CJC^T is symmetric, its operator norm is simply its largest eigenvalue, which is no larger than ma, where $a = \max_{i,j} |(CJC^T)_{i,j}|$ (Zhan, 2006, Corollary 2). What is a?

For $\mathbf{w} = \mathbf{0}$, we have $J = \frac{1}{n}I - \frac{1}{n^2}\mathbf{1}\mathbf{1}^T$, so $CJC^T = \frac{1}{n}CC^T - \frac{1}{n^2}C\mathbf{1}\mathbf{1}^T C^T$. Then

$$
\begin{aligned}
\left| \frac{1}{n}(CC^T)_{i,j} \right| &= \frac{1}{n}|C_{i,\cdot} \cdot C_{j,\cdot}| \\
&\le \frac{1}{n} \max_i |C_{i,\cdot} \cdot C_{i,\cdot}| \tag{34} \\
&\le \frac{1}{n}M^2
\end{aligned}
$$

Likewise,

$$
\begin{aligned}
\left| \frac{1}{n^2}C\mathbf{1}\mathbf{1}^T C^T \right| &\le \frac{1}{n^2} \max_{i,j} |(C\mathbf{1})_i \cdot (C\mathbf{1})_j| \\
&\le \frac{1}{n^2} \max i (C\mathbf{1})_i^2 \tag{35} \\
&\le \frac{1}{n^2}R^2
\end{aligned}
$$

Hence

$$a = \max_{i,j} |(CJC^T)_{i,j}| \le \frac{1}{n}M^2 + \frac{1}{n^2}R^2 \tag{36}$$

and so, since $\|CJC^T\| \le ma$,

$$\|CJC^T\| \le m\left(\frac{1}{n}M^2 + \frac{1}{n^2}R^2 \right) \tag{37}$$

Substituting $\|C(\mathbf{r}^+ - \mathbf{r}^-)\| \le \sqrt{m^\star} c_{range}$ from the discussion of Proposition 4 completes the proof. $\square$

A row of C corresponds to a constraint, each entry being the score that that constraint gives to one candidate. Since all of those scores are less than $c_{\max}$ (the largest absolute value of any element in C), we have $M^2 \leq nc_{\max}^2$ and $R^2 \leq (nc_{\max})^2$. Hence

$$|\mathrm{d}\Delta\lambda/\mathrm{d}t|_{\mathbf{w}=\mathbf{0}} \leq \|\mathbf{w}'\| m\sqrt{m^\star} c_{\max}^2 c_{\text{range}} \qquad (38)$$

This is a worst-case estimate, based on very weak hypotheses about C and on the blunt instrument of the vector and matrix norms, which ignore exploitable structure. Stronger hypotheses permit improvment. For example, suppose C is binary, and let $d_i = \frac{1}{n}C\mathbf{1}$ be the proportion of 1's in Row i. Each entry $(CC^T)_{i,j}$ is the number of 1's that appear in the same column in Rows i and j, and hence is at most the smaller of the two row sums, so $\frac{1}{n}(CC^T)_{i,j} \leq \min\{d_i, d_j\}$. Each entry $(C\mathbf{1}\mathbf{1}^T C^T)_{i,j}$ is the product of the row sums of Rows i and j, so $\frac{1}{n^2}(C\mathbf{1}\mathbf{1}^T C^T)_{i,j} = d_i d_j$. Consequently,

$$a = \max_{i,j} |(CJC^T)_{i,j}| \leq \min\{d_i, d_j\} - d_i d_j$$
$$\leq \min\{d_i(1 - d_j), d_j(1 - d_i)\}$$
$$\leq 1/4 \qquad (39)$$

To justify this last step, suppose without loss of generality that $d_i(1 - d_j) \leq d_j(1 - d_i)$. Then $a^2 = (d_i(1 - d_j))^2 \leq d_i(1 - d_j)d_j(1 - d_i) = d_i(1 - d_i)d_j(1 - d_j) \leq (1/4)(1/4)$, so unsquaring on both sides yields $a \leq 1/4$. It follows that

$$|\mathrm{d}\Delta\lambda/\mathrm{d}t|_{\mathbf{w}=\mathbf{0}} \leq \|\mathbf{w}'\| \frac{1}{4} m\sqrt{m^\star} \qquad (40)$$

Suppose further that the entries of C are modelled as i.i.d. Bernoulli trials with $\Pr(C_{i,j} = 1) = s$. Then $M^2 = \max_i \sum_{j=1}^n C_{i,j}^2 = \sum_{j=1}^n |C_{i,j}| = R$. If n is large, the row sums are approximately samples from a normal distribution with mean ns and standard deviation $\sqrt{ns(1 - s)}$. The expected value of the maximum of a sample of size m from the standard normal distribution $N(0, 1)$ is approximately $\sqrt{2 \log m}$ (Cramér, 1946, 374). Hence $E[M^2] = E[R] = (ns + \sqrt{ns(1 - s)2 \log m})$. As $n \to \infty$, $E[M^2]/n \to s$, while $E[R^2]/n^2 = (E[R]/n)^2 =$ $(E[M^2]/n)^2 \to s^2$. Thus $\|(CJC^T)\| \to (s + s^2)m = s(1 + s)m$, and $c_{\max} = c_{\text{range}} = 1$, so from Equation 40, we have

$$E\left[|\mathrm{d}\Delta\lambda/\mathrm{d}t|_{\mathbf{w}=\mathbf{0}}\right] \leq \|\mathbf{w}'\| m\sqrt{m^\star} \min\left\{\frac{1}{4}, s(1 + s)\right\} \qquad (41)$$

Equation 41 was checked against 10,000 simulations, generated as described in Section 4. The yoked pairs consisted of one learner that started at $\mathbf{w}(0) = \mathbf{0}$, and one that started at $\mathbf{w}'(0)$ with entries sampled from a normal distribution with mean 0 and standard deviation 0.1. In calculating the bound, $m^\star$ was set equal to m. The actual value was always less than the bound, with the minimum difference being 0.01405. The bound was usually a substantial overestimate, the median difference being 5.372 and the maximum 30.51. In the subset where the near-zero learner's initial performance was near chance ($|\lambda'(0)| \leq 1/10$) and initial improvement was near zero ($|\mathrm{d}\lambda'/\mathrm{d}t| \leq 1/10$), a total of 1075 cases, the bound proved much tighter, overestimating by a median of 0.591 and a maximum of 0.998. These cases tended to have either small m or extreme s.

7 Putting the bounds together

One way that these bounds might be applied in practice is as follows. Suppose we hypothesize that the learner's initial weights $\mathbf{w}'(0)$ are such that $\|\mathbf{w}'(0)\| \leq w$, and we experimentally measure initial performance to be $\lambda'(0) = 0$ and the initial improvment rate to be $\mathrm{d}\lambda'/\mathrm{d}t(0) = 0$. Proposition 5 then gives us a bound — call it b — on the initial improvement rate for an otherwise identical learner with $\mathbf{w}(0) = \mathbf{0}$. By Proposition 2, the slope of the hypothetical 0-learner's 2AFC curve $\lambda(t)$ never exceeds b. That curve would have started at $\lambda(0) = 0$, since $\mathbf{w}(0) = \mathbf{0}$ makes all candidates equally harmonic. Hence the hypothetical 0-learner's 2AFC curve is bounded by $\lambda(t) \leq bt$. By Proposition 3, the observed and hypothetical learner converge in weight space, which by Proposition 4 means that $\lambda'(t) \leq bt + w\sqrt{m^\star}c_{\text{range}}$. Conversely, if $\lambda'(t)$ ever exceeds this value, we know that $\mathbf{w}'(0)$ must have been more than w, contrary to hypothesis.[5]

---

[5]We also have to assume that the experiment has sufficient time resolution that learning cannot begin with an undetectably

8 When initial weights are far from zero, 2AFC performance can accelerate

If the initial weights are far from $\mathbf{0}$, then even a simple constraint set can yield abrupt learning. For $n = 4$, let $C = I_4$, the identity matrix of order 4 (i.e., 4 candidates, 4 constraints, each constraint gives a 1 to just one candidate). If we set $\mathbf{w}(0) = (x, -x, 0, 0)^T$, $\mathbf{p}^+ = \mathbf{r}^+ = (1/2, 1/2, 0, 0)^T$, and $\mathbf{r}^- = (0, 0, 1/2, 1/2)^T$, the 2AFC curve starts out flat at 0 and stays that way (longer the bigger x is), then starts climbing rapidly as shown in the black curve on Figure 3.

Figure 3: 2AFC learning curves for $n = 4$, $C = I_4$, and $\mathbf{w}_0 = (6, -6, 0, 0)^T$ (black curve) or $(6, -6, 6, -6)^T$ (gray curve), with $\mathbf{p}^+ = \mathbf{r}^+ = (1/2, 1/2, 0, 0)^T$, and $\mathbf{r}^- = (0, 0, 1/2, 1/2)^T$. Other parameters: $\eta = 1/100$.

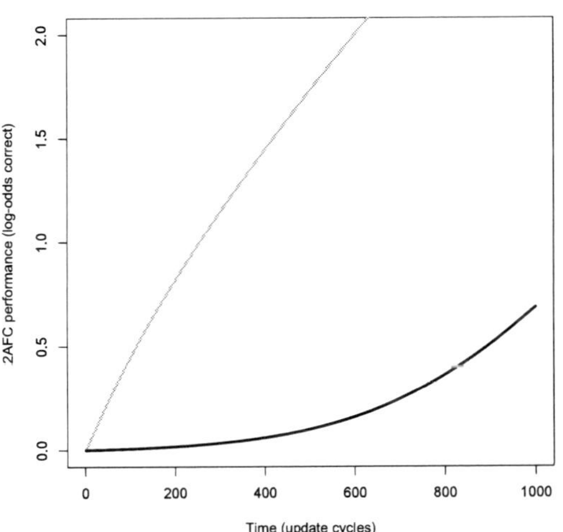

The idea behind this construction is that initially, every negative candidate is much less probable than half of the positive candidates, and much more probable than the other half, so that the outcome of a 2AFC trial is 50% likely to be correct (0 logits). The learner then spends ages laboriously hauling up the low-frequency half of the positive candidates, and letting down the negative candidates, until the low-frequency positive candidates finally start winning a

brief but huge improvment rate that would satisfy the hypothesis of Proposition 2 and thus allow later unexpected sudden improvement.

noticeable number of 2AFC competitions. The construction can be carried out for any C that makes it possible to sandwich the initial probabilities of the positive (negative) candidate between those of the negative (positive) ones by artful choice of $\mathbf{w}(0)$.

9 Discussion

Since abrupt learning has been observed in human phonological acquisition in nature Smith (1973); Macken and Barton (1978); Vihman and Velleman (1989); Barlow and Dinnsen (1998); Levelt and van Oostendorp (2007); Gerlach (2010); Guy (2014) and in the lab Moreton and Pertsova (2016), the question of when a gradual learning *rule* translates into gradual learning *performance* is pertinent. For the learner and experimental paradigm studied here, transfer from UG or from previous learning is a necessary condition for abruptness. This result spawns many further questions, among them:

▷ The non-abrupt gray curve in Figure 3 shows that not just any set of large non-zero initial weights, paired with just any training and test distribution, leads to abrupt learning in the model. Which ones do? What are the most general sufficient conditions? Phonological theory offers many proposals about the initial state of L1 or L2 learning (e.g., Demuth (1995); Gnanadesikan (1995); Smolensky (1996); Pater (1997); Broselow et al. (1998); Boersma and Levelt (2000); Curtin and Zuraw (2002); Hayes (2004); Wilson (2006); Hayes et al. (2009); Jesney and Tessier (2011); White (2014)); what predictions follow for abruptness?

▷ In human learners, is abrupt learning associated with transfer of constraint weights from UG, L1, or previous training in the lab? What is going on during apparent initial stagnation? Does it actually consist of steady *un*learning of a pre-existing grammar?

▷ Do the present results extend to other learners that are algorithmically related to this one? That is a sizable class, including not only elaborations of Max Ent gradient ascent, but also the Gradual Learning Algorithms for Stochastic OT and Harmonic Grammar (recent reviews: Boersma and Pater (2016); Pater (2016); Jarosz (2016)). Abrupt learning has been seen in some of them (see Introduction above). Differences in the conditions under which they admit abrupt learning may provide a hitherto unused way to them empirically.

References

Agresti, A. (1990). *Categorical data analysis*. New York: Wiley Interscience.

Ashby, F. G., L. A. Alfonso-Reese, A. U. Turken, and E. M. Waldron (1998). A neuropsychological theory of multiple systems in category learning. *Psychological Review 105*(3), 442–481.

Barlow, J. A. and D. A. Dinnsen (1998). Asymmetrical cluster development in a disordered system. *Language Acquisition 7*(1), 1–49.

Berger, A. L., S. A. Della Pietra, and V. J. Della Pietra (1996). A maximum entropy approach to natural language processing. *Computational Linguistics 22*(1), 39–71.

Boersma, P. (1998). *Functional Phonology: formalizing the interactions between articulatory and perceptual drives*. Ph. D. thesis, University of Amsterdam.

Boersma, P. and B. Hayes (2001). Empirical tests of the Gradual Learning Algorithm. *Linguistic Inquiry 32*, 45–86.

Boersma, P. and C. Levelt (2000). Gradual constraint-ranking learning algorithm predicts acquisition order. In *Proceedings of Child Language Research Forum 30*, Stanford, California, pp. 229–237.

Boersma, P. and J. Pater (2016). Convergence properties of a gradual learning algorithm for Harmonic Grammar. In J. J. McCarthy and J. Pater (Eds.), *Harmonic Grammar and Harmonic Serialism*, pp. 389–434. Sheffield, England: Equinox.

Boyd, S. and L. Vandenberghe (1999). *Convex optimization*. Cambridge University Press.

Broselow, E., S.-I. Chen, and C. Wang (1998). The emergence of the unmarked in second language phonology. *Studies in Second Language Acquisition 20*, 261–280.

Cramér, H. (1946). *Mathematical methods of statistics*. Princeton, New Jersey: Princeton University Press.

Curtin, S. and K. R. Zuraw (2002). Explaining constraint demotion in a developing system. In B. Skerabela, S. Fish, and A. H.-J. Do (Eds.), *Papers from the 26th Boston University Conference on Language Development (BUCLD 26)*, Somerville, pp. 118–129. Cascadilla Press.

Demuth, K. (1995). Markedness and the development of prosodic structure. In J. Beckman (Ed.), *Proceedings of the 25th Meeting of the North-East Linguistics Society*, Amherst, Mass., pp. 13–26. Graduate Linguistics Students Association.

Elman, J. L., E. A. Bates, M. H. Johnson, A. Karmiloff-Smith, D. Parisi, and K. Plunkett (1996). *Rethinking innateness*. Cambridge, Massachusetts: MIT Press.

Fischer, M. (2005). A Robbins-Monro type learning algorithm for an entropy maximizing version of Stochastic Optimality Theory. Master's thesis, Humboldt-Universität, Berlin.

Gerlach, S. R. (2010). *The acquisition of consonant feature sequences: harmony, metathesis, and deletion patterns in phonological development*. Ph. D. thesis, University of Minnesota.

Gnanadesikan, A. (1995, October). Markedness and faithfulness constraints in child phonology. Manuscript # 67, Rutgers Optimality Archive (`roa.rutgers.edu`).

Goldwater, S. J. and M. Johnson (2003). Learning OT constraint rankings using a maximum entropy model. In J. Spenader, A. Erkisson, and O. Dahl (Eds.), *Proceedings of the Stockholm Workshop on Variation within Optimality Theory*, pp. 111–120.

Guy, G. R. (2014). Linking usage and grammar: generative phonology, exemplar theory, and variable rules. *Lingua 142*, 57–65.

Hayes, B. (2004). Phonological acquisition in Optimality Theory: the early stages. In R. Kager, J. Pater, and W. Zonneveld (Eds.), *Constraints in phonological acquisition*, Chapter 5, pp. 158–203. Cambridge, England: Cambridge University Press.

Hayes, B. and C. Wilson (2008). A Maximum Entropy model of phonotactics and phonotactic learning. *Linguistic Inquiry 39*(3), 379–440.

Hayes, B., K. Zuraw, P. Siptár, and Z. Londe (2009). Natural and unnatural constraints in Hungarian vowel harmony. *Language 85*(4), 822–863.

Horn, R. A. and C. R. Johnson (1985). *Matrix analysis*. Cambridge, England: Cambridge University Press.

Jaeger, T. F. (2008). Categorical data analysis: away from ANOVAs (transformation or not) and towards logit mixed models. *Journal of Memory and Language 59*, 434–446.

Jäger, G. (2007). Maximum Entropy models and Stochastic Optimality Theory. In J. Grimshaw, J. Maling, C. Manning, J. Simpson, and A. Zaenen (Eds.), *Architectures, rules, and preferences: a festschrift for Joan Bresnan*, pp. 467–479. Stanford, California: CSLI Publications.

Jarosz, G. (2016). Learning with violable constraints. To appear in: Jeff Lidz, William Snyder, and Joe Pater (eds.), *The Oxford handbook of developmental linguistics*. Oxford, England: Oxford University Press.

Jesney, K. (2016). On the relationship between learning sequence and rate of acquisition. In G. lafur Hansson, A. Farris-Trimble, K. McMullin, and D. Pulleyblank (Eds.), *Proceedings of the Annual Meeting on Phonology 2015*, Volume 3. Linguistic Society of America.

Jesney, K. and A.-M. Tessier (2011). Biases in Harmonic Grammar: the road to restrictive learning. *Natural Language and Linguistic Theory 29*(1), 251–290.

Johnson, M. (2007, November). A gentle introduction to Maximum Entropy models and their friends. Slides from a talk, accessed at `web.science.mq.edu.au/ ~mjohnson/ papers/CompPhon07-slides.pdf` on 2013 August 6.

Kurtz, K. J., K. R. Levering, R. D. Stanton, J. Romero, and S. N. Morris (2013). Human learning of elemental category structures: revising the classic result of Shepard, Hovland, and Jenkins (1961). *Journal of Experimental Psychology: Learning, Memory, and Cognition 39*(2), 552–572.

Levelt, C. and M. van Oostendorp (2007). Feature co-occurrence constraints in L1 acquisition. *Linguistics in the Netherlands 24*(1), 162–172.

Love, B. C. (2002). Comparing supervised and unsupervised category learning. *Psychonomic Bulletin and Review 9*(4), 829–835.

Luce, R. D. (2005 [1959]). *Individual choice behavior: a theoretical analysis*. New York: Dover.

Macken, M. A. and D. Barton (1978, March). The acquisition of the voicing contrast in English: a study of voice-onset time in word-initial stop consonants. Report from the Stanford Child Phonology Project.

Maddox, W. T. and F. G. Ashby (2004). Dissociating explicit and procedural-learning based systems of perceptual category learning. *Behavioural Processes 66*, 309–332.

Moreton, E., J. Pater, and K. Pertsova (2017). Phonological concept learning. *Cognitive Science 41*(1), 4–69.

Moreton, E. and K. Pertsova (2016). Implicit and explicit processes in phonotactic learning. In TBA (Ed.), *Proceedings of the 40th Boston University Conference on Language Development*, Somerville, Mass., pp. TBA. Cascadilla.

Pater, J. (1997). Minimal violation in phonological development. *Language Acquisition 6*(3), 201–253.

Pater, J. (2008). Gradual learning and convergence. *Linguistic Inquiry 39*(2), 334–345.

Pater, J. (2016). Universal Grammar with weighted constraints. To appear in: John McCarthy and Joe Pater (eds.), Harmonic Grammar and Harmonic Serialism.

Pater, J. and E. Moreton (2012). Structurally biased phonology: complexity in learning and typology. *Journal of the English and Foreign Languages University, Hyderabad 3*(2), 1–44.

Smith, J. D., M. E. Berg, R. G. Cook, M. S. Murphy, M. J. Crossley, J. Boomer, B. Spiering, M. J. Beran, B. A. Church, F. G. Ashby, and R. C. Grace (2012). Implicit and explicit categorization: a tale of four species. *Neuroscience and Biobehavioral Reviews 36*(10), 2355–2369.

Smith, N. (1973). *The acquisition of phonology: a case study*. Cambridge, England: Cambridge University Press.

Smolensky, P. (1996). On the comprehension/production dilemma in child language. *Linguistic Inquiry 27*, 720–731.

Strang, G. (1980). *Linear algebra and its applications*. Orlando, Florida: Academic Press.

Vihman, M. M. and S. Velleman (1989). Phonological reorganization: a case study. *Language and Speech 32*, 149–170.

White, J. (2014). Evidence for a learning bias against saltatory phonological alternations. *Cognition 130*, 96–115.

Wilson, C. (2006). Learning phonology with substantive bias: an experimental and computational study of velar palatalization. *Cognitive Science 30*(5), 945–982.

Zhan, X. (2006). Extremal eigenvalues of real symmetric matrices with entries in an interval. *SIAM Journal of Matrix Analysis and Applications* 27(3), 851–860.

Using Rhetorical Topics for Automatic Summarization

Natalie M. Schrimpf
Department of Linguistics
Yale University
`natalie.schrimpf@yale.edu`

Abstract

Summarization involves finding the most important information in a text in order to convey the meaning of the document. In this paper, I present a method for using topic information to influence which content is selected for a summary. Texts are divided into topics using rhetorical information that creates a partition of a text into a sequence of non-overlapping topics. To investigate the effect of this topic structure, I compare the output of summarizing an entire text without topics to summarizing individual topics and combining them into a complete summary. The results show that the use of these rhetorical topics improves summarization performance compared to a summarization system that incorporates no topic information, demonstrating the utility of topic structure and rhetorical information for automatic summarization.

1 Introduction

Summarization is the task of creating a shortened version of an input document that retains the important information from the original text but in a more concise form. The goal of summarization is to convey the main concepts of the original document so that a summary user can understand what the document is about without reading the entire text. With large amounts of text available online, it has become increasingly necessary to find ways to allow people to quickly and easily find the information they need. Summarization is useful for this task because it condenses information into a shorter form that can be read instead of a longer text if it provides all the information a user needs or it can be read in order to determine whether the original text contains information relevant to the user's needs, allowing the user to decide which texts would be most useful. In order for summaries to achieve this goal, they must convey the important concepts from the text without including unnecessary information. Most summarization systems perform extractive summarization, which involves creating a summary by extracting complete sentences from the original document (Yih et al., 2007; Conroy et al., 2006; Wong et al., 2008; Christensen et al., 2013). The current research is also focused on extractive summarization.

Different representations of texts and text structure make different assumptions about how texts convey information and how summarization is performed. Much work on summarization does not assume anything about the structure of text. The work in this paper aims to demonstrate that attention to the linguistic structure of a text is useful in performing summarization. The type of linguistic structure and textual organization explored in this work is the notion of topic. In linguistics, there are different notions of what it means to be a topic (Lambrecht, 1996; Gundel, 1988; Blei, 2012; Griffiths et al., 2005; Van Dijk, 1977; Van Kuppevelt, 1995; Asher, 2004). Intuitively, texts are organized into topics or groups of sentences that are more related to each other than they are to sentences in other groups. A summary should include coverage of all these topics. One crucial factor that motivates grouping texts into topics for summarization has to do with summary length. A summary is a condensed form of the original text. One of the challenges of summarization is determining how to convey the same information as the original text in a more limited space.

Proceedings of the Society for Computation in Linguistics (SCiL) 2018, pages 125-135.
Salt Lake City, Utah, January 4-7, 2018

In order to convey the same information, there should be an emphasis on covering the text by including some amount of information about all of the important ideas and by limiting redundancy and in-depth coverage of a particular topic in favor of wider coverage of all topics.

In order to see how useful topics are for summarization, topic information was incorporated into a summarization system. To compare the effects of using topics versus not using topics, summarization was either performed at the level of the whole text or at the level of individual topics. Specifically, the process for incorporating topics into summarization included the following steps: divide a text into topics, summarize the text of each topic, and concatenate the summaries of each topic to create a summary for the whole text. With this method, topics are treated as independent pieces of text that contribute to the overall meaning of the text, and each topic will be represented in the final summary. This agrees with the intuition that texts can be divided into topics and a good summary should contain coverage of all topics that appear in the original text. This is a straightforward way to see how topics affect summarization.

Section 2 describes how texts are separated into topics using rhetorical information. Section 3 describes the techniques used for summarizing texts. Section 4 presents the methods and results of the experiments that were performed. Section 5 summarizes the findings and contributions of this work.

2   RST Topics

2.1   Rhetorical Structure Theory

Rhetorical Structure Theory (RST) is a framework for describing the organization of a text and what a text conveys by identifying hierarchical structures in text (Mann and Thompson, 1988). Pieces of text relate to each other in different ways in order to accomplish the writer's purpose with some pieces more central than others. Beginning with the clause level, relations can hold between successively larger spans of text forming a hierarchical structure of how all spans of the text are related to each other. One intuition behind RST is that the text structure itself conveys information beyond the information explicitly asserted by clauses in the text. Relations connect two non-overlapping pieces of text, and their combination conveys information

beyond that of the individual clauses, such as the relational proposition that the information from one clause is evidence for the information in the other clause. Relation types include enablement, circumstance, background, justification, and evidence, among others. An important part of RST relations is the distinction between nuclei and satellites. The nucleus of a relation is one of the spans of text connected by the relation that is more essential to the purpose of the writer and is comprehensible on its own without the satellite. The satellite is the element that generally cannot appear on its own but provides some type of supporting information for the nucleus. The satellite of the relation provides information that will increase the belief in the nucleus of the relation, and the effect is that the reader has an increased belief in the information given in the nucleus. In this example of an evidence relation from Mann and Thompson the information in the satellite about the program producing the correct calculation provides evidence for the nucleus which states that the program works.

> Nucleus: The program as published for calendar year 1980 really works.
> Satellite: In only a few minutes, I entered all the figures from my 1980 tax return and got a result which agreed with my hand calculations to the penny.

The evidence relation and relations in general capture information about how different pieces of the text connect to each other and work together to achieve the writer's purpose.

Past work has considered whether rhetorical information is useful for summarization (Marcu, 2000; Chengcheng, 2010; Cardoso et al., 2015; Goyal and Eisenstein, 2016). Marcu (2000) explores how to use RST structures by combining the hierarchical structure of RST with the nucleus/satellite distinction to create an ordering of the units in the text based on importance and salience. Louis et al. (2010) explore the usefulness of different features, including discourse features, for selecting content in extractive summarization. Among the discourse-based features, there are some that score text units based on how high in the discourse tree they are promoted, and others that penalize satellite units relative to nucleus units. Chen et al. (2015) combine topic information and rhetorical structure into a single model, recognizing the importance of both of these types of knowledge for understanding the structure of a document. Specifically, their goal is to model a document's intent structure by assuming that documents contain two types of words: topic words and rhetorical words. In the current work, rhetorical information is used as part of determining the division of texts into sections corresponding to topics.

2.2 Proposal for using RST Topics

As rhetorical and structural information has been shown to be useful for tasks such as summarization, there is motivation for combining this information with the idea of topics. Additionally, instead of using it directly to determine which sentences to choose for a summary, I use this information at a different point in the process. I propose using RST to inform the division of texts into topics. RST relations capture how parts of a text connect to each other to accomplish the writer's purpose. They therefore provide useful information about which sentences in a text are most closely related to each other in a more structural sense than comparing the words they contain. Grouping sentences according to how they are related in a rhetorical structure provides a way to divide texts into topics. Specifically, topic relations that indicate a change in topic provide a natural grouping of sentences.

A few RST relation types are related to topics and topic changes within the text. These types are topic shift and topic drift. Topic shift is a relation that connects large sections of text when there is an abrupt change between topics. On the other hand, topic drift is a relation that connects large sections of text when the change between topics is smooth rather than abrupt, and there is still some similarity between topics. These topic relations provide a way to partition texts into topics. Specifically, these relations can be used as dividing points, with the sections of text connected by these relations considered distinct topics. In this paper, I explore a notion of topic based on this type of structural information and the utility of these topics for summarization.

3 Summarization System

In order to test how the use of topic structure affects summarization, I explored the impact of topics on the performance of previously proposed algorithms for extractive summarization that are implemented in the Sumy Python library.[1] Specifically, several common summarizers including LexRank (Erkan and Radev, 2004), TextRank (Mihalcea and Tarau, 2004), and SumBasic (Nenkova and Vanderwende, 2005) were used. These summarization methods depend on word frequency and co-occurrence rather than using any substantial information about text structure.

Given these summarizers, the following process for summarization was used. First, the complete text was summarized by one of these summarizers. Texts were then divided into topics according to the topics in the RST annotation of the texts. Then each topic was summarized, and the outputs were combined to create a summary of the whole text. In each case, a value of 20% was used for the summarization, meaning the summarizer would return 20% of the original text, where length is measured in sentences. For example, for a text containing 10 sentences, the summarizer would return 2 as the summary. The value of 20% was used when summarizing the entire text or when summarizing an individual topic. Ideally, this will result in similar length summaries whether or not topics are used, because taking 20% of several smaller sections and combining them should be the same as taking 20% of the entire text. In addition to 20%, three other values of the summarization percentage were tested: 10%, 30%, and 40%.

4 Experiments

Experiments were conducted to see how topic structure influences summarization performance. Three conditions were tested. The first condition did not incorporate topic structure. Entire texts were summarized using the summarizers described in the previous section. The second condition used RST topics. Texts were divided into topics as described above. Each of the topics was summarized, and the outputs were combined to create a summary of the entire text. The third condition used random topics. Using the topic sizes from the RST topics, texts were randomly divided into topics of the same size. This condition provided a control to see whether topic divisions informed by RST information resulted in better summaries than random divisions or whether simply dividing a text into smaller sections improves performance.

---

[1] https://github.com/miso-belica/sumy

4.1 Data

The data for these topic summarization experiments comes from the RST Discourse Treebank (Carlson et al., 2002). This corpus contains 385 Wall Street Journal articles that have been annotated with RST structure. Dividing a text into RST topics depends on the presence of topic relations in the annotated text, specifically topic-shift or topic-drift relations. Not all texts in the corpus include topic relations in their annotations. Therefore, these experiments were limited to texts that do contain topic relations. In the corpus, there are 71 documents with topics.

Another feature of the RST Discourse Treebank is the presence of summaries for some documents. Gold-standard summaries are crucial for evaluating the output of a summarization system. For 150 documents in the corpus, there are 2 manually-created extractive summaries. Two analysts created these extracts by selecting a number of Elementary Discourse Units (EDUs) based on the square root of the total number of EDUs in the text. EDUs are the building blocks of RST structure. They are the lowest level units that are arguments of RST relations. EDUs are typically clauses.

Since gold-standard summaries are required to evaluate system-produced summaries, these experiments were performed on texts that have corresponding summaries. Of the 71 documents in the corpus that have topics, 51 documents also have extractive summaries. These 51 documents are the core dataset for the topic summarization experiments.

4.2 Division into Topics

Texts are divided into topics using RST topic relations. In the most straightforward case, all units in the text are explicitly designated as part of a topic. This case can be seen in Figure 1. The first line indicates that the text contains 31 units, as the Root spans the entire text. The next line shows that units 1-13 are part of a topic-drift relation. Skipping down to the other argument of this relation on the last line shows that the other element of the topic relation includes the rest of the text, units 14-31. In this notation, these text spans are arguments of the same relation because when combined they form a continuous sequence with the second argument starting directly after the first, and visually the two arguments occur at the same indent level. Therefore, this text

can easily be divided into two topics. The first topic begins with the first unit of the text and continues to unit 13, and the second topic begins at unit 14 and continues to the end of the text.

```
( Root (span 1 31)
  ( Nucleus (span 1 13) (rel2par Topic-Drift)
    ( Nucleus (span 1 8) (rel2par span)
           .
           .
  ( Nucleus (span 14 31) (rel2par Topic-Drift)
```

Figure 1: RST annotation with all units in explicit topics

However, in other texts, not all units within a text are necessarily included as part of an explicit topic relation. In these cases, in order to divide a text into topics the topic relations were used as dividing points. Each occurrence of a topic relation signaled the beginning of a new topic. Anything before that point is grouped together as a topic, and anything after a topic relation is grouped as a topic. In that way, all units in a text are included as part of a topic. This topic division can be seen in Figure 2. The first line shows that the text contains 88 units. In contrast to the previous example, the first relation is not a topic relation. The first explicit topic relation begins with unit 7 and ends with unit 38. The other argument of that relation begins with unit 39 and continues to unit 53. No explicit topic relations include either the beginning or the end of the text. Using the topic relations as dividing points, all units can be placed into a topic. Units 1-6 become a topic, spanning from the beginning of the text to the first topic relation, and units 54-88 become a topic, spanning from the end of a topic relation to the end of the text.

This division method creates a partition of the text into a sequence of non-overlapping topics. Using this method means that topics contain adjacent units. Each unit in the text is contained in exactly one topic. Pseudocode for the topic division process is shown in Figure 3.

```
( Root (span 1 88)
  ( Nucleus (span 1 53) (rel2par span)
    ( Nucleus (span 1 6) (rel2par span)
        ...
    ( Satellite (span 7 53) (rel2par background)
      ( Nucleus (span 7 38) (rel2par Topic-Drift)
          ...
      ( Nucleus (span 39 53) (rel2par Topic-Drift)
          ...
```

Figure 2: RST annotation without all explicit topics

```
input: RST annotation file
Topics = list of topics

# Find explicit topics in RST annotations
(1) for line in annotations:
(2)    relation = find label of relation type
(3)    span = (x, y) where x is start and y is end
(4)    if relation = 'topic-shift' or 'topic-drift':
(5)        add span to Topics

# If no topic starting with the first unit, add one
(6) minimum = lowest value in Topics
(7) if minimum != 1:
(8)    add (1, minimum-1) to Topics

# If no topic ending with the last unit, add one
(9) total_len = total number of units
(10) maximum = highest value in Topics
(11) if maximum < total_len:
(12)   add (maximum+1, total_len) to Topics

# Remove topics with overlapping starting or end-
ing points to ensure sequence of non-overlapping top-
ics
(13) for (x, y) in Topics:
(14)   if y is not smallest value for x:
(15)       remove (x, y) from topics
(16)   if there are multiple values of x for y:
(17)       if x = lowest value:
(18)           remove (x, y) from topics
(19)           add to Topics (lowest value, w-1) where
(w, z) in Topics and w-lowest value is smallest

# If unit not included in any topic, add it
(20) for i from 1 to total_len:
(21)   if i is not covered by any topic in Topics:
(22)       add (i, i) to Topics

(23) return Topics
```

Figure 3: Pseudocode for dividing into topics

4.3 Evaluation

Summary evaluation is a difficult task. There can be more than one good summary of a text, and when people are instructed to create summaries, they do not necessarily contain the same sentences. Since there is no single correct answer for what a summary should contain, evaluation typically involves comparing a system-produced summary to a manually-created reference summary. Summary quality is based on some measure of similarity or overlap with a reference summary.

ROUGE (Lin, 2004) is a measure to evaluate performance on the task of automatic summarization. ROUGE is a standard measure used in the field of summarization (Erkan and Radev, 2004; Lin and Hovy, 2003; Xie et al., 2008; Wong et al., 2008; Nallapati et al., 2016; Chopra et al., 2016). Recall-Oriented Understudy for Gisting Evaluation involves comparing a summary produced by a summarization system to reference or gold-standard summaries created by humans. Specifically, ROUGE-N measures n-gram (unigram, bigram, etc.) recall between a system summary and a reference summary. Recall refers to how many of the reference n-grams were included in the system summary. The equation for ROUGE-N is presented below.

$$\frac{\sum_{S \in \{Ref\ Sum\}} \sum_{gram_n \in S} Count_{match}(gram_n)}{\sum_{S \in \{Ref\ Sum\}} \sum_{gram_n \in S} Count(gram_n)} \tag{1}$$

In this equation, n refers to the size of the n-gram, such as unigram (1) or bigram (2). An n-gram itself is represented by $gram_n$, and $Count_{match}(gram_n)$ refers to the number of times that the n-gram $gram_n$ appears in the system summary. Therefore, the numerator is the number of matching n-grams, and the denominator is the total number of n-grams in the reference summaries.

One downside of ROUGE is that it is entirely recall-based. In general, a summary will be rewarded for including more n-grams without being penalized for containing n-grams that do not appear in the reference summary. In the extreme case, a summary that is the same length as the original text being summarized could achieve perfect recall even though such a summary would clearly not be considered a good summary, since the goal of summarization is to produce a shortened version of the input. In order to avoid this problem, summary length must be controlled. Specifically, since ROUGE-N is a word-based evaluation measure, the summary length in terms of word count must be controlled so that system-produced summaries are similar in length to the reference summaries.

Unit overlap is another evaluation measure for summarization (Steinberger and Ježek, 2012). It finds the similarity between two texts by looking at

	LR	LR-T	TR	TR-T	SB	SB-T
Avg ROUGE-1	0.496	0.588	0.554	**0.607**	0.420	0.463
Avg ROUGE-2	0.330	0.442	0.415	**0.458**	0.214	0.275
Avg Unit Overlap	0.261	**0.317**	0.260	0.289	0.241	0.260
Avg Cosine Similarity	0.668	**0.711**	0.694	0.710	0.619	0.650

Table 1: Results of using the summarizers with and without topics. LR: LexRank, LR-T: LexRank with Topics, TR: TextRank, TR-T: TextRank with Topics, SB: SumBasic, SB-T: SumBasic with Topics. Highest values for each measure are in bold.

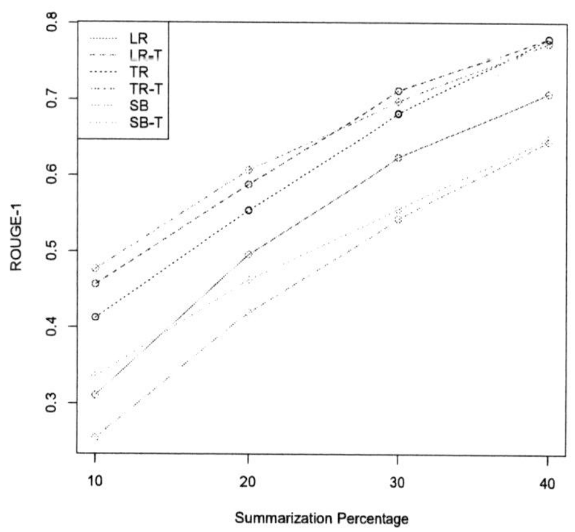

Figure 4: Values of ROUGE-1 as percentage increases

Figure 5: Values of unit overlap as percentage increases

the number of words they have in common compared to the number of non-overlapping words they contain.

$$unit\ overlap(X,Y) = \frac{\|X \cap Y\|}{\|X\| + \|Y\| - \|X \cap Y\|} \quad (2)$$

X and Y are the words in the documents being compared. In contrast to ROUGE, unit overlap penalizes an evaluated text for containing words that do not appear in the gold-standard text. A summary will not be rewarded simply for being longer.

The final evaluation measure used is cosine similarity (Steinberger and Ježek, 2012). It is a measure of similarity between documents using vectors of word frequency. Similar to unit overlap, cosine similarity takes document length into account and prevents texts from being rewarded for being longer.

To evaluate the summaries, each system-produced summary is evaluated against each of the two corresponding gold-standard summaries. Scores are calculated for each document, and the scores from all documents in the corpus are averaged to produce an overall value for each measure.

4.4 Results and Discussion

Table 1 shows the results of using three different summarizers to summarize texts with and without topics. These are the results when a summarization percentage of 20% was used. Each pair of columns shows the result of a different summarizer. The first column in each pair shows the results without using topics, and the second shows the results of using RST topics. The highest value for each measure is in bold. Looking at the results shows several interesting effects. For each measure, the highest value is achieved when using topics. The highest ROUGE values are found with TextRank, and the highest values for unit overlap and cosine similarity are found with LexRank. In these cases, using topics results in improvements in performance of around 5%. While different summarizers perform slightly better on different measures, in this paper I am interested in the fact that regardless of evaluation measure or summarizer, the inclusion of topics improves performance.

Text: [Nissan Motor Co. expects net income to reach 120 billion yen (U.S. $857 million) in its current fiscal year, up from 114.6 billion yen in the previous year, Yutaka Kume, president, said. Mr. Kume made the earnings projection for fiscal 1990, ending next March 31, in an interview with U.S. automotive writers attending the Tokyo Motor Show. The executive said that the anticipated earnings increase is fairly modest because Nissan is spending heavily to bolster its dealership network in Japan and because of currency-exchange fluctuations.]$_{\text{Topic 1}}$
[During the next decade, Mr. Kume said, Nissan plans to boost overseas vehicle production sufficiently to account for a majority of sales outside Japan. Last year, Mr. Kume said, Nissan exported slightly over one million vehicles, and produced 570,000 cars and trucks at its factories in North America, Europe and Australia. But by 1992, he added, Nissan will build one million vehicles a year outside Japan, or sufficient to equal exports. "By the end of the 1990s," he said, "we want to be producing roughly two vehicles overseas for every vehicle that we export from Japan." That will involve a substantial increase in overseas manufacturing capacity, he acknowledged, but didn't provide specific details.]$_{\text{Topic 2}}$

Summary without Topics: But by 1992, he added, Nissan will build one million vehicles a year outside Japan, or sufficient to equal exports. "By the end of the 1990s," he said, "we want to be producing roughly two vehicles overseas for every vehicle that we export from Japan."

Summary with RST Topics: Nissan Motor Co. expects net income to reach 120 billion yen (U.S. $857 million) in its current fiscal year, up from 114.6 billion yen in the previous year, Yutaka Kume, president, said. During the next decade, Mr. Kume said, Nissan plans to boost overseas vehicle production sufficiently to account for a majority of sales outside Japan.

Figure 6: Example text and summaries

Figures 4 and 5 show how the values of ROUGE-1 and unit overlap change as different summarization percentages are used. In general, values of the evaluation measures increase as the percentage increases. However, the increases depend on which measure is considered. ROUGE values increase by the largest margin and with the most consistency. On the other hand, there are smaller increases for the other measures. ROUGE has such large and consistent increases because it is recall-based, so longer summaries will always perform better. This issue will be discussed further below. The results show that topics create more of an improvement in performance when the percentage is lower and the summaries are smaller, suggesting that topics do provide useful information for summarization, and that information is the most useful when space is the most limited.

Figure 6 provides an example text along with the summaries produced when no topics are used and when RST topics are used. When no topic structure is used, all sentences in the summary come from one topic, showing how topic structure is needed to ensure coverage of all ideas in the text.

An important factor to consider when comparing the results of performing summarization with and without topics is summary length. It is possible that summarizing at the topic level could result in summaries of different lengths from the summaries produced by summarizing the entire text. Differences in length could affect these evaluation measures, particularly ROUGE, which is recall-based and therefore benefits from including more words by increasing the chances of having more words in common with the gold-standard.

One way of dealing with this potential problem is to compare RST topics with random topics. Using the topic sizes from the RST topics, texts were randomly divided into topics of the same size. While the RST topics always contain adjacent sentences, the random topics are not constrained in this way. If the topics were contiguous, they could not be both random and equal in size to the RST topics. Therefore, the random topics are equal in size but do not follow the same adjacency restrictions as the RST topics. Since the random topics are the same size as the RST topics, length should not have an effect. The model was run 25 times with random topics. Figure 7 provides a visual illustration of the results. The bars in the graph represent the mean values. The error bars show two standard deviations below and above the mean. The points represent the values when using RST topics. Comparing the mean values to the values with RST topics, the RST values are higher than the random topics for all measures. Looking at the RST values compared to the means + 2 standard deviations, the RST values are greater than or very similar to the random values, indicating that the RST values are significantly different from random.

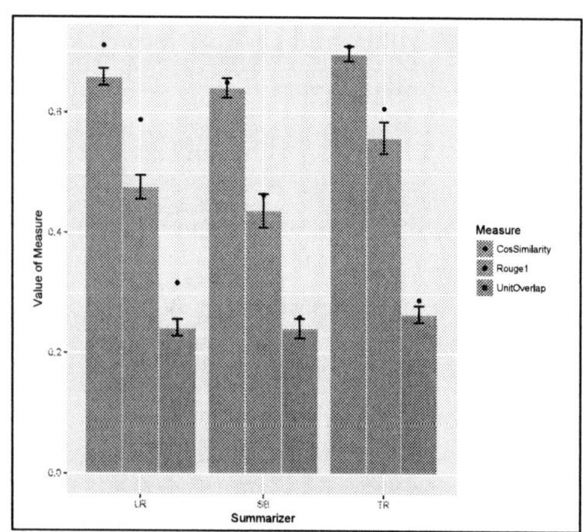

Figure 7: Results with random topics

ROUGE-1		
Factor	Estimate	P-value
Word Count	0.0004995	1.51e-08 ***
Random	-0.01885	0.31
RST Topics	0.08704	4.17e-06 ***
Unit Overlap		
Word Count	-0.0001083	0.0967
Random	-0.01616	0.2508
RST Topics	0.05705	6.32e-05 ***

Table 2: Linear Regression Results for LexRank

Another way to explore the effects of length is to consider whether the use of topics has an effect on performance separate from any effect of summary length. Table 3 shows the results of a linear regression exploring the effects of different factors on ROUGE and unit overlap to see whether length differences are having an effect. The factors considered were word count in the summary and RST Topics/Random Topics/No Topics. These are the results when using LexRank as the summarizer. The results for the other summarizers are similar.[2] As shown in the table, word count and RST topics had a significant effect on ROUGE, while random topics had no significant effect. The significance of RST topics shows that using RST topics improves performance compared to not using topics as well as compared to using random topics. As discussed above, ROUGE is affected by differences in word count, and these results show that word count was a significant factor in predicting ROUGE scores. However, the unit overlap scores are not affected in the same way, and the linear regression confirms that for unit overlap the only significant factor is the use of RST topics.

These results demonstrate the positive impact that the use of topics has on summarization performance. Specifically, dividing texts into topics using topic relations from RST results in summaries that are more similar to manually-created gold-standard summaries than summarizing texts without the inclusion of topic structure.

Given the improved summarization performance seen when using topics based on RST, it is worth considering whether other notions of topic, particularly common topic modeling methods, are useful for this task. Latent Semantic Analysis (LSA) was tested as another way to divide texts into topics, using an implementation from Gensim topic modeling software (Rehurek and Sojka 2010). An important part of LSA is the number of dimensions that are used when reducing the semantic space. Given the size of the training data and common values suggested in previous research, three values were tested for the number of dimensions: 50, 100, and 200. To divide a text into topics, the number of topics, n, to choose was taken from the RST annotation. Then this number was used as k in a k-means clustering algorithm. Clustering was performed over the sentence vectors that represent a document's sentences in the LSA semantic space. These vectors contain values for how related a document is to each of the dimensions in the model. Clustering divides the sentences of a text into k topics based on similarity of the sentence vectors. Clustering was performed using scikit-learn (Pedregosa et al. 2011). The results are presented in Table 3, which shows the mean of each evaluation measure over 10 runs of the model, using LexRank as the summarizer, with 100 dimensions in the LSA model. The values when not using topics and when using RST topics are repeated in the table for comparison.

---

[2] TextRank P-values, ROUGE: Word Count 2.21e-09 ***, Random 0.83744, RST topics 0.00345 **; Unit Overlap: Word Count 0.0713, Random 0.8942, RST topics 0.0170 *.

SumBasic P-values, ROUGE: Word Count 1.02e-10 ***, Random 0.5335, RST topics 0.0121 *; Unit Overlap: Word Count 0.2439, Random 0.7664, RST topics 0.0505.

	R1	R2	UO	CS
Mean	0.4873	0.3105	0.2546	0.6720
No Top	0.496	0.330	0.261	0.668
RST	0.588	0.442	0.317	0.711

Table 3: Results when using LSA topics compared to no topics and RST topics; Mean = mean of LSA runs

The results are similar when using different numbers of dimensions as well as the other summarizers. Looking across all summarizers and numbers of dimensions, RST topics perform better than LSA topics. The difference in performance is evident for all evaluation measures. In general, LSA topics perform similarly to using no topics at all. Overall, the types of topics found by using LSA are not very useful for a summarization system that uses topics. The results suggest that while LSA has been successfully used to classify documents and find documents related to a query (Deerwester et al., 1990; Zelikovitz and Hirsh, 2001), LSA is not sufficient to distinguish between different topics of a single document and does not find topics that improve summarization.

5   Conclusion

By performing summarization at the level of the entire text and at the level of individual topics, I investigated the influence of topic information on summarization performance. I explored a notion of topic that uses information about a text's rhetorical structure in the form of RST relations. The direct comparison of summarization when using topics versus not using topics showed that topic information improves performance. Improvements were found with several evaluation measures, including ROUGE and unit overlap. Performance also improved regardless of which summarizer was used.

The strong performance of the model when using topics has several interesting implications that highlight the contributions of this work. First, the results demonstrate the usefulness of topic structure. Conceptualizing texts as composed of a number of topics not only improves human processing of texts but also increases the quality of summaries produced by automatic systems. In this work, topics were incorporated in a straightforward way, by summarizing a text's topics and combining them to create a complete summary. The results showed that this simple method for including topic information improves performance compared to not using any topics.

Another important finding of this work is the utility of a notion of topic based on rhetorical information. The topics were based on RST relations that connect pieces of a text when the topic has changed between the sections. Using these relations to signal boundaries between topics proved to be a reasonable method to automatically separate a text into its component topics, and specifically a method that is useful for finding topics relevant for summarization. The improvements in performance seen with this notion of topic also demonstrate another way that rhetorical information such as RST can be used as part of the summarization process.

These results demonstrate the benefits of using one notion of topic for summarization and motivate further investigation into the use of topic structure, including comparisons with other methods for dividing a text into topics. This work also motivates the consideration of other ways to use rhetorical information for summarization. An area for future work is to explore how to automatically find RST-type topics without requiring a full RST annotation.

References

Asher, Nicholas. 2004. Discourse topic. *Theoretical Linguistics, 30*(2-3), pp.163-201.

Blei, David M. 2012. Probabilistic topic models. *Communications of the ACM, 55*(4), pp.77-84.

Cardoso, Paula C.F., Maria L.R.C. Jorge, and Thiago A.S. Pardo. 2015. Exploring the Rhetorical Structure Theory for multi-document summarization. In *Congreso de la Sociedad Española para el Procesamiento del Lenguaje Natural, XXXI*. Sociedad Española para el Procesamiento del Lenguaje Natural-SEPLN.

Carlson, Lynn, Mary Ellen Okurowski, and Daniel Marcu. 2002. *RST discourse treebank*. Linguistic Data Consortium, University of Pennsylvania.

Chen, Bei, Jun Zhu, Nan Yang, Tian Tian, Ming Zhou, and Bo Zhang. 2016. Jointly Modeling Topics and Intents with Global Order Structure. In *AAAI* (pp. 2711-2717).

Chengcheng, Li. 2010. Automatic text summarization based on rhetorical structure theory. In *International Conference on Computer Application and System Modeling (ICCASM)* (Vol. 13, pp. V13-595). IEEE.

Chopra, Sumit, Michael Auli, Alexander M. Rush, and S.E.A.S. Harvard. 2016. Abstractive Sentence Summarization with Attentive Recurrent Neural Networks. In *HLT-NAACL* (pp. 93-98).

Christensen, Janara, Stephen Soderland Mausam, Stephen Soderland, and Oren Etzioni. 2013. Towards Coherent Multi-Document Summarization. In *HLT-NAACL* (pp. 1163-1173).

Conroy, John M., Judith D. Schlesinger, and Dianne P. O'Leary. 2006. Topic-focused multi-document summarization using an approximate oracle score. In *Proceedings of the COLING/ACL on Main conference poster sessions* (pp. 152-159). Association for Computational Linguistics.

Deerwester, Scott, Susan T. Dumais, George W. Furnas, Thomas K. Landauer, and Richard Harshman. 1990. Indexing by latent semantic analysis. *Journal of the American society for information science*, *41*(6), p.391.

Erkan, Günes and Dragomir R. Radev. 2004. Lexrank: Graph-based lexical centrality as salience in text summarization. *Journal of Artificial Intelligence Research*, *22*, pp.457-479.

Goyal, Naman and Jacob Eisenstein. 2016. A Joint Model of Rhetorical Discourse Structure and Summarization. *EMNLP 2016*, p.25.

Griffiths, Thomas L., Mark Steyvers, David M. Blei, and Joshua B. Tenenbaum. 2005. Integrating topics and syntax. In *Advances in neural information processing systems* (pp. 537-544).

Gundel, Jeanette K. 1988. Universals of topic-comment structure. *Studies in syntactic typology*, *17*, pp.209-239.

Hyona, Jukka, Robert F. Lorch, and Johanna K. Kaakinen. 2002. Individual differences in reading to summarize expository text: Evidence from eye fixation patterns. *Journal of Educational Psychology*, *94*(1), pp.44-55.

Lambrecht, Knud. 1996. *Information structure and sentence form: Topic, focus, and the mental representations of discourse referents* (Vol. 71). Cambridge University Press.

Lin, Chin-Yew. 2004. Rouge: A package for automatic evaluation of summaries. In *Text summarization branches out: Proceedings of the ACL-04 workshop* (Vol. 8).

Lin, Chin-Yew and Eduard Hovy. 2003. Automatic evaluation of summaries using n-gram co-occurrence statistics. In *Proceedings of the 2003 Conference of the North American Chapter of the Association for Computational Linguistics on Human Language Technology-Volume 1* (pp. 71-78). Association for Computational Linguistics.

Lorch Jr, Robert F., Elizabeth Pugzles Lorch, and Ann M. Mogan. 1987. Task effects and individual differences in on-line processing of the topic structure of a text. *Discourse Processes*, *10*(1), pp.63-80.

Louis, Annie, Aravind Joshi, and Ani Nenkova. 2010. Discourse indicators for content selection in summarization. In *Proceedings of the 11th Annual Meeting of the Special Interest Group on Discourse and Dialogue* (pp. 147-156). Association for Computational Linguistics.

Mann, William C. and Sandra A. Thompson. 1988. Rhetorical structure theory: Toward a functional theory of text organization. *Text-Interdisciplinary Journal for the Study of Discourse*, *8*(3), pp.243-281.

Marcu, Daniel. 2000. *The theory and practice of discourse parsing and summarization*. MIT press.

Mihalcea, Rada and Paul Tarau. 2004. TextRank: Bringing Order into Text. In *EMNLP* (Vol. 4, pp. 404-411).

Nallapati, Ramesh, Bowen Zhou, Caglar Gulcehre, and Bing Xiang. 2016. Abstractive text summarization using sequence-to-sequence rnns and beyond. *arXiv preprint arXiv:1602.06023*.

Nenkova, Ani and Lucy Vanderwende. 2005. The impact of frequency on summarization. *Microsoft Research, Redmond, Washington, Tech. Rep. MSR-TR-2005, 101*.

Pedregosa, Fabian, Gaël Varoquaux, Alexandre Gramfort, Vincent Michel, Bertrand Thirion, Olivier Grisel, Mathieu Blondel, Peter Prettenhofer, Ron Weiss, Vincent Dubourg, and Jake Vanderplas. 2011. Scikit-learn: Machine learning in Python. *Journal of Machine Learning Research*, *12*(Oct), pp.2825-2830.

Rehurek, Radim and Petr Sojka. 2010. Software framework for topic modelling with large corpora. In *Proceedings of the LREC 2010 Workshop on New Challenges for NLP Frameworks*.

Steinberger, Josef and Karel Ježek. 2012. Evaluation measures for text summarization. *Computing and Informatics*, *28*(2), pp.251-275.

Van Dijk, Teun A. 1977. Sentence topic and discourse topic. *Papers in Slavic Philology*, *1*, pp.49-61.

Van Kuppevelt, Jan. 1995. Discourse structure, topicality and questioning. *Journal of linguistics*, *31*(1), pp.109-147.

Wong, Kam-Fai, Mingli Wu, and Wenjie Li. 2008. Extractive summarization using supervised and semi-supervised learning. In *Proceedings of the 22nd International Conference on Computational Linguistics-Volume 1* (pp. 985-992). Association for Computational Linguistics.

Xie, Shasha and Yang Liu. 2008. Using corpus and knowledge-based similarity measure in maximum marginal relevance for meeting summarization. In *Acoustics, Speech and Signal Processing, 2008. ICASSP 2008. IEEE International Conference on* (pp. 4985-4988). IEEE.

Yih, Wen-tau, Joshua Goodman, Lucy Vanderwende, and
  Hisami Suzuki. 2007. Multi-Document Summarization by Maximizing Informative Content-Words. In
  IJCAI (Vol. 7, pp. 1776-1782).
Zelikovitz, Sarah and Haym Hirsh. 2001. Using LSI for
  text classification in the presence of background text.
  In *Proceedings of the tenth international conference
  on Information and knowledge management* (pp. 113-
  118). ACM.

Sound Analogies with Phoneme Embeddings

Miikka Silfverberg and **Lingshuang Jack Mao** and **Mans Hulden**
Department of Linguistics
University of Colorado
`first.last@colorado.edu`

Abstract

Vector space models of words in NLP—*word embeddings*—have been recently shown to reliably encode semantic information, offering capabilities such as solving proportional analogy tasks such as man:woman::king:queen. We study how well these distributional properties carry over to similarly learned *phoneme embeddings*, and whether phoneme vector spaces align with articulatory distinctive features, using several methods of obtaining such continuous-space representations. We demonstrate a statistically significant correlation between distinctive feature spaces and vector spaces learned with word-context PPMI+SVD and word2vec, showing that many distinctive feature contrasts are implicitly present in phoneme distributions. Furthermore, these distributed representations allow us to solve proportional analogy tasks with phonemes, such as **p** is to **b** as **t** is to **X**, where the solution is that **X = d**. This effect is even stronger when a supervision signal is added where we extract phoneme representations from the embedding layer of an recurrent neural network that is trained to solve a word inflection task, i.e. a model that is made aware of word relatedness.

1 Introduction

Distributional word representations, or word embeddings, have attracted much attention in NLP, and their success is considered a vindication of the distributional hypothesis for lexical semantics espoused much earlier by the likes of Wittgenstein,[1]

Firth,[2] Harris,[3] and other contemporaries. Often overlooked is that this hypothesis among linguists has extended itself much wider to include phonology and grammar: "all elements of speech (phonological, lexical, and grammatical) are now to be defined and classified in terms of their relations to one another" (Haas, 1954, p.54).

Given the successes of distributional models not only in specifying semantic similarity, but also addressing proportional analogy tasks (Turney and Pantel, 2010; Mikolov et al., 2013a,b; Levy et al., 2014), we want to investigate if distributional representations of phonemes induce a similarly coherent space as lexical items do, and if the properties of such spaces conform to linguistic expectations, a question posed in another form as early as in Fischer-Jørgensen (1952). In particular, we address two questions: (1) whether learned vector representations of phonemes are congruent with commonly assumed binary phonological distinctive feature spaces, and (2) whether a proportional analogy of the type a:b::c:d (**a** is to **b** as **c** is to **d**) discovered in a phoneme embedding space is also a valid analogy in a phonological distinctive feature space, where phonemes are represented in a space of standard articulatory binary features (Mielke, 2008) such as ±continuant, ±voice, ±high, ±coronal, etc.

We address these questions using three different methods of obtaining vector representations of phonemes; two unsupervised models that associate phonemes and the contexts (neighboring phonemes) they occur in (word2vec, PPMI+SVD), and one model where we are given lemmas and inflected forms as supervised data for a recurrent neural network (RNN) encoder-

---

[1]"the meaning of a word is its use in the language" (Wittgenstein, 1953, p.43)

[2]"The complete meaning of a word is always contextual" (Firth, 1937, p.37)

[3]"distributional statements can cover all of the material of a language" (Harris, 1954, p.34)

Proceedings of the Society for Computation in Linguistics (SCiL) 2018, pages 136-144.
Salt Lake City, Utah, January 4-7, 2018

decoder model that is trained to perform such inflections from where we extract the vector representations in the embedding layer. The latter method has a weak supervision signal in that the system knows which words are truly related forms, since it is trained only on word pairs where one of the words is a result of transforming the other one according to inflectional features. Hence, this latter model can presumably better pick up on phonological alternations along distinctive feature lines that occur between phonemes; for example, knowledge of relatedness helps in determining that two forms exhibit a voicing alternation, as in the Finnish pair mato ('worm', nominative) $\sim$ ma**d**on ('worm', genitive), and hence, the segments **t** and **d** should align themselves in the embedding space parallel to other voiceless/voiced pairs that alternate similarly. We perform experiments in three languages: Finnish, Turkish, and Spanish.

2 Related Work

Local co-occurrence of phonemes and (in writing) phonemic graphemes has been widely explored in the literature for unsupervised discovery of phonological features. The observation of Markov (1913, 2006) that vowels and consonants tend to alternate in a statistically robust way in phonemic writing systems is an early observation that some articulatory features can be recovered in an unsupervised way. Algorithms for cryptographic decipherment often take advantage of such patterns (Guy, 1991; Sukhotin, 1962, 1973). Local co-occurrence counts have also been analyzed through spectral methods, such as singular value decomposition (Moler and Morrison, 1983; Goldsmith and Xanthos, 2009; Thaine and Penn, 2017), revealing that significant latent structure can be recovered, mainly with respect to vowels and consonants. Recent works along the same lines of inquiry include Kim and Snyder (2013) that presents a Bayesian approach that simultaneously clusters languages and reveals consonant/vowel/nasal distinctions in an unsupervised manner. Hulden (2017) shows that an algorithm based on the obligatory contour principle (Leben, 1973) and an additional assumption of phonological tiers being present (Goldsmith, 1976) robustly reveals at least consonant/vowel, coronal/non-coronal, and front/back distinctions from unlabeled phonetic data or orthographic data from phonemic writing systems.

Learning features directly from waveform representations (see e.g. Lin (2005))—while not addressed in this paper—is also highly relevant to the current study, and is indeed a question to which some lower-level, speech signal-based form of distributed representations may be adapted.

The idea explored in this paper—that phonemes (or graphemes) might exhibit linguistically apt correlations in an embedding space—has been implied by earlier research, for example Faruqui et al. (2016). In that work, a neural encoder-decoder model (Cho et al., 2014; Sutskever et al., 2014) was trained to perform a transformation of words from their citation forms to a 'target' inflected form and, after training, the vowels in the embedding layer of the long-short term memory (LSTM) neural model trained for Finnish were found to clearly group themselves according to known harmony patterns in the language. Li et al. (2016) take advantage of phoneme transcriptions in a neural speech synthesis application, showing improvements on this task and indicating that similar phonemes in a bidirectional LSTM (Bi-LSTM) embedding layer map close to each other. More closely related to the current work, Dunbar et al. (2015) investigate how well phonetic feature representations in English align with vector representations learned from local contexts of sound occurrence using both a neural language model and also a matrix factorization model. Their (surprisingly) negative results can be explained by the fact that the experiment was set up to compare two spaces with respect to all and only minimally differing pairs (such as: is the distinctive feature vector offset from **p** to **b** like the offset from **t** to **d** in the embedding space?) using a small specific fixed number of phonological features. By contrast, in our experiments, we learn a vector space model and examine if all phoneme-pair distances correlate globally between the embedding space and a known phonological distinctive feature space, and also whether analogies deemed to be 'good' in the embedding spaces are also 'good' in the distinctive feature space. This is less sensitive to an assumption that *all* distinctive features have correlates in the embedding space. For example, Figure 3 shows a space induced by one of our methods, where the offset from ɑ to æ (low vowels) is similar to that of o to ø (high vowels), both being back-to-front vowel transformations, but where the equivalent harmonic correspondence **u** to **y** is not represented equally prominently.

3 Models and methods

We consider three different models for learning phoneme embeddings.

PPMI+SVD These embeddings are formulated using *truncated Singular Value Decomposition* (SVD) on a matrix of *positive point-wise mutual information* (PPMI) values (Bullinaria and Levy, 2007; Levy and Goldberg, 2014). For the definition of PPMI, see Equation 1. We first compute PPMI values for co-occurrences of center phonemes and context phonemes in a five character sliding window over the training data. We then arrange the PPMI values into an $n \times n$ matrix M and apply SVD to get the factorization $M = U\Sigma V^\top$, where U and V are orthonormal, and Σ is diagonal. Let U_d denote the $n \times d$ matrix derived from $U\Sigma$ by truncating all rows to length d. Then our d-dimensional phoneme embeddings are the rows of U_d.

$$\text{PPMI}(x, y) = \max(\log \frac{p(x, y)}{p(x)p(y)}, 0) \quad (1)$$

The probabilities $p(x, y)$, $p(x)$, and $p(y)$ are derived from simple counts by maximum likelihood estimation.

word2vec Our second model is the word2vec model introduced by Mikolov et al. (2013a) for modeling semantic relatedness of words. Like the PPMI+SVD model, the word2vec model captures distributional information about phonemes. However, it explicitly constructs a language model and trains embeddings which perform well on the language modeling task. Nevertheless, Levy et al. (2014) show that the models are in a sense the same: like PPMI+SVD, the skip-gram variant of word2vec with negative sampling is also implicitly performing a factorization of a matrix of shifted PMI values of words and their context words. Although the models are similar, we decided to include word2vec because of claims that it sometimes tends to give better results on analogy tasks (Levy et al., 2014).

In our experiments, we use standard word2vec embeddings generated with the `gensim` toolkit.[4] We use the skipgram model and negative sampling with window size 1.

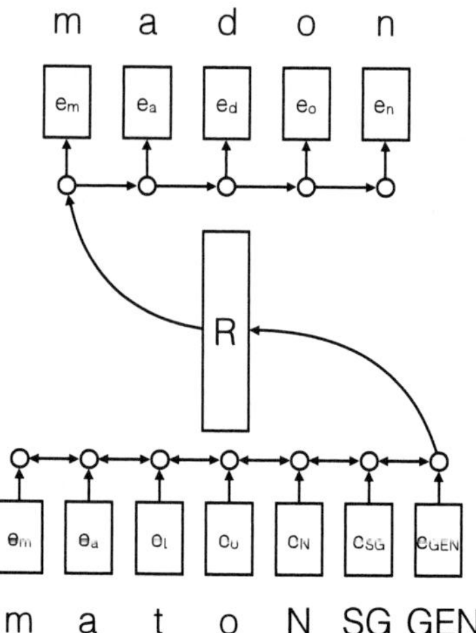

Figure 1: A word inflection system implemented as an RNN encoder-decoder. The system first encodes the input (the citation form) and the desired output morphological features "mato+N+SG+GEN" 'worm' into a single vector R using a bidirectional LSTM encoder. A decoder LSTM network then uses R to generate the output word form "madon". The system learns the appropriate phoneme embeddings, for example e_m and e_a, to aid in the inflection process. We use these as our vector representations of phonemes.

RNN encoder-decoder Our final model differs from the first two in that it learns embeddings which maximize performance on a word inflection task: the system receives lemmas and the morphological features of the desired inflected form as input and emits corresponding inflected forms. We formulate the system as an RNN encoder-decoder (Cho et al., 2014). Our system is identical to the system presented in Kann and Schütze (2016) except that it does not incorporate attention. The encoder is realized using a bidirectional LSTM model which operates on character/phoneme embeddings (see Figure 1). The same embeddings are also used by the decoder as explained more thoroughly in Kann and Schütze (2016). We first train the system and then extract the phoneme embeddings (see Figure 2) and use them as our phoneme vector representations.

The performance of RNN encoder-decoder models is known to be sensitive to the random initialization of parameters during training. In all ex-

---

[4]https://radimrehurek.com/gensim/

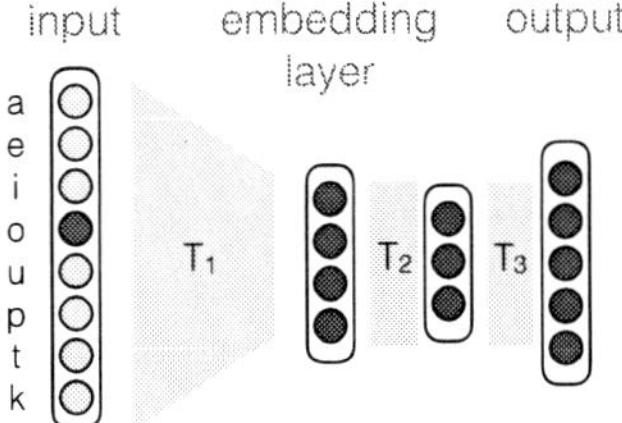

Figure 2: A neural network learns to map a one-hot input into an intermediate representation (the embedding layer). This transformation is tuned to perform well on an inflection task and yields a dense vector representation of segments.

periments, we therefore train five separate models using five different random initializations of parameters and compute similarity scores and analogy scores as averages of the scores given by individual models.

4   Data and Resources

We train all models using Finnish, Spanish and Turkish data sets from the SIGMORPHON 2016 shared task for morphological re-inflection (Cotterell et al., 2016). Each line in the data sets contains an inflected word form, its associated lemma and morphological features. For Finnish, the training data consists of 12,692 lines, for Spanish, 12,575 lines and, for Turkish, 12,336 lines. We learn embeddings for orthographic symbols occurring more than 100 times in the respective data sets. For Finnish, this set includes 25 symbols, for Spanish, 28 symbols and, for Turkish, 27 symbols.

The PPMI+SVD and word2vec models only use word forms for training. In contrast, the RNN encoder-decoder is trained on all parts of the training set: word forms, lemmas and morphological features. For all three languages, we use the training data for subtask 1 of the shared task.

There is a near one-to-one correspondence between Finnish and Turkish graphemes and phonemes. For Spanish, the correspondence between the orthographic and phonetic representation of the language is, however, less straightforward. We therefore perform a number of transformations on the training data in order to bring it closer to a phonetic representation of the language. Specifically, we transform voiced stops **b**, **d** and **g** to the voiced fricatives with the same place of articulation postvocalically (β, ð, ɣ). We addi-

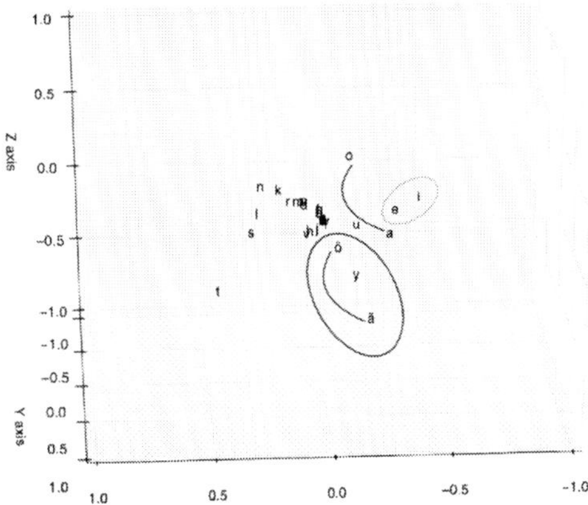

Figure 3: A vowel space for Finnish learned by collecting local phone(me)-context counts (window size 5), followed by a PPMI transform, followed by SVD, truncated to three dimensions. Neutral vowels are **e**, **i** (circled in yellow) and the harmony correspondences are **a** (=IPA ɑ) ∼ **ä** (= IPA æ), **o** ∼ **ö** (= IPA ø) and **u** ∼ **y**. The front harmonic group is circled in blue.

VOWELS		
(Syllabic), Front, Back, High, Low, Round, Tense		
CONSONANTS		
Consonantal, Sonorant, (Syllabic), Voice, Labial, Coronal, Dorsal, Pharyngeal, Lateral, Nasal, Continuant, Delayed Release, Distributed, Tap, Anterior, Strident		

Table 1: Features used in manually crafted articulatory representations.

tionally replace **ll** with ʎ, **r** with ɾ, and **c** with θ.[5]

We compare embeddings discovered by different systems to manually crafted articulatory representations of phonemes/allophones based on standard IPA descriptions in Hayes (2011). The list of the phonetic features we use is given in Table 4. We realize the representations as vectors $v \in \{0, 1\}^n$ in a *distinctive feature space*, where n is the number of distinctive features in the description (22 in our model). Each dimension in feature space corresponds to a phonetic feature such as *continuant*, *syllabic* and *voice*. Entry i in a feature vector is 1 if the corresponding phoneme is positive for the given feature. Otherwise, it is 0.

---

[5]Our code is available at `s://github.com/mpsilfvehttp/phonembedding`

	PPMI+SVD				WORD2VEC				RNN ENCODER-DECODER		
Dim	5	15	30	Dim	5	15	30	Dim	5	15	30
Finnish	0.174	0.187	**0.204**	Finnish	0.114	0.147	**0.157**	Finnish	0.378	0.408	**0.459**
Turkish	0.336	0.345	**0.363**	Turkish	**0.184**	0.178	0.177	Turkish	0.293	0.368	**0.415**
Spanish	**0.328**	0.311	0.301	Spanish	0.273	0.286	**0.289**	Spanish	0.279	0.318	**0.339**

Table 2: Correlation between feature similarities $\mathrm{sim}(\mathrm{feat}(x), \mathrm{feat}(y))$ and embedding similarities $\mathrm{sim}(\mathrm{emb}(x), \mathrm{emb}(y))$ for all unordered pairs of phonemes $\{x, y\}$ (where $x \neq y$). All correlations are significantly higher (with p-value < 0.01) than ones obtained using a random assignment of embedding vectors to phonemes.

Dim	5			15			30		
# Top Analogies	15	30	100	15	30	100	15	30	100
PPMI+SVD									
Finnish	6.40	5.83	5.50	4.07*	4.27*	4.88	4.80*	4.27*	5.26
Turkish	5.33*	4.63*	5.21*	6.87	6.43	5.97*	6.07*	6.10*	6.12*
Spanish	4.93	4.27*	4.45*	3.40*	3.53*	4.16*	**2.93***	**3.10***	**3.79***
WORD2VEC									
Finnish	4.93*	5.20	4.87	4.13*	4.07*	4.48*	3.47*	4.00*	4.47*
Turkish	4.87*	5.47*	5.74*	3.73*	4.20*	**5.11***	3.73*	4.17*	5.15*
Spanish	5.47	5.23	5.56	5.73	5.20	5.10*	5.60	5.47	5.01*
RNN ENCODER-DECODER									
Finnish	2.67*	3.70*	4.71*	**2.27***	**2.83***	**3.75***	4.00*	4.07*	4.34*
Turkish	5.00*	5.27*	5.14*	**3.00***	**4.10***	5.20*	4.60*	4.53*	5.14*
Spanish	4.47*	4.87*	4.95*	5.40	5.00*	4.83*	4.73*	4.90*	4.88*

Table 3: The embedding space is used to generate an n-best list of a:b::c:d analogy proposals. The table shows the average number of differing distinctive features between d and $\mathbf{X}$ when $\mathbf{X}$ is calculated by the same analogy is performed in distinctive feature space, i.e. a:b::c:$\mathbf{X}$, with a, b, and c given. For each language and each n, we show the best performing system in bold font. Scores which are statistically significantly better than scores for random sets of analogies are marked by an asterisk *.

5 Experiments

Correlation Our first experiment investigates the relationship between the geometries of embedding space and the distinctive feature space.

Let the embedding for phoneme p be $\mathrm{emb}(p)$, its distinctive feature vector $\mathrm{feat}(p)$, and cosine similarity of vectors u and v be given by Equation 2.

$$\mathrm{sim}(u, v) = \frac{u^\top v}{|u| \cdot |v|} \quad (2)$$

We measure the linear correlation of $\mathrm{sim}(\mathrm{emb}(p), \mathrm{emb}(q))$ and $\mathrm{sim}(\mathrm{feat}(p), \mathrm{feat}(q))$ over all unordered pairs of phonemes $\{p, q\}$ (where $p \neq q$) using Pearson's r. As a baseline, we compute the correlation of similarities of feature representations and random embeddings $\mathrm{remb}(p)$. These are derived by randomly permuting the embeddings of phonemes. That is, $\mathrm{remb}(p) = \mathrm{emb}(q)$ for some random phoneme q.

Analogy Our second experiment investigates phoneme analogies. We first score four-tuples (a, b, c, d) of phonemes using cosine similarity in embedding space as defined by Equation 3. This corresponds to a proportional analogy a:b::c:d.

$$\mathrm{score}(a, b, c, d) =$$
$$\mathrm{sim}(\mathrm{emb}(b) - \mathrm{emb}(a), \mathrm{emb}(d) - \mathrm{emb}(c)) \quad (3)$$

We then evaluate the top 15, 30 and 100 four-tuples w.r.t. phonological analogy in distinctive feature space. Our evaluation is based on applying the transformation defined by the first two phonemes a and b on the third phoneme c and measuring the Hamming distance of the result and the feature representation of d. For example, given tuple (**p**,**b**,**t**,**d**), we get Hamming distance 0. This happens because **p** is transformed to **b** by changing the value of feature *voice* from 0 to 1. When the same transformation is applied to **t**, the result is **d**, which obviously has Hamming distance 0 with

FINNISH	TURKISH	SPANISH
ɑ is to **o** as **æ** is to **ø**	**a** is to **ɯ** as **e** is to **i**	**f** is to **θ** as **p** is to **s**
ɑ is to **æ** as **o** is to **ø**	**a** is to **e** as **ɯ** is to **i**	**k** is to **ɲ** as **t** is to **ʎ**
ɑ is to **æ** as **u** is to **y**	**a** is to **ɯ** as **e** it to **y**	**p** is to **ɾ** as **ʎ** is to **l**
a is to **y** as **o** is to **ø**	**a** is to **u** as **e** is to **i**	**l** is to **ʎ** as **ɾ** is to **p**
ɑ is to **y** as **o** is to **ø**	**b** is to **k** as **f** is to **g**	**m** is to **ʎ** as **r** is to **ɲ**

Table 4: Top 5 analogies (in IPA) discovered by the best model for each languages: Finnish, Turkish and Spanish.

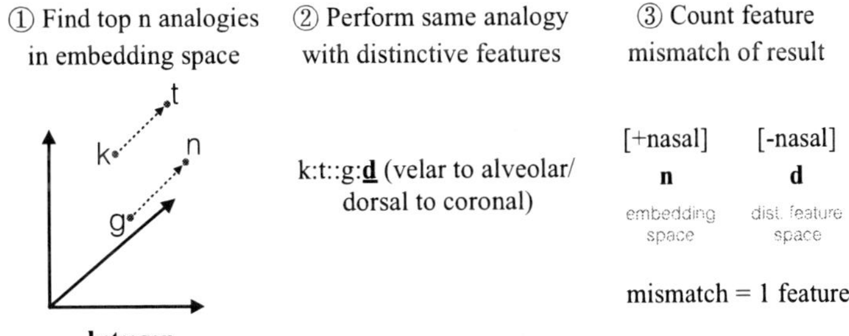

Figure 4: Illustration of the evaluation of the analogy coherence. This procedure is repeated for the top 15, 30, and 100 four-tuples in the embedding space and the average distance of the resulting analogy when performed in the distinctive feature space is reported.

Figure 5:

the fourth phoneme of the tuple in the embedding analogy.[6] We restrict tuples in two ways: (1) all phonemes in the tuple have to be distinct symbols, and (2) all phonemes in the tuple have to be consonants or all of them have to be vowels.

As baseline, we randomly select 15, 30 or 100 phoneme tuples (a, b, c, d). We then apply the transformation defined by a and b onto c and then compute the Hamming distance of the transformed image of c and the phoneme d. We restrict these random tuples as explained above.

6 Results

Table 2 shows results for linear correlation measured by Pearson's r for the similarity between phonetic representations and similarity of corresponding embedding vectors. Overall, the RNN encoder-decoder with embedding dimension 30 gives the best results. The correlation is the weak-

est for word2vec. However, all methods give a statistically significant positive correlation compared with random embeddings with p-value < 0.01 for appropriately chosen embedding dimension. For all three models: PPMI+SVD, word2vec and RNN encoder-decoder, there seems to be a tendency that higher dimension gives better correlation. This is not the case for PPMI+SVD for Spanish or word2vec for Turkish, However, in these cases, the results for all embedding dimensions are very similar. Figure 6 shows the correlation between cosine similarities of phoneme embeddings and the corresponding phonological feature representations.

Table 3 shows results for analogies as measured by average Hamming distance. Results are presented for the top 15, 30 and 100 analogies discovered by each of the systems. Overall, there is a strong trend that average Hamming distance increases in distinctive feature space when more (lower-ranked) analogies are considered in the embedding space. This is to be expected if the two spaces are coherent—as we include lower and lower ranked analogies and evaluate them, we expect them to be less fitting in the distinctive fea-

---

[6]Note that, we can only apply a transformation in co-ordinate i if the ith co-ordinates of the first and third phoneme in the tuple match. If this is not the case for some i, we do not apply any transformation for that co-ordinate. For example, if the first phoneme is [+voice], the second [-voice], and the third also [-voice], changing the third phoneme from + to − voice is not well defined.

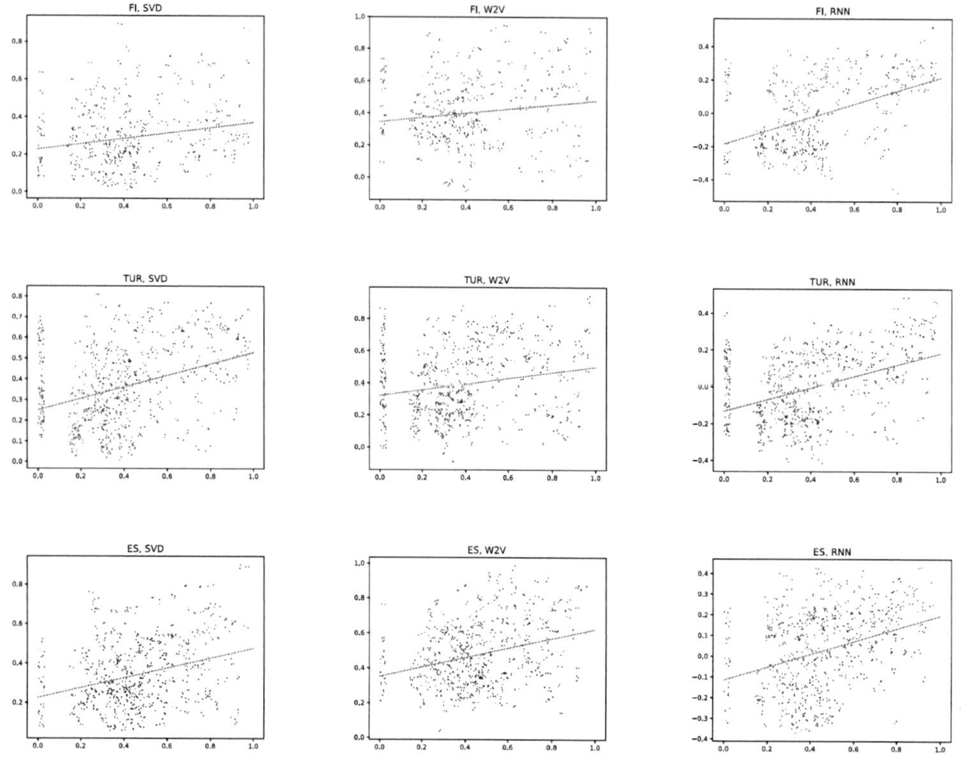

Figure 6: Scatter plots of cosine similarities of phonemes in feature space (x-axis) and embeddings space (y-axis). The figures present results for 30 dimensional PPMI+SVD, word2vec and RNN embeddings for Finnish, Turkish and Spanish, respectively. The red line represents the regression line.

ture space somewhat monotonically. The best results for Hamming distance are delivered by the 30 dimension RNN encoder-decoder for Finnish and Turkish and the 30 dimension PPMI+SVD system for Spanish. Table 4 shows a selection of top analogies for each language.

7 Discussion

The results both in comparing the geometry of the spaces learned and the alignment of analogies to distinctive features show a clear effect of distinctive features being aligned and discovered by distributional properties. The strength of the alignment appears to be somewhat language-dependent; in both Finnish and Turkish, vowel harmony effects are quite prominent and come out as many of the top-ranking analogies in an embedding space. In Spanish, by contrast, the correlation of the space is less robust, probably because there are fewer symmetrical phonologi-

cal alternations witnessed in the data, although ±continuant alternation is a prominent one (**b/β, d/ð g/ɣ**). Likewise, non-symmetric alternations in the data may distort the vector space to not align perfectly along distinctive feature lines. For example, while Finnish exhibits a **t/d** alternation (katu/kadun; 'street' nominative/genitive) the corresponding analogical labial alternation in the embedding space is **p/v** (apu/avun; 'help' nominative/genitive), not **p/b**, as one would assume by distinctive features. This is an interesting discovery since, while the analogy in the embedding space in this case does not correlate to the analogy in the feature space, this distortion of the embedding space of phonemes is arguably more "correct" than the feature-based expected one where t:d::p:b. In fact, the /b/-phoneme is only present in loanwords in the Finnish data, and the spirantization seen in **p/v** was historically present for the alveolar stop as well (**t/ð**). This analogy it-

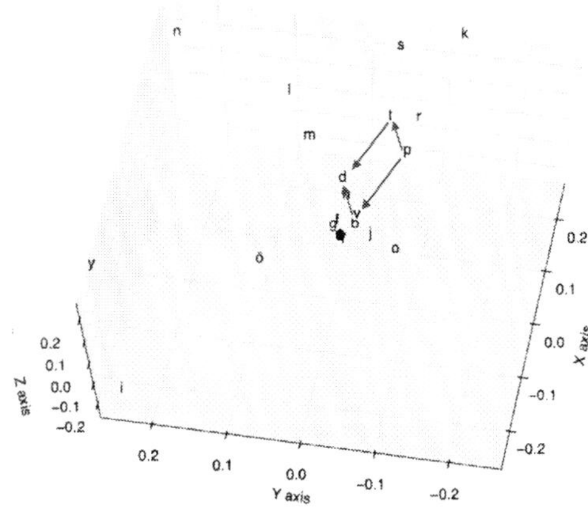

Figure 7: The phoneme space, focusing on consonants, for Finnish learned by collecting local phone(me)-context counts (window size 5), a PPMI transform, followed by SVD, truncated to three dimensions. Marked here is the (correct from a Finnish speaker point-of-view) analogy of consonant gradation **t:d::p:v̲**.

self is an example of Finnish consonant gradation which manifests itself through many idiosyncratic alternations (Karlsson, 2008), some of which are clearly captured in symmetries in the embedding space. Hence, although such mappings are often present and prevents many analogies from being 'perfect' along distinctive feature lines, embedding spaces where such seemingly 'incorrect' analogies are drawn are in fact good representations for learning tasks such as morphological inflection, since they yield generalization power to task learning, i.e. learning of phonological alternations. This flexibility to learn a vector space representation that does not always strictly conform to distinctive features is then an advantage of the representations and partly explains their recent success (Cotterell et al., 2016, 2017) in learning inflectional patterns from examples.

8 Conclusion

We have presented a set of experiments on three languages that examine how distributional properties of phonetic segments contain information about regularities in the distinctive feature alternations present in the language. In particular, we have shown a significant correlation between embedding spaces learned from either co-occurrence and distinctive feature spaces. While such embeddings can be learned from raw data without any supervision, this correlation is consistently stronger if embeddings are learned and extracted from a recurrent neural network in conjunction with a supervised task of learning to inflect word forms. Apart from a holistic inspection of the embedding spaces, we also developed an experiment that measures how well phonological analogies can be performed using the embeddings learned. While the analogies do not perfectly correlate with similar analogies in distinctive feature space, it is clear that those distinctive features that play a part in prominent phonological alternations are also latently present in co-occurrence generalizations and can be seen in the learned embedding space.

References

John A. Bullinaria and Joseph P. Levy. 2007. Extracting semantic representations from word co-occurrence statistics: A computational study. *Behavior research methods* 39(3):510–526.

Kyunghyun Cho, Bart van Merrienboer, Caglar Gulcehre, Dzmitry Bahdanau, Fethi Bougares, Holger Schwenk, and Yoshua Bengio. 2014. Learning phrase representations using RNN encoder–decoder for statistical machine translation. In *Proceedings of the 2014 Conference on Empirical Methods in Natural Language Processing (EMNLP)*. Association for Computational Linguistics, Doha, Qatar, pages 1724–1734.

Ryan Cotterell, Christo Kirov, John Sylak-Glassman, Géraldine Walther, Ekaterina Vylomova, Patrick Xia, Manaal Faruqui, Sandra Kübler, David Yarowsky, Jason Eisner, and Mans Hulden. 2017. The CoNLL-SIGMORPHON 2017 shared task. In *CoNLL-SIGMORPHON 2017 Shared Task*.

Ryan Cotterell, Christo Kirov, John Sylak-Glassman, David Yarowsky, Jason Eisner, and Mans Hulden. 2016. The SIGMORPHON 2016 shared task—morphological reinflection. *Proceedings of the 14th SIGMORPHON Workshop on Computational Research in Phonetics, Phonology, and Morphology* pages 10–22.

Ewan Dunbar, Gabriel Synnaeve, and Emmanuel Dupoux. 2015. Quantitative methods for comparing featural representations. In *Proceedings of the 18th International Congress of Phonetic Sciences*.

Manaal Faruqui, Yulia Tsvetkov, Graham Neubig, and Chris Dyer. 2016. Morphological inflection generation using character sequence to sequence learning. In *Proceedings of the 2016 Conference of the North American Chapter of the Association for Computational Linguistics: Human Language Technologies*. Association for Computational Linguistics, San Diego, California, pages 634–643.

J. R. Firth. 1937. The technique of semantics. *Transactions of the Philosophical Society* pages 36–72.

Eli Fischer-Jørgensen. 1952. On the definition of phoneme categories on a distributional basis. *Acta linguistica* 7(1-2):8–39.

John Goldsmith. 1976. An overview of autosegmental phonology. *Linguistic analysis* 2:23–68.

John Goldsmith and Aris Xanthos. 2009. Learning phonological categories. *Language* 85(1):4–38.

Jacques B. M. Guy. 1991. Vowel identification: an old (but good) algorithm. *Cryptologia* 15(3):258–262.

William Haas. 1954. On defining linguistic units. *Transactions of the Philosophical Society* pages 54–84.

Zellig S. Harris. 1954. Distributional structure. *Word* 10(2-3):146–162.

Bruce Hayes. 2011. *Introductory Phonology*. John Wiley & Sons.

Mans Hulden. 2017. A phoneme clustering algorithm based on the obligatory contour principle. In *Proceedings of The 21st SIGNLL Conference on Computational Natural Language Learning (CoNLL)*. Association for Computational Linguistics, Vancouver, Canada.

Katharina Kann and Hinrich Schütze. 2016. MED: The LMU system for the SIGMORPHON 2016 shared task on morphological reinflection. In *SIGMORPHON*.

Fred Karlsson. 2008. *Finnish: An essential grammar*. Routledge.

Young-Bum Kim and Benjamin Snyder. 2013. Unsupervised consonant-vowel prediction over hundreds of languages. In *Proceedings of the 51st Annual Meeting of the Association for Computational Linguistics (Volume 1: Long Papers)*. Association for Computational Linguistics, Sofia, Bulgaria, pages 1527–1536.

William Ronald Leben. 1973. *Suprasegmental Phonology*. Ph.D. thesis, Massachusetts Institute of Technology.

Omer Levy and Yoav Goldberg. 2014. Neural word embedding as implicit matrix factorization. In *Proceedings of the 27th International Conference on Neural Information Processing Systems*. MIT Press, Cambridge, MA, USA, NIPS'14, pages 2177–2185.

Omer Levy, Yoav Goldberg, and Israel Ramat-Gan. 2014. Linguistic regularities in sparse and explicit word representations. In *CoNLL*. pages 171–180.

Xu Li, Zhiyong Wu, Helen Meng, Jia Jia, Xiaoyan Lou, and Lianhong Cai. 2016. Phoneme embedding and its application to speech driven talking avatar synthesis. *Interspeech 2016* pages 1472–1476.

Ying Lin. 2005. *Learning features and segments from waveforms: A statistical model of early phonological acquisition*. Ph.D. thesis, University of California Los Angeles.

A. A. Markov. 1913. Primer statisticheskogo issledovaniya nad tekstom "Evgeniya Onegina", illyustriruyuschij svyaz ispytanij v cep. *Izvestiya Akademii Nauk* Ser. 6(3):153–162.

A. A. Markov. 2006. An example of statistical investigation of the text "Eugene Onegin" concerning the connection of samples in chains. *Science in Context* 19(4):591–600.

Jeff Mielke. 2008. *The Emergence of Distinctive Features*. Oxford University Press.

Tomas Mikolov, Ilya Sutskever, Kai Chen, Greg Corrado, and Jeffrey Dean. 2013a. Distributed representations of words and phrases and their compositionality. In *Neural and Information Processing Systems (NIPS)*.

Tomas Mikolov, Wen-tau Yih, and Geoffrey Zweig. 2013b. Linguistic regularities in continuous space word representations. In *Proceedings of the 2013 Conference of the North American Chapter of the Association for Computational Linguistics: Human Language Technologies*. Association for Computational Linguistics, Atlanta, Georgia, pages 746–751.

Cleve Moler and Donald Morrison. 1983. Singular value analysis of cryptograms. *American Mathematical Monthly* pages 78–87.

Boris V. Sukhotin. 1962. Eksperimental'noe vydelenie klassov bukv s pomoshch'ju EVM. *Problemy strukturnoj lingvistiki* pages 198–206.

Boris V. Sukhotin. 1973. Méthode de déchiffrage, outil de recherche en linguistique. *T. A. Informations* pages 1–43.

Ilya Sutskever, Oriol Vinyals, and Quoc V. Le. 2014. Sequence to sequence learning with neural networks. In *Advances in Neural Information Processing Systems*. pages 3104–3112.

Patricia Thaine and Gerald Penn. 2017. Vowel and consonant classification through spectral decomposition. *Proceedings of the Workshop on Subword and Character Level Models in NLP (SCLeM)* .

Peter D. Turney and Patrick Pantel. 2010. From frequency to meaning: Vector space models of semantics. *Journal of Artificial Intelligence Research* 37:141–188.

Ludwig Wittgenstein. 1953. *Philosophical Investigations [German original: Philosophische Untersuchungen]*. Blackwell, Oxford.

Imdlawn Tashlhiyt Berber Syllabification is Quantifier-Free[*]

Kristina Strother-Garcia
University of Delaware
kmsg@udel.edu

Abstract

Imdlawn Tashlhiyt Berber (ITB) is unusual due to its tolerance of non-vocalic syllabic nuclei. Rule-based and constraint-based accounts of ITB syllabification do not directly address the question of how complex the process is. Model theory and formal logic allow for comparison of complexity across different theories of phonology by identifying the computational power (or expressivity) of linguistic formalisms in a grammar-independent way. With these tools, I develop a mathematical formalism for representing ITB syllabification using Quantifier-Free (QF) logic, one of the least powerful logics known. This result indicates that ITB syllabification is relatively simple from a computational standpoint and that grammatical formalisms could succeed with even less powerful mechanisms than are currently accepted.

1 Introduction

Accounting for syllabification in ITB has become a sort of litmus test for phonological frameworks handling syllable theory. Any segment can be nucleic in ITB in some environment, making words like [tX.zNt] 'you store' commonplace.[1] Despite the seemingly bizarre syllables reported in these words, careful study shows that syllabification in ITB is predictable and follows the Sonority Sequencing

Principle (SSP)[2] almost perfectly (Dell and Elmedlaoui, 1985; Frampton, 2011; Prince and Smolensky, 1993). In this paper, I develop a QF transduction that maps underlying representations (URs) to syllabified surface representations (SRs) in ITB. This result establishes that ITB syllabification is computationally simple and local in a strict sense, a fact which is not immediately evident from previous analyses.

1.1 Motivation

Phonological processes can be thought of as functions or maps (as in Tesar, 2014) from URs to SRs. For example, the underlying string /ovɚ/ (*over*) maps to the syllabified SR [o.vɚ] in English.

A crucial question is then: what is the nature of this map? One way to characterize a map or function is to examine the kind of logic needed to express it as a transduction. Regular functions are exactly those realized by transducers in Monadic Second-Order (MSO) logic (Engelfriet and Hoogeboom, 2001; Filiot and Reynier, 2016). A strict subset of these functions correspond to transductions definable in First-Order (FO) logic, of which a strict subset are QF-definable.

Many regular functions correspond to hypothetical UR-to-SR maps not observed in the phonology of natural languages. Under certain assumptions, both rule-based theories and Optimality Theory (OT) overgenerate by allowing grammars for such unattested maps (Frank and Satta, 1998; Graf, 2010; Heinz, 2011b; Heinz and Idsardi, 2013; John-

---

[*] I thank Jeff Heinz, Adam Jardine, Mai Ha Vu, and Hossep Dolatian for insightful feedback on an earlier draft of this paper.

[1] Periods signify syllable boundaries and capital letters indicate nucleic consonants, as in Prince and Smolensky (1993).

[2] This principle has been reiterated in one form or another by Sievers (1881), Saussure (1916), Harris (1969), Hooper (1976), Selkirk (1984), and others.

Proceedings of the Society for Computation in Linguistics (SCiL) 2018, pages 145-153.
Salt Lake City, Utah, January 4-7, 2018

son, 1972; Kaplan and Kay, 1994; Karttunen, 1993; Karttunen, 1998). OT grammars cannot express *all* regular functions, so they also undergenerate in this sense (Buccola, 2013; Idsardi, 2000). In contrast, Declarative Phonology (DP) grammars are FO by definition (Coleman, 1998; Scobbie, 1991). This will be discussed further in §2.2.

While no previous theories of phonology restrict grammars to functions realized by QF maps, certain classes of QF-definable transductions are already known to characterize a variety of phonological processes (Chandlee, 2014; Chandlee et al., 2014; Chandlee et al., 2015; Chandlee and Lindell, 2016). The question of whether all UR-to-SR maps in phonology are QF-definable has strong implications for typology and learnability, as it places an upper limit on the logical complexity of phonological maps. In this paper, I develop a QF transduction for ITB syllabification, showing that this phonological function is computationally local in a strict sense.

1.2   Organization of the Paper

The remainder of the paper is organized as follows. In §2 I give a brief overview of the surface facts in ITB and previous accounts in rule-based and constraint-based frameworks. I then introduce formal word models, transductions, and logics in §3, highlighting the implications of prohibiting quantification. I develop shorthand logical predicates to characterize the input to the ITB syllabification transduction in §4. The transduction itself is defined in §5. Finally, in §6 I conclude.

2   Background on ITB

In this section I review the well-formedness principles evident from SRs in ITB and briefly summarize previous approaches to characterizing them.

2.1   The Basic Facts

Unlike most languages, ITB allows any phonetic segment to be a syllabic nucleus. The main principle driving syllable well-formedness in ITB is the SSP, which states that sonority rises monotonically from a given segment to the sonority peak of its syllable (Selkirk, 1984). Dell and Elmedlaoui (1985) report

the following sonority hierarchy for ITB[3]:

$$\text{vcl. stops} <_s \text{vcd. stops} <_s \text{vcl. fric}$$
$$<_s \text{vcd. fric} <_s \text{nas} <_s \text{liq} <_s \text{HV} <_s \text{[a]} \qquad (1)$$

The high vocoids (HVs) are [i,j,u,w]. The symbol $<_s$ denotes lesser sonority. As with the traditional notion of lesser sonority, I assume that the binary relation $<_s$ is irreflexive, asymmetric, and transitive. It is then simple to define relations $=_s$ and $\leq_s$, as in (2-3). These will be of use later.

$$=_s (x,y) \overset{def}{=} \neg <_s (x,y) \wedge \neg <_s (y,x) \qquad (2)$$

$$\leq_s (x,y) \overset{def}{=} <_s (x,y) \vee =_s (y,x) \qquad (3)$$

In addition to the SSP, there are four other principles of syllable well-formedness to note in ITB. First, all non-initial syllables must have an onset. Second, initial stops and final obstruents are forbidden from being nucleic. Third, with the exception of a small class of morphemes, the glide/vowel distinction among the HVs [i∼j] and [u∼w] is predictable based on syllable position (Dell and Elmedlaoui, 1985). That is, a nucleic HV is vocalic, as in [tag.r<u>u</u>rt] 'stable,' while a non-nucleic HV is a glide, as in [sa.<u>w</u>Lx] 'I spoke.' The latter example also illustrates the fourth well-formedness principle in ITB syllabification: the SSP is violated in glide-sonorant (GR) syllables.[4] Following another vowel, the HV in a GR syllable surfaces as a glide and forms the onset to a nucleic sonorant, preventing hiatus. Consider the UR /saulx/. The /a/ must be nucleic because it is the most sonorous possible segment. If the /u/ were also nucleic, it could have no onset. Instead, the /l/ becomes a nucleus and the /u/ becomes its onset, surfacing as the glide [w].

2.2   Previous Approaches

Dell and Elmedlaoui (1985) propose an ordered set of iterative rules to identify syllabic nuclei, each referring to a certain natural class (e.g., voiceless stops). They assign nucleic status first to instances of [a], then to HVs, then to liquids, etc., with the restriction that every non-initial syllable must have an onset. Their rules do not reference sonority directly, but are clearly applied so as to pick out the most

---

³vcl. = voiceless; vcd. = voiced; fric = fricative(s); nas = nasal(s); liq = liquid(s).

⁴As in 'glide-resonant' from Dell and Elmedlaoui (1985).

146

sonorous segments first and step down in sonority at every subsequent rule application. Any remaining segments are later assigned to coda positions. Frampton (2011) simplifies Dell and Elmedlaoui's (1985) treatment by introducing a way to simultaneously identify all points of application, making explicit reference to notions of "more sonorous" and "more left."

Prince and Smolensky (1993) offer an OT account of ITB syllabification, where GEN produces every possible syllabification of a given input form. The two main OT constraints involved in "core syllabification" penalize non-initial onsetless syllables and syllables whose nuclei are not the most sonorous segment in the syllable. The greater the absolute difference in sonority, the more the low-sonority nucleus is penalized. Additional constraints enforce the remaining well-formedness principles described in §2.1. Importantly, these constraints are all violable and the correct surface form is the one that violates the fewest highly ranked constraints. Global evaluation is required because penalties are summed over the entire candidate.

Rather than allowing SRs to violate "soft" constraints like in OT, DP grammars simply reject any SR that violates any constraint (Bird et al., 1992; Scobbie, 1991, 1996). DP relies on the Elsewhere Condition, which stipulates that, if a sequence of segments is targeted by multiple constraints, the more specific constraint applies. Lexical entries themselves are viewed as constraints, so DP does not formalize phonological grammars as UR-to-SR maps (Scobbie, 1991, 1993). There is only one level of representation and all constraints must be satisfied simultaneously. Scobbie (1993) sketches a DP treatment of ITB syllabification using constraints similar in spirit to those proposed by Prince and Smolensky (1993), but crucially differ in that they are inviolable, unranked, and defined explicitly in FO logic.

In the remaining sections, I develop a QF transduction and illustrate how ITB syllabification can be computed without recourse to global evaluation. My approach diverges from DP in three ways: i) I do not make use of lexical constraints or the Elsewhere Condition; ii) I represent syllabification as a map, requiring two levels of representation; and iii) I use strictly QF logic. This paper is therefore better situated with recent model-theoretic approaches that explicitly examine the computational characteristics of phonological generalizations independent of grammatical formalisms (Chandlee, 2014; Graf, 2010; Heinz, 2011a,b; Jardine, 2016; Rogers and Pullum, 2011).

3 Formal Background

Here I offer formal definitions of model theories, word models, and transductions, as well as an informal explanation of the differences among three logics: MSO, FO, and QF. I focus on the successor model theory, as this will be used to represent the input to the ITB syllabification transduction.

3.1 Model Theories for Words

A word model is a type of graph useful for representing relational structures. Classes of word models are defined by model theories. Given an alphabet Σ, a model theory $\mathfrak{M}$ has the signature $\langle \mathfrak{D}; \mathfrak{R}; \mathfrak{F} \rangle$ where $\mathfrak{D}$ is a domain, $\mathfrak{R}$ is a a set of relations among domain elements (nodes), and $\mathfrak{F}$ is a set of functions. For every σ in Σ there is a unary relation R_σ in $\mathfrak{R}$ that can be thought of as a labeling relation. For example, let $\Sigma = \{a, b, c\}$. Then $\mathfrak{R}$ includes the unary relations R_a, R_b, R_c. $\mathfrak{R}$ may also contain additional relations of higher arity. The following example will help to make these definitions clear.

3.2 The Successor Model Theory

The successor model theory $\mathfrak{M}^{\triangleleft}$ is defined in (4).

$$\mathfrak{M}^{\triangleleft} \overset{\text{def}}{=} \langle \mathfrak{D}; \{R_\sigma \mid \sigma \in \Sigma\}; \tag{4}$$
$$\{\mathtt{pred}(x), \mathtt{succ}(x)\}\rangle$$

The unary functions $\mathtt{pred}(x)$ and $\mathtt{succ}(x)$ pick out the immediate predecessor and successor of a given position, respectively.[5] In the general case, $\mathtt{succ}(x) = x + 1$ and $\mathtt{pred}(x) = x - 1$. To ensure the predecessor function is total, it is defined so that the initial position is its own predecessor, i.e. $\mathtt{pred}(0) = 0$. Similarly, the final position is its own successor, making the successor function total. Then in a string of n positions, $\mathtt{succ}(n) = n$.

The model for the string *ball* under this theory is denoted $\mathcal{M}^{\triangleleft}_{ball}$. Taking the alphabet $\Sigma = \{a, b, 1\}$,

---

[5]The use of unary functions (rather than binary relations) for predecessor and successor is due to Chandlee and Lindell (2016).

$\mathcal{M}^{\triangleleft}_{ball}$ is defined in (5) and represented visually in Figure 1.

$$\mathcal{M}^{\triangleleft}_{ball} \qquad (5)$$

$$\mathcal{D} = \{0, 1, 2, 3\}$$
$$R_a = \{1\}$$
$$R_b = \{0\}$$
$$R_l = \{2, 3\}$$

$$\mathrm{succ}(x) = \begin{cases} 1 & x = 0 \\ 2 & x = 1 \\ 3 & x = 2 \\ 4 & x \in \{3, 4\} \end{cases}$$

$$\mathrm{pred}(x) = \begin{cases} 0 & x \in \{0, 1\} \\ 1 & x = 2 \\ 2 & x = 3 \\ 3 & x = 4 \end{cases}$$

Figure 1: A visual representation of $\mathcal{M}^{\triangleleft}_{ball}$.

| b | $\triangleleft$ | a | $\triangleleft$ | 1 | $\triangleleft$ | 1 |
| 0 | | 1 | | 2 | | 3 |

Its domain $\mathcal{D}$ consists of four nodes, each represented as a rectangle with an index below it. Unary relations are illustrated as node labels. For example, node 1 is labeled a. This is denoted $1 \in R_a$, $R_a(1) = \text{TRUE}$, or, equivalently, $\mathrm{a}(1) = \text{TRUE}$. The successor function is illustrated by directed edges (arrows) with the $\triangleleft$ label. Thus $1 \triangleleft 2$ is equivalent to $\mathrm{succ}(1) = 2$.

3.3 A Modified Successor Model Theory

The remainder of this paper uses a slight variant of the traditional successor model theory. The key difference lies in the definition of the alphabet and the use of non-mutually exclusive position labels.

The alphabet can be conceptualized as a set of primitives – labels defined outside of the model theory itself. In traditional word models (as in Büchi, 1960), each position has exactly one label (i.e., it belongs to a single unary relation). Additionally, traditional labels are simply letters of the alphabet. The unary relations in the word models to follow are untraditional with respect to both of these conventions. In line with previous work in computational phonol-

ogy (Daland et al., 2011; Heinz and Strother-Garcia, to appear; Strother-Garcia et al., 2017), I permit each position to have more than one label. This allows us to represent phonological segments as bundles of information like phonological features, as well as syllable position (onset, nucleus, or coda), rather than disparate symbols.

Let $\mathcal{F}$ be a set of primitive phonological features. I adopt the features given in (6) for ITB.[6]

$$\mathcal{F} \overset{\text{def}}{=} \{\texttt{voice}, \texttt{vocoid}, \texttt{high}, \texttt{lab}, \texttt{alv}, \texttt{post},$$
$$\texttt{pal}, \texttt{vel}, \texttt{uv}, \texttt{phar}, \texttt{glot}, \texttt{stop}, \texttt{fric}, \qquad (6)$$
$$\texttt{nas}, \texttt{approx}, \texttt{lat}\}$$

Then the alphabet is simply $\Sigma = \mathcal{F}$. For each feature $f \in \mathcal{F}$, there is a unary relation $R_f \in \mathfrak{R}$ that represents a particular position being labeled with that feature. Let $\mathcal{R}_f$ be the set of such relations, defined in (7). As with alphabet primitives in traditional word models, $R_f(x)$ can also be written as $f(x)$ for any primitive $f \in \mathcal{F}$. For example, $R_{\texttt{voice}}(x)$ is equivalent to $\texttt{voice}(x)$.

$$\mathcal{R}_f \overset{\text{def}}{=} \{R_f \mid f \in \mathcal{F}\} \qquad (7)$$

In addition to this set of unary relations, I will make use of the binary sonority relations defined in §2.1. Let the sonority relations be members of the set $\mathcal{R}_s$, as defined in (8). Then the modified successor model theory $\mathfrak{M}$ is defined in (9).

$$\mathcal{R}_s \overset{\text{def}}{=} \{<_s, =_s, \leq_s\} \qquad (8)$$
$$\mathfrak{M} \overset{\text{def}}{=} \langle \mathfrak{D}; \{\mathcal{R}_f \cup \mathcal{R}_s\}; \{\mathrm{pred}(x), \mathrm{succ}(x)\} \rangle \qquad (9)$$

3.4 Graph Transductions

As word models are a type of graph, graph transductions can be used to represent input-output maps from one word model $\mathfrak{M}^A$ to another $\mathfrak{M}^B$. A transduction is defined with a set of formulas, one for each relation R and function F in $\mathfrak{M}^B$. These formulas are interpreted with respect the input structure in $\mathfrak{M}^A$. See (Courcelle, 1994; Engelfriet and Hoogeboom, 2001) for details.

For example, consider a transduction Γ_{ba} that changes all bs in a word model to as. Here $\mathfrak{M}^A = \mathfrak{M}^B = \mathfrak{M}^{\triangleleft}$. Then given $\Sigma = \{\mathrm{a}, \mathrm{b}, 1\}$, the transduc-

---

[6]`lab` = labial; `alv` = alveolar; `post` = postalveolar; `pal` = palatal; `vel` = velar; `uv` = uvular; `phar` = pharyngeal; `glot` = glottal; `approx` = approximant; `lat` = lateral.

tion Γ_{ba} is the set of predicates (10-14) where the superscript ω indicates the relations over the output.

When applied to the input $\mathcal{M}_{ball}^{\lhd}$, the transduction changes the label of the first position from b to a and leaves the remaining positions unchanged, as illustrated in Figure 2.

$$R_a^{\omega}(x) \overset{\text{def}}{=} R_a(x) \vee R_b(x) \tag{10}$$

$$R_b^{\omega}(x) \overset{\text{def}}{=} \texttt{FALSE} \tag{11}$$

$$R_l^{\omega}(x) \overset{\text{def}}{=} R_l(x) \tag{12}$$

$$\texttt{succ}^{\omega}(x) \overset{\text{def}}{=} \texttt{succ}(x) \tag{13}$$

$$\texttt{pred}^{\omega}(x) \overset{\text{def}}{=} \texttt{pred}(x) \tag{14}$$

Figure 2: A visual representation of $\Gamma_{ba}(\mathcal{M}_{ball}^{\lhd})$.

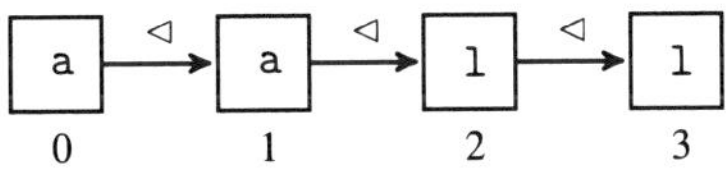

In this example, the input and output share the same model theory, but this need not be the case. As will be seen in §5, new relations may be added to the output model theory.

3.5 Logics and Locality

Statements in FO logic can use universal and existential quantifiers to quantify over elements of the domain. MSO statements can also quantify over *sets* of domain elements. For example, consider the following definitions from Jardine and Heinz (2015). First, set closure under successor is defined in (15). Then (16) defines the general precedence relation $\prec$. Captial X denotes a set, while lowercase x and y denote elements of the domain.

$$\textsf{closed}(X) \overset{\text{def}}{=} (\forall x, y)(x \in X \wedge x \lhd y) \tag{15}$$
$$\Rightarrow y \in X$$

$$x \prec y \overset{\text{def}}{=} (\forall X)(x \in X \wedge \textsf{closed}(X) \tag{16}$$
$$\Rightarrow y \in X$$

Because (15) involves universal quantification over some set X, it is strictly MSO and not FO. Sentences of MSO without quantification over sets, like (16), are FO. Sentences of FO with no quantification are QF.[7]

To see why quantification is important, compare (17) to (10), which is reproduced in (18). The former states that an output position x will be labeled a if the corresponding input position is an a *or* if there is a position labeled b somewhere in the input. Checking whether $R_a^{\omega\prime}(x)$ is true requires global evaluation of the string to see if any position is labeled b. This is due to the existential quantifier $\exists$, which makes (17) strictly FO. In contrast, (18) lacks any quantification. $R_a^{\omega}(x)$ can be evaluated independently at every position in the string.

$$R_a^{\omega\prime}(x) \overset{\text{def}}{=} R_a(x) \vee (\exists y)[R_b(y)] \tag{17}$$

$$R_a^{\omega}(x) \overset{\text{def}}{=} R_a(x) \vee R_b(x) \tag{18}$$

This example illustrates the relationship between quantification and locality. If a predicate is stated with quantification, computing its truth value requires global evaluation of the string. If the predicate is QF, truth evaluation must be possible over a substring of bounded size. A transduction defined entirely by QF predicates is a QF transduction. Thus a QF transduction amounts to a constraint-checking function that operates locally, within a bounded window of evaluation. Note that Γ_{ba} is QF, with all predicates referring to a single position.

4 User-Defined Predicates

Given a model theory $\mathfrak{M}$ and an alphabet Σ, logical predicates can be defined to make it easier to refer to certain types of information in the input word model. For example, writing $\texttt{voice}(x) \wedge \texttt{lab}(x) \wedge \texttt{stop}(x)$ to refer to a [b] is cumbersome. Instead, I use the unary predicate $\textsf{b}(x)$, defined in (19). HVs must also be defined, as in (20).

$$\textsf{b}(x) \overset{\text{def}}{=} \texttt{voice}(x) \wedge \texttt{lab}(x) \wedge \texttt{stop}(x) \tag{19}$$

$$\textsf{HV}(x) \overset{\text{def}}{=} \texttt{high}(x) \wedge \texttt{vocoid}(x) \tag{20}$$

Although I write $\texttt{stop}(x)$ and $\textsf{b}(x)$ similarly, note that the former is the labeling relation for a primitive of $\mathfrak{M}$ while the latter is a predicate derived from such primitives. I use typewriter font for primitives and sans serif font for user-defined predicates.

Note that whether a formula is MSO, FO, or QF is determined by its interpretation in terms of primitives. For example, the statement $\textsf{HV}(x) \vee \textsf{b}(x)$ is

---

[7]For formal definitions of MSO and FO, I refer the reader to Enderton (2001), Fagin et al. (1995), and Shoenfield (1967).

QF because the predicates $HV(x)$ and $b(x)$ are both QF. User-defined predicates are not meant to obscure the logical nature of the description; they are just well-defined abbreviations.

4.1 Natural Classes and Word Position

Natural classes can be defined similarly to $b(x)$. Given the primitives in $\mathcal{R}_f$, I define obs and son in (21-22).[8]

$$\mathrm{obs}(x) \overset{\text{def}}{=} \mathtt{stop}(x) \vee \mathtt{fric}(x) \tag{21}$$

$$\mathrm{son}(x) \overset{\text{def}}{=} \neg\mathrm{obs}(x) \tag{22}$$

Unary predicates can also pick out a segment's position in the word. Initial and final positions are defined as in §3.2. Then a medial position is one that is neither initial nor final. These definitions are formalized in (23-25).

$$\mathrm{init}(x) \overset{\text{def}}{=} \mathtt{pred}(x) = x \tag{23}$$

$$\mathrm{fin}(x) \overset{\text{def}}{=} \mathtt{succ}(x) = x \tag{24}$$

$$\mathrm{med}(x) \overset{\text{def}}{=} \neg(\mathrm{init}(x) \vee \mathrm{fin}(x)) \tag{25}$$

4.2 Sonority and Other Considerations

To determine syllable constituency, it is first necessary to identify sonority peaks, other positions that may be nucleic, and marked positions prohibited from being nucleic.

A word-medial sonority peak is simply a segment that is more sonorous than both its neighboring segments, as defined in (26). To be exhaustive, I also define word-initial and word-final 'peaks' in (27) and (28), respectively. Then a sonority peak (29) is any of these three.

$$\mathrm{med\_pk}(x) \overset{\text{def}}{=} \mathrm{med}(x) \wedge \mathtt{pred}(x) <_s x \tag{26}$$
$$\wedge\, \mathtt{succ}(x) <_s x$$

$$\mathrm{init\_pk}(x) \overset{\text{def}}{=} \mathrm{init}(x) \wedge \mathtt{succ}(x) <_s x \tag{27}$$

$$\mathrm{fin\_pk}(x) \overset{\text{def}}{=} \mathrm{fin}(x) \wedge \mathtt{pred}(x) <_s x \tag{28}$$

$$\mathrm{son\_pk}(x) \overset{\text{def}}{=} \mathrm{med\_pk}(x) \vee \mathrm{init\_pk}(x) \tag{29}$$
$$\vee\, \mathrm{fin\_pk}(x)$$

Frampton (2011) observes that "a slot x is 'more prominent' than an adjacent slot y ...if they are equally sonorous and x is to the left of y, unless x is initial." In other words, the leftmost segment of a sonority plateau takes prominence when it comes to assigning nucleic status, unless it is word-initial. This configuration is captured by the predicate left_prom, defined in (30). Note that word-final positions are explicitly excluded. Were this left out of the definition, every final position would satisfy left_prom due to it being its own successor and, therefore, equally sonorous to its successor (itself). Then a prominence peak is a position that satisfies either son_pk or left_prom, as in (31).

$$\mathrm{left\_prom}(x) \overset{\text{def}}{=} x =_s \mathtt{succ}(x) \wedge \mathrm{med}(x) \tag{30}$$

$$\mathrm{prom\_pk}(x) \overset{\text{def}}{=} \mathrm{son\_pk}(x) \vee \mathrm{left\_prom}(x) \tag{31}$$

Prominence peaks are typically syllabic nuclei, with three exceptions. The first two exceptions are simple: neither initial stops nor final obstruents may be nucleic. I refer to both as 'marked,' represented by the shorthand predicate mrkd in (32). The third exception occurs when a HV is preceded by another vowel, resulting in a GR syllable. The shorthand predicate GR_nuc (33) picks out the sonorant in a GR syllable, which is always nucleic.

$$\mathrm{mrkd}(x) \overset{\text{def}}{=} \mathrm{init\_stop}(x) \vee \mathrm{fin\_obs}(x) \tag{32}$$

$$\mathrm{GR\_nuc}(x) \overset{\text{def}}{=} \mathtt{vocoid}(\mathtt{pred}(x)) \wedge \mathrm{son}(x) \tag{33}$$
$$\wedge\, \mathrm{prom\_pk}(\mathtt{pred}(\mathtt{pred}(x)))$$

4.3 Syllable Constituency

Now it is easy to identify the syllable constituent for any given input segment. Predicate (34) states that a segment is nucleic if it is **a)** an unmarked prominence peak or **b)** the sonorant in a GR sequence.[9] A segment is an onset if it is not nucleic, but its successor is; this type of onset segment satisfies ons_1 (35). Additionally, a word-initial obstruent satisfies ons_2 (36) if its successor satisfies ons_1, as in the first syllable of [txZ.nas] 'store (3rd sg. fem.)'. In either case, the segment is part of an onset, thereby satisfying ons (37). Finally, a segment is a coda if it is neither an onset nor a nucleus, as in (38).

$$\mathrm{nuc}(x) \overset{\text{def}}{=} (\mathrm{prom\_pk}(x) \wedge \neg\mathrm{mrkd}(x)) \tag{34}$$
$$\vee\, \mathrm{GR\_nuc}(x)$$

$$\text{ons}_1(x) \overset{\text{def}}{=} \neg\text{nuc}(x) \wedge \text{nuc}(\text{succ}(x)) \qquad (35)$$

$$\text{ons}_2(x) \overset{\text{def}}{=} \text{init\_obs} \wedge \text{ons}_1(\text{succ}(x)) \qquad (36)$$

$$\text{ons}(x) \overset{\text{def}}{=} \text{ons}_1(x) \vee \text{ons}_2(x) \qquad (37)$$

$$\text{cod}(x) \overset{\text{def}}{=} \neg\text{nuc}(x) \wedge \neg\text{ons}(x) \qquad (38)$$

5 The ITB Syllabification Transduction

In addition to predicates corresponding to the relations in $\mathfrak{M}$, I will also define relations over the output to indicate a segment's position in the syllable (ons, nuc, cod), which is not explicit in the input. Let $\mathcal{R}_\sigma$ be the set of these three syllable constituent labels, as in (39). Then the model theory of the output will be $\mathfrak{M}'$, defined in (40).

$$\mathcal{R}_\sigma \overset{\text{def}}{=} \{\text{ons, nuc, cod}\} \qquad (39)$$

$$\mathfrak{M}' \overset{\text{def}}{=} \langle \mathfrak{D}'; \{\mathcal{R}_f \cup \mathcal{R}_s \cup \mathcal{R}_\sigma\}; \atop \{\text{pred}(x), \text{succ}(x)\}\rangle \qquad (40)$$

Armed with the predicates defined in the previous section, Γ itself is now simple to define. The transduction is completely defined with predicates (42-50). Crucially, all predicates are QF, showing that ITB syllabification is fundamentally local in nature.

5.1 Unary Relations

Because I am concerned with syllabification and not unrelated segmental processes, I assume all feature labels are preserved under Γ. Recall that $\mathcal{R}_f$ is the set of unary relations for phonological features defined over the domain of the transduction. Let $\mathcal{R}_f^\omega$ (41) be the corresponding set of unary relations over the codomain. For each feature f in $\mathcal{F}$, there is one such predicate R_f^ω, as defined in (42).

$$\mathcal{R}_f^\omega \overset{\text{def}}{=} \{R_f^\omega \mid f \in \mathcal{F}\} \qquad (41)$$

$$R_f^\omega(x) \overset{\text{def}}{=} R_f(x) \qquad (42)$$

5.2 Binary Relations

In the absence of any changes to segmental feature specification, the binary sonority relations (42-45) are also preserved from the input.

$$<_s^\omega (x,y) \overset{\text{def}}{=} <_s (x,y) \qquad (43)$$

$$=_s^\omega (x,y) \overset{\text{def}}{=} =_s (x,y) \qquad (44)$$

$$\leq_s^\omega (x,y) \overset{\text{def}}{=} \leq_s (x,y) \qquad (45)$$

5.3 Functions

The ordering of domain elements does not change, so the output functions $\text{succ}^\omega(x)$ and $\text{pred}^\omega(x)$ are similarly preserved, as in (46-47).

$$\text{succ}^\omega(x) \overset{\text{def}}{=} \text{succ}(x) \qquad (46)$$

$$\text{pred}^\omega(x) \overset{\text{def}}{=} \text{pred}(x) \qquad (47)$$

5.4 Syllable Constituents

The work of identifying onsets, nuclei, and codas in the input form is essentially already done. All that remains is to formalize the predicates that label the syllable constituents in the *output* form. These are given in (48-50).

$$\text{nuc}^\omega(x) \overset{\text{def}}{=} \text{nuc}(x) \qquad (48)$$

$$\text{ons}^\omega(x) \overset{\text{def}}{=} \text{ons}(x) \qquad (49)$$

$$\text{cod}^\omega(x) \overset{\text{def}}{=} \text{cod}(x) \qquad (50)$$

5.5 Example

To illustrate how the transduction works, consider the underlying form /saulx/ 'I spoke.' Its word model consists of five positions, 0 through 4. Each position has a set of feature labels which I abbreviate with the shorthand segment predicates s, a, u, l, and x, defined analogously to b (19). Table 1 gives the truth values for the predicates relevant to syllable structure in the word *saulx*.

The first position is less sonorous than the second, with sonority falling monotonically after that. There are no sonority plateaus, so no position may satisfy left_prom. The only prominence peak is then the single sonority peak, position 1. Because position 4 is a final obstruent, it is marked. Note that position 1 is a vowel, position 2 is a glide, and position 3 is a sonorant. This configuration means that position 3 satisfies GR_nuc and therefore satisfies nuc, even though it is not a prominence peak. Position 1 also satisfies nuc by virtue of satisfying prom_pk. Positions 0 and 2 satisfy ons_1 because their successors are both nucleic. Finally, position 4 satisfies cod because it satisfies neither ons nor nuc.

Figure 3 illustrates the resulting output form $\Gamma(\mathcal{M}_{saulx})$, also denoted $\mathcal{M}'_{saulx}$. Recall that the vowel-glide distinction is predictable from syllable constituency. Because position 2 satisfies u and ons,

Table 1: Truth table for $\mathcal{M}_{saulx}$).

x	0	1	2	3	4
$\mathsf{s}(x)$	✓	.	.	.	.
$\mathsf{a}(x)$	.	✓	.	.	.
$\mathsf{u}(x)$	.	.	✓	.	.
$\mathsf{l}(x)$	.	.	.	✓	.
$\mathsf{x}(x)$	.	.	.	.	✓
$x <_s \mathrm{succ}(x)$	✓	.	.	.	.
$x =_s \mathrm{succ}(x)$	.	.	.	.	.
$\mathsf{son\_pk}(x)$	.	✓	.	.	.
$\mathsf{left\_prom}(x)$	.	.	.	.	.
$\mathsf{prom\_pk}(x)$	.	✓	.	.	.
$\mathsf{fin\_obs}(x)$	.	.	.	.	✓
$\mathsf{mrkd}(x)$	.	.	.	.	✓
$\mathsf{GR\_nuc}(x)$	.	.	.	✓	.
$\mathsf{nuc}(x)$	.	✓	.	✓	.
$\mathsf{ons}_1(x)$	✓	.	✓	.	.
$\mathsf{ons}(x)$	✓	.	✓	.	.
$\mathsf{cod}(x)$	.	.	.	.	✓

it surfaces as the glide [w]. Thus the surface form is pronounced [sa.wLx].

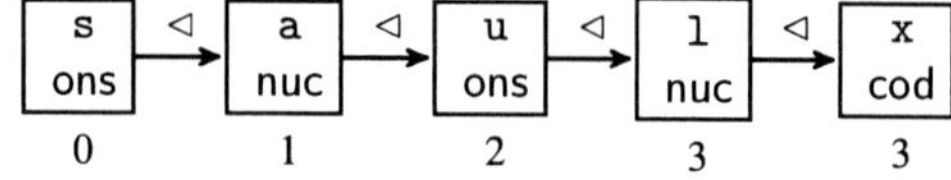

Figure 3: A visual representation of $\mathcal{M}'_{saulx}$.

6 Conclusion

I have shown that syllabification in ITB can be represented by a QF graph transduction, a formalism restricted to substantially lower computational complexity than proposed phonological grammars. Unlike these grammatical formalisms, the logical formalism makes no commitment to the implementation of the UR-to-SR map.

So which aspects of complexity are genuinely linguistic and which ones are by-products of the chosen formalism? This paper demonstrates how model theory and logic provide a foundation for studying this question. The minimal power of the logic needed to define a word model transduction is a measure of the complexity of the UR-to-SR map. Establishing that ITB syllabification is QF highlights an insight not apparent from grammatical formalisms: the local nature of computing syllable constituency in ITB is exactly what precludes the need for quantification.

This result, along with others cited previously, suggests that a fruitful avenue of future research in rule-based frameworks and OT would be to identify which properties of their machinery are responsible for their relatively high logical power. It is possible that careful modifications may increase restrictiveness in a way that makes these grammars computationally equivalent to QF transductions.

References

Steven Bird, John S Coleman, Janet Pierrehumbert, and James M Scobbie. 1992. Declarative Phonology. In *Proceedings of the XVth International Congress of Linguists. Université Laval, Québec.* Université Laval, Québec.

Brian Buccola. 2013. On the expressivity of Optimality Theory versus ordered rewrite rules. In Glyn Morrill and MarkJan Nederhof, editors, *Proceedings of Formal Grammar 2012 and 2013*, volume 8306 of *Lecture Notes in Computer Science*, pages 142–158, Berlin Heidelberg. Springer-Verlag.

J. Richard Büchi. 1960. Weak second-order arithmetic and finite automata. *Mathematical Logic Quarterly*, 6(1-6):66–92.

Jane Chandlee and Steven Lindell. 2016. Local languages. Paper presented at the 4th Workshop on Natural Language and Computer Science, in affiliation with LICS at Columbia University, NY.

Jane Chandlee, Rémi Eyraud, and Jeffrey Heinz. 2014. Learning strictly local subsequential functions. *Transactions of the Association for Computational Linguistics*, 2:491–503.

Jane Chandlee, Rémi Eyraud, and Jeffrey Heinz. 2015. Output strictly local functions. In *Proceedings of the 14th Meeting on the Mathematics of Language*, pages 112–125. Association for Computational Linguistics.

Jane Chandlee. 2014. *Strictly Local Phonological Processes*. Ph.D. thesis, University of Delaware.

John Coleman. 1998. *Phonological representations: their names, forms and powers*. Cambridge University Press.

Bruno Courcelle. 1994. Monadic second-order definable graph transductions: a survey. *Theoretical Computer Science*, 126(1):53–75.

Robert Daland, Bruce Hayes, James White, Marc Garellek, Andreas Davis, and Ingrid Normann. 2011. Explaining sonority projection effects. *Phonology*, 28(197):197–234.

François Dell and Mohamed Elmedlaoui. 1985. Syllabic consonants and syllabification in Imdlawn Tashlhiyt

Berber. *Journal of African Languages and Linguistics*, 7:105–130.

Herbert B. Enderton. 2001. *A Mathematical Introduction to Logic*. Academic Press, 2nd edition.

Joost Engelfriet and Hendrik Jan Hoogeboom. 2001. MSO definable string transductions and two-way finite-state transducers. *ACM Transactions on Computational Logic (TOCL)*, 2(2):216–254.

R. Fagin, L.J. Stockmeyer, and M.Y. Vardi. 1995. On monadic NP vs monadic co-NP. *Information and Computation*, 120(1):78 – 92.

Emmanuel Filiot and Pierre-Alain Reynier. 2016. Transducers, logic and algebra for functions of finite words. *ACM SIGLOG News*, 3(3):4–19.

John Frampton. 2011. GDE syllabification: A generalization of Dell and Elmedlaoui's syllabification algorithm. *The Linguistic Review*, 28(3):241–279.

Robert Frank and Giorgio Satta. 1998. Optimality Theory and the generative complexity of constraint violability. *Computational Linguistics*, 24(2):307–315.

Thomas Graf. 2010. Logics of phonological reasoning. Master's thesis, University of California, Los Angeles.

James W Harris. 1969. *Spanish phonology*. Cambridge, Mass.: Massachusetts Institute of Technology Press.

Jeffrey Heinz and William Idsardi. 2013. What complexity differences reveal about domains in language. *Topics in cognitive science*, 5(1):111–131.

Jeffrey Heinz and Kristina Strother-Garcia. to appear. Cluster reduction in Tibetan. In Jeffrey Heinz, editor, *Doing Computational Phonology*. Oxford: Oxford University Press.

Jeffrey Heinz. 2011a. Computational phonology part I: Foundations. *Language and Linguistics Compass*, 5(4):140–152.

Jeffrey Heinz. 2011b. Computational phonology part II: Grammars, learning, and the future. *Language and Linguistics Compass*, 5(4):153–168.

Joan B Hooper. 1976. *An introduction to natural generative phonology*. New York: Academic Press.

William J Idsardi. 2000. Clarifying opacity. *Linguistic review*, 17(2):337–350.

Adam Jardine and Jeffrey Heinz. 2015. A concatenation operation to derive autosegmental graphs. In *Proceedings of the 14th Meeting on the Mathematics of Language (MoL 2015)*, pages 139–151, Chicago, USA, July.

Adam Jardine. 2016. *Locality and non-linear representations in tonal phonology*. Ph.D. thesis, University of Delaware.

C Douglas Johnson. 1972. *Formal aspects of phonological description*. The Hague: Mouton.

Ronald M Kaplan and Martin Kay. 1994. Regular models of phonological rule systems. *Computational linguistics*, 20(3):331–378.

Lauri Karttunen. 1993. Finite-state constraints. *The last phonological rule*, pages 173–194.

Lauri Karttunen. 1998. The proper treatment of optimality in computational phonology: plenary talk. In *Proceedings of the International Workshop on Finite State Methods in Natural Language Processing*, pages 1–12. Association for Computational Linguistics.

Alan Prince and Paul Smolensky. 1993. *Optimality Theory: Constraint interaction in Generative Grammar*. Blackwell, Malden, Mass.

James Rogers and Geoffrey K. Pullum. 2011. Aural pattern recognition experiments and the subregular hierarchy. *Journal of Logic, Language and Information*, 20:329–342.

Ferdinand de Saussure. 1916. *Cours de linguistique générale*. Paris: Payot.

James M Scobbie, John S Coleman, and Steven Bird. 1996. *Key aspects of Declarative Phonology*. European Studies Research Institute, Salford.

James M Scobbie. 1991. Towards Declarative Phonology. *Edinburgh Working Papers in Cognitive Science*, 7:1–27.

James M Scobbie. 1993. Constraint violation and conflict from the perspective of Declarative Phonology. *Canadian Journal of Linguistics/Revue canadienne de linguistique*, 38(2):155–167.

Elisabeth O Selkirk. 1984. On the major class features and syllable theory. In M. Halle, M. Aronoff, and R. T. Oehrle, editors, *Language sound structure: Studies in phonology*. MIT Press, Cambridge, Mass.

Joseph R Shoenfield. 1967. *Mathematical logic*, volume 21. Reading: Addison-Wesley.

Eduard Sievers. 1881. *Grundzuge der Phonetik*. Leipzig: Breitkopf and Hartel.

Kristina Strother-Garcia, Jeffrey Heinz, and Hyun Jin Hwangbo. 2017. Using model theory for grammatical inference: A case study from phonology. In Sicco Verwer, Menno van Zaanen, and Rick Smetsers, editors, *Proceedings of The 13th International Conference on Grammatical Inference*, volume 57 of *Proceedings of Machine Learning Research*, pages 66–78, Delft, The Netherlands, 05–07 Oct. PMLR.

Bruce Tesar. 2014. *Output-driven phonology: Theory and learning*. Number 139. Cambridge University Press.

Towards a Formal Description of NPI Licensing Patterns*

Mai Ha Vu
University of Delaware
maiha@udel.edu

Abstract

This paper is a formal study of a simplified version of Negative Polarity Item (NPI) licensing requirements in two languages, English and Hungarian. In the framework of Model-Theoretic Syntax, using logical formalisms defined over tree-languages, I show that neither pattern can be described with Tier-based Strictly Local (TSL) constraints only, and suggest that they need a more complex logical formula. In particular, Hungarian patterns can be described using a combination of Tier-based Strictly 2-Local constraints over dominance relations and Locally 1-Testable constraints over the left-of relations between nodes. For English, there are no sufficient local constraints, either with or without tiers. As part of the analysis, I give a definition of a generalized tree-language that uses Tier-based 2-Local constraints over dominance relations, while it remains underspecified for left-of relations.

1 Introduction

Model-theoretic syntax is a way to study linguistic structures formally by describing them in terms of logical constraints, rather than in terms of sequences of derivational steps. While its roots can be traced back to early studies in generative grammar, it gained prominence with James Rogers' 1998 work, *A Descriptive Approach to Language-Theoretic Complexity* (Pullum, 2007).

*I thank Jeffrey Heinz, Thomas Graf, Hossep Dolatian, Kristina Strother-Garcia, and the anonymous reviewers for their thoughtful and insightful feedback on earlier drafts of this paper. All errors are my own.

Rogers' (1998) results showed that a significant portion of Government and Binding Theory can be described with a version of Monadic Second-order (MSO) constraints over phrase-structure trees. Incidentally, structures that can be described with MSO logic are members of the regular class of languages in terms of complexity (Rogers and Pullum, 2011).

It is known, however, that many regular languages are not plausible patterns in human natural language (Heinz and Idsardi, 2013). As an example, the *even-a* language, which is defined as a set of strings that can only contain an even number of *a*s, is widely considered implausible. As a result, recent work has focused on identifying *subregular* regions relevant to natural language. While progress has been made on phonotactic patterns (Heinz, 2009; Heinz, 2010; Jardine, 2016) and phonological transformations (Chandlee, 2014), less has been said in this regard about syntactic patterns.

Relevant work on syntax in this vein has been done by Thomas Graf, who has argued that most linguistic patterns, including syntactic and morphological ones, fit in the Tier-based Strictly Local (TSL) class (Graf and Heinz, 2015; Graf, 2017). While the TSL class was originally used to describe stringsets (Heinz et al., 2011), we use the class in a more abstract way, and apply it to tree-sets in the current paper.

Because trees are two-dimensional structures with two types of ordering relations in them (Rogers, 2003), the type of ordering relation over which a certain class of language applies has to be specified. The TSL tree-language as described by Graf and Heinz (2015) has TSL constraints over both the dominance and left-of ordering relations. This paper provides a more generalized definition of Tier-based Strictly 2-Local tree-grammars: tree-grammars where the constraints are Tier-based Strictly 2-Local over dominance ($\text{TSL}_2^{\triangleright}$), but can be of different complexity over left-of relations.

We then demonstrate that a particular type of pattern where the existence of one item in the structure requires the existence of another one, formalized as $a \rightarrow b$, cannot be described with TSL constraints in the sense of Graf and Heinz (2015). NPIs fall into this category of patterns, as an NPI cannot occur without a licensor.

The scope of this paper is restricted to describing well-formed surface structures, without any assumption of underlying features or syntactic movement. We are thus agnostic about any in-depth theory of NPI-licensing, and are not addressing specific proposals suggesting movement or agreement (cf. Giannakidou and Zeijlstra (2016)); neither do we look at proposed Logical Forms of these sentences, which might differ from the observed surface word orders.

Lastly, the choice of syntactic data structure needs a few words. Two common data structures used to describe syntactic structures are phrase-structure trees and derivation trees. For a detailed discussion of the two, the reader is referred to Stabler (1997). We choose to use phrase-structure trees as the data structure for the sentences discussed in this paper, instead of derivation trees. Graf (2013) gives an in-depth analysis of the nature of syntactic constraints, both over phrase-structure trees and derivation trees. He shows that representational constraints (i.e. those over phrase-structure trees), are subsumed by translocal constraints (i.e. those over derivation trees). We thus believe that modeling NPI-licensing with constraints over phrase-structure trees will not take away from the overall generalizability of our results regarding the complexity of necessary constraints in natural language syntax.

The paper is organized as follows. Section 2 states the definitions of key concepts needed to understand the discussion in the rest of the paper. Section 3 introduces the syntactic data in question: NPI-licensing in English and Hungarian. Section 4 shows that these patterns need TLT and First-Order Logic to be described. Section 5 concludes.

2 Preliminaries

2.1 Strictly Local and Locally Testable Stringsets

These definitions of Strictly Local (SL) and Locally Testable (LT) stringsets are largely based on Heinz et al. (2011), Rogers and Pullum (2011), and Rogers et al. (2013). We assume familiarity with monadic second-order (MSO) logic (Enderton, 2001).

First, k-factors over strings are defined below. Let Σ be the alphabet, and Σ^* be all strings of finite length over Σ. Then string u is a factor of string w iff ($\exists x, y \in \Sigma^*$) such that $w = xuy$. If $|u| = k$, then u is a k-factor of w. The function F_k maps a string to a set of k-factors within it:

$$F_k(w) = \{u | u \text{ is a } k\text{-factor of } w\}$$

A Strictly k-Local (SL_k) grammar for a string language is understood as a list of possible k-factors in the language, or equivalently, a list of banned k-factors.

Definition 1 *(Strictly Local Stringsets)*

$\mathcal{G}$, a Strictly k-Local description over some alphabet Σ, is a set of k-factors of $\Sigma \cup \{\rtimes, \ltimes\}$, where $\rtimes$ and $\ltimes$ mark the beginning and ending of a string, respectively.

$$\mathcal{G} \subseteq F_k(\rtimes \cdot \Sigma^* \cdot \ltimes)$$

A string w satisfies $\mathcal{G}$, iff the set of k-factors of the augmented string $\rtimes \cdot w \cdot \ltimes$ is a subset of $\mathcal{G}$:

$$w \models \mathcal{G} \Leftrightarrow F_k(\rtimes \cdot w \cdot \ltimes) \subseteq \mathcal{G}$$

The stringset licensed by a description $\mathcal{G}$ is the set of words that satisfy it.

$$L(\mathcal{G}) \overset{def}{=} \{w | w \models \mathcal{G}\}$$

A set of strings is Strictly k-Local (SL_k) iff it is $L(\mathcal{G})$ for some strictly k-local definition of $\mathcal{G}$. It is Strictly Local iff it is SL_k for some k.

Next, the definition of local k-expressions is given below.

Definition 2 *(Local k-expressions)*

The language of k-expressions is the smallest set including the following forms, with the intended semantics indicated.

- *Atomic formulae: $f \in F_k(\Sigma^*)$ is a k-expression.*

- *Conjunction: If φ_1 and φ_2 are k-expressions, then $(\varphi_1 \wedge \varphi_2)$ is a k-expression.*

- *Negation: If φ_1 is a k-expression, then $(\neg\varphi_1)$ is a k-expression.*

If w is a string and φ a k-expression, then

$$w \models \varphi \overset{def}{\Leftrightarrow}$$
$$\begin{cases} \varphi = f \in F_k(\Sigma^*) \text{ and } f \in F_k(w) \\ \varphi = (\varphi_1 \wedge \varphi_2) \text{ and } w \models \varphi_1 \text{ and } w \models \varphi_2 \\ \varphi = (\neg\varphi_1) \text{ and } w \not\models \varphi_1 \end{cases}$$

Now we can define Locally Testable Stringsets with the help of k-expressions.

Definition 3 *(Locally Testable Stringsets)*

A stringset L over Σ is k-Locally Testable (LT_k) iff there is some local k-expression φ over Σ (for some k) such that L is the set of all strings that satisfy φ.

$$L = L(\varphi) \overset{def}{=} \{w \in \Sigma^* | w \models \varphi\}$$

A stringset is LT iff it is LT_k for some k.

Notice that implicational statements can be derived from k-expressions, because $a \rightarrow b$ is equivalent to $\neg(a \wedge \neg b)$.

2.2 Tree languages

Our understanding of trees is based on the idea of *multi*-dimensional trees, as discussed in Rogers (2003). For the purposes of this paper, we exclusively work with 2-dimensional trees, and thus restrict our formal descriptions to them.

The basic intuition is as follows. Strings are one-dimensional trees, whose nodes are related to each other via one-dimensional successor relations. To add a second dimension, we first build a *local* tree (a tree of at most one depth) by connecting a single point a to each node in a one-dimensional tree S through second-dimensional successor relations (Figure 1a). The adjoined point is called the *root* in this case, and the nodes in S are the *yield*. A *composite* tree, where trees have depths greater than one, can be built by identifying the root of one local tree with some point in the yield of another (Figure 1b). In the trees in Figure 1, the solid lines represent the one-dimensional successor relations, and the dashed lines represent the second-dimensional successor relations.

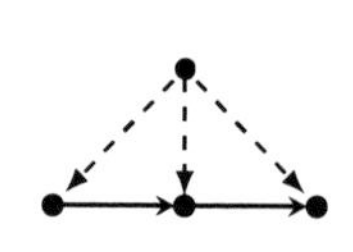

(a) 2-dimensional local tree

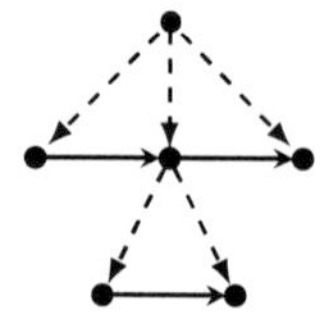

(b) 2-dimensional composite tree

Figure 1: Two-dimensional trees

We give our formal definition for two-dimensional trees within the model-theoretic framework. Model theory provides a way to describe a particular object using mathematical logic. A model requires a *signature* and a set of *logical statements*. Along with the usual logical connectives, $x \approx y$ denotes that x and y are equivalent.

The signature of the two-dimensional tree-model for linguistic trees is shown in Figure 2. Let $\Sigma = \Sigma_{Cat} \cup \Sigma_{Lex}$ be the alphabet, where Σ_{Cat} is the set of syntactic categories, and Σ_{Lex} is the set of lexical items. We write $\sigma(x)$ if node x is labeled with σ, for all $\sigma \in \Sigma$.

$$\langle \mathcal{D}, \prec, \rhd, \mathcal{L}_\sigma \rangle_{\sigma \in \Sigma}, \text{ where}$$

- $\mathcal{D}$ is the finite domain

- $\prec$ is a binary ordering relation *immediate left-of*

- $\rhd$ is a binary ordering relation *immediate dominance*

- $\mathcal{L}_\sigma$ is a set of unary relations for labeling elements in $\mathcal{D}$ with σ for all $\sigma \in \Sigma$

Figure 2: Model for two-dimensional trees

Following Rogers (2003), $\rhd^*$ is defined as the reflexive transitive closure, and $\rhd^+$ as the transitive closure of $\rhd$. This is explicitly monadic second-order definable through *Branch*: a set of nodes that are upwards closed with regard to, and linearly-ordered by the immediate dominance relation, $\rhd$. The *depth* of any tree then can be understood as the length of the longest Branch in the tree.

(1) $Branch(X) \equiv (\forall x, y)[(X(x) \wedge y \rhd x) \rightarrow X(y)] \wedge (\forall x, y, z)[(X(x) \wedge X(y) \wedge X(z) \wedge$

$x \rhd y \wedge x \rhd z) \rightarrow y \approx z]$

(2) $\quad x \rhd^* y \equiv (\forall X)[(Branch(X) \wedge X(y)) \rightarrow X(x)]$

(3) $\quad x \rhd^+ y \equiv x \rhd^* y \wedge x \not\approx y$

The predicates $\prec^*$ and $\prec^+$ are definable in a similar fashion.

(4) $\quad String(X) \equiv (\forall x, y)[(X(x) \wedge y \prec x) \rightarrow X(y)] \wedge (\forall x, y, z)[(X(x) \wedge X(y) \wedge X(z) \wedge x \prec y \wedge x \prec z) \rightarrow y \approx z]$

(5) $\quad x \prec^* y \equiv (\forall X)[(String(X) \wedge X(y)) \rightarrow X(x)]$

(6) $\quad x \prec^+ y \equiv x \prec^* y \wedge x \not\approx y$

Based on $\prec^*$, we also can also define the inherited left-of relation, $<^*$. If z is left-of w in a tree, then all nodes that are reflexively dominated by z are inherited left-of all nodes that are reflexively dominated by w.

(7) $\quad x <^* y \equiv (\exists z, w)[z \rhd^* x \wedge w \rhd^* y \wedge z \prec^* w]$

The following tree-axioms restrict all possible structures to the desired two-dimensional tree-structures described previously (and illustrated in Figure 1):

(8) There is a root that dominates all nodes:
$(\exists x)(\forall y)[x \rhd^* y \wedge \neg \exists z(z \rhd x)]$

(9) At most one parent/direct precedent per node:
$(\forall x, y, z)[[(x \prec z \wedge y \prec z) \vee (x \rhd z \wedge y \rhd z)] \rightarrow x \approx y]$

(10) Irreflexivity of $\prec$ and $\rhd$:
$(\forall x, y)[(x \prec y \vee x \rhd y) \rightarrow x \not\approx y]$

(11) Two nodes cannot be both in $\rhd^*$ and $\prec^*$ relations:
$(\forall x, y)[(x \rhd^* y \vee y \rhd^* x) \leftrightarrow \neg(x \prec^* y \vee y \prec^* x)]$

We add two final assumptions that are specific to linguistic trees. Each node can only have one label, and a node can only have a label $l \in \Sigma_{Lex}$ iff that node is a leaf (i.e. it does not dominate any other node).

(12) $\quad (\forall x)[(\alpha(x) \wedge \beta(x)) \rightarrow \alpha \approx \beta]$

(13) $\quad (\forall x)[\neg \exists y(x \rhd y) \leftrightarrow \alpha(x) \wedge \alpha \in \Sigma_{Lex}]$

As an example, see tree T1 in Figure 3b, a model-theoretic representation of Figure 3a. For this non-linguistic tree, $\Sigma = \{a, b, c\}$, with no distinction between Σ_{Cat} and Σ_{Lex}. The solid lines represent the first-dimensional successor relations $\prec$, and the dashed lines represent the second-dimensional successor relations $\rhd$.

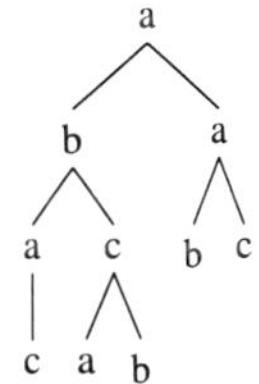

(a) Conventional representation of T1

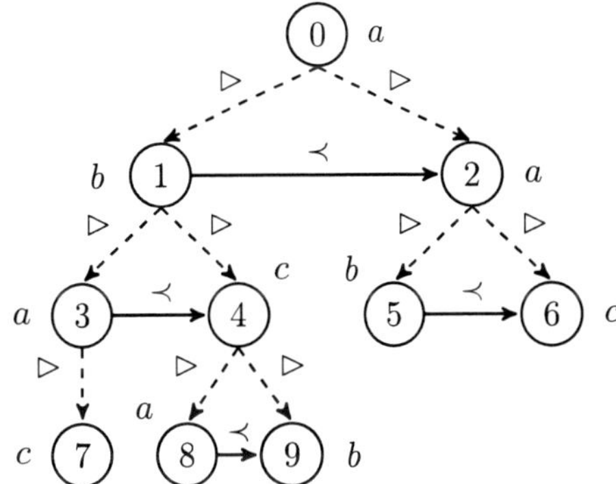

(b) Model-theoretic representation of T1

Figure 3: T1

Then TI can be described with the following list of statements:

(14) Labeling statement:
$a(0) \wedge b(1) \wedge a(2) \wedge a(3) \wedge c(4) \wedge b(5) \wedge c(6) \wedge c(7) \wedge a(8) \wedge b(9)$

(15) Statement about $\prec$:
$1 \prec 2 \wedge 3 \prec 4 \wedge 5 \prec 6 \wedge 8 \prec 9$

(16) Statement about $\rhd$:
$0 \rhd 1 \wedge 0 \rhd 2 \wedge 1 \rhd 3 \wedge 1 \rhd 4 \wedge 2 \rhd 5 \wedge 2 \rhd 6 \wedge 3 \rhd 7 \wedge 4 \rhd 8 \wedge 4 \rhd 9$

Next, we generalize k-factors to two-dimensional trees. For strings, k-factors are substrings of k length. For trees, this will mean subtrees with depth of k-1 (since the depth of the root node is 0, but one node is an 1-factor of a tree).

(17) $Subtree(X) \equiv (\exists x)(\forall y)[(X(x) \wedge x \rhd^* y) \rightarrow X(y)]$

A 2-factor can be easily defined by changing the $\rhd^*$ relation to $\rhd$ in the definition of subtrees. While this is not a generalized definition of k-factors in trees, it will be sufficient for the purposes of this paper.

(18) $2\text{-Factor}(X) \equiv (\exists x)(\forall y)[(X(x) \wedge x \rhd y) \rightarrow X(y)]$

For example, the 2-factors of T1 is the set of trees in Figure 4.

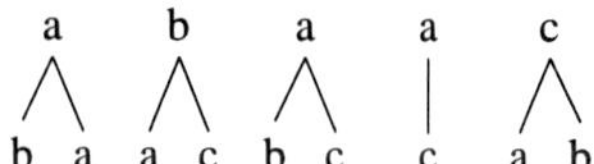

Figure 4: 2-factors of T1

In our linguistic examples, the labels will be syntactic categories (e.g. CP, NP, C', N', etc.) and language-specific lexical items. For the purposes of NPI-licensing, a specific set of lexical items are of interest only: NPIs and negation for both English and Hungarian, and CPs for Hungarian. Below we simply define the lexical items for NPIs and negation, in English and Hungarian.

(19) $\text{NPI}_{\text{eng}}(x) \equiv \text{anybody}(x) \vee \text{anything}(x) \vee \text{anywhere}(x)$

(20) $\text{neg}_{\text{eng}}(x) \equiv \text{not}(x) \vee \text{no}(x) \vee \text{nobody}(x) \vee \text{nothing}(x) \vee \text{nowhere}(x)$

(21) $\text{NPI}_{\text{hun}}(x) \equiv \text{senki}(x) \vee \text{semmi}(x) \vee \text{sehol}(x)$

(22) $\text{neg}_{\text{hun}}(x) \equiv \text{nem}(x)$

2.3 Tier-based tree-languages

Heinz et al. (2011) defined *Tier-based Strictly Local* (TSL) languages for strings. We use their definition of tiers complete with the one found in Graf and Heinz (2015) to discuss the projection of tier-trees.

A tier is denoted as $T \subseteq \Sigma$, and there is an erasing function that erases all elements in the string that are not labeled on the tier (Heinz et al., 2011).

Generalizing to our two-dimensional tree-model, a tree-tier is projected by taking only the nodes that are labeled with elements of T, while keeping all

inherited left-of relations ($<^*$) and dominance relations ($\rhd^*$) between these nodes.

For example, let $T = \{a, b\}$. Applying the erasing function to T1 (3) then yields a tier-tree (5). We say that T1 *projects* a tier-tree.

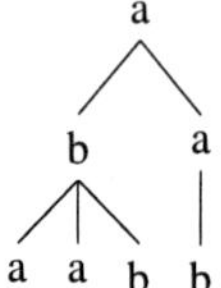

Figure 5: Tier-tree, $T=\{a,b\}$

TSL string languages were characterized by a finite list of banned k-factors over the string-tier. The equivalent is not possible for tree-languages, because in tier-trees, there is no bound on the number of daughters for a given node.

To see why, take a tree T2 such that the starting node labeled S mothers a node labeled b, and each node b mothers a node a and b (6a). In linguistic terms, node a's never dominate each other, neither are they ever sisters; the higher ones c-command the lower ones. Now suppose that the tier we want to project is $T=\{S,a\}$. We then get a tree where S directly dominates an unbounded number of a nodes, where that number is equivalent to the depth of the original tree. We thus cannot list a finite-list of banned (or permitted) k-factors over a tree-tier without knowing a bound on the depth of the tree first.

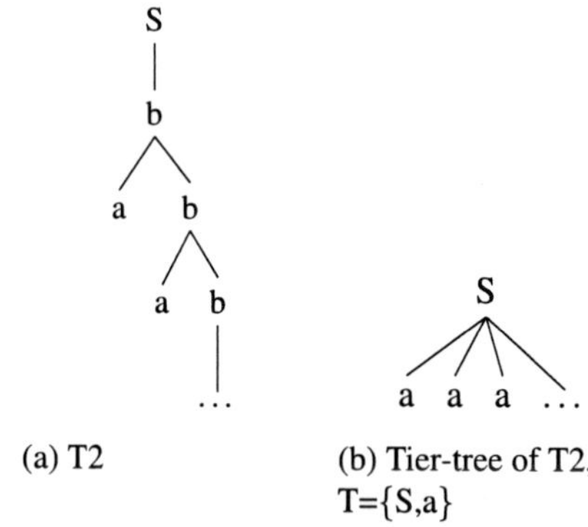

(a) T2   (b) Tier-tree of T2, $T=\{S,a\}$

Figure 6: T2 and its tier-tree

Instead, we give a general description of tree languages that are Tier-based Strictly 2-Local over the dominance relation ($TSL_2^{\rhd}$). Recall that in the framework laid out in Rogers (2003), two-dimensional trees consist of strings (i.e. one-dimensional trees) that are dominated by a single node. We use this insight to define our tier-based grammar. Informally, the grammar contains a tier as described above, and string-based grammars that apply over sisters dominated by the same node. There are potentially as many string-based grammars as nodes labeled with a syntactic category on the tier. Formally, each grammar contains a quadruple as in Figure 7.

$$G = \langle T, T_{Cat}, H, \gamma \rangle, \text{ where:}$$

- $T \subset \Sigma$ is the finite set of tier-nodes

- $T_{Cat} = (T \cap \Sigma_{Cat})$

- H is a set of string-based grammars

- $\gamma : T_{Cat} \times H$ is a bijection that maps every node labeled $\kappa \in T_{Cat}$ to a string-based grammar $h \in H$

Figure 7: Grammar of tier-trees

The grammar defined here is thus $TSL_2^\triangleright$, but there can still be different types of grammar over the left-of relations. Following Graf and Heinz (2015) then, a TSL grammar for trees is a specific instance of the grammar defined here: in this case, H must be a set of TSL string-languages.

3 NPI patterns

We understand Negative Polarity Items (NPIs) as expressions that are ungrammatical in positive declarative clauses, but they are grammatical in their negative counterpart. This understanding of NPIs echoes the one for *negative dependencies* in Giannakidou and Zeijlstra (2016). For example, English *anything* is an NPI according this definition, because it shows the following contrast:

(23)   a. *John has read anything.

       b. John hasn't read anything.

3.1 English-type

English-type NPIs are typical in English, Chinese (Lin, 1998), and Vietnamese (Tran and Bruening, 2013), among others. They are weak NPI-

languages, which means that their NPIs are licensed not only by negation, but also in questions, protasis of conditionals, and in general, downward entailment contexts (Ladusaw, 1983). For the sake of simplicity, I will focus only on the cases where English NPIs are licensed by sentential negation.

The general observation is that English NPIs must be c-commanded by negation (24-26), over an arbitrary number of clause boundaries (27).[1] The NPI item *anybody* is not c-commanded by negation (*not, nobody*) in (25) and (26), but it is c-commanded and thus licensed in (24).

(24)   John didn't see anybody.

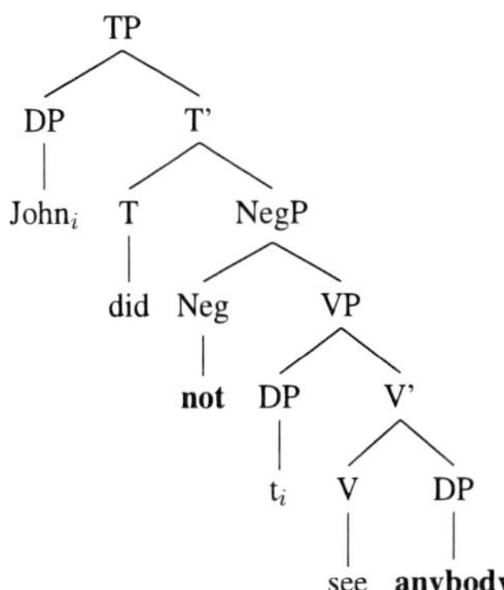

(25)   *Anybody didn't see John.

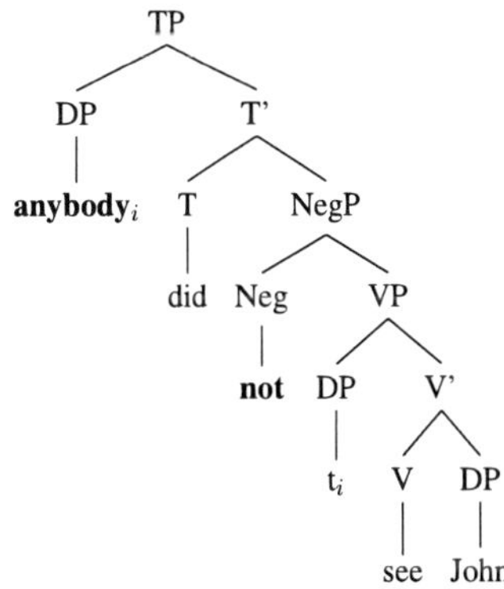

(26)   *Nobody's children saw anybody.

---

[1] A reviewer suggested that a sentence such as 'Nobody's mother understood anything I said' as a counter-evidence for the general pattern. However, if *mother* is replaced by *children*, the sentence becomes much less acceptable. Our suspicion is that 'nobody's mother' has become idiomatic, meaning 'nobody'.

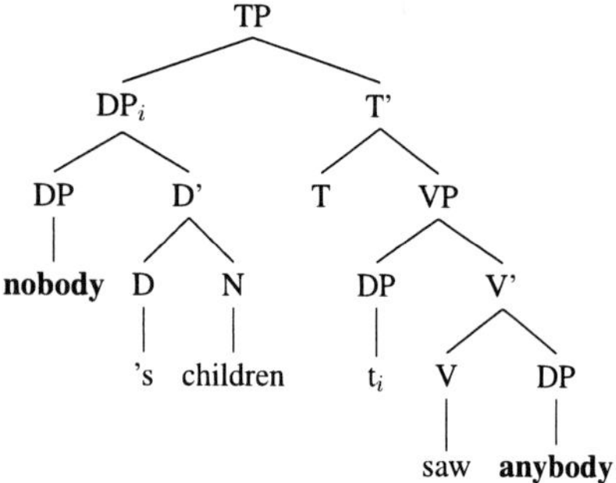

(27) [John didn't think [that Charlie saw [that Mary stole anything.]]]

A straightforward way then to formalize the English-NPI licensing requirement is to state it in first-order logic with the help of defining c-command relations.

(28) $\text{c-com}(x,y) \equiv \neg(x \triangleright^+ y) \wedge x \not\approx y \wedge \forall z[z \triangleright^+ x \rightarrow z \triangleright^+ y]$

(29) English NPI-licensing constraint:
$\forall y[\text{NPI}_{\text{eng}}(y) \rightarrow \exists x[\text{c-com}(x,y) \wedge \text{neg}_{\text{eng}}(x)]]$

3.2 Hungarian-type

Here we cite our own data collected from Hungarian, but we suspect that a similar distribution is found in Slavic languages (Progovac, 1994). Hungarian NPIs show the same contrast that is found in English:

(30) *Jancsi látott senkit.
Jancsi saw NPI.ACC

'Jancsi saw anybody.'

(31) Jancsi nem látott senkit.
Jancsi NEG saw NPI.ACC

'Jancsi didn't see anybody.'

Their similarity to English NPIs stops here. Hungarian NPIs must be licensed locally by clausemate negation (32), but there is no c-command requirement for the relation between licensor and licensee (33). We assume that the domain of licensing is restricted to CP boundaries, as NPIs are licensed in sentences with negated raising predicates (34), but not in ones with negated control predicates (35).[2]

$\overline{}$

[2]In accordance with Carnie (2013), I assume that control verbs select for CPs, whereas raising verbs select for IPs.

(32) *Jancsi nem tudta, hogy Mari semmit
Jancsi NEG knew that Mari NPI.ACC
olvasott.
read

'Jancsi didn't know that Mari read anything.'

(33) Senki nem akart el jönni.
NPI NEG want.PST PRT come.INF

'Nobody wanted to come.'

(34) Mari nem kezdett olvasni semmit.
Mari NEG started read.INF NPI.ACC

'Mari didn't start to read anything.'

(35) *Mari nem próbált olvasni semmit.
Mari NEG tried read.INF NPI.ACC

'Mari didn't try to read anything.'

The constraint can be formalized with First-order logic with the help of defining $\text{closest-CP}(x,y)$, which says that x is labeled CP, and it is the closest node labeled such to y.

(36) $\text{closest-CP}(x,y) \equiv \text{CP}(x) \wedge x \triangleright^* y \wedge \neg\exists z[\text{CP}(z) \wedge x \triangleright *+ z \wedge z \triangleright^* y]$

(37) Hungarian NPI-licensing constraint:
$\forall(y)[\text{NPI}_{\text{hun}}(y) \rightarrow \exists(x,z)[\text{closest-CP}(x,y) \wedge \text{closest-CP}(x,z) \wedge \text{neg}_{hun}(z)]$

3.3 Interim summary

The NPI patterns discussed above are summarized in Table 1.

	Negation must c-command NPI	Licensing across CP boundaries
English	yes	yes
Hungarian	no	no

Table 1: Summary of English and Hungarian NPI patterns.

4 Complexity of NPI patterns

In what follows, we re-define the NPI-licensing constraints for Hungarian and English, in the context of the $\text{TSL}_2^{\triangleright}$ grammar G defined in Section 2.3. We have two results: (1) Hungarian NPI-licensing can be characterized with the tier-based grammar, but English cannot, and (2) the string-language for the Hungarian grammar is neither SL or TSL, but it is LT.

4.1 Hungarian

Let us define the relevant tier for Hungarian NPI-licensing as follows: $T=\{\mathtt{neg}_{hun}, \mathtt{NPI}_{hun}, \mathtt{CP}\}$. Then $T_{Cat} = \{\mathtt{CP}\}$. For examples of grammatical tier-trees, see Figure 8.

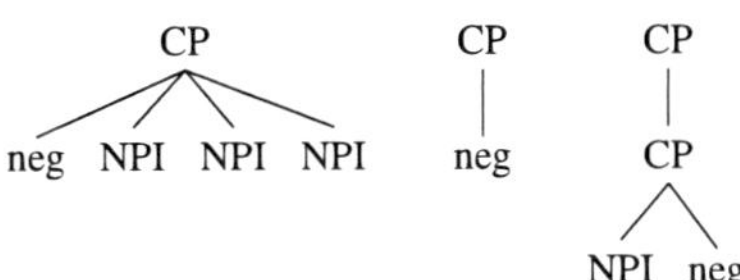

(a) Well-formed tier-trees for Hungarian NPI-licensing

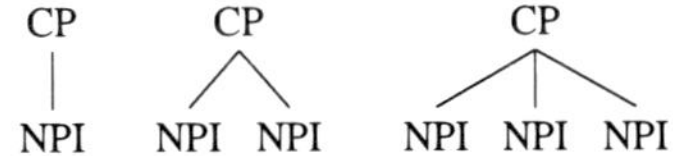

(b) Ill-formed tier-tree for Hungarian NPI-licensing

Figure 8: Well-formed and ill-formed tier-trees for Hungarian NPI-licensing

Now the question is determining the string grammar h over the nodes that CP dominates in the tier. Let us call this string-grammar h_{CP}. We show that h_{CP} is not SL, but it is LT. Consider the ill-formed set of trees where there is an arbitrary number of NPIs but there is no negation to license any of them (Figure 8b). Such trees would correspond to ungrammatical sentences of the form (38).

(38)   *Senkinek^n senkije   látott semmit.
       NPI.DAT   NPI.POSS saw   NPI.ACC

'Nobody's^n anybody saw anything.'

If h_{CP} were SL, we would be able to ban a set of k-factors to successfully exclude the ill-formed trees. This is not possible for any k. For any k-factor that successfully bans a string of k-length that consists of only NPIs, there is a well-formed string of length $k + 1$, whose $k + 1$-th member is neg.

To exclusively define well-formed trees, the use of LT logic is necessary (39). This formula is Locally 1-Testable.

(39) $(\forall x \exists y)[\mathtt{NPI}_{hun}(x) \to \mathtt{neg}_{hun}(y)]$

4.2 English

Recall that English NPI-licensing is stated as a c-command requirement: negation must c-command the NPI. This type of constraint cannot be reduced to any type of $\mathrm{TSL}_2^{\triangleright}$ grammar.

Consider the following two sentences:

(40)   *The girl, (that X said)^n that John didn't see, read anything.

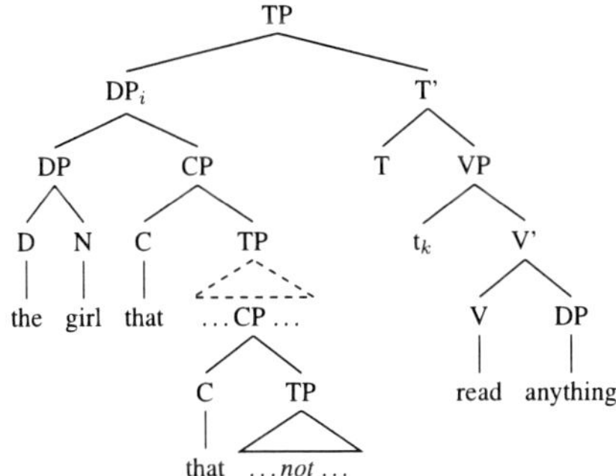

(41)   John didn't think (that X said)^n Mary stole anything.

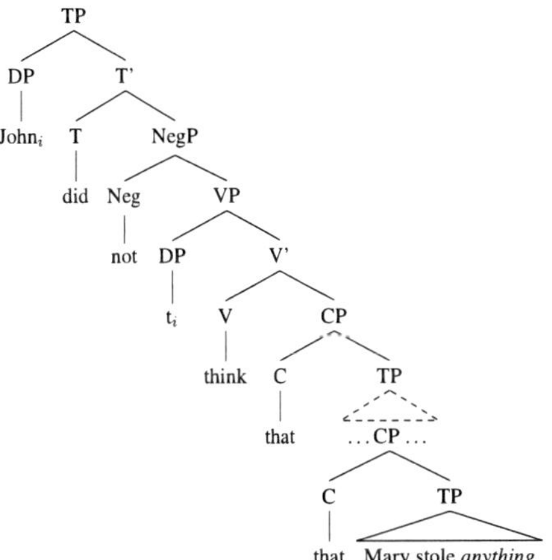

In (40), negation can be found buried inside a relative clause that has been constructed through an arbitrary number of recursive embedding, and thus it does not c-command the NPI *anything*. On the other hand, in (41), negation c-commands an NPI that is buried in the embedded clauses, and thus the NPI is licensed.

There are no local constraints that can account for the restriction, since there is no bound on the distance between the negation and the NPI. Introducing tiers does not help either, due to the c-command requirement. There is no good way to define elements for the tier to get the relevant 2-factors within the tier-tree that would help us derive the correct constraints. In fact, there is no definable tier in order to get any relevant k-factor in the tier-tree.

If the tier is defined to only include negation and NPI, the two obviously relevant elements for NPI-licensing in English, there is no way to tell apart tier-trees where negation c-commands the NPI compared to the ones where it does not. For example, both sentences (24) and (26) would yield the same tier-tree:

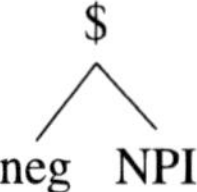

Figure 9: Tier-tree for (24) and (26), $T=\{neg, NPI\}$

Including nodes that can immediately dominate negation (NegP and DP) would again result in tier-trees of arbitrary depth. For example, in sentences (41) and (40), one would have to list all the arbitrary number of DPs that serve as subjects for each embedded clause before getting to the NPI in the sentence. We then have the problem of not being able to determine subtrees of a bounded k-depth. Thus c-command relations cannot be defined using tiers.

5   Conclusions

This paper has offered four results. First, it provided a definition of $TSL_2^{\triangleright}$ languages. Second, it showed that implicational requirements, such as the surface licensing conditions of NPIs for Hungarian and English, cannot be described with TSL constraints over both dominance and precedence relations in trees.

Hungarian, which has a clausemate-requirement, can be described with a grammar that is $TSL_2^{\triangleright}$ with LT_1 constraints over the precedence relations. On the other hand, English NPI-licensing patterns, which have a structural c-command restriction, cannot be accommodated by $TSL_2^{\triangleright}$. It is yet to be seen whether English surface NPI-licensing can be described with any logical formalism that is weaker than First-order.

These results apply to surface syntactic descriptions only. Once we consider other possible theoretical explanations for NPIs that employ either feature-agreement or movement, the complexity of these syntactic constraints might be decreased. This question is to be addressed by future research.

Our class of newly defined tree-languages, $TSL_2^{\triangleright}$, needs further study also. In particular, it would be interesting to see how the characterizations of sub-regular string languages (e.g. the Suffix Substitution Clause for SL languages, or Local Test Invariance for LT languages) hold up once the representation changes from strings to trees. It is also yet to be seen what it means for tree languages that one can mix and match different classes of languages for different ordering relations within the same tree-structure. The nature of subregular tree-languages is still largely unknown.

Lastly, we might also examine different definitions of trees. For example, Frank and Vijay-Shanker (2001) proposed to define trees using c-command as the primitive binary relation, instead of dominance. In that case, the English NPI-licensing constraint would be very easy to state by requiring that NPIs are c-commanded by a negation. We suspect that Hungarian NPI-licensing can be accounted for as well, but a careful study is needed to confirm our hypothesis.

In conclusion, these results are only preliminary to studying the computational complexity of NPI-licensing constraints. However, they show the potential of using tools from theoretical computer science to reveal the nature of syntactic phenomena. For one, it might not be immediately obvious that on the surface level, English NPI-licensing needs more powerful tools to be described than Hungarian NPI-licensing. English is unrestricted in terms of distance between the licensor and licensee, whereas Hungarian is unrestricted in terms of structural requirements as long as the licensor and licensee are within the same clause. Formalizing these constraints using logic revealed that having an unbounded distance necessitates increased complexity compared to having no structural requirement.

Studying linguistic phenomena from a formal perspective thus can give us insight into the minimal computational requirements needed for natural language. The results in turn might bear further implications on the computational complexity needed for syntactic patterns, particularly in learning and expected cross-linguistic variation.

References

Andrew Carnie. 2013. *Syntax: A generative introduction*. John Wiley & Sons.

Jane Chandlee. 2014. *Strictly local phonological processes*. Ph.D. thesis, University of Delaware.

Herbert B Enderton. 2001. *A mathematical introduction to logic*. Academic press.

Robert Frank and K Vijay-Shanker. 2001. Primitive C-Command. *Syntax*, 4(3):164–204.

Anastasia Giannakidou and Hedde Zeijlstra. 2016. The landscape of negative dependencies: negative concord and n-words. In *Linguistics Companion*, pages 1–47. Second edition.

Thomas Graf and Jeffrey Heinz. 2015. Commonality in Disparity : The Computational View of Syntax and Phonology A New View of the Power of Syntax and Phonology.

Thomas Graf. 2013. *Local and Transderivational Constraints in Syntax and Semantics*. Ph.D. thesis, UCLA.

Thomas Graf. 2017. The Power of Locality Domains in Phonology.

Jeffrey Heinz and William Idsardi. 2013. What complexity differences reveal about domains in language. *Topics in cognitive science*, pages 111–131.

Jeffrey Heinz, Chetan Rawal, and Herbert G Tanner. 2011. Tier-based Strictly Local Constraints for Phonology. In *Proceedings of the 49th Annual Meeting of the Association for Computational Linguistics*, pages 58–64.

Jeffrey Heinz. 2009. On the role of locality in learning stress patterns. *Phonology*, 26:303–351.

Jeffrey Heinz. 2010. Learning long-distance phonotactics. *Linguistic Inquiry*, 41:623–661.

Adam Jardine. 2016. *Locality and non-linear representations in tonal phonology*. Ph.D. thesis, University of Delaware.

William A Ladusaw. 1983. Logical Form and Conditions on Grammaticality. *Linguistics and Philosophy*, 6(3):373–392.

Jo-wang Lin. 1998. On existential polarity wh - phrases in chinese. *Journal of East Asian Linguistics*, 7(1982):219–255.

Liljiana Progovac. 1994. *Negative and Positive Polarity: A binding approach*. Cambridge University Press, Cambridge.

Geoffrey K Pullum. 2007. The Evolution of Model-Theoretic Frameworks in Linguistics. In James Rogers and Stephan Kepser, editors, *Model-Theoretic Syntax at 10*, pages 1–10, Dublin, Ireland.

James Rogers and Geoffrey K Pullum. 2011. Aural Pattern Recognition Experiments and the Subregular Hierarchy. *Journal of Logic, Language and Information*, 20(3):329–342.

James Rogers, Jeffrey Heinz, Margaret Fero, Jeremy Hurst, Dakotah Lambert, and Sean Wibel. 2013. Cognitive and Sub-regular Complexity. In *17th Conference on Formal Grammars*, pages 90–108.

James Rogers. 2003. Syntactic Structures as Multidimensional Trees. *Research on Language and Computation*, 1:265–305.

Edward P. Stabler. 1997. Derivational minimalism. *Logical aspects of computational linguistics*, pages 68–95.

Thuan Tran and Benjamin Bruening. 2013. Wh-Phrases as indefinites. A Vietnamese Perspective. In Daniel Hole and Elisabeth Löbel, editors, *Linguistics of Vietnamese: An International Survey*, pages 217–241. Mouton de Gruyter, Berlin.

The organization of lexicons: A cross-linguistic analysis of monosyllabic words

Shiying Yang, Chelsea Sanker, and **Uriel Cohen Priva**
shiying_yang,chelsea_sanker,uriel_cohen_priva@brown.edu

Abstract

Lexicons utilize a fraction of licit structures. Different theories predict either that lexicons prioritize contrastiveness or structural economy. Study 1 finds that the monosyllabic lexicon of Mandarin is no more distinctive than a randomly sampled baseline using the phonological inventory. Study 2 finds that the lexicons of Mandarin and American English have fewer phonotactically complex words than the random baseline: Words tend not to have multiple low-probability components. This suggests that phonological constraints can have superadditive penalties for combined violations, consistent with e.g. Albright (ms.).

1   Introduction

Lexicons can be considered mappings between word meanings and phonotactically-valid sequences of phonemes. There are several dimensions of forces shaping lexicons, based on the frequency of each item and its phonetic distinctiveness from similar items, as well as the phonotactic probability of the phonological sequences within each item. For instance, underlying pressures on the lexicon influence the frequency distribution of items within a lexicon (Zipf, 1929; Piantadosi et al., 2009); Zipf's law predicts that frequent words should be preferentially mapped to shorter segmental sequences.

In the absence of other pressures, syllables and words should be maximally distinct from one another, in order to minimize ambiguity and potential for confusion. This pressure has been demonstrated within phonological inventories; vowel systems tend to maximize the distance between vowels (Flemming, 2004), though other work has found a tendency for economy, in which each feature tends to be used for multiple contrasts, particularly among consonants (Clements, 2003; Dautriche et al., 2017). Wedel et al. (2013) demonstrate that contrastiveness is important in shaping lexicons; phonological mergers are less likely when more lexical contrasts depend on the phonological contrast. The pressure for contrastiveness has been demonstrated in various experiments, in which words with higher neighborhood density are identified more slowly than words with lower neighborhood density (Luce and Pisoni, 1998). If lexicons are not maximizing how distinct lexical items are, there must be other pressures outweighing contrastiveness.

Using two computational studies, we examine some of the factors influencing the shapes of items within lexicons, by comparing actual lexicons to generated lexicons given the same phonotactic restrictions.

1.1   Competing pressures in a lexicon

Zipf (1929) proposed the principle of least effort as a primary force shaping phonological inventories, claiming that the frequencies of sounds within a language are negatively correlated with their articulatory and perceptual complexity, given a set number of contrasts. Thus, the probability of a sound would reflect its overall perceptual and articulatory cost. Consistent with this proposal is the strong correlation between the cross-linguistic frequency of phonemes (i.e. what percentage of languages in UPSID have them) and their frequency within particular languages (Sanker, 2016).

In line with this functional view, emphasizing the communicative goal of language, Flemming's (2004) Dispersion Theory of contrast translated the trade-off between speaker and listener into three conflicting goals: "maximizing the distinctiveness of contrasts," "minimizing articulatory effort" and "maximizing the number of contrasts." He proposed that a phonological inventory would strike a balance between these goals, providing the most distinctive vowel system possible with a given number of contrasts, with articulatory effort only as motivated by achieving distinctiveness. This principle should also extend to lexicons: All else being equal, lexicons should be maximally distinct. This is additionally supported by perceptual evidence that dense lexical neighborhoods slow down processing (Luce and Pisoni, 1998).

However, lexicons seem to be less dispersed than would be expected from the pressure of maximizing contrastiveness. Dautriche et al. (2017) looked at the lexicons of four Indo-European languages and found that they were more regular ("clumpy") than expected by chance. Words were more similar to each other in these languages than in generated phonotactically-controlled baseline lexicons. This result parallels some work in the segmental domain, which shows that languages tend to reuse phonological features (Clements, 2003). However, one potential limitation of this study is that the phonotactic restrictions were tightly controlled, with environments extending out to four segments, which could have constrained the generated lexicons beyond just capturing the intended phonological constraints; in long words, it can be unclear what segmental range best captures the inherent phonotactic patterns.

In order to expand the data into an unrelated language and in particular address whether the lexicon would pattern differently in a language with shorter words and a denser lexicon, we compared generated phonotactically-controlled lexicons to the real lexicon of Mandarin Chinese in Study 1.

1.2 An explanation of phonologically clustered lexicons

In contrast to the dispersion account which bases the drive for distinctiveness on communicative efficiency, Dautriche et al. (2017) attributed their findings to a pressure for regularity that is driven by the goal of lowering cognitive costs in language acquisition and lexical access. A different possibility is that our understanding of the forces driving a language's phonotactics are flawed.

Within phonological theories that address gradient phenomena, models are generally multiplicative. For instance, in MaxEnt, as presented by Hayes and Wilson (2008), the probability assigned to a phonotactic form is e raised to the negative sum of the weighted constraint violations. Calculated differently, this is the product of the probability of each individual violation occurring.

Thus, MaxEnt treats constraints as being independent (Hayes and Wilson, 2008). However, multiple languages have constraint combinations which are more limited in combination than would be predicted from their independent probabilities (Albright, ms; Green and Davis, 2014; Shih, 2016). For example, English /æ/ and coda /z/ are attested with somewhat low frequency, but their combination is extremely uncommon, far below the product of their independent probabilities (Kessler and Treiman, 1997). Such patterns have been explained as "superadditivity"(Albright, ms) or "supercumulativity"(Shih, 2016), a phenomenon in which combinations of marked structures incur additional penalties, though their co-occurrence is not categorically disallowed.

The superadditivity effect might underlie some of the patterns of lexicons, as it would produce a faster drop-off in the occurrence of low probability forms, resulting in more clustering around higher probability forms than is predicted by models in which all phonotactic constraints are independent. Study 2 was devised to test the null hypothesis of a multiplicative grammar, in which the probability of a certain form appearing as a word is the product of the probabilities of each of its components, against a counter-hypothesis of a grammar including additional penalties for combinations of low-probability sequences; see section 3.2.

1.3 The null hypotheses: A lexicon selected by chance

Similar to the resampling procedures used by Dautriche et al. (2017), sample lexicons were generated to estimate statistics of a baseline population distribution as predicted from the phonotactic constraints and lexicon size of Mandarin, to be tested against measurements of the real lexicon. A lexicon can be thought of as a set of word forms drawn from a pool of all forms that are licit within the phonotactic constraints of a language. To draw a lexicon with k contrasting items from a constrained pool of n licit shapes, there are $\binom{n}{k}$ possibilities for lexicons; generated lexicons are drawn from this pool of possibilities.

If the lexicon is not under any pressure to maximize either distinctiveness or regularity, the sampling procedure from the pool of candidate word-forms will be random; Study 1 tests the predictions made by random sampling.

If independent phonotactic constraints are sufficient to capture well-formedness and thus predict frequency distributions in lexicons, probabilities of phonemic shapes will follow from probabilities of their subparts (Albright, ms). Study 2 tests the predictions made by independent evaluation of constraints; if constraints are independent, generated lexicons that are randomly sampled from the pool of forms based on probabilities produced by the phonotactic constraints of a language without any constraint interaction should have distributions similar to the real lexicon.

Both Study 1 and Study 2 are based on constructing phonotactically-constrained pools of words from which generated lexicons are sampled. The word-pools and the artificial lexicons are generated according to the parameters laid out in the following sections, to create baselines for evaluating what factors are influencing the real lexicons. We aim to show that real lexicons cannot be explained by randomly sampling from a constrained phonological space and that the constraints on the phonological space call for a model that includes superadditivity.

2 Study 1: Evaluating the distinctiveness of Mandarin monosyllabic lexicon

2.1 Background

Study 1 investigated monosyllabic words in Mandarin Chinese. Mandarin has a dense phonological space and limited licit syllable structures, which make it possible to enumerate all phonologically permissible forms with relatively few assumptions.

Mandarin syllables are limited to a structure with at most four phonemes: CGVX (Li and Thompson, 1987). C stands for a consonant in the onset position; G stands for a glide; V stands for a vowel; and X can either be a nasal /n/ or /ŋ/, or the off-glide of a diphthong. Every syllable must have a vowel, but all other positions can be empty (Duanmu, 2009). In addition, each syllable has one of four phonological tones. Given only these structural constraints, the phonological inventory would allow 7,600 possible syllables (Duanmu, 2009). Most words in Mandarin are monosyllabic or disyllabic, so limitations in licit syllables result in a rather small number of possible words.

If there is a pressure towards contrastiveness within the lexicon, it should be particularly apparent in a language with such a small number of phonotactically licit forms. Thus, our prediction was that the real Mandarin lexicon would be more dispersed than the randomly sampled generated lexicons.

2.2 Methods

For Study 1, we used the LDC Mandarin Lexicon and the corresponding frequency data from the LDC Mandarin Callhome training transcripts (Huang et al., 1997). Words which include the 5th tone ('neutral tone') or lack a nuclear vowel were excluded from analysis, to avoid clitics (Chao, 1968), which would be outside the scope of this analysis.

The crucial aspect of lexical contrast is phonological form, so we based perceptual distinctiveness on phonemic representations rather than phonetic measurements, using features to calculate distance between consonants and distance between formants to calculate distance between vowels. Based on misperception studies, perceptual distance between the presence and absence of a segment is highly sensitive to the segment and its environment (Tang, 2015; Sanker, 2016); such differences do not clearly fit into the same system as contrasts between phonemes, so words with different syllable structures were considered separately. Focusing just on the monosyllabic lexicon of Mandarin, we looked at CV (open syllable) and CVX (closed syllable) structures.

2.2.1 Defining the licit structures

In order to sample generated lexicons of Mandarin from the hypothesized phonological space described in 1.3, a list of well-formed syllables was generated for CV and CVX forms, to represent candidate word-forms. In order to generate such lists, all combinations of CV and CVX structures were laid out, based on the phonological segment inventory of Mandarin; then the licit word-forms of the two structures were filtered through phonotactic models, using n-grams for phonological sequences (Jurafsky and Martin, 2008).

For CV words, well-formedness was determined using a phonological bi-gram (bi-phone) model, in which the probability of a word was defined as the product of the individual probabilities for all segments given the phoneme immediately preceding each; the probability of the tone was conditioned on the vowel. CVX words were evaluated similarly, but with a tri-phone model instead of a bi-phone model due to the extra degree of freedom induced by the coda. The probability of a word was defined as the product of the individual probabilities for all segments given the two phonemes preceding each, and tone was still conditioned on the vowel. Because only monosyllabic words were considered,

there is no possibility of long-distance dependencies. Segment probabilities were based on all attested syllables in the LDC lexicon. Under this model, words with probabilities higher than 0 were considered well-formed. Beyond that, the probabilities produced by this model were not used for Study 1.

The resulting lists of forms contain 304 CV syllables (out of 360 structurally possible combinations) and 544 CVX syllables (out of 1440 structurally possible combinations), which represent the number of phonotactically licit syllables of these shapes. Of these, there are 187 monosyllabic words with CV structure attested in the LDC Mandarin Lexicon and 327 words with CVX structure. The two filtered lists of words serve as phonologically licit pools of words for the sampling procedure described in 2.2.3.

2.2.2 Defining the distinctiveness of lexicons

In evaluating dispersion within lexicons, the distinctiveness between any two segments σ_k and σ_v is denoted as $d(\sigma_k, \sigma_v)$. Comparisons were conducted with corresponding segments from the syllables being compared, e.g. comparing onsets to onsets.

In order to reflect the perceptual differences between segments, the metrics for distinctiveness differed for consonants and for vowels. For consonants, the distinctiveness between each pair of sounds was determined by the number of featural differences, which has been shown to correlate with perceptual measures of distinctiveness (Bailey and Hahn, 2005; White and Morgan, 2008). For example, $d(/p^h/, /t^h/) = 1$, because the two phonemes differ only in place of articulation; $d(/f/, /\widehat{ts^h}/) = 4$, because the two phonemes differ in place, continuance, delayed release and aspiration.

For vowels, the distinctiveness was based on the Manhattan distance between each vowel pair in the three-dimensional vowel space defined in Flemming (2004), where F1, F2 and F3 values are mapped onto a set of integers in each dimension, given the number of cross-linguistically possible contrasts making use of each dimension.[1] This choice of metric, rather than a feature-based metric, was due to perception studies suggesting that acoustic differences provide a better model for vowel perception than a feature model does (Ettlinger and Johnson, 2009). In order to have equal weighting of contrasts between consonants and contrasts between vowels, measurements of vowel distinctiveness were scaled down by $1/3$.[2]

Each tone was treated like a distinct segment, but with a binary measure of distinctiveness: 1 (different) or 0 (the same). This decision was based on the paucity of available data on tone misperception patterns among native speakers of Mandarin and based on the variation in what distinctiveness patterns are suggested by results from different tasks (Huang and Johnson, 2010).

The distinctiveness of a word from each other word was measured with the log-transformed sum of each segment's distinctiveness from the corresponding segment in the other word. For example, for a word of CVX structure S_r, a segment σ_k in position Φ_n of the syllable is denoted by σ_{r,Φ_n}. The distinctiveness between 2 syllables S_r and S_t, as denoted by $d(S_r, S_t)$, is the log-transformed sum of $d(\sigma_{r,\Phi_{pos}}, \sigma_{t,\Phi_{pos}})$ for all positions of the syllable POS (2.1). In addition, a 1 was added to the sum before log-transformation so that minimal pairs would have a distinctiveness score larger than 0.

(2.1) The distinctiveness between word S_r and S_t

$$d(S_r, S_t) = \log\left[\sum_{pos \,\in\, POS} d(\sigma_{r,\Phi_{pos}}, \sigma_{t,\Phi_{pos}}) + 1\right]$$

An average distinctiveness of all pairs of words in the given phonological system M' was calculated for each generated lexicon (2.2). The higher this number is, the more distinctions in the possible phonological space the lexicon has used.

---

[1]For example, /u/ is represented in the vowel space as [F1: 1, F2: 1, F3: 1] and /i/ is represented as [F1: 1, F2: 6, F3: 3], so /u/ and /i/ differ by 7 units in total.

[2]This scale was based on aligning the featurally-defined distinctiveness of the three Mandarin glides (/w/, /j/, and /ɥ/) with the formant-based distinctiveness of the three corresponding vowels (/u/, /i/ and /y/).

(2.2) The average distinctiveness (by word pairs) of a size N lexicon from a given system M'

$$D_{M'} = \frac{\sum\limits_{w \,\in\, W_{M'}} \sum\limits_{w \,\in\, W_{M'}} d(S_w, S_w)/2}{P(N,2)/2}$$

2.2.3 Generating baseline inventories

Baseline inventories for each syllable structure were generated in three steps. First, the summed frequency of CV (or CVX) words in the real monosyllabic lexicon was used to generate a random set of words within the phonologically licit space defined in 2.2.1. The generated lexicons were then optimized to minimize differences from the real Mandarin lexicon in lexicon size, word frequency distribution, and individual segment frequencies. By minimizing the differences in these parameters, we ensured that the generated baseline lexicons would be comparable to the Mandarin lexicon. Finally, the generated lexicons were filtered to further ensure a close match with these parameters, limiting the generated lexicons to those with a size within 5% of the original lexicon size and a correlation of at least 0.95 between their segment frequencies and the segment frequencies of Mandarin, and between their word frequency distribution and that of Mandarin.

These parameters served to hold articulatory effort constant, with variation only in distinctiveness, based on the assumption that the overall effort of a language is the mean of the effort needed for all words of the language and the effort associated with each word is the sum of the effort associated with all of its segments.

2.3 Results

Consistent with the central limit theorem and the independent sampling process, the distribution of distinctiveness scores of the generated lexicons of both CV and CVX structures conform to normality, as confirmed by the Kolmogorov-Smirnov test (CV: $p = 0.963$, CVX: $p = 0.881$).

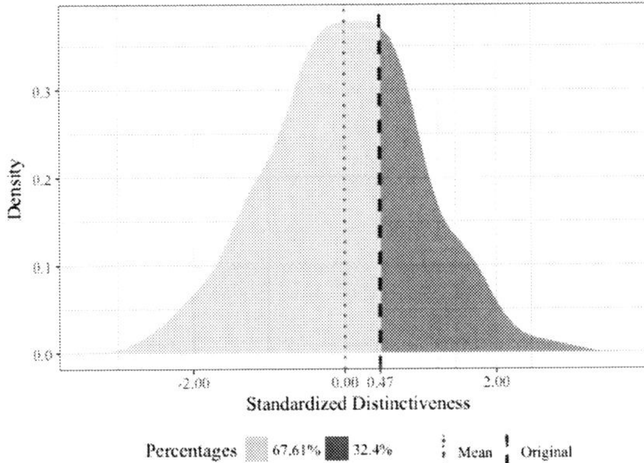

Figure 1: Standardized $D.$(distinctiveness) of 389 generated CV monosyllabic lexicons.

The shaded area in Figure 1 demonstrates the distribution of standardized distinctiveness scores of generated lexicons of monosyllabic CV words. Standardized distinctiveness of the real CV monosyllabic lexicon of Mandarin (indicated by the heavy dashed line) was greater than roughly 67.6% of generated counterparts (indicated by the light grey area). While the real lexicon is above the mean, this result is not conclusive evidence that the real lexicon differs from lexicons drawn randomly from the phonological space, given that the real lexicon is not an outlier or at all close to the top or bottom 2.5% of the distribution.

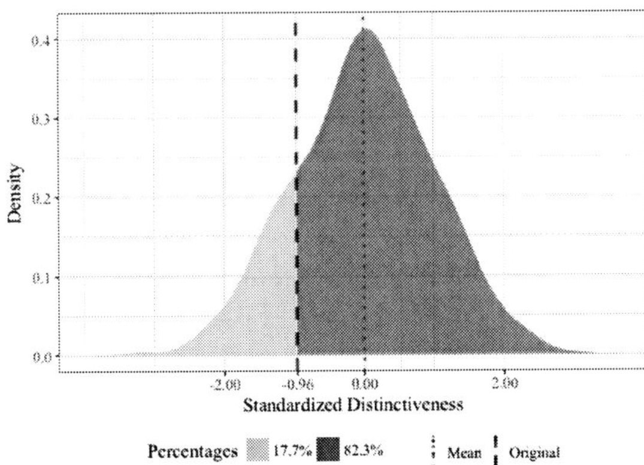

Figure 2: Standardized $D.$(distinctiveness) of 627 generated CVX monosyllabic lexicons.

As indicated by Figure 2, the distinctiveness of the real monosyllabic Mandarin CVX lexicon is better than only 17.7% of baselines. However, the real lexicon is not enough far enough towards the edge of the distribution to demonstrate that it differs from lexicons drawn randomly from the phonological space, because while it is lower than the mean, it is not an outlier.

2.4 Discussion

Mandarin words of both CV structure and CVX structure displayed similarly inconclusive patterns. Compared to randomly generated lexicons following the same parameters of phonology, word frequency, and size, the real lexicon was not an outlier in distinctiveness either in CV or CVX syllables, though the real CV lexicon was slightly better than average among the generated lexicons and the real CVX lexicon was worse. Because the CV phonological space is smaller and more saturated, it is not surprising that CV portion of Mandarin monosyllabic lexicon would be relatively more efficient than its CVX counterpart. However, in general, the results did not support the hypothesis that dispersion plays a large role in shaping lexicons, and are more consistent with the opposite pattern of clumping, as seen in Dautriche et al.'s (2017) results.

The inconclusive results might in part be due to issues with the metrics used for distinctiveness, as perceptual data suggests that different positions in a syllable are not equally salient. At least within English, listeners are most sensitive to mispronunciations in onsets, less so in codas, and least sensitive in nuclei (Franklin and Morgan, 2017), and are more accurate in perceiving onsets than codas, though this can vary depending on listeners' native language, even for the same stimuli (Sanker, 2016). Given such findings, different syllable positions might best be given different weights in distinctiveness when generating sample lexicons. Further research into Mandarin speakers' patterns of misperceptions at the word level and the segment level would further help in accurately quantifying distinctiveness.

3 Study 2: Evaluating the well-formedness of generated Mandarin and English monosyllabic lexicons

3.1 Background

Study 1 shows that a lexicon might not be as dispersed as the functional goal of communicative clarity would predict. In Study 2, we examine whether this lack of dispersion can be partially explained by gradient well-formedness constraints shaping the lexicon, disproportionately favoring words with high-probability sequences.

3.2 Methods

In Study 2, English and Mandarin were used as languages for a preliminary cross-linguistic investigation. The same LDC Mandarin Lexicon from Study 1 was used for Mandarin and the CMU Dictionary (Weide, 2008) was used for the phonemic representations for American English. CMU Dictionary entries were spell-checked with GNU Aspell to exclude rare names and borrowings from other languages. Function words and words with the rarest 1% of onsets and codas were also excluded, due to the uniqueness of their phonological structure, as many function words are clitics and can be reduced more than other words, and words with highly unusual sequences are likely to have unique etymologies that do not reflect the overall pressures of the language.

Only monosyllabic words were used. As discussed in 2.2.1, this limitation meant there were no long-distance dependencies that needed to be accounted for. Phonotactics were represented by a tri-phone model of sound sequences (as introduced in 2.2.1), with the predictability of each sound based on the two preceding phonemes. Study 2 focused on the word probabilities assigned to forms within the generated lexicons. Frequencies, as captured by n-gram models in this study, were used to approximate distributional markedness (Albright, ms). The distinction between frequency and markedness is beyond the scope of this paper.

Sampling followed a sampling procedure sim-ilar to that of Study 1. First, all combinations of segments in all possible syllable positions were laid out, producing lists of potential words. Then the real monosyllabic lexicons of Mandarin and English were used to train the tri-phone phonotactic models for each language, assigning log probabilities to all forms in the word lists based on the sum of log probabilities of each word's components. The wordlists were then filtered, only retaining forms with probabilities larger than 0, meaning that they were well-formed within the tri-phone model. Finally, in order to generate the artificial lexicons for English, words were randomly taken from the filtered English list, with the number of words of different lengths kept consistent with the real English lexicon. The same was done for Mandarin. Thus, the generated baseline lexicons had the same distribution of word lengths and the same size as the real lexicons.

Distributions of log probabilities of the baseline lexicons were compared to the real lexicons, to test whether the probability distributions of real lexicons differ from randomly generated lexicons based on phonotactic models which assume independence of subparts more than one segment apart. Logarithmic scales for probability, with probabilities of subparts combined multiplicatively, have been found previously to have a strong positive correlation with gradient well-formedness ratings and decisions about acceptability of nonce words (Frisch et al., 2000; Coleman and Pierrehumbert, 1997), though these studies did not look for patterns in where the data deviated from the model.

3.3 Results

Both in English and Mandarin, the real lexicons exhibited over-representation of high-probability forms and under-representation of low-probability forms.

The independent sampling process was essentially producing replications which could be used to bootstrap variance estimation for the estimators of interest, so standard errors and confidence intervals of estimators other than the mean were constructed with the bootstrap distributions calculated using the generated sample lexicons.

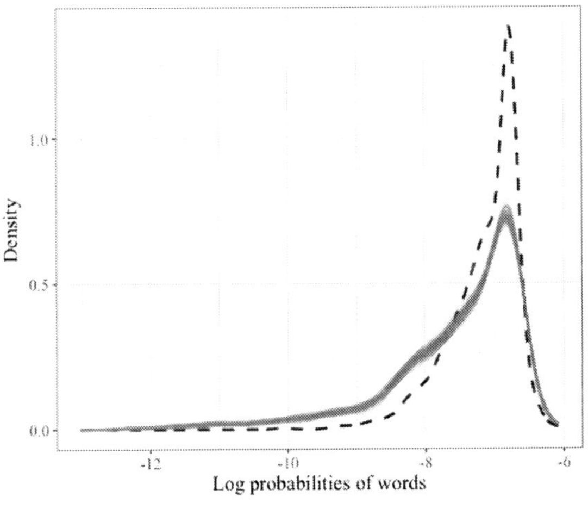

Figure 3: Probability density distributions of the original and 100 generated Mandarin monosyllabic lexicons

Figure 3 illustrates the probability density distributions of the original and generated sample Mandarin monosyllabic lexicons over word probabilities as defined in the phonotactic model. The figure demonstrates that the real monosyllabic Mandarin lexicon (indicated by the dashed line) is more clustered around the higher-probability types than the sample lexicons (indicated by the light solid lines).

Three statistics were used to test whether the distribution of log probabilities in the real lexicon is likely to come from the population distribution. The sample means were tested against the mean of the original lexicon in a two-tailed test ($t = -219.463$, $p \approx 0.000$). This shows that the mean of word probabilities in the actual Mandarin monosyllabic lexicon was significantly higher than the true mean of the population distribution generated from the null hypothesis, as measured from the generated sample lexicons.

In addition to the mean, the bootstrap percentile confidence intervals (CI) of variance and skewness of the hypothesized Mandarin population distribution were approximated. The results show that the variance of the probability distribution of the real lexicon is significantly lower than the variance of the generated popula-

tion ($\sigma^2_{original} = 0.26$, 95% CI: $(0.93, 1.18)$). The probability distribution of the original lexicon and the estimated population distribution are both left-skewed (negative skewness), but the absolute value of the skewness of the original lexicon is significantly smaller ($sk_{original} = -1.38$, 95% CI: $(-2.01, -1.70)$).

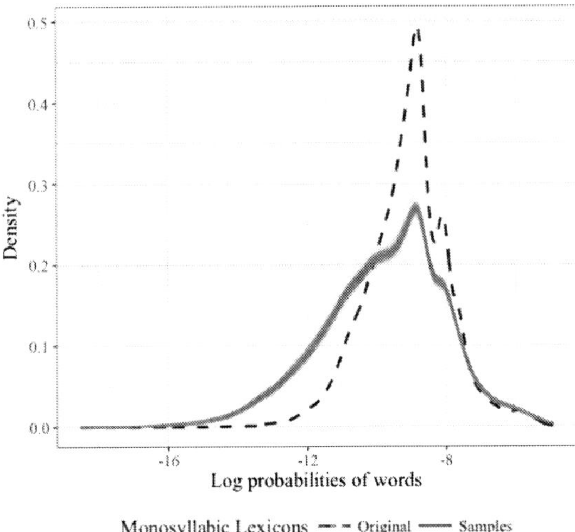

Figure 4: Probability density distributions of the original and 100 generated English monosyllabic lexicons

The English data (illustrated in Figure 4) were analyzed with the same statistical methods as the Mandarin data. As in the Mandarin results, the mean of the probability distribution of the real English monosyllabic lexicon is significantly higher than that of the population distribution generated from the null hypothesis ($t = -561.967$, $p \approx 0.000$).

The comparison in variance and skewness between the original English lexicon and the hypothesized English population distribution also exhibit results similar to the Mandarin data. The variance of the real lexicon is significantly lower than the variance of the generated population ($\sigma^2_{original} = 1.36$, 95% CI: $(3.05, 3.25)$), and the absolute value of the skewness of the real lexicon is significantly smaller than that of the skewness of the hypothesized population ($sk_{original} = -0.16$, 95% CI: $(-0.52, -0.39)$).

3.4 Discussion

If the lexicon is shaped only by local phonological constraints, as controlled for in the phonotactic models used in the current study, sample lexicons generated by the models should follow roughly the same distribution as the real Mandarin and English monosyllabic lexicons. The results of this study provide strong evidence against this null hypothesis.

Within both English and Mandarin, the real monosyllabic lexicons have higher means and smaller variance than the generated baselines, which indicates that the real lexicons make use of more high-probability word types than would be expected by the phonotactic models used. Additionally, the real lexicons were less skewed than the baselines, meaning that the probability distribution of the two real lexicons have thinner or shorter tails than their corresponding baseline lexicons, which also suggests that real lexicons tend towards higher probability words, with a fast drop-off in the frequency of lower probability words. These results seem to suggest that there is a strong superadditivity effect that penalizes words with multiple low-probability subparts, potentially in combination with a tendency to re-use high-probability sequences, as suggested by Dautriche et al. (2017).

4 General Discussion

Study 1 found that in Mandarin Chinese, dispersion is not a prominent force in the shaping of the lexicon; evidence for a pressure towards clustering was somewhat more suggestive, though not decisive. Study 2 showed that the lexicons of Mandarin and English have more words of higher probability and fewer words of lower probability than would be expected by a phonological model in which constraints are independent. This result reinforces the results in Study 1, indicating a lack of dispersion and instead a trend towards clumping within high probability forms.

These results can fit into Albright's (ms.) proposed grammar of weighted constraints, in which he suggests that inputs with multiple markedness violations have a superadditive effect that can overcome a threshold of well-formedness, resulting in forms which are unattested despite not being directly prohibited. The next step of Study 2 is to expand it to more languages, to test how consistent the effect of superadditivity is cross-linguistically. Future work should also investigate whether the observed patterns in lexicons are driven by the interaction of particular constraints, or if they result from a general pattern in how all constraints combine.

The superadditivity account and the presented evidence are consistent with Dautriche et al.'s (2017) findings that lexicons are more regular than expected. However, a pressure for "clumpiness" and a superadditivity effect make different predictions. According to Dautriche et al. (2017), regularity in the lexicon is due to re-use of phonological patterns, which should produce particularly high peaks among high-probability forms, with less of an effect on the low-probability tail. In the superadditivity account, regularity is due to combinations of markedness violations resulting in such low probabilities that many of them never appear, resulting in a shorter and thinner tail, with less of an effect on the shape of the peak. Both pressures could also co-exist. It would be informative for future work to tease apart the predictions made by each account.

References

Adam Albright. ms. Cumulative violations and complexity thresholds.

Todd M. Bailey and Ulrike Hahn. 2005. Phoneme similarity and confusability. *Journal of Memory and Language*, 52(3):339–362.

Yuen Ren Chao. 1968. *A Grammar of Spoken Chinese*. University of California Press, Berkeley and Los Angeles.

George N. Clements. 2003. Feature economy in sound systems. *Phonology*, 20(3):287–333.

John Coleman and Janet Pierrehumbert. 1997. Stochastic phonological grammars and acceptability. In John Coleman, editor, *Computational phonology: Third meeting of the ACL special interest group in computational phonology*, pages 49–56, Somerset, NJ. Association for Computational Linguistics.

Isabelle Dautriche, Kyle Mahowald, Edward Gibson, Anne Christophe, and Steven T. Piantadosi. 2017. Words cluster phonetically beyond phonotactic regularities. *Cognition*, 163:128–145.

San Duanmu. 2009. *Syllable Structure: The Limits of Variation*. Oxford University Press, New York, USA.

Marc Ettlinger and Keith Johnson. 2009. Vowel discrimination by english, french and turkish speakers: Evidence for an exemplar-based approach to speech perception. *Phonetica*, 66(4):222–242.

Edward Flemming, 2004. chapter Contrast and Perceptual Distinctiveness, pages 232 – 276. Cambridge University Press.

Lauren Franklin and James Morgan. 2017. On the nature of vocalic representation during lexical access. *The Journal of the Acoustical Society of America*, 141(5):4038–4038.

Stefan A Frisch, Nathan R Large, and David B Pisoni. 2000. Perception of wordlikeness: Effects of segment probability and length on the processing of nonwords. *Journal of memory and language*, 42(4):481–496.

Christopher Green and Stuart Davis, 2014. *Perspectives on phonological theory and development, in honor of Daniel A. Dinnsen*, chapter Superadditivity and limitations on syllable complexity in Bambara words, pages 223–247. John Benjamins, Amsterdam.

Bruce Hayes and Colin Wilson. 2008. A maximum entropy model of phonotactics and phonotactic learning. *Linguistic Inquiry*, 39(3):379–440.

Tsan Huang and Keith Johnson. 2010. Language specificity in speech perception: Perception of mandarin tones by native and nonnative listeners. *Phonetica*, 67(4):243–267.

Shudong Huang, Xuejun Bian, Grace Wu, and Cynthia McLemore, 1997. *LDC Mandarin Lexicon*. University of Pennsylvania.

Daniel Jurafsky and James H. Martin. 2008. *Speech and language processing: an introduction to natural language processing, computational linguistics and speech recognition*. Prentice Hall. Pearson Education, Inc., Upper Saddle River, New Jersey, 2nd edition.

Brett Kessler and Rebecca Treiman. 1997. Syllable structure and the distribution of phonemes in english syllables. *Journal of Memory and language*, 37(3):295–311.

Charles N. Li and Sandra A. Thompson, 1987. *The World's Major Languages*, chapter Chinese. Oxford University Press.

Paul A Luce and David B Pisoni. 1998. Recognizing spoken words: The neighborhood activation model. *Ear and Hearing*, 19(1):1.

Steven T. Piantadosi, Harry J. Tily, and Edward Gibson. 2009. The communicative lexicon hypothesis. In *The 31st annual meeting of the Cognitive Science Society (CogSci09)*, pages 2582–2587.

Chelsea Sanker. 2016. *Patterns Of Misperception Of Arabic Guttural And Non-Guttural Consonants*. Ph.D. thesis.

Stephanie S. Shih. 2016. Super additive similarity in dioula tone harmony. In Kyeong min Kim, Pocholo Umbal, Trevor Block, Queenie Chan, Tanie Cheng, Kelli Finney, Mara Katz, Sophie Nickel-Thompson, and Lisa Shorten, editors, *Proceedings of the 33rd West Coast Conference on Formal Linguistics*, pages 361–370. Cascadilla Proceedings Project, Somerville, MA, USA.

Kevin Tang. 2015. *Naturalistic speech misperception*. Ph.D. thesis.

Andrew Wedel, Scott Jackson, and Abby Kaplan. 2013. Functional load and the lexicon: Evidence that syntactic category and frequency relationships in minimal lemma pairs predict the loss of phoneme contrasts in language change. *Language and speech*, 56(3):395–417.

Robert L. Weide, 2008. *The CMU pronunciation dictionary*. Carnegie Mellon University, 0.7a edition.

Katherine S. White and James L. Morgan. 2008. Sub-segmental detail in early lexical representations. *Journal of Memory and Language*, 59:114–132.

George K. Zipf. 1929. Relative frequency as a determinant of phonetic change. *Harvard Studies in Classical Philology*, 40:1–95.

Association for Computational Linguistics
209 N. Eighth Street
Stroudsburg, Pennsylvania 18360

ISBN 978-1-5108-5551-9